THE INDIVIDUALIZATION OF CHINESE SOCIETY

THE INDIVIDUALIZATION OF CHINESE SOCIETY

YUNXIANG YAN

LONDON SCHOOL OF ECONOMICS MONOGRAPHS ON SOCIAL ANTHROPOLOGY

Volume 77

Oxford • New York

English edition
First published in 2009 by
Berg
Editorial offices:
First Floor, Angel Court, 81 St Clements Street, Oxford OX4 1AW, UK
175 Fifth Avenue, New York, NY 10010, USA

Berg is the imprint of Oxford International Publishers Ltd.

Library of Congress Cataloging-in-Publication Data

A catalogue record for this book is available from the Library of Congress.

British Library Cataloguing-in-Publication Data

A catalogue record for this book is available from the British Library.

ISBN   978 1 84788 379 7 (Cloth)
978 1 84788 378 0 (Paper)

Typeset by SAGE India.

www.bergpublishers.com

In fond memory of Professor Kwang-chih Chang (1931–2001)
– a wonderful mentor and role model

CONTENTS

ACKNOWLEDGEMENTS

During the four years of compiling this collection of essays, I have been deeply indebted to Charles Stafford, Managing Editor of the LSE Monographs on Social Anthropology, for his encouragement, patience, and untiring help, without which I would have abandoned the effort on at least two occasions. I am grateful to Stephan Feuchtwang, Arthur Kleinman, and James L. Watson for their valuable comments and advice; additional thanks go to Arthur for writing the Foreword. I am also grateful to the original publishers, who are credited in the permissions list at the end of this book, for allowing the reproduction of the essays. Nancy Hearst provided wonderful editorial assistance on many of the essays in this collection; once again, I relied on her magical skills for the two new chapters as well as for proofreading the manuscript. Professor Kwang-chih Chang's advice in 1986 was one of the crucial factors that enabled me to change from the study of Chinese literature to social anthropology. He played a key role in my early years of training at Harvard University and remains a role model for me now; hence, I dedicate this volume to his memory. Finally, I owe a special thanks to my wife Betty for being my most loyal critic and soul-mate.

FOREWORD

The author of the essays in this book, Yunxiang Yan, has lived an extraordinary life. He has been a shepherd and village storyteller in North China, an undergraduate student at Peking University, a graduate student at Harvard, and professor of anthropology at UCLA. Along the way, he has written a classic ethnographic account of gift-giving and receiving in the North China village where he lived during the frenzy of the Cultural Revolution and to which he returned to study decades later. This is complemented by a more recent study of the large emotional, relational and behavioral changes in that same village under the greatly influential impact of the economic reforms that have taken place since the late 1970s.

The individual chapters of this book – which depict changes in economic and social stratification, power, family relationships, wider kinship ties, household economy, marriage, youth culture, women's status, consumerism, and the emergence of individualism – document a great transformation in everyday life that is remaking China and the Chinese. That transformation, Yan avers, can be seen in Xiajia village and among its inhabitants, with whom Yan has lived for much longer than the usual one- or two-year ethnographic sojourn, and whose new everyday social reality, he goes on to propose, is a microcosm of what is taking place in China more generally. At its base is a shift in moral coordinates and experiences. The lived values that, on a daily basis, recreate Chinese culture in relationships, exchanges, institutions and rituals, and also in the subjective interior of personhood, are undergoing a tectonic movement which in turn is shaking and shifting the social world toward something new and different. Patriarchy is no longer so prevalent, though it has not disappeared entirely; filial reverence is losing its priority status and being replaced by the new centrality of conjugal ties and youth culture; the social status hierarchy legitimated by radical Maoism is being replaced by a new one created by the market economy and globalization; and social inequality is being reconstituted and deepened.

Most telling, Yan shows us that the Chinese culture of today is witnessing and fostering a new individualism that openly expresses aspects that were both unspoken and underdeveloped, and even politically disallowed, in past eras. That new stream of individualistic orientation and self-fashioning brings with it to the fore the material desires and practices of consumerism. It also brings an egocentric pragmatism in personal relationships that alters ties long considered to be based in cultural ethics toward a troubling "you-scratch-my-back-I-scratch-yours" pattern that can propel corruption, and a new sense of what constitutes a good life and what is thought to be good in general. Chinese society, of course, has always had a place for the individual but, in the past, that place was less aggressively pursued in public and more sociocentric in its expression. So Yan demonstrates that the self and personhood of Chinese are becoming different just as their local moral worlds are transiting to something new. That new reality, for Yan, is both troubling and hopeful.

As a chronicler of the times, Yan contributes an admirable combination of situated ethnographic detail, penetrating anthropological analysis and thoughtful marshaling of relevant and illuminating social theory. He also suggests telling comparisons with the China of earlier and different times, as well as comparisons with the West. Indeed, the cross-cultural comparisons that Yan's fine-grained descriptions and well-grounded interpretations enable go to the heart of contemporary concerns about understanding what is most at stake in our times and how it is changing who we are. Yan's chapters, then, help us not only to think about China and the Chinese, but also about America and the Americans, the West and Westerners.

In 1978, I made my first research trip to China. I had already had the deeply influential experience of living and working, together with my family, in Taiwan for three years over the previous decade. In 1978, I was impressed by the aftermath of the Cultural Revolution, China's emergence from the dangerous dominance of radical Maoism, and the new legitimacy for business practices. Above all, I was impressed by the excitement and opportunity felt by people who, amidst the grey grimness of a society which had cut itself off from the world for three decades and was still in an impoverished state, were gingerly exploring new forms of music, art, dress, food, relationships and institutions. Over the next three decades, during numerous research trips and personal visits, I would marvel at the pace and extent of the building of a modern China. Out of friendships and from research interviews, I could sense that people themselves were changing. But what I couldn't quite grasp was how to register and interpret the swirl of complex changes without ending up with simplistic generalizations or with oppositional comparisons that make polar extremes out of behaviors that, although contradictory, co-existed and spoke of a difficult to express yet for all that impressive pluralism. No single interpretative scheme seemed to fit what I was seeing and experiencing: the "blooming, buzzing" confusion that William James called genuine reality. Applied to a nation of more than 1.3 billion people, with vast differences between coastal, interior and remote regions and urban and rural settings, that confusing plurality of experience seemed to elude a single interpretative framework.

And so, I was initially skeptical of Yunxiang Yan's claim that the new Chinese modernity had a golden thread that provided coherence as well as analytic precision. It is the ethnographic details of the pictures he draws of how life is changing in Xiajia village, as well as other quite distinctive domains in which he demonstrates such change, that convinced me that he has identified a key aspect of the deep structuring of the new Chinese reality: the emergence of a Chinese form of individualism that combines global processes with local practices. Several decades ago, two influential social scientists in Taiwan – Yang Kuo-Shu and Huang Kwang-Kuo – contributed to a movement aimed at sinicizing social theory by showing that, although connections between members of social networks (*guanxi wang*) were at the core of Chinese social life, each network centered on an individual. Hence, individuals mattered even in a society characterized by collective relations and interpersonal structures. What Yan's work demonstrates is that that central individual positioning has intensified, and the new legitimacy of personal practices underlying group processes has fostered open expression of self-interest that previously had to be articulated in familistic or collectivist terms to be made culturally acceptable. It is Yan's genius as an ethnographer to be able to effectively describe scene after scene, event after event, that illustrate this point.

Of course, it is one thing to describe a local village reality and quite another to generalize to China as a whole. And yet, so persuasive are Yan's illustrations and so coherent is his analytic framework – as well as his comparisons with other, larger rural and urban realities in China – that the reader familiar with today's China will find herself or himself coming up with additional case examples to prove the point that a new form of self in its moral context is emerging in today's China.

We should not expect a social and cultural anthropologist to define the level and precise dimensions of such individualization. That will be the task of an entire community of psychiatrists, psychologists and social scientists concerned with Chinese society in our time. But what Yan has accomplished in the chapters that follow is impressive enough. For he has opened the door to a new set of questions about the lived experience of Chinese that I believe will change scholarship on the Chinese, while encouraging comparative cross-cultural studies which have been atrophying in anthropology and Asian studies.

So what will be the long-term consequences of the individualization of Chinese society? Will the Chinese Communist Party's new ideology of providing people with a good life deepen individualization still further and, by so doing, potentially shift political reality? Or will the still-potent political strictures of a non-liberal democratic state limit the scope of personal pluralism so that individualization, like globalization, is bent to the hegemonic interests of the single-party state? Previously, social science questions about China were dominated by political, economic and security concerns. Yan's contribution is part of a growing body of anthropological research that suggests that more significant developments – albeit based in political and economic change – are occurring in the forms of social life. Understanding what is happening to Chinese society may be a better long-term guide to the impressive roadmap China is constructing. And in that new cultural edifice the extraordinary infrastructure must be understood to include new ways of being a person, living a moral life and aspiring for different futures.

Arthur Kleinman
Harvard University

INTRODUCTION: THE RISE OF THE CHINESE INDIVIDUAL

The essays collected in this volume document and examine the twofold social transformation that manifests itself as the rise of the individual in social practices and the individualization of the society through structural changes of social relations. In this Introduction, I will focus primarily on the former – the rise of the individual – and will provide some updates and commentaries on the original essays based on subsequent research. The individualization of society and the theoretical implications of the Chinese case will be discussed in the concluding chapter.

A RETROSPECTIVE VIEW OF CHINA'S REFORM ERA

Regardless of the original date of publication, in essence, all the chapters in this volume are products of the 1990s. Eight articles were written in the 1990s, but they were all based on field research carried out from 1989 to 1999, although some of the essays were then updated with new materials from fieldwork carried out after 1999. Eight of the ten essays focus on the agency and action of individuals in Xiajia village, northeast China, where I lived and worked as a farmer from 1971 to 1978 and to which I then returned to conduct fieldwork in 1989, 1991, 1993, 1994, 1997, 1998, 1999, 2004, 2006 and 2008 (for a detailed description of the community, see Yan 1996: 22–42, and Yan 2003: 17–41). The remaining two essays, dealing with the impact of globalization on individuals, are based on field research in Beijing.

It is indisputable that Chinese society has undergone rapid and radical changes since the Chinese party-state officially launched its post-Mao economic reforms in 1978, and the Chinese economy has been growing at an astonishingly fast pace. Yet, the years between 1978 and 2008 do not constitute a linear pathway of China's assent to global power because the reforms represent a long story of trial by error. As a result, each of the past three decades has had its own characteristics and has had a different impact on the everyday life of Chinese people. In my view, in this respect, the 1990s were a particularly dynamic, resilient and important decade.

At a macro level, in the first decade of the reform era, both the Chinese party-state and the elite (political and intellectual alike) struggled to depart from radical Maoist socialism, as evidenced by a number of important institutional changes. These changes ranged from the establishment of the household responsibility system and decollectivization in the first half of the 1980s to a number of bold yet not necessarily successful urban reforms in the late 1980s. The rapid rise and fall of a pro-democracy movement in 1989 represents a turning point in a number of ways, one of which is that, in the post-1989 years, both the party-state and the elite bid a determined farewell to Maoist socialism. Despite the persistence of political conservatism that centered around the monopoly of power by the Chinese Communist Party, Deng Xiaoping's 1992 tour to South China, the theory of a socialist market economy and Jiang Zemin's theory of the "three represents" are the best examples of the official re-orientation or re-ideologicalization toward a market economy and capitalism.

From the perspective of market transition, the decade of the 1990s arguably was the most liberal in China in terms of the phenomenal growth of the private sector, the retreat of the party-state from its previous control over social life, the replacement of the dominance of the Communist ideology by neoliberalism, and the re-structuring of life chances and mobility channels that set hundreds of millions Chinese on the move. As a result, by the turn of the century the magical word "reform" (*gaige*, in Chinese) began to mean something quite different in practice. Instead of making changes to the previously dominant socialist institutions, more often than not reform efforts in the twenty-first century actually mean policy adjustments resulting from negotiation and contestation among the holders of economic capital and political power. As some Chinese scholars sharply note (see, for example, Sun 2004), in the third decade of the reform era there was no longer either a consensus or a mandate for reform. Instead, there emerged a sort of run-away capitalism in alliance with the strong state, which seems to be responsible for the miracle of GDP growth, the rapid increase in state revenue and capacity, the rise of China as a global player and (simultaneously) the polarization of society, the further decline of disadvantaged groups and the degradation of the environment. Under the current leadership of Hu Jintao and Wen Jiabao, various policy adjustments under the slogan of a "harmonious society" have been introduced to address these negative consequences, but it is unlikely that the Chinese mode of development as defined in the 1990s will be changed.

This book does not address China's triumphal march toward a market economy and capitalism during the 1990s; instead, it examines the changing Chinese society from a different but equally important perspective, that is, the views and experiences of flesh-and-bone individuals when coping with the institutional changes in their everyday life. This summarization is actually after-factual.

Each time I returned to my former field sites during the 1990s I could literally feel the various forms of vitality, energy and resilience among both villagers and urban residents, ranging from confusion, disillusionment, inspiration, hope and excitement, to actual action. I had some difficulties in making sense of what I was observing but I was quite sure that Chinese society in the second decade of reform was undergoing structural changes. I used the terms "dislocation," "reposition" and "restratification" to describe how the changes appeared from the perspective of an individual living through them. Central to this process, at the time, I noted the emergence of the notion of a Chinese dream, i.e. a belief that one could change one's fate through intelligence and hard work. I also observed that the meaning of the communist slogan "regeneration though self-reliance" had changed from a slogan of ideological collectivism to a slogan of individualism in everyday life competition (Yan 1994). At the time, however, I was unable to see that a great transformation in Chinese society was unfolding right in front of my eyes.

My revelation came in 2007 when I attempted to understand the patterns and trends of Chinese social change in light of the theories of second or reflexive modernity – especially the individualization thesis – of Anthony Giddens (1991), Zygmunt Bauman (2001), Ulrich Beck (1992), and Beck and Elisabeth Beck-Gernsheim (2001). I found it intriguing that, although China was still undergoing the modernization process, Chinese society was demonstrating a number of features of individualization in the age of second modernity at the same time as it bore other features of social change that belong to the modern and even pre-modern eras in the West. As a field ethnographer, I have long noted the rapid changes in mentality and behavior among Chinese individuals who increasingly have been demanding the rights of self-development, happiness and security against the backdrop of age-old moral teachings of collective well-being. Since my first fieldwork in 1989, I have been fortunate to have had various opportunities to document how individual villagers and urban residents thought and acted, and how they interacted with the various institutional changes. However, it was only when I looked back at these ethnographic materials in 2007 that I realized that my work was revealing the rise of the Chinese individual as a result of the post-Mao reform institutional changes. (For a noteworthy and new study on the Chinese individual, see Hansen and Svarverud 2009.) Although the rise of the individual in the private life sphere is one of the central arguments in my 2003 book, I had not yet appreciated its profound implications at a societal level, i.e. the individualization of Chinese society.

In the remainder of this introductory chapter, I will review the major findings of my research on this great social transformation and update the ten chapters with additional findings from subsequent field research. Five threads run through almost all the essays, each of which emphasizes one particular aspect of the rise of the individual. The presentation here is organized in the following order: institutional changes that free the individual, the agency and autonomy of the individual, the role of the party-state, the absence of individualism in the Chinese process of individualization, and the influence of globalization, especially the influence of global consumerism.

"*SONGBANG*," OR UNTYING THE INDIVIDUAL THROUGH INSTITUTIONAL REFORM

It is well known that the post-Mao reform era began with the rural reforms in the late 1970s, and the first early steps were taken by individual villagers who risked government punishment. What the party-state did at the time was nothing more than tolerate those local leaders who did not interfere with the activities of the courageous villagers (see Zhou 1996). These early initiatives stimulated work incentives by allocating both responsibilities and profits to individual producers, thus dramatically increasing agricultural output. After the fruits of these initiatives became apparent, the party-state launched an institutional reform that, by 1983, had dismantled the rural collectives nationwide and had privatized almost all collective property with the exception of farmland.

The Chinese term commonly used to describe the institutional changes throughout the 1980s is "*songbang*," a verb that literally means "to untie." All reform measures, including the most radical – decollectivization – were nothing more than untying the peasants (*gei nongmin songbang*) from the constraints of the collectives and the planned economy. The institutional strategy of untying the individual extended to the urban reforms as well. Inspired by the instant success of villager household farming, in 1984, fifty-five leaders of state-owned enterprises in Fujian province submitted an open letter requesting that they also be "untied," meaning that they would be given more decision-making and management power from the tightly controlled central planning (*Fujian ribao* 1984). Their letter, published on March 22, 1984 in the provincial newspaper, was later praised by the official media for blowing "the horn for enterprise reform."

At each step of the early reform stage, however, both the reformers and their opponents were concerned with the unpredictable consequences of granting autonomy and freedom to individual villagers (or to workers, enterprise leaders, local government agencies, and so forth), albeit for different reasons. This concern prompted a substantial amount of research at the time.

Chapter 1 of this book addresses precisely this issue. Decollectivization took place in Xiajia village in late 1983. The freed, or "untied," villagers had been going their own way in work and social life for more than five years by the time I conducted my first fieldwork in the community. I set out for myself the following research questions: Who became rich first? And what happened to the local structure of economic and social stratification? The purpose was to engage in the rather influential debate among scholars of socialist/communist countries which centered on the consequences of the transition from a planned economy to a market economy, known as the market transition debate (see especially Nee 1989; Szelenyi 1988). Therefore, the bulk of Chapter 1 includes the results of my household survey on the economic standing of villagers in 1989 and, based on these results, an analysis of the changing community stratification system from a singular socialist hierarchy based on political capital in the collective period to a dual hierarchy.

Every time I visited Xiajia village from 1989 to 2008 I updated my data on the villagers' economic standing. A second household survey, conducted in the same way as that in 1989, was carried out in 1998. About two-thirds of my findings in 1989 remained valid in 2008 and some new developments actually reinforced the earlier findings. For example, the category of "*sishuhu*" (privileged households because of their close connections with the non-agricultural sector) had completely disappeared as virtually all able-bodied villagers had access to non-agricultural employment and cash payments by working in the cities as migrant workers. The number of salaried village cadres was reduced dramatically, from thirteen in 1989 to five in 1999 and to two in 2006. After the abolition of agricultural taxes and other local levies in 2006, only the party secretary, who is also the appointed village head, and the village accountant were paid by the township government. Village cadres as a group are close to disappearing as well. Moreover, none of the ten richest household heads in 2008 was a cadre, although two still relied on the social capital that they had built up in their earlier cadre careers. Technical skills and the sizable operation of a cash economy were listed by the villagers as the two major factors that have led to the success of the current richest households. It is equally noteworthy that only two of the top ten households in 1989 remained at the top of the list in 2008, as noted by village informants who cited individual failures as the main reason.

All of the above seems to confirm the early conclusion that the transition toward a market economy indeed reduced the significance of political capital and enabled more individuals to move ahead based on their knowledge, skills, and hard work. However, the redistribution of resources and life chances through the market did not necessarily make village society more equal; in reality, it did not. For some, even the chances for social mobility did not improve. For example, eight out of the ten poorest households in 1989 remained in the bottom category in 2008. The ninth had moved out of the village to escape poverty in the late 1990s, but only fell farther down to join the poorest and lowest ranks in the city of Ha'erbin – migrant workers without steady jobs. The tenth poorest household in 1989 consisted of a bachelor and his aged mother, both of whom had died in poverty since the turn of the new century. The two households that were added to the bottom of the list in 2008 came from the group of poor households in 1989. According to my second household survey, only a handful of the poor households in 1989 managed to improve their economic standing, whereas the majority maintained their original village status, even though their absolute living standard had improved substantially in comparison with that in the pre-reform era.

Upward mobility increased from 1989 to 2008 mainly among the rich households and some middle-level households.

In retrospect, I realize that my research in the early 1990s, like that of so many others at the time, focused on the mobility of social groups to show that the market economy was fair game and thus would reduce social inequality. The other side of the equation, i.e. the inevitable results of social differentiation and individualization, was obscured by a shared urge to legitimize the market-oriented reforms. Fortunately, Chapter 1, like all the essays selected for this volume, was written as an ethnographic account and it thus contains as many details of everyday life as possible. Thus, in addition to the changing structure of stratification, Chapter 1 also tells stories about individual villagers who, after they were untied from the collective regime, began to make independent decisions and to engage in various self-chosen activities, such as refusing to present a gift at the wedding of the son of the party secretary or challenging the village cadre in a fist fight. More importantly, the public center moved from the village office to the village shop, and Giddens's (1991) village politics of life began to emerge, as the better-off villagers began to use consumption to enhance and secure their social status and to challenge the existing hierarchy. These efforts and traits of individual agency continued to develop in the subsequent twenty years and eventually moved to the central stage of village social life, as shown in the subsequent chapters.

The most dramatic change among villagers has been their attitude toward social differentiation. In 1989, many villagers complained about the rapid rise of the former class enemy, i.e. those who had been classified as landlords and rich peasants after the revolution. In fact, this was my initial motivation for conducting a household survey on social stratification. Their discontent was based on both the communist ideology of class struggle and their earlier political privileges, as revealed in the testimony of a villager quoted in Chapter 1. By the late 1990s, however, the ideology-based complaints against the former class enemy had been replaced by angry accusations of corruption against village cadres, with many villagers openly expressing their admiration of individuals from the former landlord or rich peasant families for being diligent, smart and knowledgeable. Even the grieving villager whom I quote in Chapter 1 had changed his opinion. In a 2003 conversation he admitted that there was no way that he could compete with those workaholics. Saddened by a strong sense of loss, he died in poverty in 2005, but by then one of his four sons had become an affluent shop owner. By 2008, individual ability, which can be defined as a good education, social connections or earning power, was frequently and regularly invoked by villagers in comments on the changing fortunes and misfortunes that had occurred, often in short intervals, to many village individuals. As a result, even their anger about cadre corruption was toned down to an insignificant level; some regarded corruption as a sort of individual ability and others turned a blind eye to the corruption as long as it did not block their attempts to move ahead.

The central research question in Chapter 2 is the impact of the rural reforms on the power of village cadres. This too was a primary concern in the market transition debates of the late 1980s and 1990s. In light of social exchange theory, I take a closer look at the base of cadre power in village society and identify the monopoly over resources and life chances by cadres through the core element of the redistributive mechanism of collectivization. The use of violence in the name of the mass dictatorship and the hegemony of the communist ideology were important elements in helping maintain the cadres' monopoly over resources and life chances; in return, the cadres had to offer absolute loyalty to the party-state. As a result, villagers depended on the cadres for all the things that they needed in life, i.e. Walder's "organized dependency" (1983). Institutional changes in the post-Mao reform era, ranging from decollectivization to a restructuring of village government to a disenchantment with the communist ideology, removed some elements and altered others, fundamentally reducing the villagers' dependence on cadres. Therefore, cadre power had declined to a great extent by the early 1990s. A rather simplistic but indeed important indicator of the changing power relationship that my villager friends offered me was to see who beat up whom when a quarrel developed into a fight – as evidence of naked power. Although few villagers had ever dared before to engage in a fist fight with a cadre, after decollectivization it was a common occurrence.

The most important findings again are in the ethnographic details. As time went by, many of the earlier indicators of change developed into prevailing patterns of mentality and behavior. Chief among them was an awareness of individual rights and a surge in rights-assertion activities driven by the pursuit of individual interest. Among the village cadres, in terms of both mentality and actual behavior, there was a shift from being a screw in the revolutionary machine (of the party-state) to being an interest/profit-driven agent of the government. This change accelerated throughout the 1990s. In Chapter 2, I review the careers of three party secretaries in Xiajia village, showing how the third leader in the early 1990s only wanted to play the game wisely and earn sufficient money by "cheating the state and coaxing the villagers." His successor, the party secretary who had run the village from the mid-1990s, turned out to be even worse, as I examine elsewhere (Yan 2003: 23–4). No longer depending on the cadres for resources and life chances, the villagers were demanding that they be left alone; when they were not, they often engaged in various activities, ranging from physical fights to lawsuits to public protests, to protect their interests. The pursuit of individual interests and the fight to protect individual rights continued to develop during the 1990s and beyond. In 2002, for instance, a group of villagers, after three years of petitioning and protests, finally forced the party secretary out of power on charges of corruption. The villagers' demand that they be left alone actually foreshadowed the rise of the individual in the relationship between villagers and local government.

FAMILY, KINSHIP AND THE RISING INDIVIDUAL

Unlike the first two chapters, which examine the rise of the individual in relation to social-economic institutions and the agents of the party-state, Chapters 3 and 4 focus on the relationship between the individual and the two social categories that have defined the Chinese individual for centuries, namely, the family and kinship organization. A major difference is that the rise of the individual in the private sphere began as early as the 1950s.

Chapter 3 shows that the aggregated results of the changing family structure, intra-family relations and the family ideal led to the centrality of the conjugal relationship in family life, replacing the previous central axis of the parent–son relationship; along with this structural change, the primary function of the family evolved from a corporate group for the survival of a collectivity to a private haven for individual members. The nuclearization of the family, i.e. the gradual replacement of the traditional extended family by the smaller and more intimate unit of a couple with unmarried children, has long been regarded as a global trend in the modernization of the family institution. A major argument in Chapter 3, however, is that changes in family size and structure alone do not reveal the most important part of this transition. The modernity of the contemporary family lies in the rising importance of individual desires, emotions and agencies in family life, on the one hand, and the centrality of the individual in family relations, on the other hand. In other words, no longer willing to sacrifice oneself for the collective interests and for the perpetuation of the extended family, the individual in modern society seeks her or his interest and happiness through the working of the family. In the language of the Xiajia villagers, they are seeking *shunxin* (satisfaction/happiness) and *fangbian* (convenience/freedom) in family life, both of which are defined from a personal perspective.

This is why, from the 1960s to the 1990s, so many young villagers opposed the traditional practice of extended post-marital coresidence and sought to establish their own nuclear family as soon as possible. Yet, as I observed in the 1990s, not every individual pursued independence and freedom in family life through the formula of nuclearization; a number of young villagers chose to live with the husband's parents in the form of a "stem family" but fought a similar battle from within the old structure, taking over the management of the household economy and other decision-making processes. The end results remained identical: the pursuit of intimacy, independence, choice and individual happiness prevailed and gradually became a new family ideal.

In addition to my emphasis on the role of individual agency, such as the pursuit of privacy and freedom at the expense of encountering additional economic hardships, I also note the importance of the shared notion of the ideal family and a good family life, which is derived from the individual and in turn also shapes individual behavior. This became much clearer when I revisited the village after the 1999 visit.

During my visit in 1999, for example, I was shocked to learn that Teacher Liu and his wife had been expelled by their married only son and his wife because, although the young couple did not want to live with the old couple, they still demanded the family house and most of the valuables. The case broke the hearts of many of the elder villagers because Teacher Liu held a high status and had taken various strategic moves to prevent this from occurring (see Yan 2003: 140–2). In 2008, I was equally surprised to learn that the two families had reunited in 2006 and, since then, had lived peacefully together. The key, according to a number of villagers, was that Teacher Liu had changed his opinion and behavior, giving full authority and power to his son and daughter-in-law and recognizing the strengths of the young couple in dealing with the complexities of contemporary life (including how to properly educate the grandson).

Teacher Liu's case is by no means exceptional. In 2006 and 2008, I collected sufficient data to show that intergenerational conflicts had decreased, the number of stem families had increased and the time of family division again had been delayed. The other side of the coin has been an increase in conjugal conflicts and divorce cases. All of these phenomena are the opposite of what I found in the 1990s. Many villagers whom I interviewed – old and young, men and women – were well aware of these reversals in trend and attributed them to the new family ideal, especially new notions of choice, independence, privacy and intergenerational relations. It is also intriguing that, although I paid more attention to their urban life experiences when working in the cities, many villagers identified the messages of soap operas and pop music as a major source for the changes in the family ideal. Regardless of the source, however, it is clear that the relationship between the individual and the family has been altered dramatically, with the individual freed from a number of constraints that previously had been imposed by the family.

The central issue that I explore in Chapter 4 is how individual villagers exercise their agency and act to the best of their individual interests within the institutional constraints of kinship. I borrowed the notion of practical kinship from Pierre Bourdieu for its emphasis on individual agency in practice, but I disagreed with his definition of "practical kinship" as the domestic or family kinship and "official kinship" as kinship in public life (see Bourdieu 1990: 166–87). My major finding is the fluid and flexible nature of kinship resulting from the exercise of individual agency in practice. Individuals define and redefine the kinship distance between two parties in accordance with practical needs, changing sides back and forth in forming kinship alliances and not necessarily siding with the closer kin against more distant ones. Individuals invest heavily in emotional bonding with kin and close friends, and increasingly place more emphasis on relatives of the same generation or age group, a shift that parallels the increasing importance of the personal network, known as *guanxi* in Chinese. By practicing kinship in these ways, the individual is also redefining and, in a certain sense, remaking her or his identity.

The four patterns of practical kinship continued to develop in subsequent years, sometimes with dramatic results. For example, the power struggle between the manager of a local milk collection station and his own brothers and cousin in 1997 unfolded as a violent confrontation between the two camps that continued for several years and involved several dozen individuals, including a hired hit-man. The importance of affines and friends constantly grew, as reflected in the composition of gift exchange networks, which reflected the importance of the individual who made his or her network by choice instead of by inherited kinship lines, as well as the importance of women (more on this below). As a result, emotional attachments have gained more saliency in interpersonal relations, and the number of gifts exchanged by individuals on their own behalf instead of on behalf of their families has increased rapidly as many young villagers engage in gift exchange with friends or colleagues, a new type of relationship that is more personal than familial. Quite ironically, the formalized custom of gift exchange between families, which is more kinship based, has become a more instrumental game of receiving gifts, since an increasing number of villagers are apt to reciprocate less but are keen to receive more by hosting more family ceremonies. This unconventional phenomenon emerged in the 1980s and, since then, has developed significantly in terms of both its frequency and popularity (see Yan 1996). Kinship has thus been transformed into a part of one's *guanxi* network.

This does not mean that kinship is no longer an important way of self-organization among villagers; quite the opposite, villagers still use kinship ties to build their own networks and to establish alliances in economic, social and political activities, including village elections. What has been transformed is the shift in emphasis from ancestors and the collective interests of the kin group to the individual – her or his identity and interests. In ancestor-centered kinship practices, villagers must subordinate their individual interests to those of the ancestors and the collectivity, which was a religious and ethical obligation formulated through ancestor worship as well as secular life practices. In sharp contrast, the shared connections to common ancestors are evoked in current practices only when villagers pursue their personal interests in economic or political activities and when villagers, without a religious element, utilize but no longer subordinate themselves to ancestors or the collectivity of kinship. When their personal identity and interests conflict with those of kinship group or ancestors, more individuals choose to redefine the social distance with various kin, to formulate new kinship alliances with different partners, or to openly challenge the prevailing kinship rules, hence leading to a vibrant practical kinship. If I had merely focused on the functions of kinship while overlooking who made it function and for what purpose, I might have reached the conclusion that kinship was being revitalized; however, a closer look revealed that kinship is currently evoked and respected only when it is working for the interests of the individual villagers.

STATE-MANAGED INDIVIDUALIZATION

The party-state not only plays an important role in the development of the Chinese individual but it also manages the process of individualization by drawing boundaries and regulating directions, as shown in Chapters 5 and 6. The focus of Chapter 5 is rural youth and their culture, a topic that by and large was overlooked in China studies at the time. By the early 1990s, a distinguishable youth culture, which was basically an imitation of urban values and lifestyles, had emerged in village society. Although not a counter-culture in and of itself, this urban-aspired youth culture posed a challenge to both the prevailing rural culture and to the institutionalized separation of rural and urban life under the household registration system. Influenced by the information and images received from the mass media and from their own experience of working in the cities, an increasing number of young villagers had a much stronger sense of entitlement and individual rights, and they did not hesitate to act, mostly as individuals but occasionally in small groups, to challenge the authorities in both the public and private spheres.

The making of a rural youth culture, however, was closely related to the party-state's ideology, policies, institutions and political campaigns to build a new socialist person and socialist society that can be traced back to the 1950s. The Communist Youth League, the Women's Association and the Village Militia were the major organizations that recruited and mobilized youth as the vanguard of the socialist transformation; the Marriage Law and family reforms enabled the youth to fight against parental authority; and collective farming transformed all villagers, including the youth, into individual workers under a formalized leadership outside the family and kinship circles. Formal education and later opportunities to work in the cities not only widened the horizons of the young villagers but also changed their world views, inspiring them to live in a manner similar to that of the free-willed and affluent urban youth. I also point out that the increasing awareness of individual rights and the associated anti-authority tendencies among rural youth were the unintended consequences of the early political campaigns, the original purpose of which was to make the youth loyal and obedient subjects of socialism rather than truly independent and free-willed citizens. Thus, when young villagers stood up to protect their individual rights in terms of the law or other officially endorsed tools, government officials at various levels began to complain that their activities had backfired.

Subsequent fieldwork findings supported most of these observations in the 1990s. The urbanization of youth culture and rural youth accelerated over the years due to the intensified flow of images, information, lifestyles and people across the rural–urban divide. The current generation of rural youth makes various efforts to transplant urban lifestyles into village society, including, for instance, driving sedans to shop at the village store. But the life politics sometimes also takes more creative forms. For example, a group of young couples in 2007 celebrated the May 1 Labor Day (an official long holiday in China) by holding a picnic along the village creek. They served a barbecue and sausage sandwiches, widely perceived to be foreign and modern delicacies, and they engaged in ballroom dancing in the open fields. More importantly, they gathered together as couples rather than as a same-sex group, leaving their single children at home with their parents.

A notable new development is that more young villagers have left the villages to enrich their life experiences in the cities (see also Hansen and Pang 2008). Due to increased competition in the labor market, the income of migrant workers, especially unskilled workers, has stagnated and sometimes even declined during the last two decades. Therefore, working in cities does not necessarily bring much financial gain, and this is particularly true for young villagers, because they tend to imitate urban lifestyles and consume all they earn. I have encountered many young migrant workers in cities who have said that they do not send money back to their parents, because they do not earn enough to support themselves. Some have even received monetary support from their parents in the countryside. Then what is the point of working in the cities? In their own words, it is *"kan shijie"* and *"zhang jianshi"* (to see the world and to enrich one's knowledge and experience). The twenty-year-old man whom I quote in Chapter 5 perfectly understood this new trend when he expressed his admiration of the new generation of youth:

At that time [the late 1980s and early 1990s], people were much simpler and not open-minded, myself included. I was so thrilled to meet some friends in the cities and I had a girlfriend while working in Beijing. But I worked my butt off to save money and send it back home so that we could build a large house. I rarely went to restaurants and did not buy anything for my girlfriend. Nowadays, the kids [referring to the village youth] do everything urban people do; they go to karaoke bars, Internet cafes, restaurants, and they tour beautiful places. These are all expensive things. Having a girlfriend no longer is anything new, and the question has become *how many* girlfriends one has had. Some bold guys even visit *xiaojie* [prostitutes], and some girls are working as *xiaojie*, you know . . .

Another interesting change is that, although rural youth in the twenty-first century live lifestyles radically and sometime senselessly different from those of their parents (such as the case of driving a sedan with a girlfriend to shop at a store just 300 meters down the street), the older villagers' tolerance of youth and youth culture has increased greatly. Having one's hair dyed blond, for example, does not evoke any serious objections from one's parents or the elderly, and pre-marital cohabitation among engaged couples is regarded as normal. There has even been the emergence of a small group of youth who would be qualified as what the British sociologists call the NEETs (namely, youth who are "not in employment, education or training"). They refuse to work on the farms or to seek jobs in the cities, but they still live comfortable lives by demanding money from their better-off parents, who do not object as long as the adult son (there are not yet any female NEETs) does not do anything terribly wrong, such as stealing, gambling or becoming addicted to drugs.

In the reform era, the retreat of the party-state from mobilizing the rural youth as the vanguard of the social transformation created a vacuum in public life as well as a sense of directionless among the rural youth. This was actually also the case for urban youth, as was vividly reflected in the nationwide debates on the meaning of life in 1980 and the purpose of work in 1988 (Xu 2002: 51–74, 140–7). By the 1990s, in both the country-side and the cities, this vacuum was filled with the pursuit of individual interests and material comforts. The party-state-sponsored process of making a socialist new person evolved into a new process of making a new post-socialist consumer led by both the party-state and global capitalism (for state promotion of consumerism, see Chapter 9 in this volume).

The same is true regarding the rise of village women, particularly young women who are the subject of the study in Chapter 6. The organization of the ethnographic data, the research methodology and the interpretative framework in Chapter 6 are similar to those in Chapter 5, and there is also some overlap because young women are actually part of the youth group. For the same reason, some of these ethnographic details also appear in Chapters 3 and 8. The beginning of Chapter 6 explains the main reason why I have included this essay in the volume: rural young women, defined as those between the ages of 15 and 24 years, are undergoing the most important life transition, from a teenage daughter to a young daughter-in-law. In addition, according to the Chinese custom of post-marital residence, they are moving physically into a completely new environment of family and social life. However, this is a largely overlooked group in most existing studies of Chinese family and kinship, primarily because young women were previously perceived as being powerless and unable to accomplish anything significant.

This perception is challenged by my research findings. Young women in village society are by no means powerless and they have played an active role that eventually has contributed to breaking the family hierarchy, altering the intergenerational balance of power and greatly undermining patriarchy in the private life sphere. The road to empowerment for young women is not much different from that for youth in general, except that the young women have had to work harder to earn their entitlement and rights. Consequently, they tend to play a more active role than their male counterparts in the fight against patriarchy and they tend to be much more eager to break away from the all-encompassing family and kinship collectivity. Their voice, agency and action in the transformation of private life are too important to be treated lightly.

Chapter 6 proceeds further than Chapter 5 in one important aspect, that is, in its exploration of the limitations of the party-state-sponsored process of individual making through socialism. I point out that the agency and action of young women – or "girl power" as it is referred to in this chapter – were directed by the institutional arrangements, laws and state programs to fight against patriarchal power, but they rarely challenged the androcentric culture. Moreover, girl power, although largely promoted in the sphere of private life, was always controlled in public life. Once the party-state stopped organizing and mobilizing young women in public life, girl power retreated entirely back to the private life. As a result, by the late 1990s, the primary concerns of young women had shifted to femininity, beauty, cuteness and material comforts, and the young women fought a constant battle to gain the power to manage their conjugal family. For many young women, the ideal mate in the twenty-first century is a man who is rich, knows how to live a good life and indulges his wife. To realize this ideal, more than a dozen young women in the village have married men at least ten years their senior. In several cases, a young girl first became the older man's mistress and then forced the man to divorce his wife, a phenomenon until recently commonly found only in the cities, known as "the third party."

As I argue elsewhere (Yan 2003), unlike in the West where the market functioned as the primary mover behind the rise of the individual and the transformation of the private sphere into a more intimate domain, in China it has been the party-state that created such changes by enforcing a number of top-down institutional changes to build the new socialist person and society. The role of the party-state in shaping the individual remained strong and consistent across the dividing year of 1978, albeit in different forms and in different directions before and after the post-Mao reforms. The individual arose by responding to these institutional changes rather than pursuing her or his inalienable rights through a bottom-up approach. As a result, while taking advantage of the new laws, state policies and institutional changes that generally favor the interests of youth and women, individuals have accepted the constraints imposed by the party-state and have internalized the party-state's proscribed direction for the development of the individual under state socialism. The entire process can be called "managed individualization." An apt example is the shifting focus of self-development among youth and women from public life in the Maoist era to private life in the post-Mao reform era.

The constraints remained internalized by individuals in the third decade of the reform era (1998–2008), and even the most free-spirited youth knew that they could more or less do what they wanted in their personal lives, but that they had to remain within the political boundaries drawn by the party-state. The all-familiar emphasis on the freedom of individual choice and expression bears an interesting cultural twist among Chinese youth. As Chun Shu, a high-school-dropout-turned-young writer and the hottest youth idol in 2004, explained to a Western journalist: "Our concept of freedom is different from the West's. We want the physical freedom to travel where we want, work where we want, have the friends we want. But right now we can't be so concerned with spiritual freedom" (see Beech 2004; Yan 2006).

INDIVIDUALIZATION WITHOUT INDIVIDUALISM

State-managed individualization has also led to the rise of what I refer to as the "uncivil individual" (Yan 2003: 226), an important phenomenon that is discussed in Chapter 7 in relation to the Chinese understanding of Western individualism. The ethnography in this chapter focuses on the transformation of "bridewealth," or the custom of presenting marital gifts by the groom's family to the bride's family, which is found in many societies throughout the world. In Xiajia village and the surrounding areas, the bride has replaced her parents as the sole recipient of bridewealth. This has occurred together with the newly gained freedom in mate choice, the development of romantic love and the rising power of young men and women as individuals. Despite the party-state's various efforts to ban the custom because it is considered to be feudalistic, bridewealth continues to be practiced today and its monetary value has been constantly increasing. For example, the standard size of bridewealth increased from 50,000 yuan in 1999 to 60,000 yuan in 2003 and 90,000 yuan in 2008. The bride now tightly controls the bridewealth and, because of the high divorce rate, is unwilling to share it with her husband. The young woman who demanded a matching fund from her parents-in-law in 2003 after she discovered that her sister-in-law had received more than she did (see Chapter 7 for more details) eventually divorced her husband and took all their marriage savings, sending a strong message to others in the village.

While documenting the details of change in the practice of bride-wealth over a period of fifty years, Chapter 7 focuses on two questions: first, what is the role played by individual villagers in changing the custom of bridewealth? Second, how do we understand the paradoxical results of the change whereby contemporary youth can have the cake and eat it too, namely, they have defeated parental authority and have gained freedom in mate choice and marriage, yet at the same time they also demand lavish bridewealth and a dowry from their parents? I address these two questions at the levels of individual agency and strategy, parallel changes in family life, and institutional changes at the macro level of rural society. The exercise of individual agency has not necessarily led to youth independence; rather, it has led to an increased dependence on parental support for their marriage.

Many young villagers use "*gexing*" (individuality) and "*gerenzhuyi*" (individualism) to justify their relentless selfish pursuit of monetary gain from their own parents. In a similar vein, individual villagers also often avoid fulfilling their responsibilities in the public life of village society while pursuing individual interests at the expense of others (see also Yan 2003: 162–89, 220–6). A close look at the introduction and dissemination of individualism from the West to China, however, reveals that individualism has always been understood, among both the elite and the populace, as a form of egotism, involving selfish, anti-sociable and utilitarian interests, without any consideration of other individuals' rights and interests. Other elements in Western individualism, such as liberty, equality, freedom and self-reliance, have largely been overlooked. Such an egotistical vision of individualism was condemned by the party-state during the Maoist period, but it has since gained popularity through the mass media and the ideology of consumerism in the post-Mao reform era. Village youth have obtained the misinterpreted rhetoric of utilitarian individualism through the media or through their experiences of working in the cities, and they justify their behavior as modern and individualistic.

I single out the phenomenon of the uncivil individual because it represents a radical rupture with both the traditional Chinese notion of the self and the everyday practice of many other villagers whose behavior is governed by the collective ethics of *renqing* in the local moral world. Moving to the other end of the spectrum, Chapter 8 examines the moral foundations of calculating and budgeting in the household economy, and shows that, despite so many rapid changes, some old practices continue to persist and, for a number of individual villagers, *gexing* (individuality) and *gerenzhuyi* (individualism) still carry negative connotations.

Chapter 8 presents the story of Mr. Wang, known as the bookkeeping man in Xiajia village because of his twenty-year-long practice of keeping the books, who prospered through his masterful skill in calculating and budgeting the management of the household economy. The Wang household economy consisted of four components: farming, paid services, animal husbandry and money lending. Conditioned by demand and supply as well as the macro-economic environment, the income generated by these components fluctuated over the years. Farming and paid services to fellow villagers provided the major chunk of income in the late 1980s, peaking around 1990. After the mid-1990s both began to lose money. The family sideline of raising pigs and chickens brought a steady increase of profits in the late 1990s but it also entailed much greater risks, such as the spread of animal diseases. Money lending appears to have been the most lucrative business for the Wang family, but Mr. Wang kept it low profile and made every effort to package it as part of the reciprocity culture in village society. For example, Wang provided unpaid or low-cost tractor services to villagers and increased his annual spending on gift-giving as his household income increased. By so doing, he not only created a large network of clients but he also earned the reputation of being a nice person who really cared about maintaining good relations with his fellow villagers.

This case demonstrates the importance of *guanxi* (personal networks) and *renqing* (norms and values that regulate interpersonal relations) in the cultural construction of the Chinese individual (see Yan 1996: 98–146). Like many others, Wang had to learn to fulfill various moral obligations and to strengthen emotional attachments with related individuals in the village. A stable mutuality was the key to maintaining these relations, which in turn defined Wang's personal identity and reputation in the local moral world. Therefore, a good understanding of the local notion of *suanji* (calculating and budgeting) entails a delicate balance between profit-seeking and self-cultivation, and between pursuit of individual interests and contribution to the collective good. Wang achieved such a balance and thus was widely respected in the village.

In this sense, Wang stands out as a representative of the relational person or relational self in Chinese culture (see, for example, Fei 1948; Hsu 1948; King 1985; cf. Mauss 1985), whose values bear little resemblance to either Western individualism or the Chinese understanding of Western individualism. Yet, Wang, along with many like him (most of whom were over fifty years old), was motivated by the same set of institutional changes that have promoted individualization and marketization since the 1990s, and was forced to compete with other villagers (most of whom who were in their twenties and thirties) who were guided by values of utilitarian individualism. An increasing number of young villagers, Wang's single son included, dismissed Wang's way of doing business as too conservative and criticized his way of self-cultivation for a lack of individuality (*meiyou gexing*). During my last meeting with him in 2006, Wang admitted to me that he would never be able to catch up with the tide; his self-pride that had been so apparent in the early 1990s had completely disappeared.

RIDING THE SOFT WIND FROM THE WEST

The egotistic interpretation of Western individualism, however, also originates from the West, especially from the global diffusion of consumerism that has made instant individual gratification an individual right that is almost as important as – and at least as popular as – other key notions in individualism, such as independence, choice, freedom, and self-realization. The remaining two chapters in this volume address the issue of the global influence in post-1989 China.

Chapter 9 aims to unpack the rich meanings of mass consumption and the new ideology of consumerism in China around the turn of the century. More than one-third of the essay is devoted to a historical review of the change from under-consumption during the Maoist period to three waves of mass consumption in the post-Mao era, and to the formation of consumerism as the new and dominant ideology in the late 1990s. Along with this change, the ethics of everyday life shifted from an emphasis on self-sacrifice and hard work for a greater goal, such as building the new socialist society, to a new focus on self-realization and pursuit of personal happiness in concrete and materialistic terms. In other words, what makes one's life meaningful has changed from a collective ethics to an individual-centered ethics, similar to the shift from "being good" to "feeling good" observed in US society (see Bellah et al. 1996: 75–81).

After losing interest in the party-state's grand discourse on the "four modernizations," citizens began to work to realize what they call the "family modernization" through the possession of major appliances and a comfortable lifestyle, resulting in the initial wave of mass consumption. Various efforts to create and maintain status, prestige and individual distinctiveness, however, provided a non-stop engine for the later waves of mass consumption and the increasingly strong consumerist trends. All of a sudden, the politics of lifestyle became centrally important for those self-made successful individuals who, as shown in the example of the excessively luxurious wedding motorcade in 1992, had used conspicuous consumption to gain social distinction and to subvert the existing socialist hierarchy based primarily on political capital.

Another important component of the politics of lifestyle has been the rise of a consumer rights movement in China. This too has had multiple implications. The awareness of consumer rights and the various efforts to protect them play a key role in the development of the Chinese individual as a rights-bearing citizen, which in turn is promoting more reforms toward rule of law. Individual consumer rights leaders, such as Wang Hai, also demonstrate to the public the possibility of creating one's own biography through individual actions. Yet, contrary to the wishes of many in the early 1990s, the China Consumer Association did not develop into a force of civil society. Instead, it was incorporated into the party-state through various government agencies and became one of many GONGOs (government-sponsored NGOs, a uniquely Chinese term). Consumer rights protection as a social movement has developed within government-created structures; both the consumer rights protectors as well as their opponents, such as merchants and manufacturers, must appeal to government-sponsored agencies to settle disputes. As Hooper sharply notes, Chinese individuals are asserting rights not vis-à-vis the state but vis-à-vis the market; thus she refers to the Chinese individual as a "consumer citizen" (Hooper 2005).

The two fronts in the politics of lifestyle initiated by consumerism, i.e. making a social distinction through consumption and protecting one's consumer rights through individual actions, continued to grow in the third decade of the reform era. The consumer rights movement also stimulated the development of various forms of rights-assertion movements, including sizable collective actions. Although most rights-assertion movements are ad hoc actions to protect the self-interests of the participants against the encroachment of greedy and often brutal capitalism (O'Brien and Li 2006; Lee 2007), some individuals have gone beyond the level of materialism and have taken extraordinary steps to challenge the authoritarian state. For instance, Zeng Jinyan, a 23-year-old woman married to the political dissident Hu Jia, openly protested police brutality and government-sponsored oppression. As a result, she was featured as one of *Time* magazine's 100 most influential people in 2007. Key to all of these changes is the simple fact that an increasing number of individuals are standing up for their individual rights, a common phenomenon that is rapidly developing globally.

In the 1990s, the gentle breeze of consumerism from the West also created a whole range of commercialized places that individual consumers were welcome to appropriate as their own social space. Chapter 10 takes a closer look at this process by examining the successful entry of McDonald's restaurants into the Beijing market. It focuses on two issues: (1) the interplay of the global and the local in the newly emerging fast-food sector; and (2) the emergence of a new kind of social space where individual desires, lifestyles and the pursuit of material comforts can be celebrated openly in public. The perceived American culture associated with McDonald's proved to be essential to the fast-food chain's initial success in Beijing and its subsequent victory against its Chinese competitors. To be more precise, Chapter 10 shows that the Chinese competitors lost the fast-food war in the 1990s because they paid insufficient attention to the needs of an entire generation of consumers with more individualistic demands. A good example in this connection is the popularity of McDonald's among young women and children.

Both issues had lost their original significance by 2008, mainly due to the power of the market. McDonald's and KFC (Kentucky Fried Chicken) were no longer viewed as exotic and foreign. Rather, they slowly merged into part of the local landscape of restaurant culture – so much so that many children whom I interviewed in McDonald's in Beijing in 2006 did not know the US origins of the Big Mac, and many others simply did not care about the origins of any non-Chinese food. The new sociality that emerged in the early 1990s was continuing ten years later: people from all walks of life were coming to the social space to have a good time in their personal lives and they left as individual consumers. The earlier expectation that the social space created by the consumer revolution would have political implications appears to have been mostly wishful thinking based on the historical experience of the West. As Chinese youth and children – the new consumers I describe in Chapter 10 – have become the best informed and most welcomed consumers in the twenty-first century, there seem to be few remaining social obstacles left for the thriving of the individual in the domain of consumption, except the risk of consuming faulty or fake goods.

Taken as a whole, this volume provides a sketch of the rise of the Chinese individual during the dynamic and transitional decade of the 1990s and beyond. Although most ethnographic accounts come from one rural community, the major events and the overall trend of change can be found in both urban and rural China. With variations in degree and timing, Chinese individuals throughout the country experienced a *songbang* (untying) type of institutional change and were influenced by Western values, lifestyle and globalization, all of which were either sponsored by the party-state or related to the changing state policies. With variations across regional, class, gender and age lines, most Chinese individuals obtained more rights, choices and freedom in their personal lives from the collective constraints of the family, kinship, community, work unit and, in some cases, the party-state.

At this level of abstraction, stories from Xiajia village or a McDonald's restaurant in Beijing are indicative of, if not always representative of, the rise of the individual at a national level. Regional variations can enrich our understanding of this general trend of social transformation, but they do not offset it. For example, although Xiajia village has never been a single-surname community based on highly organized patrilineal lineages, which may have made it relatively easier for individual villagers to break away from the all-encompassing categories of family and kinship, the village was quite successful during the Maoist collectivization period. Further, by and large today it remains a farming community, with insignificant rural–urban migration until very recently, both of which obviously constituted serious obstacles to the rise of the individual. These variations may shape the rise of the individual in one way or the other, but they do not change the direction of the general trend. It is in this sense that I feel confident in my claim that the chapters in this volume document a great social transformation in the everyday life of ordinary people, which has in turn individualized the society.

In the Conclusion to this volume, I will take up the question of the individualization of Chinese society, but let me end this introductory chapter with a comment about some minor repetitions in the chapters that follow. In each of the first eight chapters, there is a paragraph describing the same field site – Xiajia village. At first, I was inclined to replace these paragraphs with a single brief description of Xiajia in the introductory chapter. But I was reminded by more thoughtful colleagues that such a deletion would create a new problem when some chapters are selected for teaching, which is perhaps the major use of such a collection of essays, because the reader would have no information about the field site. This well-taken point changed my mind, and thus these paragraphs remain in their original form. For the same reason, the analyses of the new pattern of serial family division, which appear in different lengths in Chapters 3, 6 and 7, remain unchanged as well. I apologize for these seemingly inevitable repetitions.

REFERENCES

Bauman, Zygmunt. 2001. *The Individualized Society*. Cambridge: Polity Press.

Beck, Ulrich. 1992. *Risk Society: Towards a New Modernity*. Trans. Mark Ritter. London: Sage Publications.

Beck, Ulrich and Beck-Gernsheim, Elisabeth. 2001. *Individualization: Institutionalized Individualism and its Social and Political Consequences*. London and Thousand Oaks, CA: Sage Publications.

Beech, Hannah. 2004. "The New Radicals." *Asia Times*, February 2, pp. 32–8.

Bellah, Robert N., Madsen, Richard, Sullivan, William M., Swidler, Ann and Tipton, Steven M. 1996. *Habits of the Heart: Individualism and Commitment in American Life* (updated edition). Berkeley, CA: University of California Press.

Bourdieu, Pierre. 1990. *The Logic of Practice*. Trans. Richard Nice. Stanford, CA: Stanford University Press.

Fei Xiaotong. 1948. *Xiangtu Zhongguo* (Folk China). Shanghai: Guancha Press (English translation *From the Soil: The Foundations of Chinese Society*. Trans. Gary G. Hamilton and Wang Zheng. Berkeley, CA: University of California Press, 1992).

Fujian ribao (Fujian Daily). 1984. "Qing gei women songbang" (Please Untie Us), March 22, p. 1.

Giddens, Anthony. 1991. *Modernity and Self-Identity: Self and Society in the Late Modern Age*. Stanford, CA: Stanford University Press.

Hansen, Mette Halskov and Pang, Cuiming. 2008. "Me and My Family: Percep-tions of Individual and Collective among Young Rural Chinese." *European Journal of East Asian Studies* 7(1): 75–99.

Hansen, Mette Halskov and Svarverud, Rune (eds.). 2009. *China: The Rise of the Individual in Modern Chinese Society*. Copenhagen: NIAS Press.

Hooper, Beverley. 2005. "The Consumer Citizen in Contemporary China." Working Paper #12, Centre for East and South-East Asian Studies, Lund University, Sweden.

Hsu, Francis L.K. 1948. *Under the Ancestors' Shadow: Kinship, Personality, and Social Mobility in Village China*. New York: Columbia University Press.

King, Ambrose Yeo-chi [Yao-ji Jin]. 1985. "The Individual and Group in Con-fucianism: A Relational Perspective." In Donald J. Munro (ed.), *Individualism and Holism: Studies in Confucian and Taoist Values*. Ann Arbor, MI: Center for Chinese Studies Publications, University of Michigan, pp. 57–70.

Lee, Ching Kwan. 2007. *Against the Law: Labor Protests in China's Rustbelt and Sunbelt*. Berkeley, CA: University of California Press.

Mauss, Marcel. 1985 [1938]. "A Category of the Human Mind: The Notion of Person; the Notion of Self." In Michael Carrithers, Steven Collins, and Steven Lukes (eds.), *The Category of the Person*. Cambridge: Cambridge University Press, pp. 1–25.

Nee, Victor. 1989. "A Theory of Market Transition: From Redistribution to Mar-kets in State Socialism." *American Sociological Review* 54(5): 663–81.

O'Brien, Kevin J. and Li, Lianjiang. 2006. *Rightful Resistance in Rural China*. Cambridge: Cambridge University Press.

Sun Liping. 2004. *Zhuanxing yu duanlie: Gaige yilai Zhongguo shehui jiegou de bianqian* (Transition and Rupture: Structural Changes in Chinese Society since the Reforms). Beijing: Qinghua University Press.

Szelenyi, Ivan. 1988. *Socialist Entrepreneurs: Embourgeoisement in Rural Hungary*. Madison, WI: University of Wisconsin Press.

Walder, Andrew. 1983. "Organized Dependency and Cultures of Authority in Chinese Industry." *Journal of Asian Studies* 43(1): 51–76.

Xu, Luo. 2002. *Searching for Life's Meaning: Changes and Tensions in the Worldviews of Chinese Youth in the 1980s*. Ann Arbor, MI: University of Michigan Press.

Yan, Yunxiang. 1994. "Dislocation, Reposition and Restratification: Structural Changes in Chinese Society." In Maurice Brosseau and Lo Chi Kin (eds.), *China Review 1994*. Hong Kong: Chinese University Press, pp. 15.1–24.

Yan, Yunxiang. 1996. *The Flow of Gifts: Reciprocity and Social Networks in a Chinese Village*. Stanford, CA: Stanford University Press.

Yan, Yunxiang. 2003. *Private Life under Socialism: Love, Intimacy, and Family Change in a Chinese Village, 1949–1999*. Stanford, CA: Stanford University Press.

Yan, Yunxiang. 2006. "Little Emperors or Frail Pragmatists? China's '80ers Generation." *Current History: A Journal of Contemporary World Affairs* 105(692): 255–62.

Zhou, Kate Xiao. 1996. *How The Farmers Changed China: Power of the People*. Boulder, CO: Westview.

CHAPTER I

THE IMPACT OF RURAL REFORM ON ECONOMIC AND SOCIAL STRATIFICATION*

'Let some peasants get rich first' was one of the leading slogans of China's rural reforms, beginning in the early 1980s. After almost a decade, who has become rich? Who has benefitted the most? And what specific changes have resulted to the structure of social stratification in rural China? All of these questions become centrally important when we examine the consequences of rural reform. Many scholarly efforts have been made to answer these questions, but the overall picture of inequality and stratification in the past decade is still unclear.[1]

The present study will offer an account of such shifts in inequality and stratification in one north China village since the rural reform. Instead of focusing on peasant income alone, I will also examine changes in economic position, political power, and social status, i.e., the three major dimensions of social stratification. I will begin with the general background of my survey and briefly describe the status groups in the previous hierarchy of the collectives. Then I will answer the question, 'who got rich first?' by presenting the results of the village survey and will analyse the impact on the structure of stratification. I will conclude by discussing the implications of the case study beyond this village's boundaries.

THE VILLAGE SURVEY

This study draws mainly on information gathered during fieldwork in north China between January and May 1989. My decision to investigate the issue of social stratification was initially inspired by interviews with peasants during a visit to a village in Shandong Province where I had lived from 1966 to 1971. There, old friends complained that the current 'class line' was wrong and that people from 'exploiting-class' families had benefitted from the reforms much more than they themselves had. This sort of discontent was also evident in subsequent visits to villages in Hebei Province.[2] In response to this widespread dissatisfaction, I decided to conduct a systematic, inclusive household survey in Xiajia village, Heilongjiang Province.[3] The reason for choosing this field site was simple: I had lived in the village for seven years (1971–78) and knew the life histories of most residents, thus making it possible to observe the changes in their social status.

Xiajia is located on the southern edge of Heilongjiang Province. According to the household register, last updated in 1982, it has a population of 1,602 in 284 households, farming 8,310 *mu* of land, growing mostly maize and soybeans. It used to be a brigade consisting of four production teams and is now an administrative village (*xingzheng cun*). In the late 1960s and the 1970s, Xiajia was relatively successful in collective agriculture. The average value for ten work points had been kept at 1.10 to 1.30 *yuan*, which placed Xiajia among the richer villages in north China. This partially explains the delay in the village's decollectivization, which did not occur until 1983.[4]

At that date, encouraged by central government policy, peasants privatized everything, including the tractors and other heavy agricultural machines. Farmland, the fundamental means of production, was divided into two categories: ration land (*kouliang tian*) and contracted land (*chengbao tian*). Everyone in the village was entitled to have two *mu* of ration land and every adult labourer got ten *mu* of contracted land. The peasants' obligations to provide the state with cheap requisitioned grain only applied to the contracting land.

Due to its poor transport links (with only an unpaved road into the county town), there was no rural industry in Xiajia village at all during the period of collectives, and only a few grain processing factories exist now, all of them family businesses. The major income of most households still derives from farming and family sidelines. The average net income *per capita* in 1988 was 528 *yuan* (the national average was 545 *yuan*), which places Xiajia almost precisely at mid-point economically among Chinese farming communities.

THE SOCIALIST HIERARCHY WITHIN THE PRE-REFORM COLLECTIVES

Although Western scholars have recognized the urban-rural income gap and regional inequalities in Maoist China, the egalitarian image of rural life within the collectives has yet to be demystifed (about this I will have more to say below). However, it was well-known in the West that China, like other state socialist societies, was a status society, in which the structure of social stratification was based on bureaucratic 'rank order' rather than any market-based system of 'class order'.[5] So it is appropriate to follow Weber's conventions[6] by identifying the 'status groups' in the socialist collectives. In the case of Xiajia, six groups were clearly identifiable according to their prestige, privileges, and abilities to gain access to resources and opportunities in the bureaucratic redistributive system of the collectives: (i) the incumbent cadres; (ii) the retired and fallen cadres; (iii) the *shi shu hu*; (iv) the peasants of 'good class' label; (v) those of 'middle peasant' origins; and (vi) the 'four bad elements'.

Cadres

The cadres, of course, stood highest in the system of social stratification. This is not to say that the composition of the cadre group in a given collective was unchanging; in fact, as will be shown below, the distinction between being 'in office' and 'out of office' at the time of decollectivization has resulted in a significant difference for these officials' post-decollectivization economic performance. I will accordingly classify separately those cadres who were in power in 1982 or are currently holding power – namely, the post-reform office-holders – as against those who had fallen or retired from power before 1982. There are twelve such former cadres (not including cadres below the level of team head). Half of them were so-called *tugai ganbu* [cadres during the Land Reform of the 1950s]. These former cadres did not enjoy the same privileges as the cadres in power; but they were still regarded with deference and generally had access to the best jobs in the collectives. Since all of them were Party members, they also had some influence in village elections.

At the end of 1982, the eve of decollectivization, there were thirteen full-time incumbent cadres in the Xiajia brigade (cadres lower than heads of production team again are not included), and of these, ten held Party membership.[7] They enjoyed considerable political power, economic advantage, and social privilege within their little collective empire, just like their counterparts throughout rural China. And as in other places, they also played the role of patron to selected peasants – their clients.[8]

Among such clients, the political activists deserve particular attention. They tended to be assigned desirable jobs, such as tractor driver or head of a small group in a production team. More importantly, as in all villages, they enjoyed the prospect of becoming cadres themselves some day.[9] But as these activists had no stable political power or fixed economic advantage to distinguish themselves as a status group, and as the composition of the activist group was always changing along with changes of political environment, I will not regard them as an independent group in the social hierarchy of the collectives, even though their role in that hierarchy is too important to ignore.

The Si Shu Hu

There is yet another group called *si shu hu* (four types of households) that also ranks in the upper level of the village hierarchy. This category has not been recognized by earlier scholars of Chinese social stratification. *Si shu hu* include the spouses and children of state cadres, workers, teachers, and military officers, all of whom live in the village and belong to the rural population. In Xiajia, nineteen households could be counted as *si shu hu* in 1982. They enjoyed dual economic benefits – from both the state and the collective. On the one hand, given that the head of each such household was a government employee, they had a guaranteed cash income from the state; on the other hand, they received their shares of grain and other goods at low prices from the collective distribution system, even though they did not work for the collective. For this reason, in some rural areas they were called *dui lao shen* (literally, 'the gentry of the production teams').[10]

Ordinary Peasants

An important indicator of social status in the socialist hierarchy was the privilege of avoiding manual labour, especially farm work. For example, brigade cadres almost never did farm work and the heads of production teams did so only occasionally. The ordinary peasants in Xiajia accordingly called themselves 'black hands' (*hei zhuazi*), because they were continually working the land and thus exposing themselves to the sun, and the privileged were called 'white hands' (*bai zhuazi*) because they were able to avoid tanning their hands by farm work. The unequal access to opportunities and discrimination reflected in this distinction between 'white hands' and 'black hands' constituted a quite serious problem of social inequity.

While the cadres, the *si shu hu*, and some political activists occupied the upper level of the hierarchy in Xiajia, the ordinary peasants stood somewhere in the middle. According to Maoist class theory,[11] the former 'poor peasants' and 'lower-middle peasants' – those who had been impoverished before the revolution – are the only revolutionary force in the countryside, and special opportunities and jobs (e.g., as cadre or teacher) should be reserved for them. Nonetheless, a few people from former 'middle peasant' backgrounds sometimes were given these jobs by dint of their merit.[12]

Because the good class label and 'poor or lower-middle peasant' might bring marginal advantages even to ordinary peasants, in making them feel superior to others and granting them bargaining power in terms of job assignments within production teams, I have classified these peasants separately in my survey from those with the former class label of 'middle peasant'. As shall be seen, these two groups of different class labels fared differently, both before and after decollectivization.

The 'Four Bad Elements'

As can be expected, the former 'landlords' and 'rich peasants' (no-one in Xiajia bore the class label of 'counter-revolutionary' or 'rotten element') were at the bottom of the hierarchy of socialist collectives. They were considered class enemies, and were discriminated against both politically and socially. They were placed under 'mass control' and were always the first targets of attack during political campaigns. In daily life they had to accept the worst job assignments and received the least remuneration. In Xiajia 200 to 400 work points were deducted annually from the total amount they earned, which was equivalent to their giving up these work points as free labour contributed to the collectives.[13] They had no hope of ever improving their status.

There are three basic factors structuring the socialist hierarchy in Xiajia village. The first is obviously the full control of the collectives over the peasants' lives, enforced through the Party cadres' authority and power. This was the central axis of socialist stratification – a hierarchy based on bureaucratic rank, in which cadres enjoyed higher status politically and socially than their subjects. The second factor was related to the separation and inequality between the urban and rural sectors, which has been officially endorsed since the late 1950s. This makes the *si shu hu* who enjoy the 'iron rice bowl' of state employees superior to ordinary peasants who have to find their rice solely from the 'clay bowl', namely from farming. Third, the 'class line' and the virtuocratic standard in social mobility in the Maoist era provided the socialist hierarchy with a powerful ideology. This ideology transformed the 'four bad elements' into virtual 'untouchables' in the socialist hierarchy on the one hand, and on the other promised the former 'poor peasants' higher social status and spiritual superiority (born-red).[14]

In short, the socialist hierarchy was based on three sets of binary opposition, i.e., cadres :: peasants; city :: countryside; and red :: black (in class origin).[15] Interestingly enough, these three oppositions are consciously recognized by both the state authorities on one hand (represented by local government and grass-root cadres) and by the peasants on the other hand. In the official language, they are categorized in terms of the relationships between leaders and led, urban and rural, and 'we' versus 'them'. In the eyes of ordinary peasants, the first two are perceived as the opposition between the 'white hands' and 'black hands'.

RESULTS OF THE SURVEY: AFFLUENCE AND POVERTY IN THE REFORM ERA

How did the several different categories of peasant fare economically under the reforms?

In my investigation I focused on the overall economic position of every household in Xiajia village, instead of peasant income alone for several reasons. First, peasants are usually reluctant to report their full incomes. Second, as they became independent producers after decollectivization, peasants had to make their own investments for agricultural production. Therefore, the economic position of a given household was determined not only by its current income but also by accumulated family assets.

Thus two kinds of measures were utilized to examine the current economic position of every household: family assets and annual income. Assets included: 1) primary tools of production; 2) farm machinery and/or draft animals; 3) milk cows or other important capital for family sidelines; 4) private enterprises; 5) housing; 6) savings in cash and/or grain; and 7) consumer durables.[16] The net income per capita in 1988 was taken as the standard in measuring current earnings.[17] Combining the two measures, the 284 households in the village were classified into three economic levels: rich, average, and poor. In my classification, a rich household must have a per capita net income of 600 *yuan* or more, and possess all of the assets listed above. A household of average level is characterized by possession of assets 1, 3, 5, and 6 (in smaller amounts), and a net income per capita above 450 *yuan*. For the poor, only numbers 1 and 5 (but not in good condition) may apply, and per capita income will be less than 450 *yuan*. The distribution of peasants' economic status for all the social strata in the village is shown in Table 1.

Several points should be noted here. First, although scattered in all social groups, the rich households cluster significantly in certain strata. For one thing, a higher rate of rich households is found among the formerly privileged groups. As shown in Table 1, 54 per cent of the post-1981 cadres and 53 per cent of the *si shu hu* have 'gotten rich first'. At the same time, 30 per cent of the former middle-peasants among the ordinary peasantry are winners. (If we examine *all* of the households of middle-peasant label, including those who are cadres and *si shu hu*, we find that fully 41 per cent of all the former middle peasants are today rich.) Given that the average rate of attaining prosperity in the village is 16 per cent (as reflected in the bottom row in Table 1), these three groups have obviously advanced themselves. The lowest rate of prosperity is found among the ordinary peasants of 'good class' label – only 6 per cent have become rich. The performance of the 'four bad elements' looks unremarkable at first glance; but, considering their former untouchable-like status and the fact that most of them are today at an average economic level (76 per cent), their achievements become impressive.

Table 1   Economic status of Xiajia village households

Economic position	Rich	%	Average	%	Poor	%	Total
Social group							
Post-1981 cadres*	7	54%	6	46%			13
Fallen & retired cadres	2	17%	6	50%	4	33%	12
'Si shu hu'**	10	53%	8	42%	1	5%	19
Ordinary peasants of 'good class' origins	11	6%	121	67%	48	27%	180
Ordinary peasants of 'middle-peasant' origins	8	30%	17	63%	2	7%	27
'Four bad elements'	6	18%	25	76%	2	6%	33
Total	44	16%	183	64%	57	20%	284

* Including 2 households of former middle peasant background, both of whom are in the 'rich' category.

**Including 3 households of former middle peasant background, all of whom are in the 'rich' category.

Second, in scanning the column of poor households in Table 1, the rate of economic progress for different groups becomes even clearer. Among the fifty-seven poor households, none belongs to the group of post-1981 cadres and only one comes from among the *si shu hu* group. In contrast, forty-eight are from among the ordinary peasants of 'good class' origins – which renders this group the least successful, with a low rate of affluence and the second highest percentage of poor.

Finally, the performance of the group of retired and fallen cadres is interesting. Although two households in this group have become rich, the percentage of poor among them (33 per cent) is so high that, overall, this category constitutes the biggest loser since the rural reforms. Considering their former respectable status as leaders and Party members, their fall appears even more severe. For instance, a former cadre in this group who became the brigade head in the late 1960s and who was also a team head for several years found himself in such economic difficulty that during the Spring Festival of 1988 he adopted a local strategy of begging – he visited every family in the village and sent each a paper-cutting of the Chinese character for 'happiness'. Naturally, he was criticized severely by the local Party branch for 'losing face for the Party', and he has not repeated this practice. But what interests us here is the dramatic change in his status from cadre to beggar.

The unsuccessful performance of these former cadres results in part from their removal from positions of power before decollectivization, and in part from their inability to adapt to the new situation (many of them have reached old age and are illiterate). According to many informants, all cadres who were in office at the end of 1982 made their profits in various ways during the process of decollectivization, such as through access to more land or through signing lucrative contracts with the collectives. In contrast, the group of former cadres who had fallen out of power before 1982 had to sit back to wait for their share, as did the ordinary peasants. This view is supported by my survey, in which the general failure of these former cadres very strongly suggests that holding an office during and after decollectivization does make a significant difference both economically and socially. It is by no means accidental, therefore, that the five cadres who are currently in power have all attained wealth, and two of them are among the ten richest in the village.

To further illustrate the economic differentiation in the village, the ten richest and ten poorest households are listed in Table 2. Interestingly

Table 2   Distribution of the ten richest and ten poorest households

Economic position	Richest	%	Poorest	%	Total
Social group					
Post-1981 Cadres	3	23%			13
Fallen and retired Cadres	1	8%			12
'Si shu hu'					19
Ordinary peasants of good-class origins	2	1%	10	6%	180
Ordinary peasants of middle-peasant origins	4	15%			27
'Four bad elements'					33
Total	10		10		284

enough, while the social composition of the top ten families is diversified, all ten of the bottom households are clustered in one social group – ordinary peasants of 'good class' origins. This reconfirms the finding reflected in Table 1 that this group has made the least economic improvement. Two groups are missing from this list. The *si shu hu* have not been able to climb into the ranks of the top ten households because they lack strong labourers both in family farming and sidelines, as their household heads are employed by the state. The failure of the former 'four bad elements' to reach the highest level of affluence most likely results from their initial fears: according to some informants, they were among the last to respond positively to, and take advantage of, the new opportunities created by the reforms.

It becomes instructive to take a closer look at the ten richest households in the village. Among the three that are headed by post-1981 cadres, the first household head has been in power since 1967 and is currently the Party secretary in Xiajia. He earns 1,500 *yuan* a year from his position and also farms 42 *mu* of land, together with his two sons. A small tractor and two milk cows also bring in a great deal of money for his family. The household head in the second family is currently the assistant Party secretary, and his cadre career can be traced back to 1961. He enjoys higher social status partially because of his revolutionary family background: his father was an active cadre during the Land Reform, his two elder brothers became high ranking officials in the Chinese army, and one of his sons is in the army as well. As well as earning a fixed salary of 1,400 *yuan*, he also owns the only truck in the village, which his other son uses to generate a cash income in the transport business. The third family is an overlapping case: the household head has served as a brigade cadre in various positions since 1967. He became the Party secretary in the village in 1976 and retired from that position in 1987. Meanwhile, his family can also be regarded as a '*si shu hu*', as his wife (a school teacher) and his eldest son (a shop staff member) are state employees. The major source of his family's prosperity, according to many informants, is the fixed cash income from the salaries of his wife, son, and himself when he was still in office.

Among the top ten households, the only one from the group of former cadres is regarded as the most successful specialized household in milk-cow husbandry in the village. According to some informants, the family's extraordinary success results more from the kinship ties of the household head than from his own ability. His elder brother is currently the general manager in a milk product factory in the county seat and thus provides a secure market.

The two rich households from the group of ordinary good-class peasantry benefitted mostly from the professional skills of the household heads. One was a barefoot doctor in the collective and still works as a doctor in the village, lucratively. So far as I know, this person's appointment as barefoot doctor in the early 1970s was attributed not to his own professional knowledge but to the influence of his elder brother – then the Party secretary in the village. The second rich household head was a tractor driver before decollectivization who subsequently opened a small workshop for repairing agricultural machinery. Some informants asserted that the success of this individual was related to his strong friendship since the mid-1970s with Xiajia's three successive Party secretaries, for whom he provided special services.[18] But other informants argued that he was the most skilful in the village at handling machines and that his success has resulted from his own talent.

The remaining four rich households derive from ordinary peasants of middle-peasant label. They have one feature in common: all these household heads are well-known in the village to be skilled farmers and are also very good at various family sidelines, including animal husbandry, handicrafts, and cash-crop gardening. Moreover, they have a reputation of being 'decent and genuine peasants'; they have successfully maintained traditional peasant virtues within their families, such as honesty, diligence, and thrift. Two of them were criticized several times for 'pursuing the capitalist road' during the period of collectives, because they tried to develop their family sidelines and sell their family products on the black (free) market. Another of these four households, thrifty to the core, has kept using organic fertilizer since decollectivization, irrespective of the fact that most villagers use only chemical fertilizers to save on labour investment. The head in the fourth of these households is known for his sensitivity to market information and new technology. An example widely cited by my informants is that he subscribes to several agriculture-related journals and one newspaper.[19]

It is clear that there are many ways to get to the top: while political capital including social networks and fixed salaries make the four individuals with cadre background stronger in economic competition, the two with the former class labels of 'poor peasant' benefit from the specific professional skills they acquired during the collective period. Only the four individuals from the former 'middle peasant' group have made their success mainly through family farming and sidelines, the ways available to all peasants, by way of diligent work and thriftiness – the virtues supposedly possessed by all. Therefore, no one sees the success of these four households as morally questionable or accuses them of taking advantage of political power or 'back doors'.

IMPACT OF REFORM: THE CHANGING STRUCTURE OF SOCIAL STRATIFICATION

One of the more striking impacts of the rural reforms lies in the decline of village cadres' authority and power. This decline has been generally recognized and well documented among China scholars.[20] A couple of examples from daily life in Xiajia lend support to such findings.

Three years ago a young peasant felt he was being unfairly treated by the owner of a repair shop in the village and accused the then village Party secretary of giving the owner special favours. The quarrel developed into a violent conflict, and the young man not only beat the owner badly, but berated the Party secretary, challenging him to a public fight. This was the first time since the revolution that an ordinary peasant in Xiajia dared to be in violent opposition to a Party secretary and, to the amazement of all, he won the confrontation. The direct result was that the Party secretary, having lost face, was forced to resign. Ordinary villagers took this as a symbol of the collapse of the authority and power of the village cadres.

As another example, more than a dozen informants told me that in 1988 they did not give gifts to the current Party secretary to celebrate his son's marriage. Given that weddings in rural China function as one of the most important occasions to display one's prestige, it has long been taken for granted in Xiajia that the villagers present gifts to their leaders during weddings and other occasions in recognition of the latters' social status. The fact that these villagers refused to give gifts to the Party secretary on this occasion demonstrates the decline of his power in an even stronger way than does the example of violent confrontation; culturally it was more meaningful.

Parallel to the decline in the political power of cadres, the focus of public life in Xiajia village has gradually moved from the former brigade headquarters to the village shop (symbolically a locus of society). During the period of the collectives, the headquarters of production teams, in addition to their formal function in the management of production and political meetings, served as public places for informally gathering and chatting. Theoretically, the brigade headquarters should have served a similar community function, open to the public; but in practice the ordinary peasants saw the brigade headquarters as a court of village government and stayed far away. The regular visitors to the brigade headquarters consisted of cadres and political activists as well as some *si shu hu*, namely, the 'white hands'. Soon after decollectivization, the three-room brigade office and an assembly hall were demolished, and the current village office is now a small room connected to a grain processing factory. Cadres rarely stay in the office unless they have business to attend to; and there are few visitors. In contrast, the village shop has become crowded with informal gatherings by people from all walks of life. Villagers go there not only to shop but also to collect information and exchange ideas. As the shop is a place for economic transactions and one's power is reflected in one's purchasing ability, the cadres, except for the five currently in power, and the *si shu hu* have no more privileges there than do others. Interestingly enough, the village shop building has been expanded twice since decollectivization. If the former brigade headquarters might be seen as a political centre and a symbol of the privileges enjoyed by the formerly advantaged, the village shop now serves as an economic centre and symbol of the market mechanisms which have benefitted ordinary villagers.

The impact of the reforms can also be seen in peasant life styles. For instance, flashlights, pens, and cigarettes had long been the symbols of higher social status in the village – mostly the cadres and *si shu hu* had used these things during the era of collectives. The origin of this can be traced back to the Land Reform. In the eyes of peasants, the 'cadre comrades' from the urban areas had been associated with such symbols of authority. The image was reinforced again and again by the various work teams from urban areas during the political campaigns that started with the Land Reform. Gradually, these items became associated with communist cadres, the government, and urban superiority. Partially in imitation of the urban cadres and partially due to practical needs, local cadres and *si shu hu* in the village began to carry such 'equipment' and to smoke cigarettes instead of home-made leaf tobacco. During the time of economic scarcity in the 1960s and 1970s, these small commodities served to distinguish cadres and *si shu hu* from the ordinary peasants and to highlight their status differences. For instance, the higher a cadre's rank was, the bigger the flashlight he would carry. The Party secretary would have a flashlight with four D-size batteries while a team leader felt it wisest to use a less powerful one with only two batteries. This was not codified but everyone knew the rules of the game. But with the rural reforms this has totally changed. Nowadays many rich peasants have purchased motorcycles and other consumer durables, not to mention luxury cigarettes available in the village shop. The real significance here is that the symbolic meaning of luxury goods now has much more to do with one's purchasing power than one's political power.

Another interesting finding is that some of the previous advantages enjoyed under the collectives have become obstacles to prosperity. For instance, avoidance of manual labour in farming had long been a key privilege enjoyed by the cadres, the *si shu hu*, and some of the political activists, namely, the 'white hands'. Moreover, peasants with good class origins often refused to do dirty, heavy, or complex farming work and had little interest in improving their farming knowledge and skills. To avoid confrontations, team leaders simply assigned the undesirable work to the non-privileged people with 'middle peasant' or bad class labels.[21] One result was that much of the village elite and part of the ordinary peasantry of good-class labels all but forgot farming techniques while the disadvantaged were forced to improve their knowledge and skills.

After decollectivization, many young peasants who grew up in the collectives found themselves in an embarrassing situation – they neither had experience of independent farming nor were able to accomplish many of the more complex agricultural tasks.[22] In a farming community like Xiajia, failure in farming could severely damage a household's economic position, and this is one of the primary causes of poverty for the fifty-seven low income households shown in Table 1. An impressive indicator is that six farm households have been forced to sublease their land as a result of financial losses. Half of these households enjoyed obvious privileges before decollectivization. One was a discharged soldier who held Party membership and who was usually the first among the villagers to gain relief money and grain from the state.[23] The other two were former political activists, who specialized in performing various political rituals but knew little about farming.

In contrast to the former advantaged people, the former disadvantaged are benefitting from their unpleasant experiences under the collective. As indicated above, the peasants without privilege or good class origins were always assigned to do the less desirable, physically exhausting, and more skilled work. Moreover, being well aware of their vulnerable status, they had to learn to be careful about the quality of their work. After decollectivization, they proved to be among the most qualified in family farming. It is not surprising that, among the ten 'farming masters' commonly acknowledged in the village, five have the class label of former 'middle peasant' and three are from the 'four bad elements'.

The decline of the cadres' superiority was welcomed by all except the cadres themselves; but attitudes vary among villagers toward the rise of the formerly disadvantaged, especially toward the former 'four bad elements'. Some peasants attribute their success to their hard work and farming knowledge and thus expressed no objection to their rise. Others thought it unfair to allow the 'class enemies' to stand up, or *fanshen.* One person complained: 'The poor remain poor and the rich remain rich. Nothing has changed since the Land Reform'. Some even said they hoped to see a second land reform come soon.

This negative attitude toward the modest success of the former 'four bad elements' has gone well beyond any feelings of egalitarianism or any peasant envy rooted in an 'image of limited good',[24] even though both did exist in Xiajia. Rather, the anger and blame flow out of the previous system of socialist hierarchy.

Interestingly, villagers express their dissatisfaction by using the word *fanshen.*[25] Many of the peasants with good class background regarded the discrimination against the 'four bad elements' as a symbol of their own *fanshen* (or moving up), and eventually took it for granted that such people had been relegated to an untouchable-like status. It is this mentality that they themselves comprise a 'revolutionary poor', created and fostered by the communist ideology, that makes the progress of the former 'four bad elements' so unacceptable to some of the villagers in Xiajia.

Not surprisingly, most of those villagers – formerly advantaged but currently unsuccessful – still live spiritually in the shadow of the previous system of socialist hierarchy. For instance, a former activist who was once the deputy chief of the village militia told me:

> For years I didn't need to touch my hoe and sickle. You know how comfortable I was then. But now I'm in bad luck, and the worst thing is that even those 'four bad elements' have gotten ahead of me. Remember? They had to report their activities to me [in earlier decades].

According to Ivan Szelenyi, in socialist societies the state-controlled redistributive system tends to favour the officialdom, and thus 'the interests of the powerless and disprivileged can be best served with increasingly transactive (and consequently market-like) relationships in the economic system'.[26] In an examination of the impact of the second economy on the social structure of rural Hungary, Szelenyi maintains that 'the most striking development is the resurgence of the "second hierarchy", the system of inequalities based on market transactions rather than position in the bureaucratic order'. He thus traces the emergence of a dual system of social stratification.[27]

Szelenyi's thesis is supported by our case study in Xiajia village. The three basic factors that structured hierarchy in the collectives derived from one origin, namely the power of the bureaucratic system of redistribution, which is characterized by its monopoly over economic resources and opportunities for mobility. In Xiajia during the pre-reform era, as has been seen, the village cadres, the *si shu hu*, and some political activists, namely, the 'white hands', were all close to and benefitting from the redistributive system; the rest, the 'black hands', were generally excluded. The market-oriented reforms have undermined to a great extent the power of this system and opened new opportunities for these 'black hands', leading not only to a redistribution of economic position but also of social status. As a result of these changes, a dual structure of social stratification is emerging in the village, in which the socialist-bureaucratic rank order co-exists with a market-based economic class order. Although its further development remains unpredictable, it is certainly not the restoration of the pre-1949 system. As shown in my survey, the composition of today's rich households looks rather like a mixture of capable individuals from all the social groups; and without strong external intervention, no group is likely to be overwhelmingly triumphant.

IMPLICATIONS BEYOND THE BOUNDARY OF XIAJIA VILLAGE

What are the broader implications of the Xiajia case?

First, the analysis of Xiajia illustrates the necessity of studying social stratification within local rural communities, an issue that has long been neglected. Scholarly attention has focused on rural inequality and income disparities at the macro level for the pre-reform era;[28] and the hierarchy of social status and related inequalities within the socialist-era villages have yet to be adequately explored. Despite recent findings regarding the patron-client relationships between cadres and peasants,[29] an egalitarian image of the collectives still dominates Western scholarly discourse on the pre-reform era. In contrast, in the past decade a rapid increase of income differentiation in peasant communities has elevated questions of inequality and stratification to the top of our research agenda.[30] One consequence is that outside observers often gain the impression that the economic reforms have increased the inequalities in Chinese villages, while macro-level urban-rural inequalities have decreased.[31]

Perceptions of equality and inequality need to involve, as I have noted, not only income, but also status, power, and privilege. Furthermore, even if just income differentiation is analysed, we need to know, as Martin Whyte has suggested, 'whether the introduction of market-oriented reforms enables those already advantaged by the state allocation system to increasingly monopolize the new opportunities made available via the market, or whether those benefits will in large measure work to the advantage of those who were benefitting less from the state allocation system'.[32]

To accomplish these research goals we must first demystify the egalitarian image of the collectives, and then determine whether the reforms have decreased or increased social inequalities. My survey has shown that, at least in the case of Xiajia, pre-reform social life can hardly be characterized as 'egalitarian', and the collectives were perhaps no less hierarchical than pre-revolutionary communities. Moreover, the rural reforms have decreased hidden inequalities by breaking up the socialist hierarchy that had prevailed in the village.

Second, the Xiajia case may provide an alternative understanding of the position of rural cadres after the reforms, an issue that is currently under debate among China scholars. Earlier interpretations focused on cadre resistance to rural reforms and thus suggested a decline in their political power and economic position.[33] Other studies have found that rural cadres utilized their political capital for personal advantage, and thus became entrepreneurs themselves or the patrons of rich villagers.[34] A counter-interpretation was offered recently by Victor Nee, who has extended Szelenyi's analysis of economic reforms in Hungary. The argument is that a transition from redistributive to market coordination shifts sources of power and privilege in favour of direct producers rather than redistributors. Nee asserts that 'current and former cadres seem to have gained no significant returns on their cadre status'.[35]

Applying these interpretations to the Xiajia case, both have some basis in fact, but neither is sufficient to explain local developments. As indicated above, the power of the cadres has declined, and they have lost much of their superiority in social terms. But some cadres took advantage of the reforms to accumulate private wealth and in this respect they have benefitted to a great extent from their cadre status.

This being the case, how should we understand the cadres' general level of affluence under the reforms? Under a bureaucratic system of redistribution, it is natural to find that cadres (and the *si shu hu*) are taking advantage of the reforms. Unlike the bureaucratic mechanism of allocation and distribution, however, the market mechanism does not entirely preclude anyone else's chances of success due to ascribed status at birth or distance from the centre of political power. It is true that most of the cadres did succeed in market-oriented competition through ability and capital and 'connections' and power. The key point, however, is that the rural reforms were started by peasants who promoted their own interests from below and then were encouraged by the reformers from above.[36] Therefore, the most important question in examining the social consequences of the reforms should be whether ordinary peasants – and if so, who among them – have benefitted, and whether the formerly disadvantaged have improved their circumstances.

My analysis of Xiajia has shown, at a micro level, that a number of ordinary peasants – including some of the former disadvantaged – have indeed benefitted both economically and socially. In particular, in addition to the group of cadres who have advanced themselves far beyond the majority of the Xiajia residents, the peasant households of former 'middle-peasant origins have done extremely well. Given that most ordinary peasants of former 'poor peasant' origins are economically, either at an average level or remain poor, the dramatic rise of this middle-peasant group in both economic and social terms forms a challenge to the superiority of the cadres and *si shu hu*. The consequence is that the previous socialist hierarchy is being replaced by a dual system of social stratification that is characterized by the coexistence of bureaucratic rank with a market-based economic class order.

In my opinion, the most significant consequence of rural reform is that rural cadres have lost their status monopoly in the newly emerging system of social stratification. They have had to compete with their former subordinates in market-oriented agricultural production. In this sense, no matter how much rural cadres have gained in terms of wealth, abuses of power and corruption, they have been losers in the reform.

ACKNOWLEDGEMENTS

* This paper is based on field research supported by the Harvard-Yenching Institute. I owe thanks to Anita Chan, Kathleen Hartford, Jean Oi, Andrew Walder, James Watson, Tyrene White, Martin K. Whyte, and David Zweig, and the editor, Jonathan Unger, for helpful comments on earlier drafts. I am also grateful to Lida Junghans, Matthew Kohrman, and Xiaoshan Yang for editorial assistance.

NOTES

1. For a general review, see Andrew Walder, 'Social Change in Post-Revolution China', *Annual Review of Sociology*, no.15 (1989), pp.405–24.
2. During these visits, some Chinese scholars in the State Council's Research Centre for Rural Development told me that they had first noticed this problem in 1985, but had difficulty explaining it. I was interested in their use of the word 'problem' (*wenti*), and understood their difficulty, i.e., how to justify the reform politically if in some locales people of 'bad' class backgrounds were doing materially better than their neighbours of 'good' class origins. It is perhaps due to this reason that Chinese studies on rural reform purposely seem to avoid discussing the issue of social stratification and only emphasize the changes in peasant income in general, without specifying the social strata to which individual peasants belong.

3. To protect the peasant informants, the village's name has been altered, and all of the informants remain anonymous.

4. Heilongjiang was the last province in China to dismantle the commune system, and the main reason, according to Luo and others, was the relative success of collective farming. See Luo Xiaopeng et al., 'Lishixing de zhuanbian' [The Historical Change], *Nongcun, jingji yu shehui* [Countryside, Economy, and Society], vol.3 (Zhishi chubanshe, Beijing, 1985).

5. For an excellent analysis of status groups in the Chinese industrial labour force, see Andrew Walder, *Communist Neo-Traditionalism: Work and Authority in Chinese Industry* (University of California Press, Berkeley and Los Angeles, 1986).

6. Max Weber, *Economy and Society* (University of California Press, Berkeley, 1978), pp.305–307.

7. Along with the development of rural reforms, the number of cadres has considerably decreased, and by spring 1989, there were only five cadres left in village service.

8. A comprehensive examination of the cadre's role as patron is found in Jean Oi, *State and Peasant in Contemporary China* (University of California Press, Berkeley, 1989).

9. Susan L. Shirk offered an excellent analysis of political activists as a characteristic Chinese social phenomenon in her study of student behaviour in Chinese high schools, and much of her argument can be applied to rural society as well. See Shirk, *Competitive Comrades: Career Incentives and Student Strategies in China* (University of California Press, Berkeley, 1982). For discussions of political activists in rural communities, see Anita Chan, Richard Madsen, and Jonathan Unger, *Chen Village, The Recent History of a Peasant Community in Mao's China* (University of California Press, Berkeley, 1984); Huang Shu-min, *The Spiral Road, Change in a Chinese Village Through the Eyes of a Communist Party Leader* (Westview Press, Boulder, 1989); and Richard Madsen, *Morality and Power in a Chinese Village* (University of California Press, Berkeley, 1984).

10. See Chen Yizi, *Zhongguo: shinian gaige yu bajiu minyun* [China: The Tenyear Reform and the Pro-Democracy Movement of 1989] (Lianjing Press, Taiwan, 1990), p.31. At the beginning of the rural reform, a primary concern among Chinese leaders was whether the *si shu hu* would fall into poverty. To justify the reform, the reformers had to make great efforts to demonstrate that the *si shu hu*, like other peasants, actually benefitted from the reform. A good example in this connection is the famous report written by Chen Yizi which finally encouraged the top leaders in Beijing to accept the trend of decollectivization and other reforms throughout rural China. In this report,

Chen compared the rate of income increase between the *si shu hu* and other peasant households, and concluded that 'the responsibility system of house-hold production did not decrease incomes among the *si shu hu* and the *wu bao hu* [five guaranteed households]; on the contrary, it enabled them to enjoy the biggest increase of income among the peasants'. See Chen Yizi, 'Nongcun de shuguang, zhongguo de xiwang' [The Dawn in the Countryside, the Hope of China], in *Nongcun, jingji yu shehui* [Countryside, Economy, and Society], vol.1 (Zhishi chubanshe, Beijing, 1985 [original 1980]), p.44.

11. In discussing social stratification in post-revolution China, one cannot avoid referring to the class labels assigned to individual peasants in the Land Reform, i.e., the class labels of 'poor peasant', 'middle peasant', 'rich peasant', and 'landlord'. The last two plus 'counter-revolutionary' and 'rotten element' were considered bad class labels, or called the 'four bad elements'. These class labels determined people's life chances to a great extent during the decades in which the 'class line' was stressed. For a detailed explanation, see Richard Kraus, 'Class Conflict and the Vocabulary of Social Analysis in China', *China Quarterly*, no.69 (1977), pp.54–74; and James Watson (ed.), *Class and Social Stratification in Post-Revolution China* (Cambridge University Press, Cambridge, 1984). These class labels were officially abolished in 1979.

12. For example, there were two individuals of middle peasant background among the thirteen cadres, and three among the *si shu hu* in Xiajia village by the end of 1982. But it should be noted that among these three state employees, two had graduated from urban colleges and taught at the local middle school; and the third became a shop clerk by inheriting his father's position in 1979.

13. This situation was common in Chinese villages. From interviews with peasants from Guangdong Province, Parish and Whyte note that 'once a month or so they [the four bad elements] are obliged to contribute a day's free labor to the collective'. William Parish and Martin K. Whyte, *Village and Family in Contemporary China* (University of Chicago Press, Chicago, 1978), pp.99–100. The biggest reduction in payment that I have witnessed was 1200 work points per person in a year during the late 1970s, in a village of Shandong Province.

14. For a thoughtful analysis of this issue, see Jonathan Unger, 'The Class System in Rural China: A Case Study', in James L. Watson (ed.), *Class and Social Stratification in Post-Revolution China*, op.cit., especially pp.129–32.

15. The hand/mouth ratio in a family (and the life cycle as well) is certainly another contributing factor to intra-village inequalities during the collective period. But, as it plays the same role in most societies and thus cannot be seen as a unique feature of the socialist hierarchy, I will not discuss it in

the present study, even though I am fully aware of the importance of able-bodied labourers for a family's prosperity. For relevant studies, see William L. Parish and Martin K. Whyte, *Village and Family in Contemporary China,* op.cit; and Mark Selden, 'Income Inequality and the State', in William L. Parish (ed.), *Chinese Rural Development: The Great Transformation* (M.E. Sharpe, Inc., Armonk, 1985).

16. I spent a great deal of time discussing what items should be considered family assets and their importance for determining the economic position of a given peasant household. This list was finally accepted by all of my key informants.

17. As the average net income per capita in 1988 in the village is 528 *yuan*, the economic positions of peasant households are divided accordingly: above 700¥ = very good; 600–700¥ = good; 450–600¥ = fair; 300–450¥ = poor; and below 300¥ = very poor.

18. This may imply a relationship of patron and client. See Jean Oi, *State and Peasant in Contemporary China*, op.cit., pp.146–47.

19. As early as the 1950s, the advantages of the former 'middle peasants' in family farming were noticed by some open-minded Chinese officials and economists. They even discussed the future of 'middle-peasantrification' in rural China. This non-communist heterodoxy was soon eliminated by Mao's radical thought of revolutionizing China and the campaign of rural collectivization. Beginning with the late 1950s, the Party began to criticize the former middle peasants for their spontaneous tendency in going the capitalist road. For a recent discussion of the tendency of 'middle-peasantrification' in the early 1950s, see Li Boyong, 'Tudi gaige hou nongcun jieji bianhua de quxiang' [The Trend of Changes in Rural Classes After the Land Reform], *Zhonggong dangshi yanjiu* [Studies of CCP History], no.1 (1989), pp.45–47. Interestingly enough, the middle peasants in Hungary shared a similar experience as their counterparts in China, and quite similarly, they comprised the main body of successful peasant entrepreneurs after a market-oriented second economy began to play an important role in Hungary. See Ivan Szelenyi, *Socialist Entrepreneurs: Embourgeoisement in Rural Hungary* (University of Wisconsin Press, Madison, 1988).

20. See e.g., Victor Nee, 'A Theory of Market Transition: From Redistribution to Markets in State Socialism', *American Sociological Review*, vol. 54, no.5 (October 1989), pp.663–81; Jean Oi, *State and Peasant in Contemporary China*, op.cit.; Gordon White, 'The Impact of Economic Reforms In the Chinese Countryside: Toward the Politics of Social Capitalism', *Modern China*, vol.13, no.4 (1987), pp.411–40; and David Zweig, 'Prosperity and Conflict in Post-Mao Rural China', *China Quarterly*, no.105 (1986), pp.1–18.

21. Actually, this is a common problem existing in all collectives. As Oi notices, 'team leaders and work members reported that those with the not-so-good backgrounds were the most co-operative and the least troublesome. They were the easiest to control because they knew that they were the first to be criticized in the event of a campaign and therefore always walked a thin line' (Jean Oi, *State and Peasant in Contemporary China*, op.cit, p. 145, footnote 28).

22. David Zweig observed a similar phenomenon earlier in a southern province of rural China. When decollectivization was proceeding, a number of young peasants showed their reluctance to participate in family farming, because they did not know how to handle the work on their own (personal communication with Zweig). In advanced regions of southeast China, this problem was soon diminished by the rise of rural industries, which created new opportunities for the rural youths who were so eager to leave farming. But in less developed areas, rural youths' unfamiliarity with agricultural production remains a serious obstacle.

23. There were a number of peasant households, both poor and red, like the one in question in most collectives before the rural reforms. The Communist Party regarded them as the basic force of revolution and thus provided regular relief to them. An unintended result of this policy is that, being supported by the collective and the state for decades, many such households have lost their incentive to work hard and became a sort of privileged poor. As a cadre from the relief department in a county has related, 'they [the poor households] were grateful to the Party at the beginning; but over the long course they have got used to it. You have to keep giving them relief, otherwise they will complain strongly. It looks like you owe something to them. They argue, 'it is the Party not you who feed us, so how can you dare not to give us relief?' In a striking example, relief goods were sent to a poor village in Guizhou Province, but no one in the village was willing to unload the truck. Finally, some migrant peasants from Sichuan Province were hired to do the job, and they were paid by the villagers in relief cash (see *Zhongguo qingnian bao* [The Chinese Youth Daily], 2 June 1987).

24. See George M. Foster, 'Peasant Society and the Image of Limited Good', *American Anthropologist*, vol.67, no.2 (1965).

25. According to William Hinton, 'literally, it means "to turn the body" ' or "to turn over". To China's hundreds of millions of landless and land-poor peasants it meant to stand up, to throw off the landlord yoke, to gain land, stock, implements, and houses. But it meant much more than this. . . It meant to enter a new world'. (William Hinton, *Fanshen, A Documentary of Revolution in a Chinese Village*, Vintage Books, New York, 1966, p.vii.) The revolutionary meaning of this word has been emphasized by the CCP, and

fanshen was among the first Chinese characters taught in primary schools after the revolution.

26. Ivan Szelenyi, 'Social Inequalities in State Socialist Redistributive Economies', *International Journal of Comparative Sociology*, vol.19, no.1–2 (1978). p.63.

27. Ivan Szelenyi, *Socialist Entrepreneurs: Embourgeoisement in Rural Hungary* (University of Wisconsin Press, Madison, 1988), p.64 and p.71.

28. See Nicholas R. Lardy, *Agriculture in China's Modern Economic Development* (Cambridge University Press, Cambridge, 1983), and 'Consumption and Living Standards in China, 1978–83', *The China Quarterly*, no.100, pp.849–65; William L. Parish and Martin K. White, *Village and Family in Contemporary China*, op.cit.; Sulamith Heins Potter and Jack M. Potter, *China's Peasants, the Anthropology of a Revolution* (Cambridge University Press, Cambridge and New York, 1990), chapter 15; and Mark Selden, 'Income Inequality and the State', in William L. Parish (ed.), *Chinese Rural Development: The Great Transformation* (M.E. Sharpe, Inc., Armonk, 1985).

29. See Jean Oi, 'Communism and Clientelism: Rural Politics in China', *World Politics*, vol.37, no.2 (1985), pp.238–66.

30. See Andrew Walder, 'Social Change in Post-Revolution China', op.cit.; and Martin K. Whyte, 'Social Trends in China: The Triumph of Inequality?', in A. Doak Barnett and Ralph N. Clough (eds), *Modernizing China: Post-Mao Reform and Development* (Westview Press, Boulder, 1986).

31. See e.g., Sulamith Potter and Jack Potter, *China's Peasants*, op.cit., pp.337–39.

32. Martin Whyte, 'Social Trends in China: The Triumph of Inequality?', op.cit., p.120.

33. David Zweig, 'Opposition to Change in Rural China: The System of Responsibility and People's Communes', *Asian Survey*, vol.23, no.7 (1983), pp.879–900, and 'Prosperity and Conflict in Post-Mao Rural China', *China Quarterly*, no.105 (1986), pp.1–18.

34. Jean Oi, *State and Peasant in Contemporary China*, op.cit.; and Gordon White, 'The Impact of Economic Reforms in the Chinese Countryside: Toward the Politics of Social Capitalism', *Modern China*, vol.13, no.4 (1987), pp.411–40.

35. Victor Nee, 'A Theory of Market Transition: From Redistribution to Markets in State Socialism', *American Sociological Review*, vol. 54, no.5 (1989), pp.663–81.

36. See Chen Yizi, *Zhongguo: shinian gaige yu bajiu minyun* [China: Ten-Year Reform and the Pro-Democracy Movement in 1989] (Lianjing Press, Taiwan, 1990).

CHAPTER 2

CHANGES IN EVERYDAY POWER RELATIONS

In assessing the political consequences of departures from central planning, a key concern is the impact of market-oriented reforms on power relations within socialist redistributive systems. Iván Szelényi's work (1978, 1988) on social stratification in Hungary implies that the power and privilege of socialist redistributors will be undermined by the introduction of market mechanisms. Inspired by Szelényi's insight, Victor Nee (1989) developed a theory of market transition. The core of Nee's theory is that the increased scope of market allocation reduces the scope of bureaucratic redistribution, eroding the power and privilege of officials, who lose their monopoly over resources. This theory has, however, encountered much contrary evidence of the continuing influence of communist cadres at all levels. Jean Oi has proposed an alternative account that emphasizes the cadres' economic role in industrializing villages as the main root of both corruption and their legal power and privilege. She maintains that market allocation in an unreformed political system creates new opportunities for patronage and corruption, altering, but not diminishing, the power and privilege of officials who deal regularly with ordinary citizens (Oi 1989a, 1989b).

Focusing on everyday power relations in a north China village, the present study addresses the same issue, but offers a perspective different from either of the two abovementioned theories. According to Max Weber, power is "the probability that one actor within a social relationship will be in a position to carry out his own will despite resistance, regardless of the basis on which this probability rests" (Weber 1947, 152). Following this definition, I examine how people influence the conduct of others in daily life within the boundaries of peasant communities. Changes in power relations are seen as the result of interactions between cadres and ordinary villagers,[1] and attention is thus paid equally to both cadres and ordinary villagers as political actors.

From the perspective of social-exchange theory, I start with a discussion of how rural economic reforms generated a dynamic of change in power relations. Then I examine the political outcomes of these changes in two ways – namely, the altered behavior patterns among the grass-root cadres and the political mentality and actions of the villagers. To conclude the essay, I relate this village study to the general impact of reforms on cadre power, an issue raised by the two aforementioned theories.

Xiajia village, where I conducted my fieldwork from February to August 1991, is located on the southern edge of Heilongjiang Province. It is a farming community with a population of 1,564, growing mostly maize and soybeans. Owing to its poor transport links, there was no rural industry in the village during the collective era, and only a few grain-processing mills exist now, all of them family businesses. According to my survey in 1991, the average net income per capita was 616 yuan in 1990 (the national average was 623 yuan), which places Xiajia at the midpoint economically among Chinese farming communities. In other words, Xiajia will never be designated a government showcase of rural development. It is an ordinary place in every sense except for one thing: I lived in the village for seven years (1971–78) during the collective era and thus know most of its residents' life histories. I revisited Xiajia and carried out a field survey during the spring of 1989, which made it possible to discern the most recent changes when I went back yet again in 1991.

Like most rural communities in China, Xiajia has undergone dramatic social changes over the past four decades. In addition to the influences of the larger social environment, the village's fate was also closely asso-ciated with its leadership. Radical local leadership during the first decade of socialism subjected Xiajia to most, if not all, of the irrational social experiments of the Great Leap Forward. Despite these experiments and the devastation of the 1959–61 famine, by the late 1960s Xiajia had be-come relatively successful in collective agriculture, and it remained so throughout the 1970s. One of the key factors in the village's achievements, according to many informants, was good management by brigade and team leaders. The collectives in Xiajia were dismantled at the end of 1983.[2] Consequently, the number of cadres at the village level decreased from thirteen to five, including the party secretary, village head, deputy party secretary, village accountant, and head of public security. More important, as shown below, after 1983, these cadres began to play a different role in village politics.

THE BASES OF CADRE POWER IN THE COLLECTIVE ECONOMY

To examine the dynamics of current changes in power relations in village life, we must first understand the structural basis of cadre power prior to the reforms and then see what has happened to this basis since then. In this connection, social-exchange theory provides an instructive perspective.

From a social-exchange point of view, power can be seen as "the ability of persons or groups to impose their will on others despite resistance through deterrence either in the form of withholding regularly supplied rewards or in the form of punishment, inasmuch as the former as well as the latter constitute, in effect, a negative sanction" (Blau 1964, 117). Here the availability and control of resources are crucial for establishing power in social interactions. According to Richard Emerson (1962, 1972), exchange relationships are based on the predicated dependence of two parties upon each other's resources. To the extent that A is unwilling voluntarily to surrender a resource desired by B and able to use this resource to force, coerce, or induce compliance by B, A is said to have power over B. Moreover, if A can monopolize all the resources B needs, B will be dependent on A. Unless B can furnish other kinds of benefits to A as an exchange, this dependence compels B to comply with A's requests. Hence an unbalanced power relationship is established between A and B.

In his analysis of "power-dependence" relations, Emerson presented four ways for a given individual to avoid becoming involved in a power-dependence relationship. When one needs a service another has to offer, one can (a) supply him with another service; (b) obtain the service elsewhere; (c) force him to provide the service; or (d) give up the original demand. If the former is not able to choose any of the four alternatives, he has to become dependent on the latter and accept the latter's power (Emerson 1962, 31–41). Peter Blau reformulated Emerson's schema and applied it further to specify the conditions of social independence, the requirements of power, and their structural implications. According to to Blau, the conditions of independence include strategic resources (like money) for starting an exchange relationship, the available ways to escape the other's power, coercive force to compel others, and self-reduction of demands. Being complementary to the conditions of independence, the basic strategies to attain and sustain power are indifference to what others offer, monopoly over what others need, law and order, and support of a value system (Blau 1964, 118–24).

Applying this approach to examine the previous structure of power relations in Xiajia, it is evident that because cadres were able to control almost all resources in the collective economy, villagers were left no other choice but to subject themselves to cadre power. Cadre power in the prereform era was based on four main conditions.

First, collectivization provided cadres with the most efficient way to monopolize resources, from the basic means of livelihood to opportunities for upward mobility. In the collectives, Xiajia peasants worked in groups under the supervision of cadres, and their basic needs were distributed annually by the collectives. They had no right to decide what activities they would engage in. During the more radical periods, for all social activities outside the collectives, such as visiting relatives or going to nearby marketplaces, peasants also needed the formal permission of cadres. Complaints about cadres or about state policies were severely punished, and the complainants were often accused of counterrevolutionary activities. In short, peasants were deprived of all rights to basic economic, social-cultural, and political resources (see Oi 1989a, 131–55; Parish and Whyte 1978, 96–114; Zweig 1989).

Second, their loyalty to the party state helped prevent cadres from being seduced by bribery or other forms of corruption, and thus increased their overall ability to exercise power. Owing to the emphasis on political correctness and class origin in cadre recruitment, only those who closely followed the party line and their superiors' instructions could stay in power, and their political loyalty was consistently tested in numerous political campaigns. Political rewards from higher levels of government served to raise their social and political status, bringing psychological rewards and reinforcing their political loyalty. Compared to the current situation, economic corruption was not a serious problem among cadres in the collectives. Many cadres lived in conditions similar to those of ordinary villagers, and the main material privileges they enjoyed were better meals and less manual labor. The revolutionary, honest cadre was a generally accepted ideal. This probity in turn strengthened cadres' capacity to exercise power over team members (see Chan, Madsen, and Unger 1992, 26–30; Huang Shu-min 1989, 105–28; Potter and Potter 1990, 283–95).

Third, state penetration into village society established the legitimacy of cadre authority, and "mass dictatorship" provided a coercive force to compel peasants. Commune officials supervised all village work and always supported village cadres when conflicts occurred between cadres and villagers. Political struggle sessions and the use of village militia are the most common forms of mass dictatorship, and in many cases village cadres took advantage of these means to attack their personal foes (see Friedman, Pickowicz, and Selden 1991; Hinton 1983, 169–261; Oi 1989a; Siu 1989, 189–243).

A fourth source of cadre power was the hegemony of communist ideology. Cadres could enforce their authority by claiming that they represented the party's political line, and their correctness thus could not be questioned by the masses. By resorting to the official ideology, cadres were also able to justify actions that proved to be against the private interests of the peasants, such as eliminating any life chances outside the collectives. "Revolutionary ideologies, which define the progress of a radical movement as inherently valuable for its members, bestow power on the movement's leadership" (Blau 1964, 122). Moreover, the domination of communist ideology made villagers pliant to the dictates of political campaigns that empowered only the movement leaders (see Chan, Madsen, and Unger 1992; Potter and Potter 1990, 270–82; Zweig 1989).

For analytic purposes, the conditions needed for villagers to avoid cadre power are: (1) freedom of physical mobility; (2) a supply of strategic resources able to undermine cadre power; (3) personal ability to resist, or the use of protective networks; and (4) indifference to ideological mobilization. Obviously, none of these conditions existed during the collective era. There was no alternative available to villagers. The household registration system, the ban on rural-urban migration, and the requirement of official certificates to travel, all imprisoned villagers within the boundaries of the collectives (see Potter 1983, 465–99). They had little to offer cadres except bodily service, and what they did have all came from the collectives, which were run by the cadres. Under the totalitarian rulership of the CCP, personal resistance to cadre power or to ideological mobilization was virtually impossible. It would have resulted in grave political trouble.

THE DYNAMICS OF CHANGE AND MARKET-ORIENTED REFORM

The rural reforms brought fundamental changes to this seemingly immutable power structure by creating alternative resources and opportunities outside the bureaucratic redistributive system, and by attenuating the conditions that made villagers dependent upon cadres. There have been four key components of this process of change.

First, decollectivization has undermined the most important basis of cadre power: monopoly over resources. This is mainly because of the distribution of land to families and the shift to household farming. In the eyes of Xiajia residents, the most significant aspect of rural reform was the distribution of land. They always refer to the date of land distribution when discussing recent changes in village life. Farmland in Xiajia was divided into two categories: ration land (*kouliang tian*) and contract land (*chengbao tian*). Every person in the village (regardless of age or sex) was entitled to have two *mu* of ration land, and every adult male laborer received ten *mu* of contract land. Peasants' obligations to provide the state with cheap requisitioned grain and taxes only applied to contract land. The effective duration of land distribution was fifteen years, and within that period no further adjustment would take place.

For ordinary farmers in Xiajia, land is not merely a fundamental means of production; it is the most reliable source of social welfare. Control over land is nothing less than controlling one's fate. From the first day that villagers could make their own decisions about what to plant on their land and how to use the surplus, the very basis of cadre power began to crumble. It was common for villagers to express their feelings about decollectivization with a modern term: freedom (*ziyou*),[3] and they then added a footnote to it by quoting an old popular saying: "People have to obey the person who controls their rice bowls" (*duan shui de wan, fu shui guan*). An old villager once told me: "With a piece of land, you have a rice bowl of your own. It is not the iron bowl that urban people have, but you don't need to beg anybody for a bowl of rice – you dig it up from your own land."

The significance of this change is best illustrated by the simple but profound fact that more than 90 percent of the adult males in Xiajia village now have their own private seals (or "name chops"). In the past this was a privilege enjoyed only by the cadres who ran collectives. Nowadays the peasants need private seals for signing a wide variety of contracts with companies and with local government agencies. The immediate consequence of the departure from collective farming is that they have gained the status of independent legal persons.

Second, as many economists have noted, agricultural productivity surged suddenly after the switch to household farming, and living standards in rural China have generally improved to a remarkable extent. One of the most important consequences of the improvement in villagers' economic circumstances has been the eclipse of the previous social hierarchy by new patterns of economic and social stratification. This is suggested by a household survey of family incomes that I conducted during the spring of 1989 (see Table 1).

Table 1   Economic status of Xiajia village households, 1989

Economic position/ social group	Rich households		Average households		Poor households		Total households
	No.	%	No.	%	No.	%	
Post-1981 cadres	7	54	6	46	0	0	13
Fallen & retired cadres	2	17	6	50	4	33	12
Si shu hu	10	53	8	42	1	5	19
Ordinary peasants of "good class" origins	11	6	121	67	48	27	180
Ordinary peasants of "middle class" origins	8	30	17	63	2	7	27
"Four bad elements"	6	18	25	76	2	6	33
Total	44	16%	183	64%	57	20%	284

Note: As the distinction between being "in office" and "out of office" at the time of decollectivization has resulted in a significant difference for these cadres' postdecollectivization economic performance, I categorize those who have fallen or retired from power before 1982 as a separate group. Si shu hu constitute another less-known category, which includes the spouses and children of state cadres, workers, teachers, and military officers, all of whom live in the village and belong to the rural population in the household register system. The "four bad elements" are those who bear negative class labels such as landlord or rich peasant. (For a detailed explanation of the survey and the classification of the six social groups, see Yan 1992, 3–9.)

Table 1 suggests that while village cadres have taken advantage of the reforms to accumulate private wealth and have become prosperous, a number of ordinary peasants, including some of the formerly disadvantaged, have also benefited both economically and socially. In particular, peasant households of former "middle-peasant" origins have done extremely well. As a result, the previous socialist hierarchy is being replaced by a dual system of social stratification that is characterized by the coexistence of bureaucratic rank with a market-based class order. The emergence of this new structure of social stratification, which echoes what Szelényi (1988) found in rural Hungary, has contributed a great deal to a new pattern of power relations, which was quite visible when I conducted my second field survey of Xiajia in 1991.

The rise of a new group of rich peasants presented a challenge to cadre power in two ways. Many peasants, especially those who have become relatively affluent, suddenly came to possess the strategic resources (money or goods) for social exchange. According to social-exchange theory, "a person who has all the resources required as effective inducements for others to furnish him with the services and benefits he needs is protected against becoming dependent on anyone" (Blau 1964, 119). The shift in control of resources to peasant households constitutes a decline in villagers' dependence on cadres. The rise of peasants' economic well-being further broke the superiority of cadres in the previous social order and made cadres susceptible to material inducements offered by villagers (I shall return to this point later).

The third dynamic factor generated by the reforms is that the party state has begun to retreat from rural society, and mass dictatorship as a means for controlling society has gradually dissipated. A similar indicator of this change is that the village militia has disappeared – although it still exists on paper, the position of militia head has been eliminated. Everyone is so busy trying to advance their economic status that even state officials are no longer interested in monitoring villagers' behavior. In 1991, few state officials came to the village to supervise policy implementation or other work, since the local government's primary concerns were now grain procurement and tax collection.

In contrast to the retreat of the state, social networks made up of connections – referred to in Chinese as *guanxi* – have become increasingly important in village life. It is true that network-building persisted during the collective era, despite the state's efforts to transform traditional patterns of interpersonal relations in China (see Gold 1985; Oi 1989a; Walder 1986). However, since the reforms, the social scope of personal networks has expanded remarkably, involving not only kinship ties but also friends and partners both within and outside the village. As a result, gift exchange, the traditional method of cultivating personal ties, has intensified over the past decade. My survey shows that in 1990, 202 households in Xiajia village (54 percent of the total) spent more than 500 yuan apiece on gifts, with the highest reaching 2,650 yuan. Most of the gift-giving activities took place in the context of institutionalized rituals, such as weddings and funerals. If we take 500 yuan as the average expenditure, this means that most households spent nearly 20 percent of their annual incomes to maintain and expand their social networks (for a detailed account of this change, see Yah 1993).

This recent rise in network-building results from newly emerged demands for cooperation, self-protection, and self-realization among peasants, who have now become independent producers. Today, peasants have to deal with all kinds of problems in agricultural production, from purchasing seeds to selling grain. Mutual assistance during the busy season, financial aid from private loan sources, and social connections outside the village are thus all vital to the peasants' pursuit of a better life. Moreover, a larger web of personal relations provides a stronger protective network for peasants when they come in conflict with village cadres or agents of the local government.

Finally, it is widely recognized that communist ideology no longer provides a compelling basis for the legitimacy of the party state or normative values for organizing society. At the village level, the end of communist ideology is reflected clearly in peasants' cynical attitude toward politics and the state, as well as toward cadre power. They have become indifferent to political campaigns (such as the recent one called "socialist education") and suspicious of cadres' corruption. Paralleling the decline of communist ideology, many new ideas and values have been introduced into rural China, and they play an important role in changing peasant mentalities. Indeed, the flow of information into rural areas today merits much more attention than it currently receives.

Television is one important example. One evening in 1978, I joined several young Xiajia villagers in a five-mile walk to another village in order to watch the first TV set in the area. By 1991, there were 135 TV sets in Xiajia alone, including eight color sets, which translates into one set for every three households. While it is true that the TV stations are under state control, one should note that since the reforms, television programs have changed greatly. In addition to the conventional propaganda, there are many other programs introducing new values and new ideas. For instance, I found myself watching the American TV police series "Hunter" in Xiajia village, the same show having been broadcast in Boston several months before. As a consequence of such programs, during my fieldwork, I was asked to explain such things as how the U.S. Supreme Court works, why an American state governor has no right to control a district judge, and who was fighting for justice in the Gulf War.

In Table 2, I have summarized the main points discussed above. All the dynamics of change resulted directly or indirectly from rural economic reforms, especially the radical departure from central planning – namely, decollectivization and the restoration of household farming. Each of the dynamics may influence the previous order of social relations in general and thus have structural implications in a broader sense. For instance, household farming may lead to a market economy and privatization, economic development may cause social differentiation, the rapid expansion of personal networks indicates the rise of a social force, and if all these are the case, a postcommunist political culture may well be on its way.[4] Although it is hard to predict the long-term consequences of these changes, the current political outcomes can be seen clearly in two aspects of village life: changes in the interests and behavior of cadres and the new political mentalities and actions of villagers.

Table 2   Changes in power relations in Xiajia village

Requirements for cadre power before the reforms	Assumed conditions for peasant independence	Dynamics of change since the reforms	Structural implications for the future
Collectivization; monopoly of resources	Available alternatives	Decollectivization; private enterprise	Market economy; privatization
Loyalty to the party; political reward	Supply of strategic resources	Economic development; change of cadre ethics	Social differentiation; cadre corruption
State penetration; dictatorship	Capability of personal resistance; protective networks	Retreat of the state; decline of mass dictatorship	Rise of society; new social order
Hegemony of communist ideology	Indifference to ideological mobilization	End of ideology; flow of information	Postcommunist political culture

"PLAY THE GAME WISELY": CHANGING PATTERNS OF CADRE BEHAVIOR

Two questions are crucial in assessing changes in village cadres' interests and behavior. What is the criterion of a successful village cadre – political reward from the party state or personal achievement in the family economy? And what is the locus of cadres' legitimacy – the trust of their superiors or the support of the masses? Prior to the rural reforms, neither of these two questions was significant for cadres, because the former answers were the only real choices. During the collective era, the Xiajia leadership was characterized by its strong commitment to the public good, an imperious and despotic style of work, and (for much of the time) relatively successful management of collective agriculture. While enjoying various privileges, including higher work points, most cadres considered political rewards most desirable, and many cadre families were financially on a par with ordinary villagers. The reforms have changed this, however, because alternative resources and opportunities were created outside the bureaucratic system as the collectives were dismantled. Gradually, cadres changed their interests and behavior. The differences among the three party secretaries in charge of Xiajia during various periods are the best example of this.

The party secretary from 1952 to 1960 was considered the worst leader by my informants, because he was extremely loyal to higher-level officials. He endeavored to implement all the irrational policies of the Great Leap Forward, thus making Xiajia residents suffer more than their neighbors during the 1959–61 famine. Relying on the full support of his superiors and the coercive force of the village militia, he controlled Xiajia tyrannically, acquiring the nickname "Big Wolf." An example frequently cited by my informants was that he had ordered a villager tied up and beaten badly just because he had missed a meal in the collective meal hall and complained about it. While the villagers struggled with the threat of hunger in 1959, this party secretary climbed to the highest point in his political career – he was selected as a model grass-roots cadre and invited to participate in an official ceremony at the National Day celebration in Beijing. When I interviewed him about the Great Leap, he was still immersed in happy memories of his glorious past. He went into minute detail, telling me how many cities he had visited during that tour, how happy he was when he met Marshal Zhu De, chairman of the National People's Congress, and how he learned to use flush toilets in fancy hotels. Back home, however, he lived in the same conditions as the village poor, and he was widely recognized as an honest cadre, free of corruption. It seems obvious that he believed in what the party said and worked wholeheartedly for the state, which, by its ideological definition, should also have conformed with the interests of the Xiajia people. For this reason, many villagers have an ambivalent attitude toward this man: on the one hand, they hate him for inflicting famine and poverty on the village; on the other, they respect him for his commitment to public duty and his selfless character.

The party secretary from 1978 to 1987 oversaw the most dramatic turn of events: the dismantling of collectives. Xiajia's collective economy achieved great progress under his leadership during the early 1980s; in the best year (1980), the value of ten work points reached 2.50 yuan. As did his predecessor, he also resorted to coercion to exercise his power and tightly controlled the social life of villagers. He confessed to me that he could not remember how many people he had beaten during his ten-year reign as party secretary. Given this patriarchical tradition among village cadres, it was natural that he and his colleagues first resisted decollectivization and then encountered tremendous difficulties dealing with villagers who were no longer dependent on the cadres' management of production. He told me that after decollectivization, "doing thought work"[5] was no longer effective, and people did not respect the authority of cadres any more. He tried to organize villagers to carry out such projects as opening a collective enterprise and transforming a dry field into an irrigated rice paddy, but people did not respond to his call. Worse, the party did not appear to appreciate cadres' political achievements, and higher-level state officials withdrew their support of village cadres when the latter needed it most. The most upsetting incident for him was when he became involved in a public conflict with a villager in 1987. Rather than supporting him, the township government pretended to know nothing about it. "It is meaningless to be a cadre now," he said when he explained to me why he had resigned after that incident. Obviously, as a figure mediating two periods, he could not adapt to the new type of power relationships after the reforms and thus had to retreat.

The decline of appreciation for "revolutionary cadres" did not bother the next party secretary, because he simply did not care about political rewards. During one of my interviews in 1989, he gave an interesting explanation of his motives: "Society has changed now. Who cares about the party and the state? Even the top leaders in Beijing are only interested in getting rich, otherwise they should first educate their own children. Why am I doing this job? Simple – for money. I was not interested in the title of party secretary, but I do like the salary of 3,000 yuan per year. In other words, I am working for my children, not for the party." Two years later, I was told that the same cadre had designed his strategy in terms of three "nos": saying nothing, doing nothing, and offending nobody.

When I checked this with him myself, he did not hesitate to admit it. His "three-nos" strategy is best illustrated by the way he dealt with a dispute between the village vice head and a peasant, in which the latter blamed and then cursed the former in the village office, where all five cadres were present for a meeting about population control. As I was an invited visitor at the meeting, I witnessed the whole affair and was surprised when the party secretary kept silent until the end. I also found that he did not use the local phrase "sitting on the throne" (*zuo yi di*) to describe his position, even though it was the popular term used by both cadres and villagers for the act of taking the top position in the village. However, he does have something to be proud of: he has advanced his family from one of the poorest to one of the richest in Xiajia, and his two sons' families also moved to the top of the "rich list" in the past two years. This advancement, many informants suggested, was because he was party secretary.

It is clear, in short, that economic benefits have replaced political rewards as the key object of cadres' careers, and these benefits are generated within the village, not granted by political superiors. Even the party has realized that money now speaks louder than political slogans, and has adopted a market mechanism as a means of maintaining its political control over local cadres. According to Xiajia cadres, the township government has divided their salaries, which draw on local taxes paid by villagers, into a basic salary and bonuses. The bonuses make up four-fifths of their entire incomes, and are linked to the completion of specific tasks. For instance, if they accomplish the work of supervising spring plowing, they may earn one-fifteenth of their annual salaries as a reward, and if they fail they lose the same amount as punishment. Ironically, this method has not raised the cadres' motivation, because many feel manipulated by their party superiors and have thus lost their last vestige of political loyalty. As a cadre commented, "We are treated by our own party as circus dogs – you play a little game well, you get some food in return. Play it one more time, you get another tiny reward."

The locus of cadre legitimacy has also changed remarkably. During the collective era, although in theory village cadres should have been elected by the masses, few attained their positions through such means. No one could stay in power without the trust and support of higher levels of government, and unpopular leaders, like Xiajia's party secretary during the 1950s, were able to hold power as long as they were appreciated by their superiors. Therefore it was out of the question for cadres to put the support of the masses ahead of the demands of their superiors. There was only one known exception in the recent history of Xiajia. Immediately after the fall of the first party secretary in 1960, in an attempt to protect themselves, villagers (through party members) elected a demobilized soldier as the party secretary. He was a well-known anti-authoritarian character and was afraid of no one. This man stayed in power for only a couple of months and was removed from office after he made his first serious effort to resist the orders of the commune party committee. This incident might be seen as failed resistance from below, but it also demonstrates that the authority of village cadres during the collective era depended completely on higher-level officials, and the villagers could do little to affect the power structure in their village.

After the reforms, however, village cadres have gradually come to depend more on support from below than recognition from above. As a result of the reform effort to separate the party committee from government and the polity from the economy, along with the end of political campaigns, village cadres receive fewer administrative instructions and less political support. The recent reform effort to establish "autonomous village committees" based on mass elections also constituted a potential threat to their power base (see Wang 1992). One attempt at free elections was made in 1983 in Xiajia, resulting in the village head being voted out of power by die villagers. That incident scared the cadres so much that they have stifled any kind of election since then.

In addition to the changes in the broader environment, a new feeling of being salaried public servants is also affecting cadres' behavior, because their salaries draw on the money collected from peasant households in the name of "public funding." The cadres, who can no longer claim they are working for the party, feel indebted to the local people, especially when the latter repeatedly make reference to this sensitive subject during public disputes. Moreover, to carry out unpleasant tasks like collecting taxes and grain, or supervising birth control, cadres need the cooperation of their subordinates. As the current party secretary in Xiajia said, "I know that the villagers hate to feed cadres. I would too, if I were them. Collecting grain and money, forcing women to submit to sterilization, all the jobs I do are awful. The most important thing is to play the game wisely. Who knows what is going to happen after you fall out of power?"

Being aware of their newly developed dependence on their subordinates' support, village cadres have lost the incentive to enforce unpopular policies and have instead begun to play a role of mediator or middleman when the state's policies are in direct conflict with local interests, such as in the case of population control. It has long been recognized that the one-child policy causes widespread resentment among peasants. Nonetheless, it should be noted that a broad gap has always existed between this policy and its implementation. From the very beginning, the implementation of the one-child policy encountered resistance from the peasants. In the mid 1980s, the state seemed to retreat silently by allowing couples whose first child was a daughter to have another child in hopes that it would be a boy.

In Xiajia village, the implementation of the single-child policy started at the same time that the rural reforms began. Those who had a second child after April 1980 were fined 700 yuan by the commune government. Fortunately, the village office (the production brigade at that time) showed sympathy to those whose first child was a daughter by giving them a 500 yuan allowance, which meant that the fine was reduced to only 200 yuan, an amount the peasants could afford. But things soon went sour, because the local policy changed in February 1983, and the fine was raised to 1,200 yuan. In the same year, the collectives were also dismantled. Consequently, allowances were no longer available, and those who violated the one-child policy had to pay the entire amount for their second baby. This situation lasted for only one year before state policy changed again. In 1984, women who were over 29 and had a daughter as their first child were permitted to have a second child. To help villagers who wished to have sons, the village cadres had always tried to avoid asking women who had only daughters to submit to sterilization, sometimes by submitting false reports to the government.

To explain the cadres' dilemma, the head of Xiajia village said, "We are peasants, and we know exactly how painful it is for a man to have no son. We don't want to stop anybody's bloodline. This is something that could destroy our own fortune and merit. But we are also cadres, and we have to do our job. So the only way is to have one eye open and another closed [*zheng yi yan, bi yi yan*], to cheat the state while coaxing the villagers."[6] And the current party secretary told me that the secret of doing work now is *yi tuo er bian*, which means to deal with any order or policy from above, one needs first to delay implementation and then to alter it, turning the policy to the interests of the village if possible.[7] As a result of resistance by ordinary peasants and a slowdown by village cadres, the 1990 census in Xiajia village shows that none of the villagers were really affected by the one-child policy during any period. The only difference is that some of them paid for extra children and some did not.

Indeed, the cadres' double-role strategy is well reflected in the phrase "cheating the state and coaxing the villagers" (*pian shangbian, hong xiabian*). Because of increasing demand to protect private interests, cadres have deceived the state in recent years more often than in the earlier 1980s. Moreover, the phenomenon of cheating the state is by no means confined to village cadres; state officials at both township and county levels share the same mentality and strategy – otherwise, many of the village cadres' efforts could not possibly succeed. For instance, in the spring of 1991, the county government required all villages to finish corn planting before April 20. But, as Xiajia village land is located on lower ground, the ground temperature was not warm enough for planting by that date. To meet the deadline, the township cadres indicated that Xiajia cadres had completed the task in time. Although everyone knew that the work could not start until two weeks beyond the deadline, the cadres at the county level were satisfied with the report and dealt with their superiors at the provincial level in the same manner. The cadres at township and village levels were happy too, because they completed their bureaucratic duties without bothering the peasants at all. The group that benefited the most, however, were the peasants, and they did not even know what had happened.

This change can best be demonstrated in a comparison with the collective period. The implementation of government policies in the 1950s and 1960s resembled an inflation process. Cadres at every level would add their own efforts to state policies, because they had only one purpose – to be appreciated by superiors. A good example of this was the false reports on grain yields among rural cadres during the Great Leap Forward, which eventually caused high procurement of grain and the famine of 1959–61 (see Bernstein 1984). Nowadays, cadres pay much more attention to the reactions from below, and thus policy implementation has become a process of deflation. As rural cadres passively and partially carry out orders from above, central government policies lose their original meaning. This has been captured in a popular saying, "Villages cheat towns, towns cheat counties; it's cheating straight up to the State Council" (*cun pian xiang, xiang pian xian, yizhi pian dao guowuyuan*). In a sense, the new pattern of political behavior among the rural cadres might create an informal mechanism to counterbalance and resist state control of society and the negative effects of central policy.

Another interesting outcome of changes in power relations is that village cadres found themselves involved in more resistance, bargaining, and compromise in the process of exerting their power. While passively carrying out unpopular policies from above, they have become much softer when they have to interfere with the private interests of peasants, in order to avoid open resistance from the latter. A simple indicator is that incidents of cadres beating villagers have declined rapidly since decollectivization; instead, more conflicts have ended up in the reverse: cadres being beaten up by villagers. Imposing fines became the only powerful weapon left in the cadres' hands, and it was applied to almost everything the cadres carried out. However, its efficacy has diminished, because some villagers refused to pay their fines, which again led to direct confrontation between cadres and villagers.

All cadres agreed that compared to neighboring villages, Xiajia was by no means a troublesome place, and in recent years, to get a beating was not the worst of fates for cadres. In neighboring villages, cadres' houses have been set afire by peasants, and at least one cadre was killed by two outraged village youths taking revenge. In many cases, violent conflicts were caused by insignificant incidents that would not have been contemplated if the cadres had still held the same power as during the collective era. While I was doing my fieldwork in Xiajia, two cases of arson occurred, and the victims were both cadres. It seems that the local government could do little to protect the village cadres, except to compensate them economically. After the two arson cases, the township government proposed to raise the local taxes paid by villagers and use the money to buy personal insurance for village cadres, in the hope that this would make the villagers reluctant to attack the cadres' property.

In addition to the loss of their monopoly over resources, economic corruption has weakened village cadres' ability to exercise power. In one case I witnessed, a villager's application for a loan to buy chemical fertilizer was rejected by the village cadres, because funds for agricultural loans had already been diverted to pay the debts of the village. Misappropriation of state funds was nothing unusual at the village level, and the rejection of this personal application would ordinarily have been viewed as a small incident. To the surprise of all, the villager was outraged and started a public dispute with the party secretary on the street. When many people gathered to watch their dispute, the villager suddenly said that he knew where the agricultural loan had gone – it had been lent out as usury by the son of the party secretary. He also accused the village office of collecting extra taxes over the previous year and threatened to report the case to the county government. The party secretary left the spot without saying a word to defend himself. A few days later, I learned that the villager had been allowed to borrow some money from the village office, which was actually a gift to him, because both sides knew the loan would probably never be returned.

Interestingly enough, the same cadre was well known for both his bad temper toward villagers and his commitment to central policy when he was a team leader during the 1970s. People often said that, for this cadre, to curse or beat someone was as normal as eating a bowl of noodles. Despite all complaints, the villagers still supported him and recognized his authority, because he was also responsible for improving the management of the collective. During its successful period of collective farming, most cadres in Xiajia were this type of "iron fist". They ran the village in the style in which a tyrannical father controlled his family in traditional China, and their brutality was justified by their sincere devotion to central policy. Today none of the five current cadres (all of whom were in power before the reform) can boast of being "corruption free," and it is no accident that they have all improved their tempers to a remarkable extent.[8]

It is true that cadre corruption, which surged markedly after the reforms (Gold 1985; Meaney 1991), reveals that cadres still control resources in many ways and can thereby impose their wills on their subordinates (Oi 1989b; Rocca 1992). Nevertheless, the current rise of cadre corruption does not necessarily strengthen cadre power, for two reasons. First, economic corruption should be distinguished from political corruption. As Gong Xiaoxia writes: "It is after the reforms that cadre corruption began to appear more and more in economic forms. . . . Since China was a highly politicized society prior to the reforms, cadre corruption during that time presented itself mainly in political forms" (Gong 1992, 52). In the case of Xiajia, many cadres during the collective era were free of economic corruption, but they abused the villagers in more obvious ways than the current cadres. Economic corruption may increase cadres' personal wealth, but it does not allow them to compel obedience from their subordinates.

Second, corruption based on exchange of resources should be distinguished from that based on distributing resources. Because people involved in social exchange need to observe the norm of reciprocity (see Gouldner 1960), the recipient of a gift or a favor is reduced to a position inferior to the donor until the "debt" is repaid (see Mauss 1967). This is well captured in a Chinese proverb: "Eating from others, one's mouth becomes soft; taking from others, one's hands become short" (*chi ren zui ruan; na ren shou duan*). It is obvious that when a cadre receives gifts from his subordinates, his superiority is weakened, because such exchanges reduce the recipient to a position of mutual dependence. Moreover, the obligation of reciprocity implies that corruption based on exchange of resources will benefit both sides: the giver as well as the recipient. This is something quite different from transactions based on the more one-sided dependence of the collective era, when cadres distributed resources to villagers who had no real alternatives.

"LEAVE ME ALONE": POLITICAL MENTALITY AND ACTION AMONG VILLAGERS

The village power game is played out by both cadres and ordinary villagers. These days village cadres must play the game more wisely, because as indicated above, the economic reforms have broken the previous pattern of dependence and raised the position of villagers. More important, market reforms have changed the villagers' mentality as well as their living standard. New attitudes toward cadre power and authority, the rise of individualism, and an emerging conception of personal rights have also served to redefine the power game in Xiajia.

The most dramatic change is in villagers' perception of cadre power and authority. As I have explained elsewhere (Yan 1992), social life in Xiajia was previously far from "egalitarian": the collectives were perhaps no less hierarchical than the prerevolutionary community. When the cadres stood on the top of the social pyramid, fear dominated popular perceptions of cadre power. Nevertheless, villagers still placed their hopes on good leadership and respected those who led the collective to prosperity. Because cadres controlled all resources and opportunities, they represented the only hope for collective betterment. This is well captured in a popular saying of the collective era: "It's better to have a good team leader than to have a good father" (*you ge hao baba, bu ru you ge hao duizhang*).

Villagers' fear and respect of cadre power came to an end when the collectives were dismantled in 1983. By the time I conducted my first field survey in early 1989, anger and discontent over cadre corruption had reached a peak. Complaints about various kinds of local taxes and accusations of cadre misconduct were common subjects during my interviews with villagers. To my knowledge, at least two anonymous letters have been sent to the county government in an attempt to bring corrupt cadres into court. Conflicts between cadres and villagers occurred frequently when the latter felt unfairly treated, and quite often a conflict ended in violence. One such public fight in 1987, as noted above, forced the party secretary to resign. This vividly symbolizes the collapse of the authority and power of all village cadres. At that time, many villagers started showing disrespect by refusing to present gifts to cadres in ritual situations, such as weddings or funerals. The village office lost its prestige in the eyes of ordinary farmers, and the focus of public life has gradually moved from the brigade headquarters to the village retail store (for more details see Yan 1992, 15–16; Yan 1993, 167–78).

Obviously, the major reason for the sudden eruption of dissatisfaction with cadre behavior resulted from the advent of family farming, which allows villagers to control their own livelihood. A further reason is that in recent years, the diversification of life chances has raised villagers' sense of individualism and thus changed their views of cadre authority.[9] A widely cited saying in both urban and rural China is now: "A fish has its way, and a shrimp has its way, too" (*yu you yu lu, xia you xia lu*). Here, "way," *lu* in Chinese, may indicate back doors, social connections, personal skills, and so on – all the means needed to make oneself affluent. During my fieldwork, I heard both rich and poor villagers quoting this popular saying when talking about somebody who had done well economically. In Xiajia, many capable individuals have found a way to make money, such as growing cash crops, developing family sidelines, or working in the cities. One of the best chances for financial advancement in the past two years was created by the establishment of a milk-products factory owned jointly by the local government and the Nestlé company of Switzerland. Five people in the village found jobs in the factory and earned a high salary (300 yuan per month versus an average annual income of 616 yuan per capita). Several dozen villagers responded to the new demand for milk by raising dairy cows and have subsequently gained considerable benefits.

In the place of fear and respect, the villagers began to view the cadres' credibility critically, and few still trust leaders unconditionally. In the eyes of my informants, the good cadre has become a myth. When the story of

Baogong, an upright and honest official of the Song dynasty, was shown on TV, many commented cynically that Baogong could not survive in today's environment, because his honesty would hurt the interests of other cadres, and he would thus soon be removed from power or forced into corruption.

The suspicion of cadres is so strong that it sometimes causes unnecessary trouble. In a case I witnessed during my fieldwork, three men came to Xiajia to purchase pigs and cheated villagers by using a platform scale rigged to reduce the weight. Their cheating was discovered, but the villagers did not dare to claim compensation, because these three men came in a military truck and stated that they were soldiers. Finally, the village head intervened in the name of the village office and made the three cheaters return the money to the pig farmers. The villagers were not satisfied with this solution and demanded that the cheaters be punished. When the three men left, I was surprised to see some villagers accuse the village head of making a secret deal. They insisted that the village head must have accepted a bribe from the culprits.

When I asked the accusers why they were so critical of the village head, who deserved some credit for handling the problem, I was told that it was his job to resolve problems like this. After all, they said, he earned 2,600 yuan a year, and his salary was extracted from their incomes. "He is fed by us," one said. Here the practice of paying various local taxes in a direct and open way has given the peasants a new perspective from which to view their relationship with cadres. As I indicated earlier, such an awareness of themselves as tax payers not only diminishes villagers' fear of cadres, but also results in cadres realizing that they are, in fact, employed by the villagers.

In 1991, I also found an increasing cynicism about cadre behavior. While some villagers still complained and even directly confronted cadres if their private interests were challenged, their words of discontent rarely turned into action. Most villagers were tired of complaining about cadre corruption and did not even care about the size of cadre salaries. In response to my inquiries about this newly found complacency, I was frequently met with the popular saying, "It is not proper to refuse paying the taxes and procured grain; you cart them away, and leave me my freedom" (*huang liang guo shui, bu jiao bu dui; ni na li liu, gei wo zi you*). Indeed, the typical view among Xiajia residents was put into three words by an informant: "Leave me alone" (*bie guan wo*). And the most common strategy adopted by them was to fulfill their prescribed obligations to the state and local government without question and then to protect their personal interests against any additional levies.

In the early stages of my fieldwork, I took this "Leave me alone" mentality as the villagers' passive reaction to the social problems they encountered, and as a sign of their indifference to village politics, including cadre behavior. After a few months of observation, however, I became convinced that this posture concealed other meanings. "Leave me alone" conveyed a strong message – namely, awareness of personal rights and an intention to protect them. Given the heritage of patriarchal authority in Chinese culture and the influence of totalitarian rule under the party, it is not easy for the peasants to tell cadres, "Leave me alone." It could not possibly have happened during the collective period, when the only acceptable demand a peasant could make was for better leadership, and a refusal to accept cadre leadership could lead to accusations of the most serious crime – counterrevolution. It could not have happened immediately after the decollectivization either, because the peasants were still living under the shadow of socialist culture, which conferred patriarchal status on cadres. Such an expression itself symbolizes the development of a consciousness of independence and the rise of political self-confidence among the villagers.

In this regard, the increasing flow of information through TV programs and other means has, as noted above, provided the villagers with new conceptions of economic and political rights and thus encouraged them to resist the imposing power of cadres should their interests be violated. This is best illustrated in their confrontations with state officials from the township government, which usually require more courage and strength. For example, in a case of conflict with the township officials, a villager was detained by the township policemen for a few days. He was so angry that he finally refused to leave the detention room when the township cadres grew tired of him and wanted to send him away. He accused the local policemen of "violating the law and human rights" because they did not have an arrest warrant. I met him in the county seat where he was demanding justice from the county government. He showed me a booklet about the criminal law, and we also talked about the American TV detective Hunter.

It should be noted that rural cadres generally do not welcome the diffusion of political information, especially about personal rights. A state official in the township government, who was a village cadre a few years ago, complained to me that the "education of legal knowledge" was a stupid campaign launched by the state. "From ancient times, the policemen have had the right to beat people," he said. "This is the way it works. The ordinary people are just slaves, pigs. They can be ruled only by whips. Look at what is happening now. Everyone wants to have his rights, and the law protects the tough guys. The result is that these tricky people never commit crimes, but they never stop making trouble either. It just annoys the police department to death, and puts the court on the spot" (*da cuo bu fan, xiao cuo bu duan; qi si gong an ju, nan si fa yuan*).

In another interesting case I witnessed, a widow was suspected of stealing public trees. When two local policemen tried to confiscate a motorcycle from her family as a fine, a physical confrontation occurred between the two parties. The widow accused the policemen of beating her and threatened to use her personal connections in the county police department to punish the offenders. Although no one knew whether she had relatives in power or not, the local policemen decided not to risk offending higher authorities and encouraged the Xiajia village office to give the widow 50 yuan in compensation. The policemen did not, however, want to lose face in the village; and so two weeks later they detained the widow's son on a four-month old charge of gambling, and asked the widow to pay a fine of 300 yuan to free her son. Everyone, including me, thought the widow was defeated when she paid up; but, to the surprise of all, she went to the county seat and came back with a note from somebody in the county government requesting that the local police department return her money.

Many studies of the *guanxi* complex in China have focused on the instrumental function of these personal connections (see e.g., Gold 1985; Huang Kwang-kuo 1987; King 1991). The Xiajia case demonstrates that the recent expansion of *guanxi* networks may have something to do with changes in power relations and, in some circumstances, personal networks may give peasants a way to impose their will on cadres. This parallels Mayfair Yang's argument that the gift economy and personal networks have created a distribution channel outside of the bureaucratic distribution system, and thus constitute a counterforce to the power of the state (see Yang 1989; Yan 1993).

Along with their altered perception of cadre power and newly developed political self-confidence, Xiajia residents' attitudes toward the authority of the party state have also changed. They attribute all social problems, such as inflation, cadre corruption, and public disorder, to high-level state leaders. The best example is perhaps their reaction to the campaign of socialist education launched nationwide in 1990 and 1991 in rural areas. The purpose of this campaign was to clear up problems of village finance and to reeducate peasants about socialism. Xiajia was selected as one of the first villages to launch this campaign, and, as during the collective era, a work team was sent down from the county seat. When I arrived in the spring of 1991, the campaign had been under way for several months, but nothing had happened except that some slogans and posters had been placed on the walls of the village office. Not even a single meeting had been held for the campaign. When I discussed this unusually quiet campaign with my informants, they regarded it as a joke. They maintained that it was a trick by the top leaders to put the masses in the hot seat and thereby hide the serious mistakes made in Beijing. One villager put it this way: "When the people at the top fall sick, they force those at the bottom to take medicine" (*shang bian de bing, gei xia bian chi yao*). We did nothing wrong. Why do they always want to educate us?"

This attitude constitutes a sharp contrast to the ways peasants reacted to state campaigns during the collective period. At that time they told themselves: "The scriptures [state policies] were good, but the monks [the cadres at lower levels] are reciting them wrongly" (*jing dou shi haojing, xia bian de heshang gei nian wai le*). As some informants recalled, even during the famine of 1959–61, few people doubted the correctness of policies from above, and they directed all their discontent toward the village cadres. When relief grain was finally allocated to the villagers, who had suffered from hunger for several months, their first reaction was to thank the party state and Chairman Mao. In their own terms, they once had "good feelings" (*gan qing*) toward the state, but these feelings are now gone.

CONCLUDING REMARKS

Now let me return to the issue raised in the beginning of this chapter: how shall we understand and assess the impact of reforms on cadre power in Xiajia, and how does the Xiajia case relate to current debates about this issue? According to Nee's theory of market transition, if the allocation of goods and services is shifted to marketplaces rather than monopolized by the cadres in the socialist redistributive system, power "becomes more diffused in the economy and society" (Nee 1991, 267). "Therefore, the transition from redistribution to markets involves a transfer of power favoring direct producers relative to redistributors" (Nee 1989, 666). This theory is based on survey data of peasant income collected in 1985, and Nee's key argument relies on the discovery that "current cadre status, following a shift to marketlike conditions, has no effect on a household's chances of being in the top income quintile, nor in its avoidance of poverty, nor in the rate of increase of household income" (Nee 1991, 280).

It is at this point, however, that Oi (1989b) found evidence demonstrating that cadres did take advantage of the reforms by exercising their remaining power. Focusing on the policy context in which the reforms were implemented, Oi conducted a structural analysis of cadre corruption and abuse of power, and offered an instructive counterinterpretation to what Nee proposed: "The most obvious conclusion is that a freer market environment does not necessarily lead to the end of bureaucratic control nor the demise of cadre power" (Oi 1989b, 233). Oi also noted that post-reform rural politics remained clientelist in nature (ibid., 231).

It seems to me that in addition to their different conclusions, Nee and Oi also differ from each other in the ways they examine the issue. While defining power as "control over resources" and equating relative income with relative power, Nee emphasizes personal income as the criterion by which to evaluate gain and loss among cadres. In contrast, Oi pays more attention to the institutional aspect of power, with a focus on cadre corruption, and takes the extent to which cadres abuse their power in pursuing personal interest as the standard by which to measure the role of cadres after the reforms.

Applying these perspectives to Xiajia, both seem to have a basis in fact, but neither is sufficient to explain the tremendous changes in power relations. As indicated above, the power of Xiajia cadres has declined to a great extent, and they have lost much of their superiority in social and political terms. But my survey in 1989 also demonstrated that 54 percent of the cadres who were in power on the eve of decollectivization have become affluent, while only 9 percent of the villagers became rich (see Table 1). This suggests a correlation between cadres' status and their postreform economic achievements. Furthermore, this indicates that neither income nor corruption can be employed as the definitive index of cadre power in the postreform era.

A third criterion, which may be more useful in examining this issue, is the degree of peasant dependence or, to put it another way, the degree of control cadres have over resources. In studies of state socialism, it has long been recognized that the party state's power and authority are based on its monopoly over resources and opportunities, which is maintained and reinforced by the new ruling class of officials (Djilas 1957; Szelényi 1978). Such a monopoly leads to citizen dependence upon officials for the satisfaction of material needs and social mobility, a social phenomena characterized as a form of "organized dependence" by Andrew Walder (1983, 1986). In the context of village society, the fundamental feature of cadre power was villagers' dependence on cadres for the resources under their control. "Men are powerful when many want what they, the few, are able to supply or many fear what they, the few, are able to withhold," George Homans notes (1974, 197). Among many other things, the resources of living, working, resting, socializing, and self-expression are the basic needs of everyday life. These basic resources were, until the reform era, tightly controlled by village cadres, in a situation where villagers were highly dependent. It follows that by examining what happened to these control mechanisms and the degree to which ordinary peasants depend on resources controlled by cadres, one can obtain a better understanding of recent changes in power relations.

My findings from Xiajia lead me to conclude that market reforms have changed the previous balance of villagers' dependence on their leaders and, in some respects, have made cadres dependent on villagers for their incomes. The reforms have eroded cadres' previous power and privilege by breaking their monopoly over resources and by creating new income opportunities that make the accumulation of personal wealth more attractive than the political rewards offered by the party state. Their political role in village society has also changed from that of the tyrannical "local emperor" ruling the village as the agent of the party state to prudent middlemen who negotiate between the state and village society. For villagers, the reforms have ended their dependence on the collectives and the cadres who ran them, and have thereby to a great extent freed them from cadre domination. While cadres have benefited economically from the reforms, villagers have gained much more in social and political terms – that is, they have attained new individual rights (the right to work, rest, move away, and speak out). Even though the ratio of rich households to ordinary villagers is lower than that to cadres, the reforms have opened the way for the former to compete with the latter in the same market order. In short, the most significant change in power relations has been the erosion of cadres' former monopolized superiority in village life.

The Xiajia case, however, has particularities that speak to important issues of regional variation. Xiajia was and still is a farming community, with an economy characterized by agricultural production. Peasant income still derives mainly from farming and family sidelines. Unlike parts of south-eastern China, the trend of marketization and commercialization has yet to play an influential role in the Xiajia economy. Nevertheless, as everyone in farming relies on similar resources, and as land – the primary means of production – was distributed evenly among villagers at the time of decollectivization, the reforms may have produced a more profound political impact on Xiajia than on other industrial or more prosperous areas where a diversified commercial economy has emerged since the reforms. As Ákos Róna-Tas has observed in the case of Hungary, a shift to a market economy tends to have a more egalitarian effect in household farming than in larger enterprises, because agricultural production requires less political and social capital (1990, 205–7). Had there been collective enterprises in Xiajia, or if the majority of its residents had engaged in nonagricultural business, the village cadres would probably have had more resources on hand, and thus might have been able to compel or induce the villagers to respond to their power (see Oi 1990). This contradicts the prediction that the significant weakening of cadre power should coincide with a rather mature development of market transactions (see Nee 1989, 1991).

Among the various dynamics contributing to this fundamental change in power relations in Xiajia, decollectivization and the cessation of mass dictatorship have been the most crucial. As this chapter has shown, collectivization was the key institution through which cadres monopolized all economic, social, and political resources and thus controlled the life of villagers. Mass dictatorship, supported by the state and communist ideology, provided the most powerful instrument for cadres to maintain their monopoly of resources and suppress any resistance. These two mechanisms existed everywhere in rural China prior to the reforms and have subsequently eroded. I therefore regard the Xiajia case as illustrative of recent events in rural communities in China and believe that my study has implications that go well beyond Xiajia's boundaries.

ACKNOWLEDGEMENT

This paper is based on field research in 1991 supported by National Science Foundation grant number BNS-9101369. I owe thanks to James L. Watson, the participants of the conference at Arden Homestead, especially Andrew Walder, and an anonymous reviewer for helpful comments on earlier drafts. I am also grateful to Matthew Kohrman for editorial assistance.–YY.

NOTES

1. In this chapter I mainly discuss power relations between the village cadres and peasants. There is no doubt that peasant communities, especially after the reforms, are not isolated universes, and residents have to be involved in power relations with people outside their villages in both economic and social as well as political terms. But these are different kinds of power relations, involving hierarchy and inequality between rural and urban sectors. Moreover, the village cadres are usually treated like ordinary villagers when they go beyond the village boundary, because they are also "rural potatoes" in the eyes of those who are living within the system of state distribution and social welfare. Analytically, it is necessary to distinguish village cadres who do not belong to the state bureaucratic system from cadres in local government or other state organs. Hereafter, by *cadre* I mean village cadres, and I use the term *state officials* to describe the cadres within the state bureaucratic system, which begins at the "township" (*xiang*), the administrative level immediately above the village.

2. Heilongjiang was the last province in China to dismantle the commune system, and the main reason, according to Luo Xiaopeng and others, was the relative success of collective farming. See Luo et al. 1985. For a detailed introduction to Xiajia village, see Yan 1993, 17–39.

3. It is interesting that peasants in other places, such as Anhui province, also used the word *freedom* to describe their new experience as independent farmers (see Chen 1990, 31).

4. In an earlier essay, Gordon White 1987 discusses the new patterns of power and new axes or political conflict and cooperation generated by the economic reforms. He suggests that a possible political consequence of these changes might be the emergence of a new political process in rural China.

5. The term *thought work* can be applied to many means of controlling people, from personal persuasion, informal interrogation, and study workshops to public struggle sessions. The ultimate goal of doing thought work is to make the subject comply to the authority of cadres.

6. This kind of mentality is quite common among village cadres in other parts of China. Huang Shu-min reports an interesting story in which the party secretary in a South China village employed a sophisticated strategy to protect some women from abortion, meanwhile meeting the requirements of the upper-level government. See Huang 1989, 185–90.

7. This constitutes a sharp contrast to the attitude of the former party secretary during the 1950s, who told me, "When I was ruling the village [he used precisely the term *ruling*, i.e., *zuo tianxia* in local terms], if the party leader said to do one thing, I would try to complete two, or even three. We believed that if we failed, the landlords would return and take our land away."

8. In their follow-up research, the authors of *Chen Village* found a similar trend of character change among the cadres. For instance, Chen Longyong, once a tyrannical party secretary who controlled the villagers' life tightly, turned himself into a private entrepreneur and "had softened with the years" (Chan, Madsen, and Unger 1992, 315). His successor, the current party secretary, Baodai, "is fully aware that a leader's power to exact cowed compliance from the peasantry is a thing of the past, and he generally intrudes on the affairs of his neighbors only when mediation is called for" (1992, 320).

9. For an instructive study of public perceptions about life chances and the political implications for China, see Whyte 1985.

REFERENCES

Bernstein, Thomas B. 1984. "Stalinism, Famine, and Chinese Peasants: Grain Procurement During the Great Leap Forward." *Theory and Society* 13, 3: 339–77.

Blau, Peter M. 1964. *Exchange and Power in Social Life*. New York: John Wiley & Sons.

Chan, Anita, Richard Madsen, and Jonathan Unger. 1992. *Chen Village under Mao and Deng*. Expanded and updated edition. Berkeley and Los Angeles: University of California Press.

Chen Yizi. 1990. *Zhongguo: Shinian gaige yu bajiu minyun* (China: Ten Years of Reforms and the Democracy Movement in 1989). Taipei: Lianjing Press.

Djilas, Milovan. 1957. *The New Class: An Analysis of the Communist System of Power*. New York: Praeger.

Emerson, Richard M. 1962. "Power-Dependence Relations." *American Sociological Review* 27, 1: 31–41.

———. 1972. "Exchange Theory." In *Sociological Theory in Progress*, eds. J. Berger and M. Zelditch. Boston: Houghton Mifflin.

Friedman, Edward, Paul Pickowicz, and Mark Selden, with Kay Ann Johnson. 1991. *Chinese Village, Socialist State*. New Haven, Conn.: Yale University Press.

Gold, Thomas. 1985. "After Comradeship: Personal Relations in China since the Cultural Revolution." *China Quarterly*, no. 104 (December): 657–75.

Gong Xiaoxia. 1992. "Ganbu xingwei fangshi de bianhua he Zhongguo gongmin shehui de xingqi" (Changes in Patterns of Cadre Behavior and the Rise of Civil Society in China). *Zhongguo zhi chun* (China Spring) 106 (April): 52–54.

Gouldner, Alvin W. 1960. "The Norm of Reciprocity: A Preliminary Statement." *American Sociological Review* 25, 2: 161–78.

Hinton, William. 1983. *Shenfan*. New York: Random House, Vintage Books.

Homans, George. 1974. *Social Behavior: Its Elementary Forms*. New York: Harcourt Brace Jovanovich.

Huang, Kwang-kuo. 1987. "Face and Favor: The Chinese Power Game." *American Journal of Sociology* 92, 4: 944–74.

Huang, Shu-min. 1989. *The Spiral Road: Change in a Chinese Village Through the Eyes of a Communist Party Leader*. Boulder, Colo.: Westview Press.

King, Ambrose Yeo-chi. 1991. "Kuan-hsi and Network Building: A Sociological Interpretation." *Daedalus* 120, 2: 63–84.

Luo Xiaopeng et al. 1985. "Lishixing de zhuanbian" (The Historic Change). In *Nongcun, jingji yu shehui* (Countryside, Economy, and Society), 3: 121–31. Beijing: Knowledge Press.

Mauss, Marcel. 1967. *The Gift*. New York: Norton.

Meaney, Connie Squires. 1991. "Market Reform and Disintegrative Corruption in Urban China." In *Reform and Reaction in Post-Mao China: The Road to Tiananmen*, ed. Richard Baum, 124–42. New York: Routledge.

Nee, Victor. 1989. "A Theory of Market Transition: From Redistribution to Markets in State Socialism." *American Sociological Review* 54, 5: 663–81.

———. 1991. "Social Inequalities in Reforming State Socialism: Between Redistribution and Markets in China." *American Sociological Review* 56, 3: 267–82.

Oi, Jean, 1989a. *State and Peasant in Contemporary China: The Political Economy of Village Government*. Berkeley and Los Angeles: University of California Press.

———. 1989b. "Market Reform and Corruption in Rural China." *Studies in Comparative Communism* 22, 2–3: 221–33.

———. 1990. "The Fate of the Collective after the Commune." In *Chinese Society on the Eve of Tiananmen: The Impact of Reform*, eds. Deborah Davis and Ezra Vogel, 15–36. Cambridge, Mass.: Harvard University Press.

Parish, William L., and Martin King Whyte. 1978. *Village and Family in Contemporary China*. Chicago: University of Chicago Press.

Potter, Sulamith Heins. 1983. "The Position of Peasants in Modern China's Social Order." *Modern China* 9, 3: 465–99.

Potter, Sulamith, and Jack Potter. 1990. *China's Peasants: The Anthropology of a Revolution*. New York: Cambridge University Press.

Rocca, Jean-Louis. 1992. "Corruption and Its Shadow: An Anthropological View of Corruption in China." *China Quarterly*, no. 130 (June): 402–16.

Róna-Tas, Ákos. 1990. "The Second Economy in Hungary: The Social Origins of the End of State Socialism." Ph.D. diss., Department of Sociology, University of Michigan.

Siu, Helen. 1989. *Agents and Victims in South China: Accomplices in Rural Revolution.* New Haven, Conn.: Yale University Press.

Szelényi, Iván. 1978. "Social Inequalities under State Socialist Redistributive Economies." *International Journal of Comparative Sociology* 19, 1–2: 61–78.

———. 1988. *Socialist Entrepreneurs: Embourgeoisement in Rural Hungary.* Madison: University of Wisconsin Press.

Walder, Andrew G. 1983. "Organized Dependency and Cultures of Authority in Chinese Industry." *Journal of Asian Studies* 43, 1: 51–76.

———. 1986. *Communist Neo-Traditionalism: Work and Authority in Chinese Industry.* Berkeley and Los Angeles: University of California Press.

Wang, Zhenyao. 1992. "Construction of Village Committees: Background, Current Situation, and Guidance of the Government Policy." Paper presented at the 1992 annual meeting of the Association for Asian Studies, Washington, D.C.

Weber, Max. 1947. *The Theory of Social and Economic Organization.* New York: Free Press.

White, Gordon. 1987. "The Impact of Economic Reforms in the Chinese Countryside: Toward the Politics of Social Capitalism?" *Modern China* 13, 4: 411–40.

Whyte, Martin King. 1985. "The Politics of Life Chances in the People's Republic of China." In *Power and Policy in the PRC*, ed. Yu-ming Shaw, 244–65. Boulder, Colo.: Westview Press.

Yan, Yun-xiang. 1992. "The Impact of Rural Reform on Economic and Social Stratification in a Chinese Village." *Australian Journal of Chinese Affairs*, no. 27 (January): 1–23.

———. 1993. "The Flow of Gifts: Reciprocity and Social Networks in a Chinese Village." Ph.D. diss., Department of Anthropology, Harvard University.

Yang, Mayfair Mei-Hui. 1989. "The Gift Economy and State Power in China." *Comparative Studies in Society and History* 31, 1: 25–54.

Zweig, David. 1989. *Agrarian Radicalism in China, 1968–1981.* Cambridge, Mass.: Harvard University Press.

CHAPTER 3

THE TRIUMPH OF CONJUGALITY: STRUCTURAL TRANSFORMATION OF FAMILY RELATIONS[1]

During a cold night in the winter of 1990, Mr. Li, a 64-year-old man in Xiajia village, northeast China, took his life by drinking a bottle of pesticide. His suicide was hardly a mystery to the community because he had been having conflicts with his daughter-in-law and his younger son and had threatened to kill himself many times. But what struck his fellow villagers was the irony of his life as it drew to a tragic end.

According to them, Mr. Li was an aggressive person in public life and a tyrant at home. He had an exceptional ability to manage economic affairs, and as a result his family was better off than many of his neighbors; however, Li made virtually every decision at home and he never tried to control his bad temper, often beating his wife and children. His wife passed away after the marriage of their elder son, and a family division occurred when the younger son married a few years later. Following customary practice, Li chose to live with his younger son, but showed no intention of giving up his power. The wife of his younger son, however, was an independent woman who refused to take the old man's orders, and she quickly changed the power structure in this stem family. Mr. Li fought fiercely to defend his position, often bringing family disputes to the village office. He did not gain the full support of village cadres, however, because his daughter-in-law had successfully convinced the cadres that the old man's tyrannical behavior should be held in check.

During fieldwork in the spring of 1991, I investigated this family tragedy, with particular interest in the reactions of the older villagers who either had children of marriageable age or who had had experience in dealing with married sons. They all agreed that the daughter-in-law had been disobedient, and her husband should have stopped the conflict

before it got out of hand. Nonetheless, sixteen out of the 22 older informants (average age 48) suggested that the late Mr. Li should also be held
responsible. Eleven informants maintained that Mr. Li was ill tempered
and his demands were unreasonable; five informants concurred and also
commented that Mr. Li had been unwise to continue living with his son
after the disputes. Since he had accumulated a large amount of cash savings
and a good house, he could have had a comfortable retirement living alone.

This case reveals several important points. First, the rapid shift in inter-
generational power relations in Mr. Li's family suggests that the existing stereotype of the patriarchal extended family no longer holds true
in today's Xiajia village. Moreover, in her struggle against patriarchal
power, the daughter-in-law had gained moral support from public opinion
and from the village government. After the tragedy she was not the only
one to be blamed. This indicates that villagers' perceptions about what
intergenerational relations ought to be in a stem family may also have
changed. It is particularly striking that some villagers believed that economically secure parents should live in separate households if problems
arise with married sons in a stem family. Until the 1980s it would have been
disgraceful for parents to live alone in their late years because it would
have indicated their failure to raise filial children. From the perspective
of individual villagers it was apparent that the newly emerged centrality of the husband-wife relationship in the domestic sphere (the rise of
conjugality, as I prefer to call it) represents one of the most important
changes for rural Chinese families in the past half-century.

Contemporary discussions of the family in rural China revolve around
the increasingly important role that family labor plays in the rural economy since the onset of the economic reforms in the late 1970s. As Whyte
(1992a) summarizes, "tradition-restoring" and "modernizing" speculations
are the two major themes that have, alternatively, dominated the initial
explanations for the responses of the rural family to the market-oriented
reforms. The former maintains that the re-emergence of the family as a
production unit creates new incentives to delay family division and thus
leads to larger and more complex households; the latter focuses on non-
agricultural employment opportunities created by the reforms and argues
that these new opportunities lead to a continual shift away from the traditional family structure and values (Whyte 1992a:317–18).

Further studies in the 1990s have revealed more complicated patterns
of family behavior that reflect distinctive characteristics of the regional

economy, ethnic cultures, overseas connections, local histories, and the influence of state policies (see especially Cohen 1992; Johnson 1993; Harrell 1993; Lavely and Ren 1992; Selden 1993). But like the earlier studies, most analyses continue to focus on changes in family size and household composition. Although the younger generation's demands for conjugal independence have been recognized in some of these studies (see e.g., Cohen 1992; Selden 1993), the nuclearization of the family, together with a few important customs such as postmarital residence and family division, remains the ultimate standard by which family change is measured in rural China (a notable exception is Whyte 1995).

Missing from these studies are the internal dynamics of family life that are not necessarily reflected in the genealogical composition of a household.[2] Everyday cooperation, negotiation, and competition over such issues as power and influence, emotional attachment, moral obligation, and economic resources among individuals within a family are at least as important as family size and household composition (Yanagisako 1979:85). Moreover, the family is also a cultural construct, "a 'socially necessary illusion' about why the social division of obligations and rights is natural or just" (Coontz 1988:14). A new perception about what a family ought to be may shape behavior within the family and transform the family institution. Thus the pursuit for economic interest is insufficient to explain all changes in family life. This is particularly true when the general standard of living has been significantly improved and people can make choices in accordance with necessity and personal preference.

In an attempt to explore the internal dynamics of family life, this article focuses on the increasing importance of the conjugal relationship in a north China village. As noted by many scholars, the traditional Chinese family is characterized by the centrality of the parent-son relationship in family life and the superiority of this relationship over all other family relations, including conjugal ties (Fei 1947; Freedman 1966; Levy 1949; Yang 1965). Such a traditional family configuration, as I will demonstrate in the following pages, has been altered in the 1990s: the horizontal, conjugal tie has become both the central axis of family relations and the foundation of the family ideal shared by most villagers. After examining the relationship between family structure and economic stratification, I argue that villagers' aspirations for conjugal independence have played a role equally important to their concern for economic interest in the process of household formation. Next, this article explores how the current practice of family division promotes the development of conjugality. It then analyzes an obvious shift in the power balance between the older and younger generations in stem families, focusing on family management and the waning of parental power. Finally, I briefly discuss the sociocultural factors that have contributed to the rise of conjugality.

This case study is relevant to Goode's (1963:1) classic thesis that industrialization and urbanization lead to a shift from an extended family system to a conjugal family system; that is, "toward fewer kinship ties with distant relatives and a greater emphasis on the 'nuclear' family unit of couple and children." Goode's argument has been challenged by a series of historical studies demonstrating that nuclear families prevailed long before industrialization in Western Europe (Laslett 1971; Laslett and Wall 1972; Mitterauer and Sieder 1982; Stone 1975). Furthermore, evidence from developing countries reveals that extended families may be well suited for market economies undergoing industrialization (Chekki 1988; Conklin 1988; Dasgupta, Weatherbie, and Mukhopadhyay 1993; Gallin and Gallin 1982). However, the most important part of Goode's thesis is his interpretation of the worldwide trend toward the centrality of conjugality in family life, rather than the dualism of extended families versus nuclear families. In this connection, the data from rural north China show that there has indeed been a shift toward conjugal independence along with the development of rural economy, although the rise of conjugality does not always show a correlation with changes in family structure and post-marital residence.

The present study is based on data collected during fieldwork in Xiajia village, Heilongjiang Province, in 1989, 1991, 1993, and 1994. Like other villages in the surrounding area, Xiajia was established by migrants from central China during the nineteenth century and it remains a multi-surname farming community, growing mainly maize and soybeans. Prior to the 1949 Communist revolution, lineage organizations existed among major surname groups, but their power was never as strong as that along the southeast coast (cf. Baker 1968; Freedman 1966; Potter 1970; Watson 1975; Watson 1985). The absence of strong lineage organizations allowed the family (in many cases, the extended family) to play a leading role in organizing individuals' activities both within and outside the household, and affinal ties constituted a major component in a family's social network. Since the revolution, the importance of family networks has remained unchanged, and family loyalty and obligations to family members continued.

Yet, as demonstrated below, the organization of life within the family has been changing during the past five decades and it underwent a breakthrough in the 1990s. Economically, Xiajia was successful during the collective period (1956–80), but it has encountered a problem of development stagnation in the postcollective era, mainly resulting from its lack of industrial enterprises and its distance from the main roads and market towns. Nonetheless the community has still managed to maintain itself at the average national level in terms of household income and agricultural productivity (for more details about the community, see Yan 1996a: 22–42).

THE CHANGING PATTERNS OF FAMILY COMPOSITION

The following numerical indicators were generated from a comparison between 1980 household registration data and my 1991 household survey data in Xiajia village (see Table 1). In 1980, three years before decollectivization, there were 1,469 people in the Xiajia collectives, living in 276 families; eleven years later, there were 1,542 people in 368 families. Thus, during the past decade, Xiajia village has increased by 73 people and 92 new households.[3] This means that the number of households grew much more rapidly than the population. Accordingly, the size of families became smaller, and the average number of family members dropped from 5.3 in 1980 to 4.2 in 1991. A change of this nature, as suggested by Davis and Harrell (1993:7), could have been the result of the strict control of population growth by the state. However, a closer look at the structural composition of Xiajia families reveals that there has been a more significant change; that is, a trend toward a simpler, husband-and-wife-centered form of family organization.

Table 1 Family structure in Xiajia village, 1980 and 1991

Family structure	1980		1991	
	Number	Per cent	Number	Per cent
Nuclear family	162	59	264	72
Stem family	88	32	82	22
Joint family	11	4		
Incomplete family	15	5	22	6
Total	276	100	368	100

The tables use conventional labels for family types: a nuclear family refers to a married couple with unmarried children; a stem family is a married couple or a surviving spouse in each of at least two generations, and unmarried children; a joint family is defined by the presence of at least two married brothers, with or without unmarried children. An incomplete family is one which does not fall into any of the other categories, such as a one-person family or a family of a widow or widower.

An examination of Table 1 shows that the percentage of conjugal families in Xiajia increased from 59 per cent (N = 162) in 1980 to 72 per cent (N = 264) in 1991, with a net increase of 12 per cent. Stem families, however, remained almost the same in absolute terms (from 88 to 82), but the overall percentage of stem families decreased from 32 per cent in 1980 to 22 per cent in 1991, resulting from the rapid growth of nuclear families. The more interesting indicator is the joint family. There were eleven joint families in 1980, 4 per cent of the total number of families in the village; but there were none in 1991.

These figures show that in the past fifteen years the rapid increase in the number of nuclear families in Xiajia village has been accompanied by the stable persistence of the stem family. This pattern actually fits well with the national trends as reported by large-scale surveys (see ZGNCJTDCZ 1993:13, 82–83); it has also been found in other parts of rural China (Fang 1992; Harrell 1993; Selden 1993). A satisfactory study of family change, therefore, should be able to explain both the popularity of the nuclear family as well as the persistence of the stem family.

China scholars generally agree that the traditional Chinese family is a corporate organization characterized by a common budget, shared properties, and a household economy with a strict pooling of income. A key feature of this corporate unit is its flexibility and entrepreneurial ability to make the best of family resources (such as capital and labor) and of external opportunities. The variations in family structure, therefore, are ultimately determined by the economic self-interest of the domestic group as a corporate enterprise (Cohen 1976; Freedman 1979; Gallin and Gallin 1982; Harrell 1982). Many recent studies of contemporary rural China also use this corporate model to explain current changes in family structure (see e.g., Cohen 1992; Harrell 1993; Johnson 1993).

As so many people have chosen to live in nuclear families, one may infer that the nuclear family must be the best form for Xiajia residents to develop the household economy in the postreform era. A further analysis of the relationship between family structure and economic stratification, however, reveals the opposite case; the extended families (stem and joint families) enjoyed a significantly higher economic level in both the collective and postcollective periods. Based on annual income and family assets, Xiajia households can be classified as rich, average, and poor (see Table 2).[4] In 1980, 11 per cent (N = 10) of the stem families and 36 per cent (N = 4) of joint families were rich, while only 4 per cent (N = 6) of the nuclear families fell into this category. In 1991, 17 per cent (N = 14) of the stem families were rich; by contrast, only 10 per cent (N = 27) of the nuclear families were rich. At the other end of the spectrum, 32 per cent (N = 52) of the nuclear families in 1980 were poor, while only 6 per cent of the stem families belonged to this category. Although the gap became smaller in 1990, the number of poor nuclear families remained 17 per cent higher than that of the stem families.

Table 2   Family structure and economic stratification in Xiajia village, 1980 and 1991

Family structure	Percentage of rich		Percentage of average		Percentage of poor		Number in total	
	1980	1991	1980	1991	1980	1991	1980	1991
Nuclear family	4	10	64	53	32	37	162	264
Stem family	11	17	83	63	6	20	88	82
Joint family	36		55		9		11	
Incomplete family			53	18	47	82	15	22
Average Percentage in Village Total	7	11	69	51	24	38	276	368

The Xiajia case clearly presents a challenge to the corporate model of the Chinese family: since the extended family has proven itself economically more functional than the nuclear family, why have a growing number of people chosen to live in nuclear families since the 1980s? Here the emic views of ordinary villagers are quite illuminating. When asked the reasons for choosing to live in a nuclear family, most Xiajia residents answered with two words: *shunxin* (satisfaction/happiness) and *fangbian* (convenience). The former is not difficult to understand, as many villagers assert, "Life is always happier when you can manage the family life yourself" (*rizi zong shi ziji guozhe shunxin*). In other words, the power to make decisions and the joy of conjugal independence can make one feel happy. This feeling of satisfaction and happiness cannot be generated from family wealth alone. It is inevitable that when young couples begin their own conjugal households they are short of many things: capital, production tools, savings, and in some cases even adequate housing. However, most young couples use the word shunxin to describe their feelings after family division. As a young woman who just established her own conjugal household explained, "It is true that there is a lot of property in the old house, but it is not ours. It belongs to his [her husband's] parents and brothers. Look around this small house. Every single item is ours! I am so happy."

The second term, fangbian, however, is more complicated and can only be understood in relation to shunxin. When villagers explain that one may feel more fangbian in a nuclear family, this does not merely mean convenient in terms of making things easier, as the word usually indicates. In most newly established nuclear households, the couples frequently encounter inconveniences when they need extra hands to do household chores, when they lack necessary capital for the household economy, or when they need someone to take care of their newborn child. In this context the word fangbian actually refers to the notion of family privacy, and a couple's demand for fangbian represents an effort to reduce the accessibility of the conjugal space by others (Laslett 1973). In a nuclear family a couple may have more convenience to develop conjugal intimacy, to be left alone, and to make decisions without parental intervention. Because of these special kinds of fangbian, life in a nuclear family is considered to be more shunxin, namely, happier.

It is easy to understand why young villagers, especially young women, complain that they cannot spend much time with their spouse when they live with the husband's parents and unmarried siblings. As a young woman put it: "You always feel as though you are being watched; there are eyes around the house all the time." However, older villagers also said that they too felt "inconvenience" (bu fangbian) of a similar kind because, as parents, they had to set a good example in everyday life and thus had to remain self-disciplined at all times. A middle-aged man provided a simple example. During hot summer days he likes to wear only his shorts when at home, but after his son married (and brought in a daughter-in-law) he had to dress more formally, no matter how hot it became. Thus, when his son moved out last year he felt happy that he had recovered his freedom (specifically, to wear shorts at home). An interesting development in this connection is that in recent years many villagers have remodeled their homes, separating the bedrooms from the living room and creating more bedrooms for individual use. The common explanation for this re-arrangement of the domestic space, again, is fangbian, which is actually the villagers' way of saying "more privacy." Here we can see a reflection of the classical case whereby the individual's claim for private space within the family reflects a historical trend whereby the family becomes more like a private institution revolving around the center of conjugality (see Laslett 1973; Prost 1991:62–67).

FAMILY DIVISION AND THE DEVELOPMENT OF CONJUGALITY

The direct, immediate result of strong desires for conjugal independence is that the time of family division has been advanced considerably, and the customary coresidence of newlyweds with the groom's parents has begun to lose its significance. This change has in turn reinforced the popularity of conjugality in family life. In pre-1949 China, a family did not grow automatically out of marriage; instead, it was first conceived within an extended family by virtue of the marriage of a young couple, and then it was born when the extended family divided into two or more families, known as family division (*fenjia*). As many have noted, the Communist revolution and collective farming did not undermine patrilocal residence in rural China, nor did it change the traditional way of household formation (Lavely and Ren 1992; Parish and Whyte 1978:131–38). In today's Xiajia, as in other parts of rural China, newlyweds normally live in the groom's parents' house for a period of time before they move out to set up their own homes. Closely related to a new form of family division are changes in the duration of the coresidence period and the timing of the family division.

A key feature of the conventional form of family partition (fenjia) is that when all the sons have married, the parents of the household divide the family estate equally among the sons, and then live with one married son in a stem family. Ideally, the time of the family division should be delayed as long as possible, usually until after the death of the father or after his retirement as household head. As in many parts of rural China, this form of family division had been practiced in Xiajia for many generations. This conventional form of family division had the effect of suppressing conjugal independence in a stem family, since young couples remained under the supervision of the husband's parents and lacked the private space necessary for more intimate conjugal relations. By the time the couple finally established their own conjugal household, they were already middle-aged and their own children were teenagers, which means that it would have been too late for the couple to develop a closer conjugal relationship.

Since the late 1960s, however, a new form of family division has emerged in Xiajia, whereby the first married son sets up a separate household with his wife soon after their marriage, leaving his parents and younger brother(s) in the old household. The second married son repeats this pattern after his marriage, and the process continues until all sons are married. In most cases the youngest son stays with his parents after his marriage, thus forming a stem family.[5] The villagers in Xiajia distinguish this new type of family partition from the conventional one by calling it *danguo* (to live independently) as opposed to fenjia (to divide up the family). The family estate remains undivided in the parents' home because there are still unmarried siblings who need financial support from the family. This form of family division is referred to by Cohen (1992:370) as "serial division" and it has been reported in other parts of rural China as well (see e.g., Harrell 1993:100; Huang 1992:30; Selden 1993:148–49).

During the collective period (1956–1983), young couples who wished to leave the family through serial division (danguo) were entitled to only their shares of the rationed grain and cooking fuel (all allocated by the collective), their personal belongings (such as clothing and simple production tools), and the savings from their wedding gifts (bridewealth and dowry). As some couples recalled, they had to start their own households with little support and had to rent or borrow a small room from a relative or fellow villager. It would take them five to ten years to build a house of their own. Thus, another local term for this form of family division is *jingshen chuhu*, which literally means "to leave the family naked" (that is, with no family property).

Until the early 1980s, the socially accepted timing for the serial division (danguo) in Xiajia village was after the birth of a couple's first baby, while many waited until the marriage of the husband's younger brother. Since decollectivization in 1983, however, the time of partition has become increasingly early. According to my survey in 1991, nearly one-third of the newly married couples in Xiajia established their own households before they had children, and more than 40 per cent did so right after the birth of their first child. The trend continued to accelerate: by 1994, more than 40 per cent of the newlywed couples established an independent household prior to the birth of a child, and nearly 80 per cent of the family divisions occurred prior to the younger brother's marriage. In 1991 the earliest family division occurred seven days after the wedding; by 1994 there were two couples who did not bother to observe the traditional custom of patrilocal coresidence at all; immediately after their wedding they moved directly into a new house and began their independent households.

As a result of this accelerated trend in earlier family divisions, a growing number of newly established conjugal families consist of young couples who have yet to produce children. I call these "husband-wife families," as opposed to the conventional type of nuclear families which emerge from delayed family division after couples have had children (see Selden 1993:148–49). In 1994 twelve newlyweds had established conjugal households in this way, including two young men who are the single sons in their respective families. This would have been unthinkable in the recent past.[6]

The redistribution of family property in the current practice of family division basically follows the early pattern as described above, yet it has become a much more complicated and elaborate event, due to the increase in family wealth in recent years and the decollectivization of farm land.[7] The family-owned grain stock is divided on a per capita basis, and the young couple may take their own shares, together with their personal belongings (as explained above). Major family estates, including draft animals, tractors, and dairy cows, are usually kept in the parents' house if unmarried sons still reside there. Cash savings are never divided, even in the last round of serial family division, because, as some villagers put it, the parents want to retain their own "financial security." In the case of debts resulting from the young couple's marriage, the groom's parents (and their unmarried sons) take the responsibility to repay them. The old house is retained by the parents and will be given to the son who agrees to live with his parents; but this rule does not apply to new houses built exclusively for newlyweds. In short, in the 1990s a married couple is entitled to keep whatever they received from their marriage (clothing, furniture, cash, new house, etc.) and their share of the husband's family grain stock. This means that the amount of bridewealth and dowry is highly significant for young couples.

Documentation of the changes in marriage transactions from 1946 to 1994 in Xiajia village (Yan 1996a) reveals that over the past four decades bridewealth and dowry have been transformed from a form of marital gift exchanged between two families into a new form of premortem inheritance for marrying children (cf. Goody 1973). The latest development in the practice of bridewealth is the groom's parents' conversion of all gift items into cash, which is then given directly to the bride. This, plus the dowry a bride receives from her own parents, is considered by all parties involved to be a conjugal fund. As this conjugal fund constitutes a major part of the property that a couple can claim when they depart from the groom's parents' household, rural youths have made strenuous efforts to raise the standard amounts for the bridewealth and dowry, resulting in the rapid escalation of marriage costs (Yan 1996a: 176–209). This in turn reinforces the current practice of family division that gives the departing couple little share of the family estate, since they have already withdrawn it in the form of bridewealth and dowry.

The division of land is a new feature of family division in the post-reform era. In late 1983 the Xiajia collectives were dismantled during a nationwide campaign of reform. All collective property, including heavy agricultural machinery, was sold to individuals. Farmland, the fundamental means of production, was divided into two categories: subsistence-grain land (*kouliang tian*) and contract land *(chengbao tian)*. Everyone in the village, man and woman alike, was entitled to two *mu* of subsistence-grain land, and every adult male laborer (from age eighteen to 59) received ten *mu* of contract land (1 *mu* = 0.16 acre). The villagers' obligations to provide the state and local governments with cheap requisitioned grain, taxes, and various levies only applied to the contract land. This formula of land redistribution was based on an egalitarian principle (which is gender biased, because women received only subsistence-grain land) that gave each qualified individual, instead of the family, an equal share of the farmland.

As time passed, however, the original egalitarian principle led to new forms of social inequalities. To put it simply, male villagers who were eighteen or older gained a share of contract land equal to that of their fathers, but their younger brothers did not. Since decollectivization, the biggest problems associated with family division relate to land which is legally owned by the state and allocated to individuals as users. Because younger villagers insist on maintaining their rights to land that was granted in 1983, families that divided after that date have adopted a simple solution: land belongs to and will pass to the person to whom it was allocated in 1983. In other words, the family recognizes and follows the official arrangement of individual rights to land, including the daughters' right to their share of subsistence-grain land. This solution works perfectly for the young because it enables them to start their conjugal household with adequate land resources (they need to pay tax and grain procurement, which is based on the contract land, to the state). In the case of intravillage marriages, the bride also brings her own share of subsistence-grain land, and it becomes a part of the new conjugal household's land. (Land is not alienable between villages.)[8]

The serial form (danguo) of family partition has had a profound influence on the villagers' perception of and aspirations for conjugality in several respects. First, as mentioned above, this type of partition transforms the conventional marriage transaction into a new form of wealth devolution and thus gives the prospective bride and groom an incentive to demand a higher amount of bridewealth and dowry, which encourages the extraction of as much property as possible from their natal families. This naturally promotes the development of conjugal solidarity between the young even before they become a married couple.

Second, since the main body of the family estate remains undivided in this new form of family division, a newlywed couple has fewer incentives to remain in the old house. The earlier they leave to set up their own conjugal household, the more chance they have to take advantage of the opportunities outside of the old household. The younger sons tend to follow the example of their elder brothers in demanding more funds for their own marriages (the most obvious indicator of this is new houses, which have become a necessary part of bridewealth in recent years). This in turn weakens the parent-son solidarity in family life.

Third, for security reasons parents have also shown a tendency to create their own conjugal fund, by keeping all cash savings at their disposal. Thus, the notion of conjugality is promoted and developed even among the senior generations. As a result, some parents now encourage all of their married sons to move out, thereby setting up their own conjugal family, or an "empty nest," as it is called in the West. In Xiajia village this new trend was set by a tailor who took the initiative to let his four sons move out after their marriages; he then lived only with his wife. Many villagers admired his decision, and now others have followed his example. There were eight households consisting exclusively of senior couples in 1991, and the number had increased to seventeen by 1993.

THE DEMOCRATIZATION OF FAMILY LIFE IN STEM FAMILIES

Thus far analysis has focused on nuclear families, trying to show that it is the pursuit of conjugal independence that has led so many villagers to chose adaptation, regardless of its disadvantages with respect to economic performance. What about the persistence of the stem family, the total number of which has remained stable during the reform era (from 88 in 1980 to 82 in 1991)? Are the villagers who have chosen to live in stem families less enthusiastic about conjugality than their counterparts in nuclear families? Or have they been overwhelmed by their parents' authority and power? Both of these speculations may be valid for some individual cases. Nonetheless, survey data on stem families in Xiajia village reveal that a shift in power and authority from senior to junior generations has occurred in most stem families as well. As a result, conjugality has taken a central place in family relations, and family life in stem families shows a tendency toward democratization.

In order to understand the exercise of parental power and authority in stem families, three questions must be addressed. 1) Who is the recognized family head in official documents and important daily life ceremonies, the father or the son? 2) Who controls the family resources and makes decisions, the parents or the young couple? 3) Where does the married son stand when his wife has conflicts with his parents?

The first two questions are designed to examine the changing power relations in family life in both nominal and practical terms. There are two leadership roles in Chinese family life: the family head (*jianzhang*), who represents the family to the outside world; and the family manager (*dangjia*), who is in charge of the overall management of the family as an enterprise (Cohen 1976; Levy 1949; Yang 1965). In most cases these two roles are played by the senior male (the father) in a nuclear or extended family. However, when seniority and managerial capability do not coincide, a more competitive yet less senior person plays the role of family manager. As Cohen (1992:363) points out, the distinction between these two terms is far more important than semantic, because it also "provides for the family the cultural basis of the coexistence and reconciliation of ultimate aspirations and practical management." Whether a father remains as family head, therefore, says much about the current ideal which the family wishes to present to the outside world, while the question about decision-making may reveal the actual power balance between senior and junior generations in a stem family.

Of the 82 stem families in Xiajia village in 1991, 33 (40 per cent) were headed by fathers, mostly in their late fifties, and the remaining 49 households were headed by married sons. By contrast, 54 (61 per cent) out of the 88 stem families in 1980 were headed by parents.[9] This means that the power shift to the younger generation in stem families had become obvious by the 1990s. The change can been seen in both official documents, such as household registration or house certificates, and important everyday rituals. For instance, older men presenting gifts to the hosts at weddings or funerals often ask the bookkeeper to enter their son's name into the gift records, clearly demonstrating who the real family head is.

Due to the increased importance of building family networks and keeping up with the fast-changing trends in the market-oriented economy of the 1990s (Yan 1996a:74–97, 229–38), a family head must be more presentable to the outside world than in the recent past; as family representative he or she must dress properly, talk skillfully, and make connections effectively. The old-fashioned, conservative fathers in stem families, therefore, are not well qualified for such tasks; many of them have also found their knowledge to be out of date. As a 56-year-old man put it, "I am good at growing crops, but farming won't make much money. I know how to offer sacrifices to our ancestors [he is a local ritual specialist], but this is superstition and not allowed in our new society. The last thing I want to do is to talk with policemen or officials, but now one has to deal with these people every day. It is better to let my son do it [as family head]."

With respect to resource control and decision-making, in 1991 only 26 (32 per cent) out of the 82 stem families were actually run by parents. While my 1980 data do not reveal exactly how many fathers were actually in charge of the 88 stem families at that time, all informants confirmed that more fathers were family managers during that period. Given the much higher number of parental family heads in 1980, it is safe to speculate that more parents were in charge of stem families in the 1980s than in the 1990s. Looking at the data from another angle, younger couples were in charge of 56 (68 per cent) out of the 82 stem families in 1991. In these 56 families the young members enjoyed almost the same conjugal independence and power as their counterparts in nuclear families, plus they had the advantage of parental support for household chores and resource allocation; their aged parents were their dependents, having little influence in decision-making or resource allocation.

Furthermore, in the 26 stem families which were both headed and managed by parents in 1991, most parents could hardly be described as patriarchal tyrants; instead, parental power was expressed in moderate terms due to both the self-restraint of the parents and the strong resistance from young people. In 1991, five older villagers who played the double role of family head and family manager explained how difficult it was to run a stem family. For instance, a father had to talk with his son and daughter-in-law on eight separate occasions in order to convince them that it was too early for the family to purchase a motorcycle. In 1993 and 1994 even more parents complained about the difficulties in running a stem family. As an older woman said, "You cannot imagine how smart they [the young people] have become nowadays. They want me to be in charge, but I have to do everything; cook for the family, raise chickens and pigs, keep the family savings, and baby sit for their children. What do they do! They do nothing except watch TV and complain. I am an old servant in the family." This young couple worked in a local factory and indeed rarely helped with the household chores when they returned home from work. What really bothered the mother was that only her son handed over his salary to her while her daughter-in-law kept all of her own salary as private money (*sifangqian*), special savings which can only be accessed by the daughter-in-law or her husband. This is why the mother saw herself as a family servant instead of a family manager.

Many parents have to make special efforts to communicate with their adult children and to meet the latter's demands in order to keep the family together. In 1991 more than half of the parents who were supposedly in charge of the 26 stem families openly admitted that they could not impose their will on their married sons and daughters-in-law; instead, they discussed important issues in formal or informal family meetings where the young members' opinions were taken into serious consideration. The parents all stressed that family harmony could only be achieved by agreement among all family members. (This parallels with findings among Taiwan families; see Gallin and Gallin 1982:148–50; Thornton and Lin 1994.)

Mr. Gao, a very capable man and probably the most powerful father in Xiajia village, told me that in addition to family meetings for important issues, he also purposely spent leisure time with his two adult sons watching TV, listening to popular music, or playing mahjong. During the 1990 Chinese Spring Festival, he organized a party for his family and relatives visiting from other villages and cities. At the party he asked his children, nephews, and nieces to perform; to give a speech, sing a song, or tell a joke. He then asked his single daughter (who was nineteen and studying in an occupational school) to comment on the strengths and weaknesses of every family member. When commenting on her father, to everyone's surprise she criticized him for not treating her mother well, saying, as quoted by Mr. Gao, "In my memory you rarely talked with my mother unless you had to; you always went out after dinner, spending time with your colleagues instead of with my mother. [The father had been an important leader in the village.] Now you have retired from office and have begun to spend more time with us, but you still do not spend time with my mother." The daughter's open criticism, as Gao recalled, shocked him and moved his wife to tears. For a while, everyone else at the party was speechless. Since that event Mr. Gao has tried to improve his conjugal relationship, which he had neglected for many years. Gao's success was admired by many fellow villagers who agreed that parents could do more to improve family harmony. Although Gao's family party is uncommon, his effort does illustrate some villagers' aspirations for a new type of stem family wherein power is shared between parents and adult children, intrafamily relations are built on a more equitable foundation, and conjugal intimacy is promoted.

Another important issue concerns a married son's loyalty and support when his wife quarrels or has a conflict with his mother. From this we can determine whether the parent-son relationship is more important than the conjugal tie. According to older villagers, in the past a man always firmly stood by his parents' side, regardless of who he thought was right. Filial piety is singled out as the primary reason for taking such a position because children are supposed to show respect and obedience to their parents under all circumstances, and a daughter-in-law is always in the wrong if she dares to talk back to her mother-in-law. Another reason is that the wife is brought into the family from the outside and remains an outsider with respect to her in-laws; in conventional reasoning it is wrong for a man to make an alliance with an outsider against his own parents (see ethnographic and theoretical accounts in Freedman 1979; Levy 1949; Wolf 1972). They reconfirm the notion that when the patrilineal ideology prevails and when the parent-son relationship remains the central axis of family relations, the married son can hardly defend his own wife. Has this changed in the 1990s?

Generally speaking, when asked about their sons' position, the majority of parents state that their sons never take their side. This accusation, however, is denied by almost all of the 32 married sons whom I interviewed, although their explanations for this vary. Nearly two-thirds of the sons said that it depends on the specific situation – sometimes their parents are right and sometimes their wives are right. "We just support the person who is right," many said. Interestingly enough, their parents dismissed this explanation without hesitation. As an old woman commented, "This is all bullshit. They just try to make excuses for themselves. At each and every time, they can find a reason for their wives to be right and for their parents to be wrong. This is true, and I can speak for all parents." The remaining one-third of the married sons, however, prefer to stay neutral when their wives are involved in conflicts with their parents. Some said that they would simply leave the house for a while, thus avoiding the necessity of taking sides in an argument.

It seems that informants were answering my questions using different frames of reference. Most parents based their answers on the family quarrels and disputes they had actually experienced and thus emphasized that their married sons always sided with their wives instead of with their parents. Some parents pointed out that staying neutral in a family quarrel is nothing more than a married son's strategy to support his wife. By contrast, most married sons gave an "ought to be" answer; namely, the socially accepted attitude toward this issue rather than their actual experience or actual behavior pattern. The ideal-behavior type of answer is still enlightening, for it reveals the place of conjugality in current family ideology. Based on the information presented above, it is clear that the previous dominance of the parent-son centrality is waning; in its stead the conjugal tie has attained at least equal importance.

To clarify their responses, I went back to the married sons and asked for examples of family quarrels or disputes and how the married sons had behaved in such incidences. To avoid embarrassing the informants, I did not ask about their own experiences but discussed other cases with them. It turned out that when reviewing the disputes of their neighbors, the married sons gave answers that were very close to those of their parents. In virtually all cases of family conflict, married sons supported their wives openly, directly or indirectly. Comparing their stories about other married sons with their earlier responses about what they thought ought to be, it seems that those who claim they only support the person who is right tend to support their wives against their parents, and those who want to be neutral tend to adopt an indirect way of supporting their wives, such as by offering moral support in private. Interviews with married sons who live in nuclear families indicated that their attitude toward the issue of family quarrels is the same as the majority of those who live in stem families; namely, a man should support the person who is right (whether his mother or his wife) depending on the specific situation. Again, in actual context, these married sons tend to unconditionally support their wives; the very fact that they live in nuclear families already illustrates this point, since most family divisions result from unresolvable family conflicts.

THE SOCIAL CONTEXT OF CONJUGAL INDEPENDENCE

The most important factor contributing to the waning of parental power is the change in the mode of social organization during the past half-century. This change has terminated many of the public functions previously performed by the family, undermined parental authority to a great extent, and created conjugal space at home. Unlike the previous emphasis on the domestic mode of production (e.g., Sahlins 1972), the "mode of social organization" approach encompasses a range of social activities (such as socialization, education, and migration) having the same analytical status as production; thus the tendency to explain family changes in terms of economic determinism may be avoided. As Thornton and Fricke (1987:749) note, particular attention should be paid to the "transformation of the family mode of organization by the proliferation of social structures outside the family that have come to perform or direct many of the activities formerly carried out by family units."

In pre-1949 Xiajia village, as in other parts of rural China, most (if not all) social activities were organized within the family and kinship networks, where power and authority were based on the superiority of the senior generation over the junior generation, the older over the younger, and men over women (Cohen 1976; Freedman 1966, 1979; Levy 1949; Thornton and Lin 1994; Watson 1975, 1982; Wolf 1972; Yang 1965). This familial mode of social organization experienced the most dramatic change when collectivization campaigns terminated familial ownership of land and other means of production in the mid-1950s, directly weakening the power base of parents as they had much less family property at their disposal during family division. During the subsequent 25 years, Xiajia village became a production brigade with four production teams. Agricultural production was organized by the collectives, and individual villagers were assigned various tasks by their team leaders instead of by parents or lineage leaders. Parental authority was further challenged in public life when the experience and knowledge of the older villagers became outmoded in their encounters with ideological education, political campaigns, and the introduction of agricultural machinery, chemical fertilizer, pesticide, and other innovations. The development of formal education also weakened the family's organizational role. By the mid-1980s, 75 per cent of boys and 48 per cent of girls in Xiajia village had completed junior high school, while virtually all school-age children were enrolled in primary school. This means that most village teenagers normally spend at least six years in school, participating in social activities outside the family for at least six hours a day. As a result of these changes, village youth have gained the right to participate in public life, to have more freedom in socializing with the opposite sex, to have increasing autonomy in mate choice. All this supports a national trend in favor of conjugality as discussed in early studies (see Parish and Whyte 1978; Salaff 1973).

This trend has continued in the postcollective period (1983 to the present), because decollectivization restored only family farming, not the entire familial mode of social organization. In agricultural production, although specific farming work is organized within the family, the household economy as a whole is directed by state policy and market demands. This situation can hardly be regarded as a complete restoration of the domestic or familial mode of production. Moreover, due to the diversification of the rural economy and increasing opportunities for outside employment, many villagers engage in nonfarm work in industrial or semi-industrial organizations. In Xiajia village, for instance, 106 laborers regularly worked outside the village in 1991 for periods longer than three months per annum; this figure increased to 167 people by 1994. Furthermore, the organization of work constitutes only one aspect of the mode of social organization (admittedly a very important one), and there are many other areas where villagers' activities are organized by nonfamilial modes of organization, such as participation in public life, formal education, and leisure activities.

In contrast to William Goode's (1963) argument that the state regulation of family life is usually a consequence of industrialization and urbanization, Davis and Harrell (1993:5) assert that in China, "state power and policies have been the creators, not the creations, of a transformed society."

This is particularly true with regard to the development of conjugality. In addition to the above-mentioned social changes which are all closely related to state policies and government intervention in one way or another, the marriage law (1950 and 1980), the state-sponsored family reform in the 1950s and 1960s, the constant attacks on ancestor worship, and the dismantling of lineage organizations have all worked against parental authority and power. Meanwhile, youth autonomy in mate choice and marriage has been protected by law and encouraged by government directives during the past five decades (Whyte 1992b, 1995). Contrary to state goals, these policies have not altered or weakened villagers' commitments to their families, as noted by many scholars (Davis and Harrell 1993; Whyte 1995); but they have had the effect of weakening parental authority, thus encouraging the development of conjugality.[10]

Prosperity is another important contributing factor to the current popularity of conjugality in Xiajia families. Most studies of Chinese families have focused on how the family as a production unit enables its members to develop the household economy; few ethnographers, however, have considered how the family as a unit of consumption may affect members' everyday lives. Consumption was probably not an important issue when general living standards were low and most rural families were struggling at a subsistence economic level. From 1978 to 1984, peasant net income grew at an enviable annual rate of 17.6 per cent, and general living standards in rural areas improved considerably. Although the growth of peasant net income slowed in the late 1980s, it recovered in the early 1990s. Overall, living standards in rural areas have continuously improved since the late 1970s (State Statistics Bureau 1988; Chai 1992; Ma and Sun 1993:259–62). As a result, consumption has taken an important place in rural family life. The most common agenda during family gatherings concerns the purchase of consumer durables, house construction or remodeling, and planning stylish family ceremonies such as weddings or funerals. Qiu and Wan (1990) suggest that the first wave of consumerism in China was actually triggered by the sudden increase in peasant consumption.

Consumption and lifestyle are particularly significant for younger villagers who grew up during the reform era. Unlike their older siblings and parents, they have been greatly influenced by the prevailing trend of consumerism since the late 1980s and thus they have a different perception of what constitutes the "good life." For these rural youth, old-fashioned peasant thrift (i.e., reducing expenditures to the minimum level) is not necessarily an asset because it does not generate wealth or make life more enjoyable. Many rural youth have the notion of *nengzheng huihua* (meaning "capable of making money and knowing how to spend it"), which was a leading slogan promoted by economic reformers in the 1980s (Yan 1996b). A simple yet interesting piece of evidence from Xiajia village shows that, in general, young people in nuclear households spend more money on food and clothing than do their parents or older siblings; they are also more likely than older villagers to follow consumer trends, such as replacing black-and-white televisions with color sets, or purchasing motorcycles.

From a conjugal/individual perspective, a well-to-do extended family is characterized by a larger amount of accumulated family property and a stronger labor force, but it does not necessarily mean a better quality of everyday life because individuals have less access to family property and less power over consumption. The desire for consumption and the increase of purchasing power have therefore created an important motivation for young villagers to live apart from their more conservative and old-fashioned parents. By the same token, parents who are accustomed to saving and to avoiding consumption beyond necessity also feel uncomfortable living with their trendy adult children and prefer to have them leave the house when the parents can no longer control them.

Finally, demography is important in the current change in family relations. Life expectancy for both men and women in China has been extended from 40.8 years to 69.4 years during the past four decades (United Nations 1993:234). With the improvement of living standards and medical care, villagers are much healthier than before. A 50-year-old man or woman in the 1940s was old and not expected to play a significant role in farming; nowadays many villagers in their sixties are healthy and strong enough to work in the fields. (In Xiajia, as in many other rural areas, a large proportion of the land is farmed by older villagers because many youths have left to seek employment in the cities.) Moreover, rural youth currently tend to marry earlier than during the collective era, in part because of their newly attained prosperity and in part due to the loosening of the legal marriage age by the new marriage law (Ocko 1991; Palmer 1995). As a result, many parents (particularly among well-to-do families) are in their forties when their eldest son gets married. In 1993 the youngest father-in-law was only 39 years old and the youngest grandfather 42, while newly married couples were in their late teens or early twenties.

These middle-aged, healthy, and vigorous parents (even grandparents) are unlikely to retire from family management and thus are more likely to become involved in conflicts with the younger generation, should they all live together (see Davis-Friedmann 1991:82). A possible solution for both generations, therefore, is to live apart; hence the emergence of empty-nest families in recent years. Furthermore, most parents in the 1990s were village youths themselves in the 1970s and thus enjoyed more autonomy than did their parents in the 1950s. Influenced by their own experiences as rebellious youth (Yan 1996b), they have demonstrated more tolerance toward conjugal independence of the next generation when they became the parents of married children in the 1990s. The very concept of parenthood, therefore, is changing and needs to be redefined in discussions of family relations in contemporary China.

CONCLUSIONS

The cases examined in this essay demonstrate that by the early 1990s conjugal independence had become an accepted feature of family ideology for the majority of Xiajia residents. Similarly, the horizontal, conjugal tie has replaced the vertical, parent-son relationship as the central axis of family relations in most households – nuclear and stem alike. This marks the triumph of conjugality over patriarchy, a structural transformation of domestic life in both ideology and institutional arrangement. The transformation is a consequence of social changes whereby several generations of villagers have gradually redefined the family ideal and adjusted their behavior accordingly.

The Xiajia case reveals the interplay between a changing family ideal on the one hand and a changing power balance between the older and younger generations on the other. The most important result is the dramatic rise of conjugality in family life, instead of the structural change from extended family to nuclear family (*pace* Goode 1963). In Xiajia, as in many other parts of rural China, nuclear and extended families coexisted in the past, coexist today, and will very likely continue to coexist in the near future, due in large part to the absence of a well-developed social support system for the elderly (Fang 1992; Zeng, Li, and Liang 1992; ZGNCJTDCZ 1993). The internal changes in intrafamily relations, therefore, might be more important than changes in the formal structure of families. Furthermore, by focusing on the internal dynamics of family life rather than structural composition, the full complexity of the institution emerges. The Chinese family is indeed a vehicle for the performance of public functions, but it is also a private haven where the private lives of individuals unfold or, as Xiajia villagers put it, a home where couples can feel that life is fangbian (convenient) and shunxin (happy).

NOTES

1. I owe special thanks to Deborah Davis, James Watson, Martin Whyte, and the anonymous reviewers of *Ethnology* for helpful comments on early drafts. I am also grateful to Nancy Hearst for editorial assistance.
2. Some studies of family life in urban China have documented important changes in this aspect (see, e.g., Davis-Friedmann 1991; Honig and Hershatter 1988; and Jankowiak 1993). Changes in rural family life, as demonstrated by the Xiajia case, are similar to those in urban China, although the former occurred in a less dramatic fashion.
3. These figures do not include the population of a small neighboring village which officially has been part of the Xiajia administrative system since the 1950s. Moreover, a number of families moved out of the village between 1980 and 1991, which also contributes to the slow increase in population.
4. Household net income alone is not an accurate measure of a rural family's economic position because villagers need capital to invest in agricultural production. My survey used both household income and family assets to determine economic position. The second measurement includes primary tools of production, farm machinery and/or draft animals, and important capital for family sidelines such as dairy cows, private enterprises, housing, savings, and consumer durables. For a more detailed account, see Yan 1992:8–14.
5. As a family is very likely to have multiple divisions under this new form of division, the developmental cycle of the family has also changed (Yan 1997).
6. A development associated with the trend of early family division is that after married sons establish their own conjugal households they maintain close relationships with and actively participate in joint activities with their parents and siblings. A new pattern of networking and co-operation among postdivision nuclear families has been formed (Yan 1997). See also Croll's (1987:488–95) analysis of the "aggregate family" and Judd's (1994:173–87) discussion on the blurring of household boundaries in rural north China.
7. It is "decollectivized land," and not "privatized land," because legally it is still the collective's land, and individual villagers have only a user's right to the land allocated to them during a contracted period granted by the local government and protected by state policy. The duration of the contracted period, however, was extended from fifteen years to 30 years and now is up to 50 years.

8. However, when younger sons (who were under eighteen in 1983) started to claim the family division in the early 1990s, they could only take away their own subsistence-grain land from the old house (which is all they were given in 1983). Most fathers are still physically strong enough to farm their own contract land and they also need to do so for the unmarried sons at home. Only those older villagers who were about 50 in 1983 and who have reached retirement age in the 1990s may decide to pass their contract land on to their sons (in most cases the youngest sons) in a family division. The situation can be far worse for those who were born after 1983, because they did not even get the subsistence-grain land. When they are ready to set up their own conjugal household they will be landless (but this will not become an issue until the next century).

9. Depending on the senior male's age, health, and personality, in the past there were always some stem families headed by a married son instead of the father. But this number was quite small.

10. It is important to distinguish family structure from family relations. Some state policies, such as the emphasis on the obligation to support aged parents, tend to reinforce traditional family obligations and encourage the persistence of stem families. But this does not indicate official support for parental power; on the contrary, as shown in the Xiajia case, the majority of stem families are run by the younger generation and the parents are their dependents.

BIBLIOGRAPHY

Baker, H. 1968. *Sheung Shui, a Chinese Lineage Village*. Stanford.

Chai, J. C. H. 1992. Consumption and Living Standards in China. *China Quarterly* 131:721–49.

Chekki, D. A. 1988. Recent Directions in Family Research: India and North America. *Journal of Comparative Family Studies* 19(2):171–86.

Cohen, M. L. 1976. *House United, House Divided: The Chinese Family in Taiwan*. New York.

———— 1992. Family Management and Family Division in Contemporary Rural China. *China Quarterly* 130:357–77.

Conklin, G. H. 1988. The Influence of Economic Development on Patterns of Conjugal Power and Extended Family Residence in India. *Journal of Comparative Family Studies* 19(2):187–205.

Coontz, S. 1988. *The Social Origin of Private Life: A History of American Families, 1600–1900*. London.

Croll, E. 1987. New Peasant Family Forms in Rural China. *Journal of Peasant Studies* 14:469–99.

Dasgupta, S., C. Weatherbie, and R. S. Mukhopadhyay. 1993. Nuclear and Joint Family Households in West Bengal Villages. *Ethnology* 32(4):339–58.

Davis, D., and S. Harrell. 1993. Introduction: The Impact of Post-Mao Reforms on Family Life. *Chinese Families in the Post-Mao Era*, eds. D. Davis and S. Harrell, pp. 1–22. Berkeley.

Davis-Friedmann, D. 1991. *Long Lives: Chinese Elderly and the Communist Revolution.* Stanford.

Fang, X. 1992. Nongcun jiating jiegou biandong quxiang de shequ fengxi (Directions of Change in Rural Family Structure: A Case Study). *Shehuixue yanjiu (Sociological Studies)* 2:114–21.

Fei, X. 1947. *Xiangtu zhongguo (Folk China).* Shanghai.

Freedman, M. 1966. *Chinese Lineage and Society: Fukien and Kwangtung.* London.

———— 1979 (1961). The Family in China, Past and Present. *The Study of Chinese Society: Essays by Maurice Freedman*, ed. G. W. Skinner, pp. 273–95. Stanford.

Gallin, B., and R. Gallin. 1982. The Chinese Joint Family in Changing Rural Taiwan. *Social Interaction in Chinese Society*, eds. S. Greenblatt, R. Wilson, and A. A. Wilson, pp. 142–58. New York.

Goode, W. 1963. *World Revolution and Family Patterns.* New York.

Goody, J. 1973. Bridewealth and Dowry in Africa and Eurasia. *Bridewealth and Dowry*, eds. J. Goody and S. Tambiah, pp. 1–58. Cambridge.

Harrell, S. 1982. *Ploughshare Village: Culture and Context in Taiwan.* Seattle.

———— 1993. Geography, Demography, and Family Composition in Three Southwestern Villages. *Chinese Families in the Post-Mao Era*, eds. D. Davis and S. Harrell, pp. 77–102. Berkeley.

Honig, E., and G. Hershatter. 1988. *Personal Voice: Chinese Women in the 1980s.* Stanford.

Huang, S. 1992. Re-examining the Extended Family in Chinese Peasant Society: Findings from a Fujian Village. *Australian Journal of Chinese Affairs* 27:25–38.

Jankowiak, W. 1993. *Sex, Death, and Hierarchy in a Chinese City: An Anthropological Account.* New York.

Johnson, G. 1993. Family Strategies and Economic Transformation in Rural China: Some Evidence from the Pearl River Delta. *Chinese Families in the Post-Mao Era*, eds. D. Davis and S. Harrell, pp. 103–36. Berkeley.

Judd, E. 1994. *Gender and Power in Rural North China.* Stanford.

Laslett, B. 1973. The Family as Public and Private Institution: An Historical Perspective. *Journal of Marriage and the Family* 35(3):480–94.

Laslett, P. 1971. *The World We Have Lost.* London.

Laslett, P., and R. Wall (eds.). 1972. *Household and Family in Past Time.* Cambridge.

Lavely, W., and X. Ren. 1992. Patrilocality and Early Marital Co-residence in Rural China, 1955–85. *China Quarterly* 130:378–91.

Levy, M. 1949. *The Family Revolution in Modern China.* Cambridge MA.

Ma, H., and S. Sun (eds.). 1993. *Jiji Baipishu, 1992–93* (The White Book of Economics, 1992–93). Beijing.

Mitterauer, M., and R. Sieder. 1982. *The European Family: Patriarchy to Partnership from the Middle Ages to the Present.* Oxford.

Ocko, J. K. 1991. Women, Property, and the Law in the People's Republic of China. *Marriage and Inequality in Chinese Society*, eds. R. Watson and P. Ebrey, pp. 313–46. Berkeley.

Palmer, M. 1995. The Re-emergence of Family Law in Post-Mao China: Marriage, Divorce and Reproduction. *China Quarterly* 141:110–34.

Parish, W., and M. Whyte. 1978. *Village and Family in Contemporary China.* Chicago.

Potter, J. M. 1970. Land and Lineage in Traditional China. *Family and Kinship in Chinese Society*, ed. M. Freedman, pp. 121–38. Stanford.

Prost, A. 1991. Public and Private Spheres in France. *A History of Private Life, vol. 5*, eds. A. Prost and G. Vincent, transl. A. Goldhammer, pp. 1–43. Cambridge MA.

Qiu, X., and D. Wan. 1990. Jin shinianlai woguo xiaofei xingshi de jiben huigu yu zhanwang (Brief Review of the State of Consumption in the Past Decade and Its Prospect in China). Xiaofei Jingji (Consumption Economics) No. 2.

Sahlins, M. 1972. *Stone Age Economics.* New York.

Salaff, J. 1973. The Emerging Conjugal Relationship in the People's Republic of China. *Journal of Marriage and the Family* 35(4):705–17.

Selden, M. 1993. Family Strategies and Structures in Rural North China. *Chinese Families in the Post-Mao Era*, eds. D. Davis and S. Harrell, pp. 139–64. Berkeley.

State Statistics Bureau. 1988. *Zhongguo Noncun Tongji Nianjian (Statistics Yearbook of Rural China).* Beijing.

Stone, L. 1975. The Rise of the Nuclear Family in Early Modern England. *The Family in History*, ed. C. Rosenberg, pp. 13–57. Philadelphia.

Thornton, A., and T. Fricke. 1987. Social Change and the Family: Comparative Perspectives from the West, China, and South Asia. *Sociological Forum* 2(4):746–79.

Thornton, A., and H.-S. Lin (eds.). 1994. *Social Change and the Family in Taiwan.* Chicago.

United Nations. 1993. *World Population Project: The 1992 Revision.* New York.

Watson, J. L. 1975. *Emigration and the Chinese Lineage: The Mans in Hong Kong and London.* Berkeley.

—— 1982. Chinese Kinship Reconsidered: Anthropological Perspectives on Historical Research. *China Quarterly* 92:589–622.

Watson, R. S. 1985. *Inequality among Brothers, Class and Kinship in South China.* Cambridge.

Whyte, M. K. 1992a. Introduction: Rural Economic Reforms and Chinese Family Patterns. *China Quarterly* 130:317–22.

—— 1992b. Changes in Mate Choice in Chengdu. *Chinese Society on the Eve of Tiananmen*, eds. D. Davis and E. Vogel, pp. 181–214. Cambridge MA.

—— 1995. The Social Roots of China's Economic Development. *China Quarterly* 144:999–1019.

Wolf, M. 1972. *Women and the Family in Rural Taiwan*. Stanford.

Yanagisako, S. J. 1979. Family and Household: The Analysis of Domestic Groups. *Annual Review of Anthropology* 8:161–205.

Yan, Y. 1992. The Impact of Rural Reform on Economic and Social Stratification in a Chinese Village. *Australian Journal of Chinese Affairs* 27:1–23.

—— 1996a. *The Flow of Gifts: Reciprocity and Social Networks in a Chinese Village*. Stanford.

—— 1996b. *Rural Youth and Youth Culture in North China*. Paper presented at the Workshop on the Transformation of Social Experience in Taiwan, Hong Kong, and China, Academia Sinica, Taipei, Taiwan, August 25–31.

—— 1997. *Money and Morality in Family Politics: The Case of Family Division in a Chinese Village*. Paper presented at the Annual Symposium of the Center for Chinese Studies, University of California at Berkeley, March 21–22.

Yang, C. K. 1965. *Chinese Communist Society: The Family and the Village*. Cambridge.

Zeng. Y., W. Li, and Z. Liang. 1992. Zhongguo jiating de xiangzhuang, quyu chayi, ji biandong qushi (The Current State, Regional Variations, and Trend of Change in the Chinese Family Structure). *Zhongguo Renkou Kexue (Population Science in China)* 2:1–12.

ZGNCJTDCZ (Zhongguo nongcun jiating diaochazu). 1993. *Dangdai Zhongguo Nongcun Jiating (The Family in Contemporary Rural China)*. Beijing.

CHAPTER 4

PRACTICING KINSHIP, REMAKING
THE INDIVIDUAL

In August 1966, my father was wrongly accused of having been a capitalist prior to the 1949 revolution (he actually had been a small shop owner), and as a result of the Red Guards' efforts to make Beijing politically pure and clean during the Cultural Revolution, our family, like many other families in similar situations, was forced to leave the capital city and relocate in my father's natal village in northern China. This village is a patrilineal community where all the male members share the same surname, Yan. At that time, "class struggle" was the primary concern of the Communist Party leaders; so it became national practice in everyday life. Chinese people were divided into various good-class categories (those who had been exploited and oppressed before the revolution) and bad ones (those who had been exploiters and oppressors); the former were mobilized by the state to monitor and struggle against the latter. Hence, in our village there were the members of the good class, the supposedly revolutionary Yans, and the members of the bad class, the allegedly antirevolutionary Yans. Because my father was labeled a capitalist, he and, by virtue of our kin relationship, our entire family were considered politically polluted and thus we were all excluded from many social activities in which only good-class people were allowed to participate.

An odd thing occurred in the first autumn (1967) following our relocation to the countryside. My father's aunt (the mother of his patrilineal cousin, who, based on complicated kinship terminology, I called "sixth grandmother") died at the age of seventy-seven. She was survived by a large number of children, grandchildren, and great-grandchildren. Because of her age and because she had so many descendants, an elaborate funeral, based on local customs, was called for. Unfortunately, she died during the peak of the Cultural Revolution when the young Red Guards were sweeping through the whole nation to attack traditional culture and customs, including life-cycle rituals. After intensive discussions among themselves, as well as negotiations with the village authority, the family members of the deceased finally decided to provide the deceased woman with an appropriate funeral, which she so much deserved. To show their willingness to go along with the new customs proposed by the Communist leaders, the family members agreed to reduce the length of the ritual to two days (instead of the three or seven days that it should have been) and observe only the most important ceremonial procedures, while omitting many others, including the traditional white mourning dress and musical band.

Much to the surprise of our family, my father was also called on to participate in the funeral and play his role in all the major rites as a close nephew of the deceased, despite the fact that he was a political outcast. During this public event, my father became kin to those good-class villagers, some of whom were village cadres, political activists, or even Red Guards. Because his generational rank was quite senior, he was addressed by all but a few individuals by such terms as "uncle" or "grandfather" – terms that definitely should not have been used to address a class enemy. He later recalled that initially he had felt uncomfortable with such a sudden change of position in public life, and the other villagers had also felt the same way. But as the ritual proceeded, most people seemed to forget the political boundaries between the good- and bad-class categories.

During the second night, a final farewell ceremony was performed in front of the deceased, who had been placed inside her coffin. Members of the entire sublineage assembled in the courtyard, with the males on one side and females on the other. The participants were lined up in rows based on their generational rank. Although I had successfully avoided the major part of the funeral (I was thirteen years old at the time and quite afraid of the ceremony), an older cousin took me from my home and literally threw me into the crowd of mourners, who were kneeling in rows and kowtowing when the ritual specialist gave the order. I remember being completely terrified by the performance and forgetting to do what I had been told. Then someone lifted me by the ear and carried me past several rows to place me in the second row in the front. Then he kicked the back of my knees. I next found myself kneeling on the ground along with more than a dozen men in the row, all of whom I was used to addressing as "cousin" in everyday life, regardless of their age. Following their example, I proceeded to do what they did during the rest of the ritual.

Even after I grew up, I always had a feeling of fear whenever I recalled my experience during that night. As time passes, however, I no longer fear the ghosts or my older cousins; what I still fear is perhaps the mystic power of the funeral itself, as well as the strange feeling that I am one of the Yans and thus bound to all the other Yans regardless of whether I like them or not.

Now looking at the event in retrospect, I realize that it actually reveals a complex situation of kinship practice in that particular historical moment. On the surface, it shows once again the tremendous power of patrilineal ideology and kinship norms, as villagers felt compelled to recognize their kinship position in public and perform the funeral in accordance with traditionally defined kinship norms, despite the state-sponsored, antitradition radicalism during the Cultural Revolution. As a result, the political boundaries between the good and bad classes were blurred publicly by the kinship ties during the ritual – perhaps a small victory for the villagers' passive resistance to the penetration of state power.[1]

Nevertheless, a closer look reveals interesting changes, which occurred during the funeral. First, the state had obviously reshaped the practice of kinship to such an extent that the villagers had to consider many factors when deciding whether or not to perform a proper funeral. During my 1991 fieldwork in the village, interestingly enough, I was told by a couple of villagers that my seventh uncle (the son of the deceased lady) had indeed encountered some trouble after the funeral, even though he had confessed his guilt for practicing a traditional ritual in front of a portrait of Chairman Mao Tse-tung right after the event. Second, the villagers had to make modifications to their ritual practice, such as shortening the duration of the funeral and simplifying the ritual procedures. Finally (and perhaps more important), despite the fact that the mourners acted as a collective during the funeral, each individual had to make a decision before and during the process whether to respond to the event socially, politically, and emotionally (admittedly a child's decision did not count much, as illustrated by my own case). For instance, although most members of the sublineage participated in the funeral, several young and radical villagers refused to attend the ritual so as to demonstrate their firm revolutionary standpoint.

These changes reveal the other side of kinship relations: that is, in practice, kinship relations are actually a set of rather flexible interpersonal relations negotiated by individual agents in response to social changes that occur in the larger setting. Here, individual agency is as significant as external factors, such as state policies and social changes. A newer kind of theoretical eye is also critical for a better understanding of the current patterns of kinship practice in China. The fluid and flexible nature of kinship as well as the negotiated, processual features of kinship practice, which are recently discussed at length by anthropologists working on non-Western societies (see, for example, Astuti 1995; Carsten 1995), have been by and large ignored in existing studies of Chinese kinship. As Charles Stafford (2000) correctly points out, a formalist approach, which emphasizes the centrality of patriliny, has obscured in anthropological accounts the lived experience of Chinese kinship.

It is, therefore, necessary and important to study kinship in the context of practice, or to borrow one of Pierre Bourdieu's terms, to reexamine kin relations as practical kinship. It should be noted that in this essay, the phrase "practical kinship" is used differently from Bourdieu's original definition (1977, 33–38; 1990, 166–87). Bourdieu's dichotomy of official and practical kinship is rather problematic because it merely continues the long-existing division between public kinship organization and the domestic family established by E. E. Evans-Pritchard and Meyer Fortes.[2] Still, Bourdieu's emphasis on practice and individual agency is note-worthy, and practical kinship also seems to be an appropriate appellation. Hereafter I will borrow the term, but I will use it in my own way – namely, to refer to the fluid and flexible nature of kinship in practice, not in opposition to official kinship.

In the following, I introduce the kinship organization of the village where I conducted fieldwork and locate practical kinship in terms of the local category of guanxi networks. I argue that both community and kinship relations tend to be incorporated into person-centered guanxi networks. I then examine some features of current kinship practices, including the elasticity of kinship distance, the uncertainty of kinship alliance, the active role played by women, and the shift in emphasis from cross-generation links to same-generation connections. I conclude the essay by discussing three major factors that contribute to an understanding of the kinship system in rural China – that is, social change, scholarly models, and the changing practice of kinship itself.

KINSHIP ORGANIZATION AND GUANXI NETWORKS
IN XIAJIA VILLAGE

The present study is based on data collected during a series of field studies in Xiajia village, Heilongjiang Province, in 1991, 1993, 1994, and 1997. According to the household register of 1991, Xiajia had a population of 1,564 in 365 households, and it remains today a farming community, growing mainly maize and soybeans. As a result of constant immigration throughout its history, the village currently consists of more than thirty agnatic groups. The largest one is the Xia, which has 104 households, a fact well reflected in the name of the village, which literally translates as "Xia's home." Besides the Xia, there are seven sizable agnatic groups, such as the Xu and the Wang, each with more than 15 households.

Prior to the 1949 Communist revolution, the significance of patriliny and agnatic solidarity was ritually demonstrated and reinforced during the *Qingming* festival (grave sweeping). The Xia lineage collectively owned land and trees near the ancestral tombs. During the Qingming festival, Xia males gathered to visit their ancestors' tombs, located six kilometers away from the village. After the visit, a banquet was provided at the home of the lineage head. Similar gatherings were held on the eve of Chinese New Year when the year-end, grand-ancestor worship ritual was performed at the homes of the senior males of each sublineage. Other major agnatic groups in Xiajia village had similar practices, but their scale was smaller compared to that of the Xia. These agnatic groups were also the major organizational form of social and economic activities for most ordinary villagers. The overall power of lineage organization in Xiajia village, however, was never as strong as that along the southeast coast (see Freedman 1966; J. Watson 1975; R. Watson 1985).

The Communists took the southern region of Heilongjiang Province during 1946–1947, so Xiajia villagers witnessed the dramatic social changes three years prior to the founding of the People's Republic of China. In Xiajia and the surrounding area, land reform was launched in late 1946 and collectivization, another radical social engineering project sponsored by the state, began during the mid-1950s. When the collectives in Xiajia were dismantled as part of the economic reform program at the end of 1983, once again the order of social life in the village was altered to a great extent (see Yan 1992). The average per capita net income in Xiajia village was 616 yuan in 1990, which when compared to a national average of 623 yuan, places it at the midpoint economically among Chinese farming communities.

During the postrevolution era, especially after the high tide of radical collectivization – aimed at destroying traditional patterns of social organization – the power of the patrilineage in Xiajia was considerably diminished. The ancestral land and trees were redistributed among villagers during the land reform, and a public cemetery was established outside the southeastern gate of Xiajia. The Xia and other groups whose ancestral tombs were far away from Xiajia began to bury their dead in the public graveyard. The Qingming visits to the ancestral tombs and associated banquets no longer took place. Domestic ancestor worship during the spring festival continued until the Cultural Revolution (1966), and it was resumed in the early 1980s. Nevertheless, it was performed within the lineage subbranch (*fang*) at the home of a senior agnate, and there were no organized, lineage-wide activities in public settings. A major reason for the decline of ancestor worship was the state-sponsored attack on lineage organization along with the ideological campaign against feudal values and superstition. Some core notions of lineage ideology, such as filial piety, male preference, and generational superiority, were also attacked during repeated political campaigns. Despite all these efforts and the state's hostility toward large-scale kinship organizations, the importance of kinship per se has not declined. Instead, the practice of kinship has been moved onto a new stage in which kinship ties have been absorbed into the more general and open-ended structure of guanxi networks.

The Chinese notion guanxi, which may be translated roughly as social networks, contains multilayered meanings and has been a central concern among China scholars in recent decades. Existing scholarly accounts tend to regard guanxi as an element in a uniquely Chinese normative social order (see, for example, King 1991; Kipnis 1997; Hwang 1987) or treat it as a practical means for advancing specific personal interests (Walder 1986; Yang 1994). My study in Xiajia shows, however, that villagers perceive their guanxi networks as the very foundation of society – the local moral world in which villagers live their lives. As such, guanxi constitutes a total social phenomenon in the Maussian sense because it provides one with a social space that at once incorporates economic, political, social, and recreational activities (see also Kipnis 1997). In a given guanxi network, the immediate family and closest agnates and affines make up a "core zone" of social connections; good friends and less close relatives who can always be counted on for help form a larger "reliable zone"; and finally, an "effective zone" embraces a large number of distant relatives and friends in a broader sense (see Yan 1996, 98–102).

A careful analysis of patterns of gift exchange, the most central means of building up and maintaining guanxi in everyday life, shows that the overall structure of the guanxi networks in Xiajia is characterized by a heavy reliance on friendship ties, as opposed to (official) kinship relations, the involvement of a large number of fellow villagers, and the active role of affines.[3] For instance, kinship ties make up 37 percent of the donors in villagers' gifting networks; by contrast, nonkin relationships, which include fellow villagers, friends, and colleagues, occupy a total of 62 percent of the donors. Within the system of kinship ties, affines occupy 21 percent, outnumbering the agnates (9 percent) more than twofold. More important, Xiajia villagers have gone beyond the boundary of the kinship system to build networks through all kinds of personal relations based on friendship: friends, colleagues, and fellow villagers (locally called *tunqin*, which literally means relatives by coresidence). In other words, most relationships in guanxi networks, such as affines, friends, and colleagues, are not inherited from their parents or ancestors but are made or cultivated by villagers themselves, who want to do something with these connections for their practical concerns (Yan 1996, 105–21). It is this stress on extended relatedness, as opposed to inherited or blood-based relatedness, that draws my attention because the former has to be made and maintained, and therefore, heavily depends on individual choice and agency. The increasing significance of extended relatedness, or nonkinship relations, in guanxi networks has in turn affected both the practice of kinship and villagers' perception as well as our view toward it.

THE FLOW OF PRACTICAL KINSHIP

Looking at kinship practice from the perspective of guanxi networks, it becomes clear that kinship relations are fluid and transformative. It is true that close kin tend to form the core of an individual's network; but in many cases, close kin can also be transformed into a more marginal status in guanxi and, as a replacement, best friends can be brought into the core zone of guanxi. Below are some recent findings from Xiajia village.

The Elasticity of Kinship Distance

It should be noted that the patrilineal ideology remains influential in some crucial areas of contemporary village life, such as in the reckoning of descent and inheritance of family properties. Thus, agnatic ties are still considered more essential and closer in distance than any other kin relations. In practice, however, villagers must frequently evaluate and reevaluate kinship distance in accordance with their ongoing interactions with relatives, and when they do this, agnatic ties may not necessarily be at the top of their list. For instance, I repeatedly asked my informants a simple question: "Who is closer to you – your brother or your wife's brother?" Many informants regarded this as a difficult question, and most responded that they were closer to their brothers yet had a better relationship with their wives' brothers, which was reflected in more frequent mutual help and the exchange of more generous gifts. Here, the difference between a closer and better relationship exemplifies the differences between kinship ideology and practice.

Such a difference became more obvious when the practice of socialism basically destroyed the organizational infrastructure of the patrilineage as well as its ideology, thereby offering more room and flexibility for villagers to choose with whom they would ally themselves. Under this new circumstance, affines, as opposed to agnates, tend to be more desirable. As reflected by the gift lists, there are twice the number of affines involved in gift exchange as there are agnates (except among the Xia families); in addition, affines present the more valuable gifts. Even for families of the Xia lineage, the dominant patrilineal group in the village, affines still constitute the main body of donors within the kinship relations (for more details, see Yan 1996, 112–14).

It should also be noted that while emphasizing the importance of affines, Xiajia villagers seem to have a narrower definition of patrilineal kinsmen. When asked to identify the donors on their gift lists, they were reluctant to include all lineage men in their inner cycle of guanxi networks, which was quite different from their positive attitudes toward affines. According to Mr. Xia, a knowledgeable informant who has been the host of ancestor worship rituals in his sublineage for many years, his significant agnates include only those who are the descendants of his great-great-great-grandfather (which is a local understanding of the five mourning grade system in official Chinese kinship). Those beyond the boundaries of this five-generation circle are similar to fellow villagers (tunqin), even though they share the same surname, Xia. When I pointed out that they were the descendants of his remote ancestors, he laughed and said: "Close neighbors are better than remote relatives" (yuanqin bu ru jinlin).

The Uncertainty of Kinship Alliances

As kinship distance is increasingly redefined in accordance with individual discretion, the making of kinship alliances has become a less predictable business in contemporary village society. The old rule that one should always stand with one's own brothers against outsiders as well as against less-close relatives sometimes no longer holds. Under certain circumstances, friendship has proven to be more reliable and valuable than close kinship.

A good example of this connection is the case of a political battle that was reaching its peak when I revisited Xiajia village in the summer of 1997. Basically, a group of villagers led by the former village party secretary were trying to remove the current party secretary from office, and they had made various efforts toward this end (including direct confrontation, sending reports to upper-level party organizations, and filing suit against the current party secretary for embezzlement and adultery). This political battle had split a number of villagers who otherwise were closely related by either agnatic or affinal ties, such as the five siblings of the Xu family. Among them, the eldest brother was one of the firmest opponents to challenge the current party secretary, the third brother remained neutral, the second and fourth brothers were the closest allies of the current party secretary, and their younger sister allegedly was having an extramarital affair with the current party secretary.

During my interviews with the Xu brothers, they defended their various positions in accordance with their different perceptions of their relations with the two party secretaries. The eldest brother decided to side with the former party secretary for two reasons: they were cross-cousins; and the extramarital affair between the current party secretary and his younger sister had damaged the reputation of the Xu family. The second brother had been the best friend of the current party secretary for a long time and had been promoted to village head by the latter prior to the outbreak of the political battle. So he decided to help his best friend against the former party secretary – his own cross-cousin. The youngest brother simply followed in his second elder brother's footsteps because, as he put it, they had been on good terms ever since he was a child. By the time I left Xiajia village, however, it was said that the youngest brother had been won over by the eldest brother and had joined the ranks against the current party secretary.

In another case, which occurred during 1996 and 1997, a man had to shift his loyalty toward close kin several times. Through family connections, this man had obtained a well-paid and lucrative position to supervise the local milk collection station for a dairy factory jointly owned by the Nestle company and a Chinese partner. When more hands were needed, not surprisingly, this man hired his elder brother and his brother's son. He soon discovered that they were taking the favor for granted and did not work hard. Later, when he was under tremendous pressure from some local bullies and did not get the expected help from his brother and nephew, he fired both of them and hired his wife's brother, who was a young and militant discharged soldier. Within a few months, he found himself in trouble again – his wife's brother was more ambitious than he had thought and actually started to take over the station. So he had to get rid of him, too. When the latter refused to leave, he asked his best friend, a nonrelative, to help. When I left Xiajia village in the late summer of 1997, the struggle between this man and his wife's brother was still at its peak, and both had invited their respective friends to join the fight. The involvement of outsiders (friends) was considered by some older villagers as scandalous. They commented that it was all due to the influence of money; without so much money at stake, the relatives would have remained on good terms.

Although not always as dramatic as the above two cases, there are many other examples of alliance making that do not follow the recognized rules of kinship: that is, villagers do not always ally with their closest relatives within the pool of their networks. For instance, a number of villagers chose not to let their own close kinsmen (father, brothers, or uncles) farm their land when they departed to the cities for industrial work. Instead, they offered the land to their friends or less-close relatives with whom they had maintained better relationships. (Farmland still belongs to the state, yet in practice, individual villagers have exclusive users' rights, which are granted by the state for thirty-five years. Such land transactions are thus possible.)

The Flattenization of Kinship

Another feature of current kinship practice is the slow process of the flattenization of kin relations. By "flattenization," I mean a shift in emphasis from cross-generation links to same-generation connections – a process that parallels the increasing importance of affines and friends in villagers' networks as well as the shifting balance of power from the senior generation to the junior one within individual families.

It is widely agreed among scholars that the fundamental kin relationship in Chinese society is that of patrilineal descent. Individuals from different generations are bound closely by the everlasting link of patriliny, which expresses itself in terms of both consanguinity and reciprocity. As Hugh Baker notes, in traditional Chinese society, the living individual is "the personification of all his [*sic*] forebears and of all his descendants yet unborn. He exists by virtue of his ancestors, and his descendants exist only through him" (1979, 26–27). Thus, "all the living are in the shadow of their ancestors" (Hsu [1948] 1967, 243). Consequently, the link between the living and dead has received the most scholarly attention, and cross-generation kin relations, such as parent-child ties, have always been regarded as more significant than same-generation relations, such as that between siblings.

In contemporary Xiajia village, though, it is the connections among individuals of the same generation that constitute the core of the guanxi network within which kinship is practiced. Elsewhere I examine the shift of power from the senior to the junior generation, and along with it, the replacement of the vertical, parent-son relationship by the horizontal, conjugal tie as the central axis of family relations and the foundation of the family ideal shared by most villagers (see Yan 1997). As more and more young couples leave their husbands' parents to establish their own conjugal family soon after their marriage, they have to start building their own social networks from scratch. In this aspect of family life, many young women prove to be more successful than their husbands because they have a ready resource to turn to – their natal families. As a result, noninherited, same-generation connections – such as affines, friends, and colleagues – constitute a major part of individual villagers' guanxi networks, particularly those of young villagers. A common feature shared by affines, friends, colleagues, and fellow villagers in these guanxi networks is that they are all lateral (or horizontal) connections between families rather than vertical filiation within families, such as agnatic ties. These relations represent alliances that are created by individual villagers and maintained through mutual indebtedness in social exchange.

Moreover, because these same-generation connections are maintained by and revolve around a couple in a given family (as opposed to a group of ancestors), the notion of kinship authority also has been redefined. Generational rank and age seniority, the very basis of authority in the Chinese kinship system, have become less important in comparison to individual capabilities for getting things done. It is common that in everyday cooperation among relatives and friends, the leaders are younger and better educated, while the senior people have to play a secondary role. And these young villagers are much more interested in indulging their own children than in worshiping their ancestors. The previous kinship authority structure based on generational seniority and age rank has weakened, as vividly demonstrated by the waning of ancestors.

Women and the Changing Kinship Practice

As indicated by the flattenization of kinship connections, women take an active part in maintaining family networks in everyday life, which is itself a new development of the Chinese kinship system. As I demonstrate elsewhere, women not only participate in gift exchange activities as household representatives but have also created several new rituals revolving around human reproduction – childbirth, abortion, and female sterilization (see Yan 1996, 53–55). Through these rituals, which are by and for women, village women can build up their own social connections and thus successfully go beyond the traditional boundaries of the male-centered kinship web.

In terms of kinship distance, understandably, women's criterion of closeness does not always fit that of their husbands', nor that of the patrilineal kinship ideology. Because of the crucial role played by wives, one's relationship with one's wife's sister's husband is considered quite significant in local practice. The closeness of this kind of relationship is reflected in its local term, *lianqiao*, which literally means men who are linked by a bridge – namely, the bridge of the sororal relationship between their wives. Unlike the relationship between brothers, men linked by their wives' sororal relationship have no inherited conflicts of interest, and mutual assistance and cooperation can be easily supported and facilitated by their wives (see Judd 1989). The analysis of the gift lists shows that the most generous gifts can be expected from one's wife's sisters' husbands, and in daily life, they are also among the first to offer help. For instance, the most lucrative crop in the area is watermelon, but it requires larger capital investments and depends on unpredictable market demands. Therefore, villagers prefer to plant watermelon together, working with one or two partners, in order to share the risks. In 1991, seven out of the nine watermelon farmers in the village cooperated with their wives' sisters' husbands in various forms, while no one worked with their own brothers. When asked why, they told me that it was easier to work with one's wife's sisters' husbands because they were more reasonable and trustworthy.

In addition, it is at least inaccurate to portray women's kinship activities only within the domestic or private domain. Ethnographic evidence from Xiajia village reveals that women are critical in many aspects of the public domain. In the above-mentioned case of political struggle between the former and current party secretary, a key figure is the younger sister of the Xu family. As explained earlier, by kinship ties she is close to the former party secretary, but she also is emotionally involved with the current party secretary. Because of her intimate relationship with the latter, she was assigned several important jobs at various times, such as supervising the village election in 1996 and managing a small village enterprise. Because of the Xu sister's deep involvement in the activities of the village office, her eldest brother and his friends tried hard to win her over from the opposite camp. Nevertheless, she chose to stand firmly with her lover – the current party secretary – despite public opinion and tremendous pressure from her kin. In this highly publicized case of village politics, the kinship alliance was defeated by the individual bonds between the two lovers.

It is true that village women usually do not fill as dramatic a role as the Xu sister did; instead, they transform kinship practice in a more subtle yet equally effective way, as shown in the case of the ghost festival ceremony. Local custom traditionally forbade women to participate in the visit to the ancestor tombs of their natal families during the ghost festival (on the fifteenth day of the seventh month in the lunar calendar). This taboo, however, was broken by a woman single-handedly. In 1995, a young daughter-in-law thought it was unreasonable that she should be prevented from visiting her deceased grandfather, whom she loved very much. So she went to the graveyard of her natal family and burned paper money in front of her grandfather's tomb, just like a man would do. She seemed to be a perfect candidate to break the traditional taboo since she was well-known for being an independent, capable, and sometimes ill-tempered young woman in the village; as well, she was considered to be responsible for encouraging her husband to leave his parents and set up his own conjugal family shortly after his wedding. No one dared to stop or blame her. And the following year, more women took her lead. When I visited Xiajia village in 1998, I saw as many women as men burning paper money in the graveyard during the ghost festival. It was also interesting to find that married women prefer to visit the ancestor tombs of their natal families before they attend to their husband's families' ancestral tombs. When I learned that the daughter-in-law of my landlord had visited her late father's tomb first, I was told by my landlord that this was nothing new. "This is why nowadays girls are better than boys [to their parents]," commented my landlord.

THE EMOTIONAL DIMENSION OF KINSHIP PRACTICE

In my earlier study of gift-giving networks (see Yan 1996, 139–45; see also Stafford 2000), I examined how Xiajia villagers were emotionally attached to some close relatives and good friends for a very long time. They described these attachments in terms of the expression of *ganqinghao*, which means having good feelings toward one another. They maintain that interactions in daily life (*wanglai* in local terms) do not necessarily imply the existence of good feelings between two parties because in many cases, people are obligated to interact with kin they do not like. This is particularly true in cases of gift exchange at such ritual situations as weddings or funerals. For those who do have good feelings toward one another, though, their interactions are greatly intensified. In addition to routinized gift exchange, people with good feelings visit one another quite often, spend spare time together, and emotionally depend on one another, too. In local terms, this type of intimate interaction is called *zoudong*, literally meaning "walking and moving," a metaphor for mutual visits.

The local distinction between wanglai and zoudong reveals an interesting relationship between kinship norms and practices. On the one hand, the morality and principle of kinship require the maintenance of certain kinds of formal relations along with the completion of the institutionalized and prescribed task of interacting with one's kin (wanglai). On the other hand, one can also find room to develop emotional ties with select people in terms of more intimate, informal, and nonritualized interactions in daily life (zoudong), which is often the case with practical kinship.

In 1991, one informant told me that he had not visited his father's youngest sister for more than ten years, even though she was married to a Xiajia man and lived in the same village. The reason, according to him, was due to a personality conflict: he could not stand his father's sister's bad temper, and she had not treated him well when he was a small boy. "We did not have good feelings toward each other from the very beginning," the informant concluded. Nevertheless, he had to fulfill his obligation of ritualized gift giving and the prescribed visits during the Chinese Spring Festival, which could not be affected by individuals' emotional concerns. As a compromise, he sent his wife to represent him on these occasions and increased the value of his gifts in an effort to show his respect (this is a common strategy frequently used by many villagers). In this case, the emotional quality of kinship practice works in a negative way – whenever the informant can make his own choice, he avoids interacting with his father's sister, who has been excluded from the core zone of this man's guanxi network.

As a result of the recent changes in kinship and the larger social settings, the emotional dimension of kinship practice has now become more important because with less-constraining forces of official ideology and institutional principles, the personalities and emotional ups and downs of individual agents are more easily reflected in their interactions with one another. A simple example is the case of the above-mentioned political struggle in Xiajia village where the youngest Xu brother decided to support his second-oldest brother merely based on his good feelings toward the latter, and the Xu sister firmly sided with her illicit lover regardless of her own brothers' attempts to win her over to the other camp.

One of the reasons that I have found Bourdieu's notion of practical kinship unsatisfactory is that he completely ignores the role of emotionality in kinship practice. In his discussions of the "usefulness" or "utility" of practical kinship, he rarely explores the possibility that people may also need to build up (which in fact they do) kinship networks for moral/emotional support, in addition to a number of more practical purposes. This is best illustrated by Bourdieu's analysis of the working of practical kinship in marriage negotiations (1977, 34–35; 1990, 168–86), in which his notion of practical kinship turns out to be nothing more than pragmatic kinship. The Xiajia case shows that once individuals can make their own choices, personal and emotional elements indeed play a central part in kinship practices. Without taking into consideration the emotionality of individual agents, one runs the risk of reducing people in the real world to abstract rational actors who are driven merely by the desire to maximize utility of whatever resources they hold.

SCHOLARLY MODELS, SOCIAL CHANGE, AND KINSHIP PRACTICE

How should the current patterns of kinship practice in rural north China be understood? Are they recent developments resulting from the Communist revolution or merely new to scholarly eyes that have now been liberated from the constraints of the previously dominant structural-functional model of kinship study? The answer is not a simple yes or no; both the kinship practice of Chinese villagers and our scholarly practice of kinship study are changing within the context of the ever changing society at large. It follows that all three elements have to be considered: the scholarly models, social change, and the dynamics of kinship practice itself.

Some of the above-mentioned kinship practices may have existed for a long time, but they were neglected by scholarly scrutiny because students of Chinese kinship did not look for them. In my opinion, most studies of Chinese kinship fall into one of two lines of inquiry. The first might be loosely called the Confucian model, whereby scholars stress the pervasive influence of Confucian ideas and values – such as filial piety, chastity, and ancestor worship – on Chinese kinship. A well-known example is Francis Hsu's *Under the Ancestors' Shadow* ([1948] 1967; for a recent and sophisticated analysis of the role of Confucian values in Chinese kinship, see Chun 1996).

The second approach was established by Maurice Freedman, who creatively applied the African model of lineage organizations in social anthropology to China and developed a "lineage paradigm" of Chinese society (1958, 1966). This paradigm "assumes a fundamental model of Chinese society in which the ideology of patrilineal descent takes precedence over all other principles of social organization" (J. Watson 1986, 274). Shifting away from the previous emphasis on Confucian values, Freedman and his followers focused on the working mechanisms of lineage property and organization. Since the 1960s, this paradigm has been applied to all major studies of powerful patrilineal organizations in south China (see, for example, Potter 1968; J. Watson 1975; R. Watson 1985).

The limitations of the lineage paradigm were noticed by those who worked in regions outside the patrilineal belt of south China, notably in Taiwan. They challenged the universality of the lineage model in Chinese societies by demonstrating that matrilateral and affinal relationships are as essential as agnatic ties, and that kinship is not the only working system that binds people together in Taiwan (see, for instance, Diamond 1969; Gallin and Gallin 1985; Harrell 1982; Pasternak 1972; Sangren 1984).

Recognition that other kin relations are equally as significant as agnatic ties, however, does not take one far beyond the lineage paradigm. The key issue here is that both the Confucian model and lineage paradigm tend to focus on the fixed norms, rules, and moral expectations of kin groups defined by demonstrated genealogy; thereby, they stress the centrality of a kinship collectivity represented by powerful ancestors and tend to study only those social facts that reflect durable structural principles. Missing is the role played by individual agents in their everyday cooperation, negotiation, and competition with one another over issues such as emotional attachment, moral obligation, power and influence, and economic resources – the specific processes that are not necessarily reflected in the genealogical composition of a kin group (see Yanagisako 1979, 184–89). In other words, an emphasis on how kinship functions to sustain the social structure may have precluded scholarly inquiries into how villagers in everyday life make their kinship system work for them.

As indicated above, when asked, Xiajia villagers would say one's own brothers are closer than one's wife's brothers. This fits well with the patrilineal ideology, which has been underscored in most studies of Chinese kinship. Still, in practice many villagers do the opposite – in some cases they prefer to cooperate with their brothers-in-law (one's wife's brother or one's wife's sister's husband) in economic activities and to maintain closer ties with them in social activities; in other instances they shift back and forth between different categories of kin. Moreover, women may have had a different standard of kinship distance long before the Communist revolution, as manifested in the long-existing doubts of a daughter-in-law's loyalty toward her husband's family. This can be, nevertheless, easily dismissed by the structural-functional model as insignificant because it belongs to individual acts taking place within the domestic sphere and thus has no effect on social structure.

The obstacle of previous scholarly models, however, should not be overstated because kinship practice itself also changes over time in response to the changes in society at large. It is therefore also possible that some previously insignificant or probably latent social actions have now become more important and salient, such as, again, the active role played by women and youth in village life. As far as the Xiajia case is concerned, two major social changes are particularly noteworthy: the practice of socialism after 1949 and the impact of the market-oriented reforms in the recent two decades.

As explained in the first section, the socialist state was especially hostile to traditional lineage organization and kinship ideology. Through administrative means and political campaigns, the state was generally successful in eliminating organized lineage activities for nearly three decades, greatly shaking the foundation of traditional kinship ideology. The state also made efforts to transform the organization of social life in rural China – such as reforming life-cycle rituals. Villagers had strategized their acts accordingly in order to cope with a powerful and revolutionary political authority, as shown in the anecdote at the beginning of this chapter. Furthermore, through collectivization and other political campaigns, the state successfully mobilized women and youth to become a major force in the socialist transformation of rural society. As a result, a clear shift in the balance of power from the senior to the junior generation has been identified throughout rural China (see White 1995; Yan 1997), a distinguishable youth subculture has emerged (see Yan 1999), and women, particularly young women, have become a major social force challenging patriarchal traditions in the sphere of private life (see Yan 1998). The rise of these previously marginalized players in the Chinese kinship system certainly has had a profound influence on the current practice of kinship. A good example in this connection is the political struggle between the current party secretary, who was supported by a group of youth, and his predecessor, who was supported mostly by middle-aged males. According to older villagers, fifty years ago the active and public involvement of the young woman (the Xu sister) in this political conflict would have been impossible from the very beginning.

Second, the introduction of both commodity production and a market-oriented economy during the past two decades has created new life aspirations for villagers, especially for rural youth, to pursue their individual needs, sometimes at the expense of the interests of larger kin groups. This is evidenced by the dramatic rise in the centrality of the conjugal relationship and the decline of parental power in family life that I have documented elsewhere (see Yan 1997). The ongoing process of commercialization has created more latitude and instrumentality for individual maneuvering in dealing with interpersonal relations as well. A directly related development is the increasing importance of friendship in an individual's social network (that is, guanxi network). Commodity production and market-related activities require connections beyond conventional kinship ties and village boundaries; the number of one's outside connections and friendship ties thus has become an obvious sign of social capital in village society (see Yan 1996). In many cases, these newer ties can be absorbed into the core zone of existing guanxi networks without causing any conflicts, but in other instances, they may also prove to be hostile to kinship ties, such as in the above-mentioned fight between the brothers and relatives over control of a milk station in Xiajia village. In these new forms of kinship alliances, individual economic power has replaced generational seniority and age rank as the new basis for social hierarchy. And due to the unpredictable changes in business interests and expansion of individual guanxi networks, some of the old kinship obligations and behavioral norms have been undermined, too. All of these may partially contribute to the new developments noted above.

It is incorrect and unnecessary, therefore, to single out either the shift in the scholarly model or consequences of social change as the major factor contributing to the current changes in descriptions of kinship practice in rural north China. Some developments are due to social changes (as discussed above) and others to the rediscovery of some old social practices as a result of our shift to a new theoretical emphasis. It is more likely that, in practice, there are consistent interactions of all these factors, thus leading to the ever changing practice of kinship study itself.

The real challenge now is to determine how to go beyond the old scholarly models and develop new ones that can conceptualize or theorize current patterns of kinship practice. As indicated at the start of this essay, fluidity and flexibility are definitely the most important features of current kinship practice, which seems to revolve more around strategic individuals than a representational collectivity. In other words, kinship ties are better viewed as a set of differentially valued relations, which may mean different things relative to one another in different contexts.[4] The relativity of kinship relations may be a key to understanding the nature of an ever changing kinship system. In this connection, two Chinese notions – *chaxu geju* and guanxi – are particularly noteworthy.

The term "chaxu geju" was first coined by the famous Chinese sociologist Xiaotong Fei more than half a century ago. To describe the different structural principles in Chinese society, he wrote: "In Chinese society, the most important relationship – kinship – is similar to the concentric circles formed when a stone is thrown into a lake" ([1947] 1992, 63). In such a network of concentric circles, "everyone stands at the center of the circles produced by his or her own social influence. Everyone's circles are interrelated. One touches different circles at different times and places" (62–63). Fei refers to such a mode of social origination as chaxu geju, translated as the "differential mode of association." Through this concept, Fei argues that Chinese society is not group oriented but egocentric – a view quite different from that of mainstream China studies. The most intriguing point of the notion chaxu geju is that the relational links – namely, the concentric circles – are valued differently by the person in the center, and accordingly, the norms of social interactions and moral judgments also vary when they are applied to discrete categories of people in these circles. Unfortunately, Fei's 1947 book remained unnoticed in the West until the late 1980s, and during this period, the study of Chinese kinship was dominated first by the Confucian model and then the lineage paradigm. The relativity of kinship relations, as well as other relations in Chinese society, has thus also been overlooked until recently.

Unlike Fei's chaxu geju (differential mode of association), guanxi was first a term used by ordinary people in their everyday lives; in recent years, guanxi also has become a key category in scholarly analyses of Chinese society and culture. My study of the Xiajia case shows that at least during the past two decades or so, there has been a tendency for both kinship and community relations to be absorbed into person-centered guanxi networks. In everyday social practices, guanxi networks provide the moral world as well as channels of opportunity for individual agents. And to a great extent, it is the individual agents who determine which strings – kinship and nonkinship alike – in a given network are pulled in dealing with various issues in social and personal lives. More important, a fundamental feature of guanxi is that it exists only in the process of practice, and as such, can counterbalance the previous emphasis on the normative/structural aspects of the kinship system in Chinese society.

NOTES

The present study is based on fieldwork supported by the Research Council of the Academic Senate, University of California, Los Angeles, and the Chiang Ching-Kuo Foundation for International Scholarly Exchange. I am grateful to Carol Delaney, Gillian Feeley-Harnik, Kath Weston, and other participants at the Mallorca conference for their comments on the early draft. Special thanks are due to Susan McKinnon and Sarah Franklin for their insightful and detailed suggestions for the revisions of this essay.

1. I should add that the funeral improved my father's status in public life for only two days; afterward, he was back in the outcast position and later humiliated at a public meeting by several young villagers who regretted what they had had to do during the funeral.

2. To surmount the shortcomings of both objectivist and subjectivist tendencies in kinship studies, Bourdieu proposes a distinction between official and practical kinship: the former refers to the abstraction of norms, rules, and regulations of kin groups, while the latter refers to the transformation of such an abstraction into strategies of practice by active agents in everyday life. Although the function of official kinship is to order the social world and legitimate that order, it is practical kinship that is used by individual agents to achieve social goals in everyday life (Bourdieu 1977, 33–38; 1990, 166–87). Despite the fact that Bourdieu always stresses the centrality of individual agency in practice, such an arbitrary division between official and practical kinship actually precludes the importance of individual agency in political, public life. Moreover, since practical kinship – as defined by Bourdieu – is confined to the domestic sphere, which does not have much political significance, it also tends to ignore women's active role in gender politics in particular and kinship practice in general (see Yanagisako and Collier 1987).

3. My inquiry into guanxi networks began with a collection of villagers' gift lists. In Xiajia village, as in most rural communities in China and some other East Asian societies as well, villagers always write a gift list for each major family ceremony they host – a document that records the names of the gift givers as well as a description of all gifts received. Families carefully keep these gift lists and use them for future reference when reciprocal gifts need to be offered. From a researcher's point of view, a gift list may serve as a repository of data on the changing nature of interpersonal relations and a social map that vividly displays guanxi networks. In my 1991 fieldwork, I collected 43 gift lists based on a stratified selection of households and put them into a computer database, containing a total of 5,286 individual gift transactions. For more details about gift lists, see Yan 1996, 49–52.

4. Here I am particularly in debt to Susan McKinnon for probing me to think along these lines.

REFERENCES

Astuti, Rita. 1995. *People of the Sea: Identity and Descent among the Vezo of Madagascar.* Cambridge: Cambridge University Press.

Baker, Hugh. 1979. *Chinese Family and Kinship.* New York: Columbia University Press.

Bourdieu, Pierre. 1977. *Outline of a Theory of Practice.* Translated by Richard Nice. Cambridge: Cambridge University Press.

———. 1990. *The Logic of Practice.* Translated by Richard Nice. Stanford, Calif.: Stanford University Press.

Carsten, Janet. 1995. The Substance of Kinship and the Heat of the Hearth: Feeding, Personhood, and Relatedness among Malays in Pulau Langkawi. *American Ethnologist* 22, no. 2:223–41.

Chun, Allen. 1996. The Lineage-Village Complex in Southeastern China: A Long Footnote in the Anthropology of Kinship. *Current Anthropology* 37, no. 3:429–40.

Diamond, Norma. 1969. *K'un Shen: A Taiwanese Village.* New York: Holt, Rinehart and Winston.

Fei, Xiaotong. [1947] 1992. *From the Soil: The Foundations of Chinese Society.* Translated by Gary Hamilton and Wang Zheng. Reprint, Berkeley: University of California Press.

Freedman, Maurice. 1958. *Lineage Organization in Southeastern China*, London: Athlone.

———. 1966. *Chinese Lineage and Society: Fukien and Kwangtung.* London: Athlone.

Gallin, Bernard, and Rita Gallin. 1985. Matrilateral and Affinal Relationships in Changing Chinese Society. In *The Chinese Family and Its Ritual Behavior*, edited by Hsieh Jih-chang and Chuang Ying-chang. Taiwan: Institute of Ethnology, Academia Sinica.

Harrell, Steven. 1982. *Ploughshare Village: Culture and Context in Taiwan.* Seattle: University of Washington Press.

Hsu, Francis L. K. [1948] 1967. *Under the Ancestors' Shadow: Chinese Culture and Personality.* Reprint, New York: Doubleday and Company.

Hwang, Kwang-kuo. 1987. Face and Favor: The Chinese Power Game. *American Journal of Sociology* 92, no. 4:944–74.

Judd, Ellen. 1989. Niangjia: Chinese Women and Their Natal Families. *Journal of Asian Studies* 48, no. 3:525–44.

King, Ambrose. 1991. Kuan-hsi and Network Building: A Sociological Interpretation. *Dacdalus* 120, no. 2:63–84.

Kipnis, Andrew. 1997. *Producing Guanxi: Sentiment, Self, and Subculture in a North China Village.* Durham, N.C.: Duke University Press.

Pasternak, Burton. 1972. *Kinship and Community in Two Chinese Villages.* Stanford, Calif.: Stanford University Press.

Potter, jack M. 1968. *Capitalism and the Chinese Peasant.* Berkeley: University of California Press.

Sangren, Steven. 1984. Traditional Chinese Corporations: Beyond Kinship. *Journal of Asian Studies* 43, no. 3:391–415.

Stafford, Charles. 2000. Chinese Patriliny and the Cycles of *Yang* and *Laiwang.* In *Cultures of Relatedness: New Approaches to the Study of Kinship,* edited by Janet Carsten. Cambridge: Cambridge University Press.

Walder, Andrew. 1986. *Communist Neo-Traditionalism: Work and Authority in Chinese Industry.* Berkeley: University of California Press.

Watson, James L. 1975. *Emigration and the Chinese Lineage: The Mans in Hong Kong and London.* Berkeley: University of California Press.

———. 1986. Anthropological Overview: The Development of Chinese Descent Groups. In *Kinship Organization in Late Imperial China, 1000–1940,* edited by Patricia B. Ebrey and James L. Watson. Berkeley: University of California Press.

Watson, Rubie S. 1985. *Inequality among Brothers: Class and Kinship in South China.* Cambridge: Cambridge University Press.

White, Martin. 1995. The Social Roots of China's Economic Development. *China Quarterly* 144:999–1019.

Yan, Yunxiang. 1992. The Impact of Rural Reform on Economic and Social Stratification in a Chinese Village. *Australian Journal of Chinese Affairs* 27:1–23.

———. 1996. *The Flow of Gifts: Reciprocity and Social Networks in a Chinese Village.* Stanford, Calif.: Stanford University Press.

———. 1997. The Triumph of Conjugality: Structural Transformation of Family Relations in a Chinese Village. *Ethnology* 36, no. 3:191–212.

———. 1998. Girl Power: Young Women and Family Change in Rural North China. Paper presented at the workshop, Women and Modernity in Twentieth-Century China, 6 March, University of California, Santa Barbara.

———. 1999. Rural Youth and Youth Culture in North China. *Culture, Medicine, and Psychiatry* 23, no. 1:75–97.

Yang, Mayfair Mei-hui. 1994. *Gifts, Favors, Banquets: The Art of Social Relationships in China.* Ithaca, N.Y.: Cornell University Press.

Yanagisako, Sylvia J. 1979. Family and Household: The Analysis of Domestic Groups. *Annual Review of Anthropology* 8:161–205.

Yanagisako, Sylvia J., and Jane F. Collier. 1987. Toward a Unified Analysis of Gender and Kinship. In *Gender and Kinship: Essays toward a Unified Analysis,* edited by Jane F. Collier and Sylvia J. Yanagisako. Stanford, Calif.: Stanford University Press.

CHAPTER 5

RURAL YOUTH AND YOUTH CULTURE

Traditional Chinese society was characterized by the subordination of the young and women to the dominant patrilineal ideology and power structure. Age, generation, and sex served as the three basic elements constituting the Chinese hierarchy system in both the public and the domestic domains (Baker 1979: 15–21; Fei 1992 [1947]: 84–86, 118–119; Freedman 1966). Moreover, there was no intermediary stage between childhood and adulthood in a person's life course; according to custom, a child was not considered a full person. Thus, one remained an unreliable, immature child until marriage and one would be stigmatized if one remained in such a non-status for too long (Waltner 1986; Watson 1989). Therefore, *nianyou wuzhi* (meaning "young and ignorant") was used either as the rationale for not taking youngsters seriously or as an excuse for any of their wrongdoings.

It was at the turn of this century that the word "youth" (*qingnian*) gained more social meaning. The student movement in the 1920s demonstrated for the first time that youth were an important social force (Chow 1960; Levy 1949). During the 1930s and 1940s, the KMT did not fully exploit the potential of the youth group; in contrast, the CCP was an attractive political force to Chinese youth in all walks of society for several decades (Yang 1965). After 1949, the CCP and the state continued to mobilize youth in both rural and urban areas as the main force for the socialist transformation of society and for economic development.

Rural youth as a social group, however, seem to have been overlooked in China studies. Previous discussions are more concerned with the urban sent-down youth in the countryside (see e.g., Bernstein 1977; Rosen 1981). A noteworthy exception is Fred Blake's study of love songs and youth culture during the Great Leap. He argues that the CCP tried, and to a certain extent succeeded, in communicating socialist values to the young by using popular songs and through new patterns of courtship, thus recruiting an energetic and disciplined labor force for economic development (Blake 1979: 51). Equally important, Chan, Madsen, and Unger (1984) note the active role of both rural youth and sent-down urban youth in village politics; Parish and Whyte (1978) systematically examine the impact of socialism on rural life, including the life experience of rural youth (for discussions on young women, see Johnson 1983; Stacey 1983). These studies deal mostly with the period from the 1950s to the 1970s and do not treat rural youth as an important social group. The life experience of contemporary rural youth and their relations to older villagers, who were youths in the earlier scholarly accounts, remain largely unexplored.

I use the term "rural youth" to refer to young villagers between the ages of sixteen and twenty-five. By "youth culture" I mean a set of beliefs, values, and behaviors shared by contemporary young villagers, which are, in some respects, recognizably different from the mainstream ideas and patterns of behavior of adult villagers. It should be noted that this chapter is not about "juvenile delinquency" which is perhaps one of the most common topics in youth studies (see Wulff 1995: 2–6); instead, I focus on the emergence of a youth culture as defined above in several rural communities. Thus, deviant behavior among a small number of individual youngsters in the same communities, such as alcoholism, gambling, and petty thievery, is not the main concern of this article (for relevant research, see Bakken 1993; Ngai 1994). Moreover, due to limitations in my fieldwork, most of the youngsters whom I interviewed are young men; as a result, the following discussions are primarily about the male subculture.

The present study is based on data collected from fieldwork conducted in Luohou village in Hebei province, Northgate village in Shandong province and Xiajia village in Heilongjiang province, over a period from 1989 to 1994. Although I rely heavily on ethnographic evidence collected from Xiajia village, my conclusions about rural youth and youth culture are supported by data from the other two villages and further confirmed by my reading of secondary sources in Chinese scholarly works and newspaper reports.

Among the three villages, Luohou in Hebei province is currently the most advanced economically. With a population of 2,002, it is located beside a highway connecting the county and Baoding city. It has benefited significantly from the rise of rural industries both within the village and in the surrounding areas. Only 32 percent of its households engage primarily in farming. Northgate village in Shandong province has about 1,700 people; it was extremely poor during the collective period. Since the economic reforms, many people, most of them young, have left the village to work in urban areas, thus improving the village economy a great deal. It remains, however, the poorest among the three villages I studied. Xiajia village is the place where I stayed for the longest time and where I conducted my doctoral research. Xiajia was quite successful in collective farming in the 1960s and 1970s and it remains a farming community to the present. There are no industrial enterprises in the village, except for a few grain-processing services. Until the late 1980s the majority of its 1,600 residents worked full-time in the fields maintaining the village economy at an average level. The biggest change in recent years is that more and more young villagers have sought urban employment; most were driven out owing to the lack of farming land.

ASSESSING THE CURRENT SITUATION: "YOUTH PROBLEM" OR YOUTH CULTURE?

My interest in rural youth culture was first aroused by an unexpected encounter with several village teenagers during my 1989 fieldwork. In an effort to find a good site for my doctoral research, I surveyed six villages in three provinces between January and May, 1989. When I went to Luohou village in Hebei province I was accompanied by a friend from a government research institute under the State Council. Because of my partner's official position and our introduction letter which was endorsed by a research center under the State Council, we were enthusiastically received by the local governments at both the prefecture and the county levels. We arrived at the village before dark, accompanied by a county official, and, as expected, we dined with the village cadres. It was arranged that we were to stay in the village party secretary's three-room house – more specifically, in a separate room shared with his son, a 17-year-old high school student. When we arrived at the teenager's room at about 10:30 p.m. we found him still up playing cards with his friends. His father, the party secretary, ordered the boys to stop their game because, in his words, "These two uncles [meaning my partner and I] from Beijing need to rest." But his son had no intention of quitting and he argued with his father that it was still early and that they wanted to finish the game.

Their argument continued for a period of time. My partner and I, of course, tried to ease the tension and comfort our host, the party secretary, so we said that it was all right for the boys to continue their game for a while because, in any case, we would not immediately go to sleep. The father left us and, to my surprise and amazement, the four young men continued to play for another hour, totally ignoring the fact that we had gotten into our beds and were trying to sleep.

I was immediately intrigued by this unexpected encounter because these young villagers did not show us any special respect, even though we were received as government officials from Beijing by the local cadres. Rather, they showed their indifference to both the father/party secretary's order and our unexpected visit. During that evening I clearly felt that the son hated our intrusion into his room and his privacy. My guess proved to be correct when I tried to make friends with him the next day. He explained: "My father is stupid. He doesn't realize that I have already grown up and I want to be left alone. He should have first asked me before sending anybody to sleep in my room."

Such an attitude conflicts sharply with what is known as age-generation superiority in Chinese culture, according to which this teen-ager's behavior would be considered extremely unfilial and morally wrong. In my subsequent surveys I discovered that examples of such a generational gap were prevalent in everyday life since the late 1980s, leading, in some respects, to serious social tension between village youth and their elders. For men and women who are thirty-five or older, today's village youth are simply headaches to everyone except themselves; the youngsters, however, have their own complaints about the older people who refuse to understand the new generation.

In public life, young villagers tend to be much more argumentative and disobedient, often causing conflicts with older villagers. The most severe criticism of village youths, however, comes from the village cadres. There have been numerous confrontations, some involving violence, between young villagers and cadres. In an extreme case which occurred in Northgate village, a 19-year-old man was caught gambling and fined heavily by the local police department. He then confronted and accused the village head for leaking this to the police. When their dispute became fierce, he pulled out a knife and chased the village head, threatening to kill him. The panic-stricken village head, who finally climbed a tree to escape, was surrounded by the furious young man and many onlookers.

When I interviewed the village head in 1991 he recalled the incident with a great deal of bitterness and embarrassment. "What else could I do except retreat?" he explained, "nowadays these kids are very strong physically but they have nothing in their heads. They are afraid of no one, not even the police. Spoiled by their parents, they have become a bunch of hooligans."

Conflicts between the young and the aged are equally common in the domestic sphere. The main complaint from elders, as can be expected, is the unfilial behavior of the young. Filial piety has long been recognized as one of the key concepts in Confucian ethics and one of the major principles structuring Chinese social life (Weber 1968). An important component of the notion of filial piety is the unconditional obedience of the young to their parents and to their senior kin. The term "father" conveys a sense of authority, demanding respect and obedience. In this connection, a father-son quarrel in Xiajia village is illuminating for our understanding of how shaky age-generation superiority has become in the domestic domain. When a father could not silence his son during a family discord, he yelled: "Don't forget I'm still your father!" Without thinking, the son yelled back: "Nowadays it's hard to tell who's whose father!" The dispute ended quickly, as the son soon realized he had said something extremely stupid. Apparently they both had used the word "father" as a metaphor for the ultimate authority at home. This episode quickly became well-known in the community, and many of my informants cited it as an example of the current state of family relations.

Parents of unmarried young adults and teenagers also complain that village youths sometimes have become too liberal in their interactions with peers of the opposite sex. The more open-minded, active youths usually have their own small groups of close friends with whom they spend most of their spare time, watching TV, enjoying pop music, playing basketball or the newly imported game of billiards. The first time I saw young villagers playing billiards was in Luohou village, Hebei province, during my 1989 fieldwork. I was accompanied by two village cadres, but our presence did not attract the attention of the village youths who were concentrating on their game. I was particularly impressed by the fact that there were several girls standing around the billiards table, but no one seemed to notice. I was less surprised after witnessing many similar scenes during my subsequent fieldwork in all of the three villages. In Northgate village, a middle-aged village musician is known for being especially nice to the peers of his young son and daughter. Regularly eight to ten village youths stay at his house; as a result, his home is nicknamed "the youth club." When an old friend of the musician heard that teenage girls and boys always play together at this unofficial "youth club," he prohibited his youngest son from going there, causing difficulties in the relationship between the two friends.

Another common criticism about the village youths is their materialistic orientation. Older villagers complain that today's young villagers are only interested in enjoying a good life. Almost without exception, the young dislike working in the fields and always try to avoid heavy manual labor. But they like to hang out on the streets, displaying their new clothes and leather shoes, and spending money on things that formerly were only consumed by urban people, such as expensive shampoo and cassettes (Hong Kong and Taiwan pop singers are as popular among village youth as they are among urban youth). A former village party secretary told me that his cigarettes only cost 0.39 yuan per pack, while his son's cigarettes cost ten times more – 3.9 yuan per pack. An old woman said she simply could not understand why her grandson, a young man, spends so much time in front of the mirror, and why he wears good clothing and leather shoes even to herd the cows in the fields. "Even a young girl should not be like that," she concluded. To meet their increasing material needs, a number of youngsters have engaged in petty thefts, stealing food and household items from their neighbors.

As might be expected, the village youths see nothing wrong with their behavior, and when I interviewed them they all complained that their parents, and sometimes their elder siblings, were very domineering and intrusive. They feel particularly annoyed when older people try to lecture them, because there is nothing new in the lectures. They also think the older villagers simply do not know how to live a good life. In their opinion, thrift, hard work in the fields, and devotion to either Confucian ethics or the communist ideology will no longer help them enjoy a good life. As a 20-year-old man elaborated:

> My parents always tell me what I should do, how I should talk with people, and what kind of family I should have in the future. This is all rubbish. They do not realize how pitiful their lives are and how little they know about the world. My father has never gone more than 200 kilometers away from the village, and my mother only visited the

county seat twice. They know probably no more than thirty people outside the village, all of whom are our relatives. True, I am young and not strong enough yet; but I have worked in five cities in the past three years, including Beijing, and I am acquainted with several hundred people. Yesterday my mother tried to teach me how to talk properly with a girl, because she is trying to find a wife for me in her parents' village. But she does not know that I had a girlfriend when I worked in Beijing and I know everything about women. Isn't this funny!

This young man makes an interesting point. Due to the quickly improved living conditions, the flow of information, new values, and the opportunities to work in cities, village youths in the 1990s have embraced a whole new world which was never available to their elder siblings and parents. They are obviously more knowledgeable than the aged, more open-minded than their elder siblings, and in some respects, more competitive socially than their elder siblings and parents.

It is also understandable that the young have complaints toward their elders, because they feel that older people refuse to understand them and insist on shaping them in accordance with outdated ideas. Indeed, there is a tendency among older people to refuse to accept the fact that village youth in the 1990s are remarkably different from those in the 1970s or earlier. By denying this new development, they come to regard the characteristics of today's youth as problematic, hence the common expression, the "youth problem."

Actually, even in the above complaints and criticisms of the village youths, there are some positive aspects. For instance, most young villagers demonstrate an anti-authority tendency. In public life, this tendency has led to their more critical attitude toward the corruption of the village leadership and the unpopular policies of the government. Unquestionably they are more materialistic, but many young villagers are more strongly aware of their own individual rights and are more willing to defend their own interests from outside intervention. All these new characteristics may work as a counter-balance to the mechanism of state power and as a means to check cadre corruption. For instance, in the spring of 1991, the village leaders in Xiajia decided to sell a large number of public trees for lumber, in order to balance the budget. When the buyers arrived with their trucks, the village leaders found more than a dozen young villagers already at the site. The leader of the crowd, a 21-year-old, told the cadres that public trees belonged to everyone in the village, thus the cadres had no right to make the decision alone, without consulting with public opinion. He declared that the masses [the villagers] had decided to sell the same number of trees as the cadre had sold, but the money was to go to the masses. The dispute soon attracted a huge crowd of villagers who, after listening to the young protesters' explanations, became very angry about the cadres' secret deal to sell the public trees. Under pressure from public opinion, the cadres finally gave up their plan.

In the private domain, although they are less obedient to older people, many young men have shown a willingness to treat women in a more equal way, and young women are more active in defending their own rights at home. A more egalitarian type of family life centered around the conjugal relationship has emerged among these young villagers (see Yan 1997). As mentioned above, young villagers also differ from their elders in terms of their strong desires to pursue happiness in personal life. Although the notion of happiness is frequently defined by material comforts, such as fashionable clothing, good housing, and better jobs, the pursuit of personal happiness also challenges the previously dominant communist ideology which denies individual interests in the name of the collective and promotes asceticism in material life.

In my opinion, what has been occurring is the rise of a youth culture rather than a "youth problem" as some village cadres perceive it. The intriguing point is that this youth culture is actually a projection of elements of the urban culture in a rural context, which has taken the form of youth culture only because of the special social conditions in rural China.

As is commonly understood in the West, youth culture refers to a set of values and customs shared by a contemporary youth group, which is, quite often, different from the generally accepted mores among adults. Therefore, youth culture concerns notions of adolescent rebellion and counterculture (see Berger 1974; Musgrove 1965). As Virginia Caputo recently notes, most previous studies of youth cultures are concerned with such topics as definitions of style, musical tastes, unemployment, sexuality, delinquency, and resistance. As a result, adolescent resistance and juvenile delinquency have dominated the discourse on youth culture for quite a long period of time (1995: 21). Helena Wulff maintains that such a narrow focus on the passive role played by youth should be broadened by more anthropological studies of youth cultures from different parts of the world. "[Y]outh culture does not only consist of resistance and delinquency on the part of white teenage boys in Western cities. Youth culture is what young people are concerned with, and there is more culture agency in it than most earlier studies have acknowledged" (Wulff 1995: 15).

Following these recent insightful views in youth studies, I focus on the concerns of the majority of rural youth in their everyday life and the social meanings of these concerns. I discovered that in general the emerging youth culture in north China villages does not represent a counterculture. On the contrary, rural youth attempt to follow the mainstream culture of the cities, and to imitate the life styles of urbanites whom they regard as modern and fashionable. Their tastes in fashion and entertainment, their pursuit of individual independence and happiness, and their indulgence in material benefits would be regarded as moderate and thus "normal" in an urban context. Yet in Xiajia village these do not match the dominant culture shared by most adults, which has until recently been based on a mixture of a traditional peasant economy and collective farming under the socialist planned economy. The interesting point is that, due to the increasing gaps in material life and the birth-ascribed status differentiation between rural and urban residents during the first three decades of socialism (see Potter 1983: 465–484; Yan 1994: 15.18–19), urban life styles have long been considered superior and more modern than their counterparts in the rural areas. Such a perception is shared by villagers of all age groups. The only difference is that most older villagers have accepted the existing social inequalities between urbanites and themselves and regard the attempt of rural youth to imitate urban life styles as unrealistic and counter-productive. In contrast, rural youth are not willing to accept such inequitable realities and they want to claim their rights to enjoy better lives. The conflict between youth culture and the mainstream culture in Xiajia village, therefore, results mainly from the gap between ideals and reality, and between those who accepted the existing social inequalities and those who do not. It is misleading to suggest that the youth culture at its current stage of development is a resistant "counter-culture."

Nevertheless, urban ideals and behavior patterns do set contemporary rural youth apart from their elders, especially their pursuit of a more materialistic, individualistic, and modern life style (the fashions, of course, change quickly). Their strengths are based on these new aspirations and nontraditional life experiences; consequently, they are willing to try something new. Although the rural youths may not be able to realize all their dreams, the new values and ideas will have a profound impact, not only on them, but also on future generations.

In my 1989 fieldwork in Northgate village in Shandong province, I lived in the same room with three village youths for several days. It was in the late evenings when we all got into our beds and turned off the lights that I had the chance to understand these three brothers who were between fourteen and twenty years old. They talked about their wildest dreams: what kinds of jobs they would like to do, where they would like to go (they were already playing with the idea of tourism), and what kind of women they wanted to marry (the youngest did not participate in this discussion). For instance, the eldest brother vowed that he would marry a beautiful woman with a middle-school education and that he would not marry until he had secured a nonagricultural job. And the youngest one was only interested in traveling around the country, doing nothing.

I was particularly impressed by the two older brothers' aesthetic standards of female beauty, i.e., slim bodies and well-developed breasts, which, not too much earlier, had been regarded as signs of unsuitable wives. Older villagers believed that female breasts do not fully develop until they are touched by men. Thus a flat chest was considered a symbol of virginity. Slim women were considered less healthy and infertile, thus not good wives for the villagers. When I discussed the ideas of the brothers with their father, he shook his head and could not believe how his boys come up with such stupid ideas. There was clearly a huge gap in terms of ideas and values between the father and his sons.

The father, however, was not particularly worried about his sons' untraditional ideas, because, as he put it, "They will become smarter and more realistic when they taste the bitterness of life." Indeed, the eldest brother was not able to realize his dreams at all. When I returned in 1991 I found him remaining in the village to farm, married to a healthy, hard-working yet old-fashioned girl. His two younger brothers, in contrast, had been much luckier. Due to the increasing opportunities for rural-urban migration, they both found relatively secure employment in Beijing, thus partially realizing their dreams; meanwhile they also acquired many new aspirations. When they came to visit my hotel room in Beijing in 1993, I could hardly recognize them – they dressed like native Beijing youth, spoke with a Beijing accent, and, to my greatest surprise, they arrived by taxi! This case reveals both the marginality and flexibility of rural youth culture, which has had to adjust itself along with changes in the society at large. Quite often, youngsters must give up their ideals, due to the harsh realities of rural life such as poverty. But when possible they also show their courage to try new ways of life.

THE FORMATION OF RURAL YOUTH CULTURE AND THE PARTY-STATE

In reviewing the previous studies of family life in China, Martin Whyte suggests that we should not divide the collective and post-collective periods, because many of the current changes did not begin with the reforms (Whyte 1992: 320). This is certainly the case with respect to the youth culture in rural China. The contemporary youth culture did not surge ahead overnight in the post-Mao era; instead, it is the result of a long process of gradual development, beginning with land reform and developing during the collective period. The Chinese Communist Party (CCP) and the state played a determinant role in the formation of a youth culture, a process which can be examined in terms of politics, economics, and society.

Youth Organization and Political Participation

The CCP is known for its power to mobilize Chinese youth during the revolution period; its key mobilization strategies are ideological education and organizational work – both of which were particularly effective amongst the young up until the late 1970s. Well-known youth organizations include the Communist Youth League, the Women's Association, and the Basic Militia, all of which are affiliated to and led by the Party.[1] There were, however, other less formal yet equally important organizations which provided an arena for village youth to play an important role in public life. Study groups, for instance, were very important in public life, especially when ideological influence was strong, as during the "Studying Mao's Work" campaign in the early 1960s and the "Criticizing Lin Biao and Confucius" campaign in the early 1970s. Xiajia village also had a well-organized performance troupe to entertain villagers in slack seasons, which also served as a propaganda team during political campaigns. The troupe maintained itself for more than twenty years, but its membership changed constantly, with the majority of members always in their early twenties. Its influence among village youth, however, went far beyond its members; actually, it served as a center of popular culture for village youth, before being replaced by TV sets, cassettes, etc., in the post-Mao era.

Breaking the age-based hierarchy and seeking upward mobility were important factors motivating village youth to participate in political campaigns. When land reform was launched in Xiajia village in 1947, the two most active men were seventeen and eighteen years old; both were extremely poor, unmarried, and with no status, thus making them the bravest fighters in the struggle meetings against landlords and other members of the old elite. Because of their outstanding performance, they were soon promoted to be leaders of the village militia. One of them recalled in 1991: "All of a sudden I found myself an important person; everyone, including my own father, took me seriously after I joined the Communist Party." Young activists remained a rich source for recruitment of village cadres throughout the collective period. A close look at the beginning age of cadre's careers in Xiajia village shows that among the seven successive party secretaries, six began their careers before the age of twenty: two at sixteen, one at eighteen, and the rest at the age of nineteen. With one exception, each became the top leader in the village in his early thirties. At the lower ranks more than two-thirds of the village cadres were between twenty and thirty years old, a pattern echoing the observations of Parish and Whyte in south China (1978: 101–102).

Until the late 1970s, the youth group was the most easily mobilized by the communist ideology, as shown in studies of youth participation during the Great Leap Forward (Blake 1979) and the Cultural Revolution (Chan, Madsen, and Unger 1984). Ever since land reform, village youths in Xiajia have been active participants in political campaigns and other public/collective activities, such as voluntary work during late evenings. The first half of the 1960s was a golden age for idealistic youths. During my interviews in 1991 and 1993–94, villagers who were in their late forties or early fifties recalled fondly and nostalgically their experiences during the 1960s, which of course reflects their critical view of the youth in the 1990s. The most memorable things they recalled were the village performance troupe, the voluntary work, and the struggle meetings against the corrupt cadres during the "Four Cleans" campaign. An informant concluded: "In the 1960s we youth all had endless energy and good thoughts. We just wanted to do good things for the collectives and for everyone in the society." In 1963, a middle-aged woman became seriously ill and needed a blood transfusion. Soon thereafter the village

Party Branch and Youth League jointly issued a call for blood donors, and sixteen young men and women lined up in front of the village office. When I interviewed the blood donor in 1991, he told me that at that time he felt extremely honored to be chosen, adding: "The woman's family class label was middle-peasant. Had she been a poor peasant, I am sure there would have been more people willing to donate blood." Given the strong fear of losing blood shared among most Chinese, especially villagers, it is clear that there was indeed a very active youth culture which responded rapidly to the party-state's mobilization.

Collective Farming

Although there is little resemblance to urban employment, collective farming has expanded social space for the young. As the family ceased to be a production unit during the collective era, paternal leadership in agricultural production was replaced by the leadership of village cadres, so youngsters spent most of their working hours under the supervision of people other than their fathers. Unless he was a cadre, the father would occupy the same status as his sons, and they all had to follow the instructions of the team leaders. Moreover, the introduction of agricultural machinery, chemical fertilizer, pesticides, and other innovations rendered the older peasants' knowledge of farming mostly out of date. Most of the new, nonagricultural posts in the collectives, such as school teachers, tractor drivers, barefoot doctors, and members of the Experimental Team for Scientific Farming, all required a certain level of formal education; therefore these positions had to be filled by the young villagers. The new order in production management inevitably undermined paternal power and authority within the family. As a result, a sense of autonomy and demand for self-development among the youth grew.

The work-point system in the collectives individualized the contributions made by each member of a household to the family economy, and thus fostered a consciousness of individual identity among the young. Under the accounting system in the collectives, one's daily contribution was recorded in terms of work points which were then transferred into a cash value after the harvest. The intriguing point is that the records of work-points were open to the public and were annually posted on the walls of team headquarters. Therefore one's income and contribution to his/her family was publicized in a crystal-clear manner. This made an important difference to the young, because their fathers could no longer deny or understate the contributions made by other members to the family economy, as was usually the case in the traditional family farming. Because of their advantages in adapting to collective farming and in learning new skills, many young members could earn more work points than their fathers, and their competence was demonstrated to the public every year when the accounting books were posted. Consequently, as they became aware of their important contribution to the family economy, the young people gained an individual consciousness about their positions and as a result they were less obedient to the parental authority at home. As an old villager put it, "the young kids quickly developed bad tempers once they could earn their own rice."

Formal Education

As many scholars have pointed out, the expansion of formal schooling has created significant social space for youth to develop peer connections outside their family networks; it has also equipped them with more knowledge and new ideas (see, e.g., Thornton and Fricke 1987: 755–758). Again taking Xiajia village as an example, most boys and girls graduated from primary schools during the 1960s. The village school added its own junior high program in the late 1970s and opened a preschool class for children aged five to seven in 1975. By 1985–86, 75 percent of boys and 48 percent of girls in Xiajia had completed junior high, while virtually all school-age children enrolled and graduated from primary school. Graduates of senior high school were rather common during the same period. School enrollments went down in the second half of the 1980s, but this mostly affected high school students because many chose to seek employment in the cities rather than to continue their studies.

As a result, most village teenagers spend six to nine years in school, participating in social activities with peers outside the family sphere. Although the collective preferences of the young vary depending on the changes in the larger social setting, from reciting quotations from Mao's works to wearing printed T-shirts to tastes in pop music, the end result is the same: the youngsters now constitute a distinct group. Moreover, as mentioned above, the better education of the younger generation also helps them to adapt to technological reforms and to enhance their work competence, particularly as the Chinese economy has become more market-oriented and more nonagricultural jobs are available.

Marriage Law and Family Reforms

From early on the CCP advocated reforms relating to family life, including freedom of mate choice, late marriages, simplified weddings and other rituals, gender and generational equality in family relations, and freedom to divorce and remarry (for an account of early experiments, see Hu 1974; see also Ocko 1991; Yang 1965). As Parish and Whyte, among other scholars, correctly point out, there has been a gap between the official ideology and the actual implementation of government policies. "Thus over time there have been recurring waves in the marriage reform field, with fairly superficial press accounts of positive models in some periods, and more intensive local pressure, with some sanctions applied to particular negative examples, in other periods" (1978: 161). They conclude that there are both changes and consistencies in family life; for rural youth, the biggest change is increased youth autonomy in mate choice and the increasing importance of conjugal relations within the family.

Similar to Parish's and Whyte's observations in south China, state-sponsored family reforms, the implementation of marriage laws, and the increasing opportunities for village youths to work and socialize with peers of the opposite sex have no doubt led to more freedom in mate choice in the villages which I studied. I can add that this trend continued and, in some aspects, even accelerated after the early 1970s – the time that Parish and Whyte were conducting their research interviews. As a result, in the 1990s the youth have enjoyed much more autonomy in this area of their life (see Yan 1997). Understandably, almost every change in marriage custom initially provokes parental disapproval and generational conflicts in one way or another, but they are gradually accepted as "normal." In a 1961 case in Xiajia, for instance, the party secretary's daughter insisted on marrying a young man of her own choice; he happened to be poor and addicted to gambling. To stop their daughter's crazy romance, the parents tried both tough and soft methods, including threatening to cut her off from the family should she become involved with this person. The daughter was very determined and, as a Communist Party member herself, she knew how to seek support from the upper-level government agencies. Eventually she won the battle but paid a high price: she married the man she loved but her father refused to see her for the next two decades; he only forgave her when he was dying in 1993. In contrast, in 1990 a strong-minded girl became engaged to a boyfriend from the same village, despite some parental disapproval. After the ritual she frequently stayed in her fiancé's home and walked arm in arm with him on the streets in Xiajia village, just like a pair of urban lovers. This caused a huge wave of criticism and gossip from the older and conservative villagers, mostly women, but her behavior was welcomed and imitated by her peers. During my last visit to Xiajia in 1994, it was quite ordinary to see engaged young couples displaying intimacy in public.

A Brave New World Since Decollectivization

The 1980s probably was the first politically peaceful decade in rural China. The only memorable drama was decollectivization, in which village youths did not have much of a role to play. Once again the family became the unit of production, and the youngsters had to learn family farming under guidance from their fathers and elder brothers. This has led scholars to speculate about the revival of traditional family culture, including oppression of the young. For various reasons, however, this did not occur; instead, the early trends to building a youth culture have continued, albeit in different ways. Actually, the current characteristics of village youths described in the first section of this paper emerged in the late 1980s. There are not many differences between the youth in the second half of the 1980s and their younger brothers in the 1990s. Both groups have demonstrated strong anti-authority tendencies and inclination toward materialism and consumerism, as well as a strong sense of their individual rights.

Two factors are important in understanding the continuing growth of youth culture; they are both related to state policies. First, the distribution of land during decollectivization recognized the full membership of village youth in public life, which represents a radical departure from traditional views. When decollectivization took place in Xiajia in the winter of 1983, the land was divided into two categories – *kouliangtian* (ration land) and *chengbaotian* (contract land) from which taxes and other levies would be extracted. Everyone was entitled to have a share of ration land, but only male laborers were given contract land. Every man of age eighteen or above was allocated an equal share of land, and those who were aged sixteen to seventeen were given a half share. This means that the village youths who were eighteen or above all received a share of land equal to that of the older villagers. One's marital status did not affect the redistribution of land. Given the importance of land in Xiajia villagers' life, this format of land redistribution has enabled the village youths developed a sense of ownership, and their status as adults in both public and private domains was enhanced.[2]

Second, soon after decollectivization there appeared new opportunities for young villagers to work in cities. The party-state began to loosen up its early ban on rural-urban migration in 1981–82, issuing new policies to allow villagers to seek employment and temporary residence in cities in 1985 (Li 1993: 110–111). Since then millions of villagers are on the move every year; by 1993 the number of rural migrants to the cities exceeded 100 million. Village youth of both sexes constitute the main body of this great wave of internal migration (Yan 1994: 15.7). In Xiajia village, eighty-one young villagers worked outside for at least more than three months in 1991, and this figure increased to 142 when I revisited in 1993 (the total numbers were 106 and 167 respectively). As indicated above, urban employment has opened a completely new world for the village youth; they have experienced, sometimes against their will, new life styles which older villagers have not heard of. They have also been exposed to the new ideas and information which grew quickly in the cities after the party-state relaxed its tight control over popular culture. As a result, the cultural gap between those who have moved out of the village and those who have stayed behind has been enlarged considerably, and in many respects, this is reflected in the youth culture in village society.

Unintended Consequences

The foregoing analysis shows that the state-sponsored ideological mobilization, youth organizations, collective farming, and formal school education are the major means by which the party-state successfully moved young villagers away from the influence of kinship power in the public domain and, for quite a long period, transformed village youth into the most active supporters of the party agenda in political campaigns and into a valuable source of labor force in economic development. The party-state, therefore, has played a major role in contributing to the full membership of village youth in public life and in creating a youth subculture. There are, however, two consequences which may not have been expected by the CCP leaders; that is, the anti-authority tendencies and the awareness of individual rights on the part of youth in the post-Mao era.

Comparing several generations of rural youth under socialism, we can see the gradual development of anti-authority sentiment. The young villagers in the 1950s, like most other groups, were loyal followers of their leaders whom they believed to be the true representatives of the CCP. This generation did not challenge the age-generation hierarchy outside the directives of the party-state. The next generation of village youth, as mentioned above, was known for its idealism. Under the leadership of the party-state, the youth in the 1960s also actively participated in campaigns to criticize village cadres who were scapegoats for the failure of the Great Leap and the ensuing famine.

The village youths in the 1970s had close ties to the Cultural Revolution – they were either young participants in the Cultural Revolution or the "beneficiaries" of its legacy. The Youth League and other organizations were replaced by the Red Guard organizations which soon became factionalized and fought with one another. These rebellious youths were given their first opportunities to challenge the authorities – to challenge the village cadres in public life and elder kin in private life. There were numerous cases where young villagers humiliated village cadres in struggle meetings. Although there were no cases of reporting on their parents, several youths publicly denounced their uncles or other close kin who were the targets of such struggle meetings.

When the initial political storm of the Cultural Revolution had subsided, the young villagers quickly divided into different groups. A small number of them were absorbed into the village leadership or assigned some of the more desirable jobs such as tractor drivers or school teachers. A larger number of youth became a new generation of trouble-makers, rebelling against the cadre leadership and taking advantage of public resources. In local words, they were called *ci'er tou* which literally means "thorny-head" In addition, the Youth League and other former youth organizations were not able to revive their former strength.

Anger over social inequalities and corrupt leadership grew among the village youth in the post-Mao era. Direct and violent confrontations between village youth and cadres escalated (for more details, see Yan 1995: 230–237). What makes contemporary youth different from their predecessors is that they distrust and tend to challenge all authorities, not merely a few targets hand-picked by authorities at higher levels. Their anti-authority tendencies are accompanied by an indifference toward the communist ideology and political mobilization. An interesting indicator is that since the 1983 decollectivization the CCP branch in Xiajia village has received only one application from someone wishing to join the party; the applicant was the son of an important cadre who is well-known to have ambitions to become party secretary himself.

Due to the state's retreat from its radical socialist programs, diminishing cadre power to monopolize resources, opportunities of working in cities, and increasingly easy access to new ideas/information, today's village youth have become ever more aware of their individual rights and have learned to use the legal system to protect themselves and to challenge local authorities (Li and O'Brien 1996; Yan 1995: 234–235). Although the development of youth culture did not constitute a direct political threat to village cadres (as it does not carry any political agenda), the general anti-authority tendency among young villagers and their frequent confrontation with cadres in social life have indeed intensified the weakening of power and authority of village cadres. It is therefore not accidental that cadres complain about the "youth problem" much more than anyone else.

The Long-Term Effects of Youth Experience

As already mentioned, there are at least four generations of rural youths who had quite different experiences from their own parents: 1) the illiterate and newly awakened youth in the 1950s; 2) the idealistic youth in the 1960s; 3) the post-Cultural-Revolution, "thorny-head" youth of the 1970s; and 4) the more individualistic and materialistic youth in the post-Mao era. By the early 1990s, the youth who sang love songs during the Great Leap (Blake 1979) had become grandparents, and the young activists who were fond of voluntary work and political campaigns (Parish and Whyte 1978; Chan, Madsen and Unger 1984) had become parents with marriage-age children.

The youth experience of these grandparents and parents has affected their current attitudes toward contemporary youth. Each generation has undergone its own particular kind of "breakthrough" with respect to the rural youth culture and in shaking the age-generation superiority; the next generation down the road has also enjoyed more youth autonomy and independence than its elder siblings. Consequently, when these youths became elder siblings and parents they demonstrated more tolerance toward the autonomy of the next generation. This is what I call the long-term effects of the youth experience. I believe it has also contributed significantly to the rise of a youth culture in the post-Mao era. A good example in this connection is the changing attitude toward premarital sex among engaged young couples.

I attended a wedding in a neighboring village of Xiajia in July 1991. The bride was nineteen and the groom only eighteen. As they both were too young to marry according to the Chinese marriage law, their parents had to use their connections to get official approval for the marriage certificate. The reason for such a rushed and early marriage was the bride's unexpected pregnancy. The bride and groom had been classmates in both primary and middle school and they had developed their "good feelings" – as they put it – toward each other at school. After they became engaged in 1990 they had spent much more time together, visiting and staying at each other's home. Because of their young age, neither of their families ever considered an early wedding, until the bride's mother learned, in June 1991, that her daughter was three months pregnant. As I note elsewhere (Yan 1996: 193–194), from the 1970s engaged young couples in this region enjoyed more freedom to be together and they could even take long-distance trips on their own and stayed in hotels as married couples. As a result, more and more engaged youth have had premarital sexual experiences, and older villagers have also become more tolerant toward this increased intimacy. In this case, while the young bride was blamed by her parents for her careless and improper pregnancy, she still received support from her family, including a large dowry worth 3,000 yuan. The pregnancy provoked some negative comments about the bride among some older people but it did not go beyond the line of ordinary gossip, and she was still regarded as a good girl in the community. This constitutes a sharp contrast to a similar case in Xiajia village in the early 1950s, in which the pregnant bride was condemned as a bad woman by both her own family and her husband's family as well by the village community.

In discussing the 1991 case, several older informants recalled how strict the rules had been when they were young. A 45-year-old man told me that when he secretly developed a close relationship with a girl who later became his wife in 1967, both were very nervous and cautious. He said: "We often went to the fields during the nights and stayed there for a long time. I touched her body many times but did not dare to go further, because we both knew if she became pregnant our reputation would be ruined." Because of his own experience, this man told me, he was very lenient to his two sons when they reached the same age. Incidentally, the fiancée of his elder son became pregnant in 1990. "It was an emergency but not a disaster. We had to make them get married as quickly as possible. That was all," the man concluded with a smile.

To get a sense of how many engaged youths might have had premarital sex I studied the *Records of Birth Control Implementation* in Xiajia village to examine the wedding dates and the dates of the first baby-delivery of every woman in the village since 1979 (the data are updated twice a year). Among the forty-nine couples who married between 1991 and 1993, thirteen had babies within eight months after their weddings, and of these thirteen couples ten of them had babies within seven months. This shows that, conservatively speaking, during this period 20 percent of the newly-weds engaged in premarital sex. How do villagers see this change? A national survey shows that 24 percent of villagers regard premarital sex among the engaged young couples as something "permissible" or "unimportant" (ZGNCJTDCZ 1993: 53). It is clear that premarital sex, taboo in the 1960s, has become a rather common practice among engaged couples in the 1990s.

In conclusion, a youth culture has now emerged in north China villages, and village youths have become an important social group in their own right. In an attempt to move rural youth away from the previous social control of the family and kinship organizations, the state has played a key role in the formation of this youth culture. But there have been unintended consequences as the contemporary rural youth have demonstrated more anti-authority sentiments. At the individual level, the meaning of youthfulness in rural life has to be redefined, and a new stage in the life course – the youth period – was created between the stages of childhood and adulthood. The rise of a youth culture also reveals an important aspect of the transformation of social experience in mainland China, that is, the diversification of rural society due to the formation of the youth group. The long-term implications of these changes, however, remain to be explored in future studies.

ACKNOWLEDGMENTS

I am grateful to Harvard-Yenching Institute, the National Science Foundation, The Chinese University of Hong Kong, and the Luce Foundation for making my fieldwork in these villages financially possible.

NOTES

1. Theoretically, only the Youth League is exclusively a youth organization. But in reality, only young villagers are active members in the Women's Association and Basic Militia, unlike the situation in the cities. In villages, older women rarely participate in any public activities, which makes the Women's Association an organization for young girls. The militia organization is divided into the ordinary, basic, and armed militia. The ordinary militia does not make much sense as an organization, because virtually all adult males with good class labels are members. The elite group is the Basic Militia which consists of young men aged 18 to 25, plus a few experienced discharged soldiers in their late twenties or early thirties. The Armed Militia is usually organized at the commune level, with each village contributing a few members. The Basic Militia was a very important force during the 1950s and 1960s, because it legitimized oppressive actions. So every party secretary in Xiajia made a special effort to appoint his own man as the head of the Basic Militia.

2. To secure confidence and investment by villagers in their land, the Chinese state has extended the promise of no policy change several times, from fifteen years to thirty years and now for fifty years. This certainly has stabilized the situation and works well for those who received land in 1983. But the lack of landed resources is a problem among the young villagers who were born after 1967. During my last visit in 1994 I found that most migrant laborers in their early twenties had missed the opportunities of land redistribution and thus had only ration land to farm. This will be an even more severe problem for those who were born after 1983 because they do not even receive their ration land. Presently, out-migration and temporary work in the cities seem to be the only option for village youths in the 1990s.

REFERENCES

Baker, Hugh 1979 *Chinese Family and Kinship*. New York: Columbia University Press.

Bakken, Borge 1993 Crime, Juvenile Delinquency and Deterrence Policy in China. *Australian Journal of Chinese Affairs* 30: 29–58.

Berger, Brigitte 1974 *Readings in Sociology: A Biographical Approach*. New York: Basic Books, Inc.

Bernstein, Thomas 1977 Urban Youth in the Countryside: Problems of Adaptation and Remedies. *China Quarterly* 69: 75–108.

Blake, Fred C. 1979 Love Songs and the Great Leap: The Role of a Youth Culture in the Revolutionary Phase of China's Economic Development. *American Ethnologist* 6(1): 41–54.

Caputo, Virginia 1995 Anthropology's Silent 'Others': A Consideration of Some Conceptual and Methodological Issues for the Study of Youth and Children's Cultures. In Vered Amit-Talai and Helena Wulff, eds., *Youth Cultures: A Cross-Cultural Perspective*. London: Routledge, 19–42.

Chan, Anita, Richard Madsen, and Jonathan Unger 1984 *Chen Village: The Recent History of a Peasant Community in Mao's China*. Berkeley: University of California Press.

Cohen, Myron 1992 Family Management and Family Division in Contemporary Rural China. *China Quarterly* 130: 357–377.

Chow, Tse-tsung 1960 *The May Fourth Movement: Intellectual Revolution in Modern China*. Cambridge, MA: Harvard University Press.

Fei, Xiaotong 1992 [1947] *From the Soil*, trans, by Gary Hamilton and Wang Zheng. Berkeley: University of California Press.

Freedman, Maurice 1966 *Chinese Lineage and Society: Fukien and Kwangtung*. London: Athlone.

Hu, Chi-hsi 1974 The Sexual Revolution in the Kiangsi Soviet. *China Quarterly* 59: 477–490.

Johnson, Kay Ann 1983 *Women, the Family and Peasant Revolution in China*. Chicago: University of Chicago Press.

Levy, Marion 1949 *The Family Revolution in Modern China*. Cambridge, MA: Harvard University Press.

Li, Lianjiang and Kevin O'Brien 1996 Villagers and Popular Resistance in Contemporary China. *Modern China* 22(1): 28–61.

Li, Qiang 1993 *Dangdai Zhongguo shehui fenceng yu liudong (Social Stratification and Mobility in Contemporary China)*. Beijing: Zhongguo jingji chubanshe (in Chinese).

Musgrove, F. 1965 *Youth and Social Order*. Bloomington: Indiana University Press.

Ngai, Ngan-pun 1994 Youth Deviance in China. In Maurice Brosscau and Lo Chi Kin, eds., *China Review*. Hong Kong: The Chinese University Press.

Ocko, Jonathan K. 1991 Women, Property, and the Law in the People's Republic of China. In Rubic Watson and Patricia Ebrey, eds., *Marriage and Inequality in Chinese Society*. Berkeley: University of California Press.

Parish, William and Martin Whyte 1978 *Village and Family in Contemporary China*. Chicago: University of Chicago Press.

Potter, Sulamith H. 1983 The Position of Peasants in Modern China. *Modern China* 9(4): 465–499.

Rosen, Stanley 1981 *The Role of Sent-Down Youth in the Chinese Cultural Revolution: The Case of Guangzhou*. Berkeley. Center for Chinese Studies.

Staccy, Judith 1983 *Patriarchy and Socialist Revolution in China*. Berkeley: University of California Press.

Thornton, Arland and Thomas Fricke 1987 Social Change and the Family: Comparative Perspectives from the West, China, and South Asia. *Sociological Forum* 2(4): 746–779.

Waltner, Ann 1986 The Moral Status of the Child in Late Imperial China: Childhood in Ritual and in Law. *Social Research* 53(4): 667–687.

Watson, James 1989 *Self Defense Corps, Violence, and the Bachelor Sub-Culture in South China*. In Proceedings of the Second International Conference on Sinology. Taipei: Academia Sinica.

Weber, Max 1968 *The Religion of China*. New York: The Free Press.

Whyte, Martin 1990 Changes in Mate Choice in Chengdu. In Deborah Davis and Ezra Vogel, eds., *Chinese Society on the Eve of Tiananmen: The Impact of Reform*. Cambridge, MA: Harvard University Press.

———— 1992 Introduction: Rural Economic Reforms and Chinese Family Patterns. *China Quarterly* 130: 317–322.

Wulff, Helena 1995 Introduction: Introducing Youth Culture in Its Own Right: The State of the Art and New Possibilities. In Vered Amit-Talai and Helena Wulff, eds., *Youth Cultures: A Cross-Cultural Perspective*. London: Routledge, 1–18.

Yan, Yunxiang 1994 Dislocation, Reposition and Restratification: Structural Changes in Chinese Society. In Maurice Brosscau and Lo Chi Kin, eds., *China Review*. Hong Kong: The Chinese University Press.

———— 1995 Everyday Power Relations: Changes in a North China Village. In Andrew Walder, ed., *The Waning of the Communist State: Economic Origins of Political Decline in China and Hungary*. Berkeley: University of California Press, 215–241.

———— 1996 *The Flow of Gifts: Reciprocity and Social Networks in a Chinese Village*. Stanford: Stanford University Press.

———— 1997 The Triumph of Conjugality: Structural Transformation of Family Relations in a North China Village. *Ethnology* 36(3): 191–212.

Yang, C.K. 1965 *Chinese Communist Society: The Family and the Village*. Cambridge, MA: The MIT Press.

ZGNCJTDCZ (Zhongguo nongcun jiating diaochazu [Survey Group of Chinese Rural Families])

———— 1993 *Dangdai Zhongguo nongcun jiating (Rural Families in Contemporary China)*. Beijing: Shchui kexuc wenxian chubanshe (in Chinese).

CHAPTER 6

GIRL POWER: YOUNG WOMEN AND THE WANING OF PATRIARCHY

Although there are still many issues under debate among students of the Chinese family, it is widely agreed that the decline of parental authority and power is the most visible and significant change that has occurred in the domestic sphere in rural China since 1949. Such a trend began in the heyday of socialist transformation during the 1950s (Yang 1959) and continued in both the collective period (Parish and Whyte 1978) and the post-collective reform era (Davis and Harrell 1993; Bossen 2002). Thus far, most studies see the decline of parental power and authority as a result of a set of social changes occurring in larger social settings, such as the implementation of the new marriage law and other government policies, the state-sponsored attack on patrilineal ideology and kinship organization, and public ownership that disabled the family as a unit of production. The contribution of individual agency to the shifting power balance across generational line, especially the role played by young women, however, has been by and large underplayed, if not completely ignored. To balance the previous emphasis on external, social causes, this article explores the active role played by young women to redefine intergenerational power relations in particular and other dimensions of private life in general.

Throughout this article the term "young women" is used to refer to rural women between the ages of 15 to 24, or as defined by social terms, those who are going through the transition period from a teenage daughter to a young daughter-in-law. For a rural woman, this is the most difficult and important period in her life, full of changes and challenges (Wolf 1972). In the areas where this study was conducted, young women in this age group are referred to as *guniang* or *yatou*, which may be translated as "girls" in English. But guniang or yatou refer only to unmarried young women. Once a young woman marries, she is no longer a girl; but has been transformed into a daughter-in-law (*xifu*) and an adult woman.

In a traditional family, young women were marginal outsiders with only a temporary position, as daughters married out and new daughters-in-law entered the domestic group under the rules of patrilineal exogamy and patrilocal post-marital residence. Thus, daughters were commonly regarded as a drain on family wealth and new daughters-in-law were seen as a potential threat to the existing family order. In comparison to their male siblings, girls were statusless, powerless, and somewhat dangerous; they could acquire a proper place in the domestic sphere only by becoming mothers (Baker 1979; Freedman 1966; Watson 1985, 1986; Wolf 1972; Bossen 2002).

As a result of their anonymity in family life, young women have drawn little scholarly attention thus far and, admittedly, they also constitute the most difficult age group to study for a male researcher. Male informants are the usual sources when conducting fieldwork. When I tried to reach female informants, I found myself more often talking with older women, the supposedly more knowledgeable and certainly more powerful woman in a household, typically the mother (or mother-in-law) who manages the household budget. However, from the numerous complaints about their daughters, daughters-in-law, and recollections of their own life histories, and also from more serious complaints by men about women in general, I came to realize that ever since the 1950s young women have been perhaps the most active agents in initiating significant changes in intergenerational relations and patterns of family life.

This article will demonstrate that, over a period of five decades, several generations of young women have challenged patriarchal power in terms of mate-choice, marriage negotiation, and family division, thus altering the domestic sphere. The second part of the present study explores the social context in which these young women have developed their identities and have progressed from voiceless dependents to active agents in family life. The conclusion discusses the limitations to girl power and explains how these limitations may also contribute to the emergence of such a power. Data for this article were collected from fieldwork in Xiajia village, Heilongjiang province, northeast China, in 1989, 1991, 1993, 1994, 1997, 1998, and 1999, as part of a larger project, being an ethnographic account of the transformation of private life in this rural community from 1949 to 1999 (Yan 2003), wherein the rise of power of young women is merely one of the many important changes that occurred to the domestic sphere.

With a population of 1,492 in 1998, Xiajia village had been fairly successful in collective farming prior to the implementation of the de-collectivization reforms in the early 1980s; today it still remains a farming community. The heavy reliance on farming has been one of the major obstacles to economic development in the village, keeping the average per capita income slightly below the national average during the 1980s and 1990s. But the villagers' livelihood has been closely tied to the market through raising cash crops, household sideline businesses, labor migration, and the impact of the mass media and urban consumerism.[2]

GIRL POWER AND CHANGES IN PRIVATE LIFE

Examining the major changes in the private lives of Xiajia villagers shows that there are many areas in which young women have played a major role in changing pre-existing patterns of family life, such as establishing wife-centered family networks after marriage, altering the previous standard of kinship distance, and creating new rituals that celebrate women's reproductive power or the importance of their natal families (Yan 1996:53–54 and 2001:234–36). Mate-choice, marriage transaction, and family division, however, are particularly noteworthy, because young women challenged patriarchal power in these areas, and their efforts have had profound influence on current patterns of family life.

Mate-Choice and Courtship

As noted by many scholars of contemporary rural China, the autonomy of rural youth in mate-choice has been steadily increasing since the 1950s, although the trend varies a great deal depending on the region and the time period (see, e.g., Chan, Madsen, and Unger 1992 [1984]; Parish and Whyte 1978). But scholars have not yet noted that in rural China, youth autonomy in mate-choice is reflected mainly in the increasing power of young women as a result of two factors. First, the current customs of courtship and marriage proposal allow young women to make the final decision regarding mate-choice; second, there has been an artificial shortage of women in rural areas, which has put young women in a more advantageous position.

In Xiajia village, as in many other communities in the surrounding area, youth autonomy in mate-choice emerged during the late 1950s, but it remained limited by certain local customs and ritual procedures. With inter-village marriages, agreement for a match had to be worked out in stages. Usually, it started with initial inquiries from the male's side about the suitability of the intended young woman. Then there was a preliminary meeting in which the young couple would see each other and talk for a while. While the inquiries and meetings were arranged between the parents and the go-between, the opinions of the young couple were an important basis for the next move. If they made a good impression on one another, their parents would seek further information and negotiate the marriage finances for the proposed engagement. But even though daughters normally did not formally initiate their choices at an early stage, they could veto proposed mates whom they did not like.

In cases of intra-village marriages, things were simpler, as the two young people may have known one another from childhood. Interestingly enough, village endogamy appears to be the preferential form since the 1950s. During recent decades, one-fifth of Xiajia men found wives within their own village. Some of the marriages within the village took place after a brief dating period.

The young women's power to veto a marriage proposal was first recognized after the implementation of a new marriage law in the early 1950s, which was gradually routinzied as part of local custom. A young woman can exercise her veto power many times until she finds a suitable match and she can use this power to change slightly the rules of the game, such as by defying her parents' will, or even selecting a husband by herself. In general, securing the daughter's consent is a basic element of any marriage proposal and, to my knowledge, since the early 1970s all parents have recognized a daughter's right to reject an undesirable suitor.[3] A survey in 1993 of 78 marriages since the late 1980s revealed no cases in which the bride had been forced into a marriage by her parents or by anyone else. Furthermore, more than two-thirds of these young women had previously refused marriage proposals at least once.

Naturally, parents are reluctant to give up their power to manage the marriages of the younger generation, as this is perhaps one of the most efficient means of controlling their adult children. During the 1950s, each time a young woman tried to use her veto power to test the waters, she inevitably provoked parental disapproval, and generational conflicts occurred. Gradually, such actions became accepted during the 1960s and 1970s and have been considered the norm since the 1990s. The most common source of conflict is when a young woman wants to marry someone whom her parents strongly oppose. However, as shown in the following three cases, parental power in this respect has also been declining.

In a 1961 case, the local Communist Party secretary's daughter insisted on marrying a young man who was poor and addicted to gambling. To stop this romance, the parents tried both tough and soft methods, including the threat to oust her from the family. The daughter was determined, however, and as a Communist Party member, she sought support from upper-level government agencies. Eventually she married the man but paid a high price. Her father refused to see her for the next two decades and forgave her only when he was dying in 1993.

A similar case occurred in the early 1970s when a young woman from a cadre's family fell in love with a young man in her production team and asked her family to approach his family. But her family strongly opposed the idea because the young man's family had a bad class label. After a long struggle, she finally married the man, but her husband was not welcomed in her family until after they had a child.

In the third case, a strong-willed young woman became engaged in 1990 to her boyfriend from the same village, despite her parents' disapproval. After the engagement, she frequently stayed at her fiancé's parents' home; the two would walk together arm in arm on the village streets, just like a pair of urban lovers. This caused much criticism and gossip from the older and more conservative villagers, especially older women, but was welcomed and imitated by their peers.

In addition to the decision-making, which is the most important aspect in mate-choice, another important change in courtship results from young women's pursuit of freedom and intimacy. The early trend of youth autonomy in mate-choice developed into a "romantic revolution of courtship" by the end of the 1990s (Yan 2003: 64–85), characterized by three major developments. The first is an increase of intimacy in courtship and post-engagement interactions, including the increasing popularity of premarital sex. To a certain extent, premarital sex for engaged couples has become socially accepted, and has transformed the post-engagement time from a preparation for marriage to a passionate and erotic period of romance. Second, contemporary young women pay more attention to their future spouse's individual characteristics, such as physical appearance, respect and caring, emotional expression, and communication skills. Third, young women of the 1990s tended to be more open and vocal in expressing their emotions. In addition to conventional ways of caring, many young women expect a direct and passionate expression of love from young men. Pop culture and mass media seem to be the most obvious and direct influence on the development of the language of love and intimacy, which both enriches and alters the discourse on an ideal mate and the practice of mate-choice. Here the new emphasis on communication skills, particularly on whether one is able to speak *fengliu hua* (romantic talk) shows that the imaginative/subjective world of youth is expanding, and the idealization of the partner is emerging as an important part of mate-choice.

These three major changes are all related to the subjectivity construction among village youth, a development that was not documented in Parish and Whyte's 1978 study. In comparison to their parents and older siblings, Xiajia youth of the 1990s preferred to control their own fate; they enjoyed making decisions and had a strong sense of entitlement to claim their rights. It is interesting that during both the collective period and the post-reform period, village women played a leading role in pursuing romantic love and the freedom of mate-choice. In most cases of free choice that occurred in Xiajia village, young women were far more active than their male counterparts, either by directly confronting parental authority or by using their veto power to resist parental interference. Similarly, in almost all cases of engagement break-ups, the initiators were women.

Marriage Negotiation

An important phenomenon of family life in rural China is that, despite all the reforms made by the state and despite radical changes in the organizational modes of production and reproduction, the practice of bridewealth – that is, the flow of gifts in cash and in kind from the groom's family to the bride's family – still continues. In fact, the cost of bridewealth has been increasing in the past two decades in both the wealthier and poorer areas of China. The interpretations of this phenomenon include the persistence of cultural tradition and the need to compensate for the loss of a female laborer, but missing is the role played by young people, especially young women.

My interviews with older village women and a study of engagement documents reveal a process by which several generations of young women transformed the institution of bridewealth. Bridewealth in Xiajia village consists of two parts: money and material goods (Yan 1996:176–209). Until recently, monetary gifts were given by the groom's parents to the bride's parents, and material gifts were purchased by and remained with the groom's parents, to be placed in the new couple's room. During the 1950s and 1960s, engaged young women were not directly involved either in negotiating or in purchasing marital gifts, but they tried to protect their interests by monitoring the preparation of the material gifts prior to the wedding date. They adopted many strategies to detect whether the groom's family kept to their side of the bargain, such as trying to pick out the items themselves or sending someone to check the gifts before the wedding day. If the groom's family spent too little on the material goods, the bride might refuse to attend the wedding.

The bride's role became more active after a local custom, *zhao dinghunxiang* (taking engagement photos), emerged. Beginning in the early 1970s, engaged young women participated in purchasing material goods for their own betrothal. The bride and groom went to a nearby city (either the county seat or the provincial capital, Ha'erbin) to buy clothes and other personal items on the gift list. They also sat for an engagement picture in a photo studio. More important, most couples spent a night or two together at a hotel. The village office (the production brigade during the 1970s) issued them an official letter which entitled them to rent a single room in a hotel as a couple. Along with the custom of having an engagement photo, brides gradually began to take control of the actual purchase of the material goods and, accordingly, new categories of material gifts were created and the value of these goods increased.

By the 1980s, the monetary gift in bridewealth, which was given directly to the bride's parents, was insignificant in comparison to the material gifts purchased first under the supervision of the bride and later entirely controlled by the bride. That is, the bride took over the major part of the bridewealth by purchasing these goods. A more radical change followed.

In 1984 a young woman demanded, for the first time in the village, that her betrothal gifts be converted into a lump sum of cash given to her.

Of that amount she spent only a small portion for her wedding. This behavior was regarded by many as absurd and scandalous because at that time a bride could only control a small part of the bridewealth as trousseau money spent during the shopping trip.

The bride made such a bold request because the groom had four younger brothers waiting to be married and the economic status of the groom's family was below average. Although she had grown up in a similarly poor family, she was confident and forthright by local standard. The young couple grew up in the same village and, by the time of engagement, the groom was already dependent on her to make decisions. Thus, the groom's family complied with her demands because their son was afraid of losing her. Her parents initially protested her aggressiveness, but they backed down, knowing their daughter had always been determined.

This new and strange change of the bridewealth, *ganzhe* (converted bridewealth), occupied the center of village gossip for only a short while because villagers regarded this case as too unconventional to be taken seriously. But in the following year, 1985, there was a rumor that there would be no extra land allocated for house construction. Those planning marriages at that time worried about not being allocated a plot, so many grooms suggested that their brides ask only for cash as betrothal gifts, following the 1984 ganzhe model that was still fresh in their minds. The large amount of cash that a bride would receive was to be used by the young couple to purchase construction materials, after which the village office would allocate them a plot of land. This idea was welcomed by parents on both sides because they too were worried about the proposed government policy. As a result, ganzhe quickly became popular, and this model has been followed by young villagers ever since. By the summer of 1997, most villagers with whom I spoke considered converted bridewealth to be a normal practice, and a number of more articulate youth had resorted to the rhetoric of individualism to justify this.

Since the emergence of ganzhe, young women have shown unprecedented enthusiasm to negotiate marital gifts with potential in-laws. In a 1991 case, for example, the toughest negotiator at the engagement table was the prospective bride. She insisted on a ganzhe gift of 5,500 yuan when the groom's family had offered 4,000 yuan. Ultimately, 5,000 yuan was agreed to, plus 500 yuan to be paid to the bride for her serving cigarettes and wine at the wedding. When she returned from the engagement ceremony she had pocketed 3,000 yuan and she expected to receive the remaining 2,500 prior to the wedding.

In the 1990s it became common for engaged young women to possess relatively large amounts of cash (several thousand yuan or more). My informants claim that more than half the families in Xiajia village have to borrow money in order to arrange their sons' marriages and, ironically, more than half of these families borrow the money from betrothed young women.

The most significant implication of this change in bridewealth to ganzhe has been the transformation of a marital gift exchanged between two families into a new form of pre-mortem inheritance. The converted bridewealth, which is controlled completely by the bride, plus the dowry she receives from her parents, is considered by all parties involved as a conjugal fund. As this conjugal fund constitutes a major part of the property that a couple can claim when they depart from the groom's parents' family, rural youth have tried to raise the standard amounts for the bridewealth and dowry, resulting in a rapid escalation of marriage costs. Young women have played a key role in initiating and institutionalizing this important change in family life.

Post-Marital Residence and Family Division

The timing of family division is another indicator of how young women have changed family life. According to older villagers, prior to the 1949 revolution most people tried to delay the time of family division as long as possible, usually after the death of the father or after his retirement as household head. By the 1970s, the socially accepted time of family division was after the marriage of the husband's younger brother – which usually involves three to five years of co-residence of the newlyweds with the groom's parents – or at least after the birth of a young couple's first child. In contrast, my 1991 survey shows that nearly one-third of the 36 newly married couples in Xiajia village since 1989 had established their own households before having children, and almost half did so right after the birth of their first child. The trend continued, and by 1994 more than 40 percent of the 49 newlywed couples over the previous three years had established an independent household prior to the birth of a child, and nearly 80 percent of the family divisions occurred prior to the younger brother's marriage. The earliest family division occurred seven days after the wedding in 1991, and by 1994 there were two couples that did not even bother to observe the custom of patrilocal co-residence. Immediately after their wedding they moved into a new house and set up their independent households.

As a result of this rapid change to an earlier family division, a growing number of newly established conjugal families consists of young couples who have yet to bear children. In 1994, twelve newlywed couples had established conjugal households in this way, including two young men who were the only sons in their respective families. This would have been unthinkable previously.

These figures poorly reflect the actual impact on the parents of early family division or of an only son's departure. A concrete example may be more illuminating. Mr. Fang has four sons. The eldest was named Gold (*jin*), the second was named Silver (*yin*), the third Full (*man*), and the youngest Storehouse (*ku*). Together their names mean a storehouse full of gold and silver. This expresses the most common wish of all Chinese villagers; that is, to have sons for security in old age. In Mr. Fang's case, however, things went contrary to his will. During the past decade, he and his wife had to finance all their sons' marriages, which had become increasingly costly. When the youngest son became engaged in 1990, the old couple thought they had reached the end of their bridewealth obligations. They were soon disappointed because the prospective youngest daughter-in-law demanded a separate new house prior to the marriage and an early family division after the marriage. In less than two months after the youngest son's wedding, Mr. Fang and his wife were living alone in their old house, back to their financial condition when they had first established their household more than 30 years earlier. When we discussed his family history, Mr. Fang said, "All the gold and silver have been taken away by my sons. What is left is only a shaky, empty storehouse, guarded by an old man and an old woman. It was just like a dream, a bad dream."

As can be expected, older villagers blame their young daughters-in-law instead of their sons for the rush to an early family division. Many older villagers complained that it was always the young daughter-in-law who initiated and actually managed everything, from the early tough demands for a large bridewealth to the request for an early family division. They saw their married sons as too weak to stand up for their own parents; instead, young men always followed the orders of their wife.

This has always been an issue in Chinese family politics. A new daughter-in-law has long been viewed as a threat to family order by both senior males and older women, and especially by mothers-in-law. In an extended family, daughters-in-law are always blamed for causing conflict between married brothers, which would lead to family division (Cohen 1976; and Freedman 1966). The difference in the 1990s is that young women can (and do) initiate early family division without resorting to any devious strategies, such as using gossip and sly maneuvers. In many cases, engaged young women openly declare their intention to live independently long before the wedding and they even pressure their parents-in-law into offering help, such as by specifically requesting a fully decorated and equipped (with major appliances) new house as part of their bridewealth. Sometimes, young women's insistence on an early family partition appears to be economically irrational. In one case, the parents did all they could to satisfy the demands of the bride of their only son, including offering the largest converted bridewealth at that time and allowing the young couple to keep their income for themselves after their marriage. As the groom's father was a well-respected school teacher and the mother had made a small fortune in developing businesses, many villagers expected the young couple to stay with the husband's parents. But the bride demanded family division only three months after the wedding, without any reason other than that she felt it was inconvenient to live with her in-laws.

The most important implication of early family division is the radical reduction in the time of post-marital co-residence. As findings from a large-scale survey show, co-residence has become a ritual performance rather than a long-term domestic arrangement in many areas of rural China (Lavely and Ren 1992:391). In Xiajia village, until the late 1980s, young people's demands for early division still frequently caused family disputes, as many parents regarded early family division as a sign of their failure to raise filial sons and thus they opposed any attempt to shorten the duration of co-residence. Some parents even threatened to end the parent-child relationship if their son insisted on moving out too soon. Nowadays, however, parents have begun to deal with the issue by helping their married son move out. By the late 1980s and early 1990s, ironically, prolonged co-residence indicated a negative image of parents who are unable to help their married son set up an independent household (Potter and Potter 1990:219).

THE ROAD TO EMPOWERMENT

The role that young women play in defining important moments in their lives represents a remarkable change in comparison to their previous situation in the traditional Chinese family, whereby they could not even have a proper personal name for themselves (Watson 1986). However, the power and agency of rural young women did not surge ahead overnight in the post-Mao era, but has been the result of a long and gradual development, beginning with land reform, developing over the collective period, and continuing in the post-collective era. In this long process, generations of young women responded to state polices, social reforms, and new economic opportunities which helped them gain more independence from parental control. From early on the state advocated reforms relating to family life, including freedom of mate-choice, late marriages, simplified weddings and other rituals, gender and generational equality in family relations, and freedom to divorce and remarry.[4] These policies and reforms had a positive influence on improving the social status of young women. Of the other external empowering factors, collective farming, women's participation in public activities, and better chances for social mobility through marriage appear to have been quite important.

Front-Line Women in Collective Farming

Although it bears little resemblance to urban employment, collective farming has expanded young women's power. Since the 1950s, young women have become an important part of the labor force. In Xiajia village, female laborers were divided into three groups in accordance with their age, marital status, and working capacity. The unmarried young women and the newly married women were called *yixian funu* (front-line women), young women with small children were called *erxian funu* (second-line women), and the rest were called *sanxian funu* (third-line women). Only the young women, namely, the front-line women, participated in agricultural production as full-time laborers, partly because they were young, energetic, and without the burden of much household chores, and partly because collectives did not need so many female laborers on a full-time basis. The other two groups of women were mobilized to work only during the busiest seasons, such as during the spring planting and the autumn harvest. Since decollectivization in the early 1980s, unmarried young women leave the village in search of jobs in the cities, while married women stay home and do the household farming. The same is true regarding women's participation in other public activities, such as political meetings and voluntary work during the collective period. The social mobilization of women is thus more relevant to young women rather than to older, married women.

As the family ceased to be a unit of production during the collective era, paternal leadership in household farming was replaced by leadership of village cadres. Thus, youngsters spent most of their working hours under the supervision of people other than their fathers. Unless he was a cadre, the father would occupy the same status as his sons and daughters, and they all had to follow instructions from the team leaders. The new order in production management inevitably undermined paternal power and authority within the family. As a result, there was a growing sense of autonomy and demands for self-development among young women in the village.

Moreover, the work-point system in the collectives individualized the contributions made by each member of a household to the family economy, thus fostering a consciousness of individual identity among the young. Under the accounting system of the collectives, one's daily contribution was recorded in terms of work points which were then transferred into a cash value after the harvest. The records of work points were made public by annually posting them on the walls of the production team headquarters. That a youth's contribution to the family was publicized in a clear manner made an important difference to the youth, especially to young women, because a father could no longer deny or understate the contributions made by others to the family economy, as was possible traditionally. Usually, a young woman could earn 1,800 to 2,000 work points per year, while an average male adult earned 2,800 to 3,000 points (the difference mainly resulting from the local custom that women in Heilongjiang province usually do not work in the fields during the long winters). But it was not uncommon that a capable young woman earned more work points than a weak male laborer.

During the entire collective period, there were always some families in which young women were the major bread-winners. This occurred for reasons such as the senior male members worked outside the village, the boys were too young to work, or there were no male laborers in a family. Consequently, as they became aware of their importance to the family economy, young women became increasingly conscious of their importance, and this awareness led to their increasing pursuit of autonomy. By the same token, the parents from both their natal family and their husband's family gradually ceded patriarchal power over the young women. This resulted in the changes described above, in the increased autonomy and power of young women in mate-choice, marriage negotiation, and family division.

Active Participants in Public Activities

Probably the most dramatic change to have occurred to young women in the village during the collective period is the opportunity to receive a formal education. As Thornton and Fricke (1987:755–58) have pointed out, the expansion of formal schooling increases peer connections outside family networks, and introduces youth to knowledge and new ideas, resulting in their empowerment. This is particularly true for rural young women. In Xiajia village, most boys and girls graduated from primary school during the 1960s. The village school added a junior high program in the late 1970s and opened a preschool class for children aged five to seven in 1975. By 1985–86, 75 percent of the boys and 48 percent of the girls in Xiajia had completed junior high school, while virtually all school-age children were enrolled and ultimately graduated from primary school. Graduates of senior high school became common during the same period. School enrollments declined in the second half of the 1980s, but this mostly affected high school students because many chose to seek employment in the cities rather than continue their studies. In short, most village teenage girls spend at least six years in school, and also participate in social activities with boys outside the home. It is noteworthy that the better-educated young women tend to be more active in mate-choice, marriage negotiations, and demanding early family division. In other words, the more years they spend in school, the less likely they will become the traditional type of good daughters-in-law. This is actually a repeated comment made by many older villagers. It is also the better educated young women who tend to enjoy a more intimate and equal relationship with their husbands in their own conjugal families, and they are more likely to be praised as good wives by their husbands and peers.

During the collective period, young women had more opportunities than older women to participate in public activities. They constituted the core members of the Women's Association and of the Youth League. Some young women were also recruited into more selective small organizations, such as the Youth Scientific Research Team or the village troupe that combined traditional entertainment with political propaganda. Although female members had to quit once they married, there were always eight to ten young women active in the performing group. The troupe also served as a center of popular culture for village youth and as a model for young women in particular, before it was replaced by television sets and music cassettes in the post-collective era.

After decollectivization in 1983, the Youth League, the Women's Association, and other village organizations gradually stopped functioning, and organized public activities declined rapidly. In the 1990s government-sponsored public activities ended. Young women, along with other age groups, found themselves returning home and working on family farms individually. The shrinking public sphere and the disappearance of public activities no doubt constitute a drawback for young women in terms of participation in public life. However, other new developments sustain the growth of girl power.

The most important development in the post-collective era are the new opportunities to work in the cities. The state began to loosen its ban on rural-urban migration in 1981–82, which allowed villagers to seek employment and temporary residence in cities in 1985 (Li 1993:110–11). Since then, millions of villagers have moved to cities every year; by 1993, the number of rural migrants to the cities was estimated to exceed 100 million. Village youth of both sexes constitute the main body of this great wave of internal migration (Yan 1994). In Xiajia, 81 young people worked outside the village for at least more than three months in 1991; in 1993 this figure had increased to 142. Among the village youth who went to work in the cities, slightly less than one-third were young women, for whom urban employment opened a new world, seeing life styles that are unheard of in the village. They have also been exposed to the ideas and information that grew rapidly in the cities after the state relaxed its tight control over popular culture. In addition, most young women were able to save a large portion of their wages for their dowries. More important, along with the gradual improvement of living standards in the village, the new generation of youth has shifted from seeking temporary work in cities and earning money for basic needs to exploring the world beyond the village and experiencing a different life. This is particularly true for young women, as fewer of them still need to make important economic contributions to their natal families in the late 1990s.

A second new development has been the emergence of a youth culture in village society and the increased influence of one's peer group.[5] By the 1990s, rural youth had their own cultural tastes and life aspirations quite different from those of their parents and older siblings. Accordingly, rural youth also now have their own social space where they interact with their peers and where older villagers feel uncomfortable and unwelcome, such as the pool tables and dance parties (Yan 1999). For example, two shop owners in Xiajia village began to sponsor regular dance parties in their courtyards in 1994, hoping to attract more young customers. Now young men and women hang out there in the evenings, and such activities have sometimes led to courtship and marriage. Although some parents were strongly opposed to the dance parties, they could do nothing to stop the practice because the village party secretary, who is in his mid-thirties, was also a frequent participant. Other forms of youth culture continued to emerge and thrive. The latest one is a small Internet Bar that was opened inside a village shop in the summer of 2006, in which young men and young women play games and chat on line with six computer stations. Two young women told me that they often chat on line with friends they met when they worked in cities.

The Mobility of Young Women, Courtship, and Marriage

Young rural women have enjoyed more advantages than their male counterparts in courtship and marriage since the 1949 revolution. This female superiority is best illustrated in their power to reject marriage proposals and to renege on engagement agreements, which acts are rare for young men. It also reflects the fact that young women introduced ganzhe which enabled them to take full control of marriage transactions, while young men have not achieved anything close to this. While the value of young women as laborers increased during the collective era (Parish and Whyte 1978), this cannot explain why they have continued to have the edge over young men after decollectivization.

Another contributing factor may be young women's greater mobility under the household registration system. Since the late 1950s, the household registration system divided the Chinese population into rural and urban residents, but only urban residents could enjoy a variety of state social welfare benefits. The legal ban on rural-urban migration confined villagers to their own communities, making it impossible for a villager to achieve the higher status of an urban resident. Moreover, due to the economic inequalities between regions and even between villages, it was also extremely difficult for villagers to move to better regions. Potter and Potter (1990:306–07) note that serving in the armed forces, becoming a party cadre, obtaining a higher education, or marrying a worker with an urban registration status were the few possible avenues of villager mobility. They also point out that the first three opportunities were rare and overwhelmingly available only for males (Potter and Potter 1990). Marriage, on the other hand, was a much more common and accessible opportunity for rural young women, due to patrilocal residence.

Although there were no laws or regulations against a husband moving into his wife's community after marriage, it was women who customarily relocated through marriage. By the same token, a local community had no right to refuse accepting an in-marrying woman, even if she was from a much poorer community. This meant that a young woman could choose to better her life by looking for a husband from a more prosperous village. In fact, the general economic conditions of a potential husband's village constituted an important concern for many young women when they made decisions regarding marriage. Once young women began to marry out to better places, young men in the community had to look for brides from villages that were economically worse off than their own. In other words, young women could move up in the hierarchy of residential communities (determined first by the rural-urban dichotomy and then by the economic conditions of each settlement) by marrying into better communities, while men had to take women from the lower levels of the same hierarchy. As Xiajia village is a relatively better off place, it only suffers from losing women to the nearby market town and the county seat, while receiving women from many other villages. Young women are also in a more advantageous position than young men in marriage, for they can always choose to marry up, while young men have to work hard to avoid marrying down.

THE LIMITATIONS TO GIRL POWER

During the past five decades, several generations of young women have exploited social changes brought about by state policies and socialist practices to alter their position in the domestic sphere from statusless outsiders to new players in family politics, an important phenomenon that I call the rise of girl power. Favorable social conditions for the rise of girl power include marriage law, family reforms, collective farming, formal education, and the social mobilization of women. However, equally important have been the young women who took advantage of new opportunities to challenge the patriarchal order of family life. Many young women took the initiative in courtship and dating, to explore the previously forbidden area of premarital intimacy. Young women have been particularly active in negotiating marital gifts, especially after the introduction of the new custom of converted bridewealth that allows them to pocket most of the bridewealth. And, to a great extent, the daughter-in-law now determines the duration of post-marital residence and the power balance across generational lines in a stem family.

An emphasis on young women in this study by no means indicates the lack of agency of rural young men. Young women alone could not have made all these changes, and as far as the shifting power balance between the senior and junior generations is concerned, there is usually a supportive fiancé/husband behind each powerful young woman. In most cases of dispute or conflict between a young woman and her parents-in-law, the young woman can count on her husband's support (Yan 2003). In marriage negations, it is also common that a young man encourages his girlfriend to request a higher amount of bridewealth from his parents, or request early family division even before their marriage. In this sense, girl power is merely a manifestation of youth power, which constitutes, as I argued previously (Yan 1999, 2003), one of the most profound social changes in rural China since the 1949 revolution.

Nevertheless, mostly due to their previous marginality, young women have been particularly receptive to new family ideals based on gender equality, and more active in pursuing autonomy and independence in the domestic sphere than their male counterparts. Their rising power has also been more effective in challenging and changing the existing patriarchal hierarchy.

It should be noted that the traditional Chinese family was designed so that most, if not all, duties and obligations in everyday life fell on the shoulders of the daughter-in-law, and thus, for all pragmatic concerns, her status had to be kept low and her agency could not be awakened. This is why the development of agency and individuality among young women could give a fatal blow to the patriarchal family. As a witty villager put it, "When the daughter-in-law enters the family home, the father's power is knocked down" (*erxifu yi jin jiamen, fuquan jiu bei dadao*).

There are, however, two major limitations to the further development of girl power, both of which relate to young women's previous marginal and temporal status in private life. First, girl power grows out of the wider social context whereby the power balance is shifting from the senior generation to the junior generation in the domestic sphere, and it challenges patriarchal power instead of androcentric power. Because of this, girl power has not brought about radical changes in gender equality. In all areas – mate-choice, marriage negotiation, and family division – girl power mainly reflects a young woman's ability to impose her will on her prospective or actual parents-in-law, such as with bridewealth or early family division. Young women have altered the traditional expectation of virtuous daughters-in-law and the earlier unfair treatment of new daughters-in-law. In their own natal families, however, young women rarely challenged their parents except in the matter of mate-choice, which is justified by their economic contributions to their natal families. Precisely because girl power mainly poses a threat only to prospective in-laws, young women can easily pursue their goals without much resistance from their own parents or even from their prospective husbands. In other words, young women's challenge to patriarchal power is realized when they physically move from their own natal families to those of their husbands and as they socially transform themselves from daughters to daughters-in-law. In this sense, girl power is actually the power of young women as new daughters-in-law, and it is limited to the cross-family, inter-generational dimensions of domestic life.

Because it challenges only the patriarchal power of one's in-laws, girl power has another limitation, its temporality. Once young women achieve their goals of acquiring a larger bridewealth, keeping the property under their control, and establishing their own independent households via an early family division, they tend to become increasingly conservative. Gradually they merge into their roles as mothers and then mothers-in-law and thus transform themselves once again, becoming the supporters and protectors of existing family values and patriarchal power. This traditional pattern is captured by the popular saying, *"duonian de xifu aocheng po"* (meaning that after years of suffering as a daughter-in-law, one finally becomes a mother-in-law). However, an important difference since the 1980s is that the power balance has irreversibly shifted to the junior generation, and the next generation of young women is bound to be more self-confident and powerful in pursuing individual interests and initiating changes in family life. Being a mother-in-law in the 1990s often means nothing more than being the target of girl power. Thus, the transition from daughter-in-law to mother-in-law also represents a change from empowerment to powerlessness for an individual young woman. Nevertheless, girl power as a social phenomenon is still on the rise.

NOTES

1. This article is based on fieldwork supported by the Wenner-Gren Foundation for Anthropological Research, and a 2003–04 Fellowship from the American Council of Learned Societies. My thanks to Professor Leonard Plotnicov and anonymous reviewers for their valuable comments on the early draft.
2. For details about the history and current state of the community, see Yan (1996, 2003).
3. The last case of an arranged marriage against a young woman's wishes took place in 1971.
4. For an account of early experiments, see Ocko (1991) and Yang (1965).
5. See Yan (1999) for the growth of youth culture in the rural context over the past five decades.

BIBLIOGRAPHY

Baker, H. 1979. *Chinese Family and Kinship*. Columbia University Press.

Bossen, L. 2002. *Chinese Women and Rural Development: Sixty years of Change in Lu Village, Yunnan*. Rowman & Littlefield Publishers, Inc.

Chan, A., R. Madsen and J. Unger. 1992 [1984]. *Chen Village under Mao and Deng*. University of California Press.

Cohen, M. L. 1976. *House United, House Divided: The Chinese Family in Taiwan*. Columbia University Press.

—— 1992. Family Management and Family Division in Contemporary Rural China. *China Quarterly* 130:357–77.

—— 1999. North China Rural Families: Changes During the Communist Era. *Etudes Chionises* 27(1–2):59–153.

Davis, D., and S. Harrell (eds.). 1993. *Chinese Families in the Post-Mao Era*. University of California Press.

Diamant, N. 2000. *Revolutionizing the Family: Politics, Love, and Divorce in Urban and Rural China*. University of California Press.

Freedman, M. 1966. *Chinese Lineage and Society: Fukien and Kwangtung*. Athlone.

Johnson, K. A. 1983. *Women, the Family, and Peasant Revolution in China.* Chicago University Press.

Lavely, W., and X. Ren. 1992. Patrilocality and Early Marital Co-residence in Rural China, 1955–85. *China Quarterly* 130:378–91.

Li Q. 1993. *Dangdai Zhongguo shehui fenceng yu liudong (Social Stratification and Mobility in Contemporary China).* Zhongguo jingji chubanshe.

Parish, W., and M. Whyte. 1978. *Village and Family in Contemporary China.* University of Chicago Press.

Ocko, J. K. 1991. Women, Property, and the Law in the People's Republic of China. *Marriage and Inequality in Chinese Society*, eds. R. Watson and P. Ebrey, pp. 313–46. University of California Press.

Potter, S. H., and J. M. Potter. 1990. *China's Peasants: The Anthropology of a Revolution.* Cambridge University Press.

Stacey, J. 1983. *Patriarchy and Socialist Revolution in China.* University of California Press.

Selden, M. 1993. Family Strategies and Structures in Rural North China. *Chinese Families in the Post-Mao Era*, eds. D. Davis and S. Harrell, pp. 139–64. University of California Press.

Thornton, A., and T. Fricke. 1987. Social Change and the Family: Comparative Perspectives from the West, China, and South Asia. *Sociological Forum* 2(4):746–79.

Watson, R. 1985. *Inequality among Brothers, Class, and Kinship in South China.* Cambridge University Press.

——— 1986. *The Named and the Nameless: Gender and Person in Chinese Society.* American Ethnologist 13(4):619–31.

Wolf, M. 1972. *Women and the Family in Rural Taiwan.* Stanford University Press.

Xu A. (ed.). 1997. *Shiji zhe jiao Zhongguoren de aiqing he hunyin (Love and Marriage among Chinese at the Turn of the Century).* Zhongguo shehui kexue chubanshe.

Yan, Y. 1994. Dislocation, Reposition, and Restratification: Structural Changes in Chinese Society. *China Review*, eds. M. Brosseau and L. C. Kin, pp. 15.1–24. The Chinese University Press.

——— 1996. *The Flow of Gifts: Reciprocity and Social Networks in a Chinese Village.* Stanford University Press.

Yan, Y. 1999. Rural Youth and Youth Culture in North China. *Culture, Medicine, and Psychiatry* 23:75–97.

——— 2001. Practicing Kinship in Rural North China. *Relative Values: Reconfiguring Kinship Studies*, eds. S. McKinnon and S. Franklin, pp. 224–43. Duke University Press.

Yan, Y. 2003. *Private Life Under Socialism: Love, Intimacy, and Family Change in a Chinese Village, 1949–1999.* Sanford University Press.

Yang, C. K. 1959. *The Chinese Family in the Communist Revolution.* MIT Press.

—— 1965. *Chinese Communist Society: The Family and the Village.* MIT Press.

CHAPTER 7

THE INDIVIDUAL AND TRANSFORMATION
OF BRIDEWEALTH

With few exceptions, anthropologists treat the exchange of marital gifts as a collective strategy employed by the elders of two corporate groups through which 'households attempt to adjust labor needs, the transmission of property, and status concerns' (Schlegel & Eloul 1988: 305). This is particularly true of the institution of bridewealth since it is regarded as both reflecting and shaping the corporate structure of unilineal descent groups (see Goody 1973; Harrell & Dickey 1985) as well as, from a political economy perspective, being the outcome of the prevailing mode of production (Gates 1996; Meillassoux 1981). Such an emphasis on the collective and corporate aspects of bridewealth transfer derives from the received wisdom that marriage in traditional societies is not a personal affair between two individuals but instead involves two kin groups (lineages or families) and thus constitutes a community (public) event. Accordingly, the role of individual agency in marriage transfers rarely warrants serious scholarly scrutiny, and the bride and groom as flesh-and-bone individuals are normally absent in ethnographic accounts of bridewealth or dowry. However, along with the rise of youth autonomy in mate choice, the nuclearization of the family, and the decline of parental power and authority, marriage transactions will inevitably undergo radical changes, and, according to a widely accepted theory of family change, bridewealth should eventually fade away (see Goode 1963).

Anthropologists have also fallen short in theorizing about rapid changes in the systems of marriage transactions that occurred during the twentieth century in many parts of the world. Most ethnographic accounts dealing with changes in marriage transactions try to explain the changing size and content of African bridewealth systems in terms of the impact of the market economy or labour migration (see, e.g., Buggenhagen 2001; Grosz-Ngate 1988); others reduce the complexity of marriage transactions to a simple consideration of cost and benefit in exchange (Bell & Song 1994). A noteworthy exception is the bargaining model offered by Ensminger and Knight (1997), who argue that the rising power of the young generation and the new alternative offered by Islamic ideology changed the social norms of bridewealth among the Orma in Kenya. Despite the centrality of game theory and rational choice in their model, however, Ensminger and Knight still regard the bride's and the groom's families as the basic units of marriage negotiations and property transfers, paying little attention to the agency of individual brides and grooms in the process.

Ethnographic evidence from rural north China reveals the importance of the role of the individual and the transformation of marriage transactions for anthropological studies of contemporary practices of marriage and kinship. Whereas village youth have gained power and independence in mate choice, marriage negotiations, and post-marital residence, the custom of bridewealth remains intact, with the standard value of bridewealth increasing more than tenfold since the 1980s. More importantly, it is now the bride, not her parents, who receives the bridewealth and, working together with the groom, she takes the lead in bargaining for the highest possible amount of bridewealth from the groom's parents, often pushing the parents deeply into debt. To justify their demands for lavish bridewealth, village youth resort to the notion of individual property rights and the rhetoric of individualism, effectively transforming the bridewealth institution into a new form of property division.

What makes the Chinese case even more intriguing is that the socialist state has made repeated efforts to restrict the practice of bridewealth as part of its attempt to modernize the Chinese family. Marriage payments were legally banned as early as 1950, and various education and political campaigns were launched to attack the feudal custom of bridewealth from the 1950s to the 1990s (Croll 1981, Parish & Whyte 1978). The most recent example is the socialist spiritual civilization campaign in the late 1980s and early 1990s, in which, as Kim (n.d.) documents, bridewealth was targeted as one of the major feudal customs to be eliminated. Admittedly, the Chinese state is not alone in its effort to reform the custom of bridewealth for the sake of modernization. Muslim and French colonial authorities tried to limit the circulation of bridewealth in Senegal (Buggenhagen 2001: 386), and the government of Mali enacted a law to reduce the value of marriage transactions (Grosz-Ngate 1988: 511). Nowhere else, however, has the state been so committed to changing the traditional patterns of marriage or has it invested such great political and economic resources. This is because the Chinese state regards marriage reform as part of the socialist transformation of society, an important goal of the communist revolution (Croll 1981). In addition, the state used its entire propaganda apparatus to condemn Western individualism as the selfish and corrupt ideology of the capitalist class in order to promote collectivism and construct the new socialist person (Wang 2002).

Ironically, by the end of the twentieth century, the state seemed to have failed on both fronts, as high bridewealth and lavish dowries reappeared all over rural China, and the centrality of individual interest was celebrated by the majority of Chinese youth. The transformation of bridewealth reflects the negotiations between individual villagers and a powerful state over the meaning of marital gifts and personhood.

The present study is based on fifteen years of fieldwork in Xiajia village, Heilongjiang province, northeast China.[1] With a population of 1,492 in 1998, the village had been fairly successful in collective farming before the implementation of decollectivization in the early 1980s and it remains a farming community today. Heavy reliance on farming has been a major obstacle to village economic development, keeping average per capita income slightly below the national average during the 1980s and 1990s. Yet the villagers' livelihood has been closely tied to the market through cash crops farming, household sideline business, labour migration, and the impacts of mass media and urban consumerism. By the late 1990s, labour migration was the most important channel of cash income, and an increasing number of unmarried young women had joined the labour force, accounting for about one-third of the out-migrant seasonal workers.

In Xiajia village and the surrounding areas, marriage negotiations usually result in the writing of a formal engagement contract called the *caili dan* ('list of betrothal gifts'). This contract, two copies of which are produced during the engagement ritual, records all marital gifts for a given marriage. During my 1991 fieldwork, I collected fifty-one engagement contracts across several decades and conducted structured interviews with their owners to gather background information. I updated the data using the same methods during subsequent fieldwork in 1994, 1997, 1999, and 2004.

The present study consists of two parts. First, I will briefly review the changing practice of bridewealth in Xiajia village over five decades, examining the active role of the bride and groom in the marriage negotiation. It should be noted that the local system of marriage transactions also involves a dowry which too has undergone changes, but this study focuses only on bridewealth (for details see Yan 1996: 176–209). Second, I analyse multiple factors that have contributed to the transformation of bridewealth, situating the role of individual agency in the context of social changes in both the domestic and public spheres, which are closely related to the prevailing state ideology of modernization and the national policies of family reform.

THE TRANSFORMATION FROM BRIDEWEALTH TO THE WEALTH OF THE BRIDE

In Chinese societies, marriage transactions involve both bridewealth and dowry, although dowries are often subsidized through the bridewealth paid by the groom's family to the bride's family (Cohen 1976; Watson 1984), a complicated practice characterized by Jack Goody (1973) as 'indirect dowry'. Referring to the different types of marriage transactions in Chinese culture, Hill Gates criticizes the concept of indirect dowry as a counterproductive simplification of diversified practices across the boundaries of class, region, and time (1996: 134–5). Indeed, the prescriptive definitions of scholarly terms sometimes fail to capture the rich meanings of local practices. A closer look at the content and destination of marital gifts in local practice shows that neither 'bridewealth' nor 'indirect dowry' expresses the full meanings of marital gifts offered by the groom's family, because both anthropological terms, by definition, refer only to properties exchanged between the groom's and bride's families, overlooking that which is transferred across generations within the same household.

The Changing Local Practice of Bridewealth

According to Xiajia villagers, marriage transactions provided by the groom's parents are called *caili*, literally meaning 'colourful gifts', but better translated as 'marital gifts'. When asked what constitutes *caili*, villagers always replied: money and goods. The monetary gifts were presented by the groom's family to the bride's family, constituting what anthropologists call bridewealth. Ideally, the bridewealth was supposed to be used by the bride's parents to subsidize the dowry, but they can decide how much to retain to meet other family needs. The material gifts include a great variety of goods, such as furniture, beddings, and major appliances. It is the responsibility of the groom's family to purchase the material gifts that will furnish the conjugal chamber. Because these material gifts do not move between two families and are meant to be used by the newlywed couple as a conjugal unit, I refer to them as the 'conjugal endowment'. In other words, the local practice of marital gifts by the groom's family includes the inter-family betrothal gifts and the intra-family conjugal endowment. Table 1 summarizes their changing composition from the 1950s to the 1990s.

Table I   Marriage finances by the groom's family, 1950–99 (RMB yuan)

Periods	BM	T	PRS	CB	F	B	MA	CE	Total expenses
1950–4	200								200
1955–9	280								280
1960–4	300	100	20			50			470
1965–9	200	300	20			100	120		740
1970–4	300	300	50		70	100	150		970
1975–9	400	400	200		200	200	300		1,700
1980–4	400	700	300		500	300	500		2,700
1985–9				4,500	1,000	800	1,000		7,300
1990–4				7,200				4,000	11,200
1995–9				20,000				8,500	28,500

Key: BM = betrothal money (liqian); T = trousseau (mai dongxi qian); PRS = payment for ritual service (zhuangyan qian); CB = converted bridewealth (ganzhe); F = furniture; B = bedding; MA = major appliances (dajian); and CE = converted endowment (ganzhe).

The content of bridewealth in the 1950s was simple, including only a sum of cash called *liqian* and a set of routine gifts such as foods and wine. The routine gifts were not subject to negotiation and were not entered into the formal engagement contract. The Chinese word *liqian* literally means 'ritual money', but a better translation is 'betrothal money' since the term ritual in this context refers to the engagement ceremony. Ideally, the betrothal money is to subsidize the bride's parents' preparation of the dowry, including the trousseau items. Nevertheless, throughout the 1950s and 1960s it was not unusual for parents to use the betrothal money to pay for a son's marriage. Since the betrothal money was controlled by the bride's parents, a higher bridewealth often benefited the parents instead of the bride.

From the 1960s to the 1970s, to cope with the increasing pressure against traditional marriage transactions during a series of political campaigns, including the Cultural Revolution, several new categories of betrothal gifts were devised to benefit the bride directly. The first was called *mai dongxi qian* ('money to buy things'), which I translate as 'trousseau money', to purchase clothes, shoes, and other minor items for the bride. As an attempt to reform the custom of bridewealth, the trousseau money, however, was not given to the bride's parents. The groom's family directly used the money to buy the trousseau items, which were then sent to the bride's family to give to the bride.

Second, the 'money for filling the pipe' (*zhuangyan qian*) was given directly and exclusively to the bride for her service of filling the tobacco pipes of her senior in-laws during the wedding. I refer to this as 'payment for ritual service'. Like the trousseau money, the amount of this gift increased considerably during the late 1970s and early 1980s. In addition, the groom's family eventually relinquished control over the purchase of the trousseau items to the young couple. These developments reflect the increasing importance of the bride in marriage transactions.

Beginning in the mid-1980s – shortly after the collectives were dismantled and villagers resumed household farming – all monetary gifts were subsumed under a new category – *ganzhe*, referring to the conversion of material goods into monetary terms. In the context of marriage transactions, *ganzhe* implies the conversion of the three categories of betrothal gifts into a lump sum of cash. The total amount was recorded on the engagement contract and the cash was given directly to the bride during the engagement ritual. Hereafter I refer to *ganzhe* as 'converted betrothal gifts'.

Similar changes occurred in the provision of material gifts by the groom's family. During the 1950s, only very basic bedding items were supplied by the bride's family as part of her dowry. The demands for material goods for the conjugal unit began in the late 1960s and grew rapidly in the 1970s. Furniture was added as a necessary part of marriage expenses, as well as demands for the well-known 'four big items' (bicycle, sewing machine, wristwatch, and radio).

More items were added to the conjugal endowment throughout the 1980s, and by the early 1990s the bride was requesting that all material gifts be converted into cash. Following the earlier model of *ganzhe* money (the converted betrothal gifts), the cash was given to the bride herself. Villagers call the new practice *daganzhe* (meaning 'grand conversion'), which includes all the previous categories of bridewealth; accordingly, I use the term 'converted bridewealth' to describe the current practice of grand conversion. By the end of the 1990s the converted bridewealth regularly included a new house and sometimes important means of production, such as a small tractor or a dairy cow.

Thus, over the past five decades marriage finances provided by the groom's family evolved from a simple, single category of betrothal money into six categories of monetary and material gifts. At the end of the 1990s, the six-category system was transformed to the simple single category of *daganzhe*. The creation of each new category was indicative of the emergence of a new relationship in marriage transactions and constituted an important step in the ongoing process of change. Moreover, despite the party-state's severe criticism of bridewealth, average expenditure per marriage climbed from 200 yuan in 1950 to 50,000 yuan in 1999 (including a new house), and, as I discovered in January 2004, it had exceeded 60,000 yuan by the end of 2003.

However, the practice of high bridewealth does not always imply 'marriage by purchase', as is argued by the official media. The bride's parents do not necessarily benefit from the rise in bridewealth. In fact, the recent rise in marriage payments in Xiajia village resulted mainly from the creation of new categories of bridewealth that privileged the bride. Moreover, the practice of *ganzhe* (converted bridewealth) has impaired the inter-household exchange, undermined parental power in marriage transactions, and reduced the importance of the affinal relationship between in-laws of the senior generation. The organizational principles that are articulated through the practice of converted bridewealth centre on the notion of conjugality instead of patriliny. Furthermore, the innovation of *ganzhe* enables the bride to have direct control over the marriage finances provided by the grooms family, which practically transformed bridewealth into the wealth of the bride in a literal sense. The wealth of the bride strengthens her post-marital status as she uses the wealth as the most important fund for the new conjugal family; consequently, gender dynamics in family life have also changed to a great extent among young villagers who married during the 1980s and 1990s (see Yan 2003: 86–111).

The Bride in Bridewealth

As the direct beneficiary of the transformation of bridewealth, the bride, since the mid-1980s, has been motivated to participate actively in the negotiation of the marriage transactions. In a case I witnessed in July 1991, the toughest negotiator at the engagement table was the prospective bride. She insisted on a *ganzhe* gift of 5,500 yuan even though the groom's family had only offered 4,000 yuan. By the time she returned from the engagement ceremony she had already pocketed 3,000 yuan and expected to receive the balance prior to the wedding.

In another striking example, a bride wanted the grain-processing factory of the groom's family to be included on her bridewealth list. The groom in this case had an unmarried brother, and, in the end, each son received half-ownership of the factory. New and unconventional items continued to be added to the list of betrothal gifts throughout the 1990s, such as a plot of land, a dairy cow, or a tractor. The inclusion of the means of production into bridewealth shows that the ultimate intention of the couple is to accumulate a productive fund for their conjugal family.

The ever-increasing demand for lavish bridewealth often caused conflicts over the redistribution of family property between young women and their in-laws. In one of the most dramatic cases, in 2003 a daughter-in-law demanded that her parents-in-law pay her a matching fund after she realized that the fiancée of her younger brother-in-law was about to receive 4,000 yuan more than she had received two years ago. The parents-in-law rejected her request on the grounds that the 4,000 yuan difference was due to the 'natural inflation' of bridewealth (which is true). This began a period of disputes and fights in the household, and when I revisited the village in 2004 she was still not on speaking terms with her parents-in-law.

The deeper motivation for young women to pursue costly bridewealth is to build for the future prosperity of the conjugal family, bride and groom together. Thus, there is usually a supportive groom behind each aggressive bride during the negotiation with his parents. According to a well-known story in the village, in 1989 a young man encouraged his girlfriend to demand a large amount of bridewealth from his parents. He told the girl: 'Just be tough. Ask for 4,000 yuan in *ganzhe*, and don't bargain.

Otherwise, you won't be able to get any money from my mothers pocket'. In the end, the couple got all they demanded and, only a few months after their wedding, they left the groom's family to establish their own household. This case is no longer extraordinary because recently many young couples have acted similarly without revealing their true intentions. This means that young villagers now begin planning their conjugal family as early as courtship.

The Rhetoric of Individualism

On the surface, the scarcity of economic resources appears to be the root of these problems. By the end of the 1990s, average household annual income in Xiajia village was approximately 6,500 yuan, yet the average cost of a marriage for the groom's family was about 50,000 yuan, including both the converted bridewealth and the new house for the newlyweds. Even without any consumption expenses, an average family needed to work for more than seven years to be able to pay for a son's marriage. If a family had two or more sons, the entire household economy would be tied down by marriage expenses for twenty years or more. Sibling rivalry often developed into open hostility as competition intensified by escalating demands for lavish bridewealth for each couple.

Economic scarcity, however, is more a perceived problem than a real cause of the competition for large bridewealth. As a number of older villagers noted, their families were much poorer when they were married but their parents could still provide the bridewealth because they were not as greedy as the contemporary youth. In their time, it was scandalous for a bride to set the terms of the bridewealth; instead the parents on both sides negotiated a reasonable amount.

In contrast, the current generation has a much stronger sense of entitlement for bridewealth and better housing, claiming that they had made contributions to the family economy and what they were requesting in the form of bridewealth was their due. As several young couples explained, the family is like a production team with a collective bank account; each person makes a contribution to the family economy in the same way one makes a deposit in a bank account. Therefore, their bridewealth is nothing more than the withdrawal of their own deposits. Moreover, because they will not receive anything else under the new form of family division (more on this below), bridewealth is their only chance to recover their deposits.

Several articulate youth also resorted to an assertion of individuality to justify their demand for larger bridewealth, insisting that they were merely exercising their individual rights to recover their deposits in the family estate and this was a matter of personal freedom and independence (*geren ziyou he duli*) or of having individuality (*you gexing*). When asked what was meant by 'having individuality', a 22-year-old woman with a secondary school education replied:

You gexing is to do whatever you want to do and not to care what others think of you. This is a must in today's world because people are mean and competitive. For example, when I asked my parents-in-law for a *ganzhe* of 36,000 yuan two years ago, many people accused me of being a selfish money-grubber and warned me not to hurt the feelings of my future parents-in-law. My inlaws even sent someone try to persuade my parents. I did not care what the others said and I got the money. Look what has happened since then – I have a lovely son, two dairy cows, all the modern appliances in my house, and a good husband who listens to me! My parents-in-law respect me and often help me with household chores. I would not be able to have all this had I not had individuality (*you gexing*). Girls in our village all admire me.

My subsequent interviews with seven young man and women in early 2004 proved that this young woman was not boasting at all – she is indeed widely regarded as a strong and modern woman with individuality (*gexing*) and they also agreed that having *gexing* is the best way to realize the goal of family modernization (*jiating xiandaihua*). According to them, being able to outdo one's peers in terms of a lavish bridewealth is an important marker defining one's individuality and success. Interestingly, those with a better education or experience working in cities openly claimed that the aggressive pursuit for monetary and material objects showed the strength of one's *gexing* or individuality. The two individuals who had no experience of city life and had not finished primary school were reluctant to define *gexing* in this way and viewed selfishness as a serious moral flaw. Although these individual testimonies are too few to have any statistical significance, they probably show the influence of what Macpherson (1962) calls 'possessive individualism'[2] from the outside world, mostly from the market economy and an urban lifestyle.

The young villagers' self-claimed individuality became problematic when I brought up these issues with the parents who had paid the converted bridewealth during the 1990s. They all dismissed as unfounded the young villagers' justification of withdrawing their own deposits. According to these informants, a healthy and hard-working male labourer in the village earns an average of 3,000 yuan per year. Assuming that he starts to work full-time at the age of 17 and marries at age 23, he will make only 18,000 yuan during these six years, not counting his consumption expenses. 'Even if my son had not eaten anything for six years,' reasoned a 51-year-old father during an interview in 1999, 'the money he earned would still be less than one-third of the 52,000 yuan I spent on his marriage last year'.

Who makes up for the difference between the average accumulated income of 18,000 yuan that a young man can earn by the time of his marriage and the approximately 50,000 yuan required for his marriage? The answer is the family group, including parents and younger siblings. The newlywed couple are unable to repay any of this because they customarily move out of the groom's parents' house to set up their own conjugal household shortly after their wedding, thus no longer contributing to the parents' household economy. According to the villagers, among younger siblings, sisters contribute much more than they recover in the form of dowry, but they will eventually get even by demanding higher bridewealth from their parents-in-law. The youngest brother may end up in a disadvantageous position because the pool of family income will have been considerably diminished by the time of his marriage; his only way to compensate for this is to ask for even more bridewealth. In this case, the parents will have to borrow a significant amount of money to pay for the bridewealth and, according to current practices, will be responsible for repaying the resultant debts.

Equipped with this simple economic rendering of the bridewealth transaction, I returned to the young villagers and pointed out that, without the help of their parents and younger siblings, they might not be able to get married at all, much less be independent. Most agreed, but quite a few added that it was their parents' and younger siblings' duty, just as they had helped their elder brothers. In other words, these young villagers believe that their parents are obligated to support them financially but have no right to interfere with their autonomy in mate choice and postmarital residence.

UNDERSTANDING THE TRANSFORMATION: THE INDIVIDUAL, THE FAMILY AND THE STATE

The Xiajia case calls for a careful reconsideration of most existing anthropological accounts of bridewealth because they overlook the role of the agency of the individual brides and grooms. A mere recognition of the rising power of rural youth, however, cannot explain the continuing importance of the traditional custom of bridewealth in contemporary household economy. In other words, why has the rise of youth autonomy in marriage choice and marriage transactions not eliminated the custom of bridewealth once and for all, as modernist theory predicts?

To understand better the transformation of bridewealth, one cannot separate the macro and micro causes. It is often the combined consequences of social changes at both levels that result in the new social norm. Moreover, it often takes a particular type of individual at a particular historical moment to break the old norms and to establish new norms; individuality and individual agency thus become a crucial link between the macro and the micro.

Agency, Psychology and Individualism

The first *ganzhe* case occurred in 1984 when a young woman in the village demanded that her betrothal gifts be converted into a lump sum; she then pocketed the cash and spent only a small proportion of the money to prepare for her wedding. This unprecedented behaviour was regarded by many as scandalous.

This woman was motivated to make such a bold request because her husband-to-be had four unmarried brothers and the economic status of his family was below average. Although she too came from a poor and low-prestige family, she was smart, confident, and quite individualistic by local standards. The young couple had grown up together, and by the time of their engagement her future husband was already very dependent on her to make decisions. In the end, the groom's family complied with her demands because their son was afraid of losing her.

This new and strange settlement of the bridewealth deal between the bride and the grooms family, however, was the centre of village gossip for only a short while because villagers regarded this case as too abnormal to be taken seriously. What the villagers did not expect was that in the following year, 1985, rumour had it that no land would be allocated for house construction. Those planning marriages at that time worried about not being allocated a plot of their own; following the 1984 *ganzhe* model that was still fresh in their minds, many grooms suggested that their brides ask only for cash as betrothal gifts. This was then used by the couple to purchase construction materials. Once they had construction materials, the village office would allocate them a plot of land. Parents on both sides welcomed this plan because they too were worried about the impact of the new policies. As a result, converted bridewealth (*ganzhe*) rapidly became popular and has continued to this day. By the summer of 1997, most villagers with whom I spoke regarded converted bridewealth as a normal practice.

This short history of *ganzhe* or converted bridewealth shows that the social position of the first challenger to the existing social norm and the timing of her challenge are important to understand changes in social norms. The young woman in 1984 was successful not only because she had the upper hand in dealing with her in-laws but also because the marginal position of both families enabled her to avoid social sanctions. The public did not react strongly because the defiant behaviour of a marginal individual or family could hardly have any impact on social norms, which were normally guarded by the more well-respected individuals in well-to-do families. Nevertheless, the young woman's bold act actually realized a long-held wish shared by many young women who, for various reasons, had not dared to make such a request. Thereafter, many young women followed her lead by demanding complete control over the transaction and consumption of bridewealth.

At the level of individual psychology, the rhetoric of utilitarian individualism that village youth obtained through mass media and urban experiences helped them legitimize their pursuit of lavish bridewealth. The first woman who requested *ganzhe* in 1984 was called *zisi* or selfish, as were other individuals who subsequently raised the amount of bridewealth through marriage negotiations, refused to practice the customary post-marital co-residence with the husbands' parents, or fought with siblings over the redistribution of family wealth (see Yan 2003: 140–61). Nevertheless, in one way or another, they were able to shrug off the moral criticism and continue their unconventional and materialistic pursuits against the interest of their parents. As they eventually received the material rewards and remained unharmed in terms of their reputations and social standing, they became role models for others in the community.

Interestingly, over the past two decades, the sanctioning power of accusing someone of being selfish has become insignificant, because village youths now regard selfishness as a necessity for success in the market economy. Contemporary youths justify their behaviour in terms of *you gexing* (having individuality), *xiandaide* (being modern), and possess *duli he ziyou* (independence and freedom).

During my 2004 visit to Xiajia village, I asked my young informants to define *gerenzhuyi* (individualism) and to evaluate its role in their lives. Individualism was commonly defined as being selfish (*zisi*) or being able to do whatever one pleased. Most informants thought individualism or selfishness was not good yet definitely necessary for survival, while two or three openly praised it as morally good because it promotes one's individuality (*gexing*).

The village youths' understanding of individualism as selfishness and their use of individualism to justify their pursuit of lavish bridewealth constitute an interesting contrast to the Western philosophy of individualism, in which the balance between rights and duties is a core value. Modern individualism in the West can be defined in a number of ways depending on one's perspective. Political and religious individualism tends to focus on social contract, liberty, equality, freedom, and self-improvement; economic individualism emphasizes utilitarian pursuits, competition, self-interest, and hedonism (see Dumont 1986; Lukes 1973; Musschenga 2001). Yet independence and self-reliance are the two common basic elements in almost all definitions of individualism, regardless of orientation (Triandis 1995: 31). In a way, a sense of self-reliance is the most important foundation of individualism (Hollan 1992; Macfarlane 1978; Macpherson 1962). Perhaps this is also why there is no such custom of bridewealth in the history of England (see Macfarlane 1986: 277–8). Individualism also includes a self-constraining side that recognizes the equal rights of other individuals and leads to the promotion of other core values, such as equality and liberty. In other words, individualism is not only about the self; it also regulates the relationship between the self and other equal individuals (Dumont 1986; Lukes 1973; Triandis 1995).

It is precisely at this point that the young villagers in Xiajia are not individualistic in the idealized sense of the term because they do not meet the criteria of being self-reliant and self-constraining, as indicated by their argument that the new converted bridewealth is the obligation of parents and younger siblings and that individualism is equated with selfishness. At first glance, their relentless quest for bridewealth resonates with certain elements of modern individualism, such as utilitarian pursuits for self-interest, competition for status, and hedonism. Their pursuit of independence, however, is at the direct expense of the independence of their parents and younger siblings. This perceived absence of self-reliance enables them to feel entitled to extract financial resources from their parents for the sake of their personal happiness and at the same time to claim to be independent and individualistic. The disjunction between independence and self-reliance thus becomes the cornerstone of the utilitarian individualism of these young villagers.

In Western societies, such as the contemporary United States, young people also receive financial aid from parents for a wedding and, more importantly, for a down-payment on a house. However, there are at least three differences. First, few American youth claim that receiving money from their parents is a sign of their independence; instead, they acknowledge it as parental help. Second, parents can decide to help or not to help, because such help is not perceived to be a part of parental duty in American society. Third, the dominant ideology of individualism in the larger society does not encourage youths to extract money from their parents' pockets, nor do they compete with peers in this respect.

In face of the aggressive youths, do parents have their agencies? Why must they forgo parental power but still financially support their adult children? A number of older villagers told me that they were not fooled by the young people's rhetoric and could clearly see their real motivations. Yet they conceded to the young generation because of their 'parental hearts' (*fumuxin*). The local term 'parental heart' implies unlimited parental love and benevolence, which are the strongest motivations for parents to work for their children. No matter how much their children have disappointed them or even abused their love and care, parents are still concerned with their children's well-being. Chief among their concerns is a proper marriage for their children, especially their sons, and they have no choice but to try their best to satisfy their sons' excessive demands for lavish bridewealth.

The local notion of 'parental heart' contains two components: one is emotional and the other is moral. There is no doubt that parental love plays a key role in the parents' altruistic behaviour toward their children, but they are pressured by a special moral obligation, that is, good parents must help their children to marry in style. The task of helping children to marry defines not only parenthood but also the very notion of the person. At a deeper level, the task reveals the most important responsibility of a Chinese person in family life, that is, to assure the continuity of the descent line. Defined as a relational being, the Chinese person is not an autonomous individual by virtue of birth; instead, she/he must fulfil various roles in life to become a full person (see, e.g., King 1985; Kipnis 1997; Yan 1996). This is why parents who help their children to marry in style are always congratulated by fellow villagers for accomplishing the mission (*wancheng renwu*). In contrast, those who have failed in this respect are looked down upon in the community; conversely, adult children can, and some indeed did, accuse their parents of being morally inadequate for not completing the 'task' well.

In other words, at the level of individual psychology, the two generations justify their own behavioural patterns in terms of two different sets of moral discourse, characterized by the self-centred notion of *you gexing* (having individuality) and the family-orientated notion of *fumuxin* (parental heart), respectively. Under the impact of the market economy and the national pursuit of modernization, the modern notion of individuality overshadows the traditional notion of parental heart. The two notions never engaged in debate; instead, they each serve to legitimize the current practice of bridewealth.

Changing Norms of Family Behaviour

The transformation of bridewealth did not occur in isolation; instead, it is related to a number of important changes at the level of family life, among which youth autonomy in mate choice, the new form of family division, and the new dynamics in inter-generational reciprocity are the most noteworthy.[3]

A close examination of 484 marriages entered into by male villagers from 1949 to 1999 in Xiajia village reveals a gradual yet constant shift from arranged marriage to free-choice marriage (see Yan 2003: 42–63). Arranged marriages declined from 73 per cent in the 1950s to none at all in the 1990s; virtually all engagements since the 1970s have been based on mutual consent of two young individuals after a period of romantic love or intensive interactions following an initial introduction through a third party. Moreover, intimacy has become an integral part of the courtship process, and nearly 20 per cent of engaged couples admitted to having engaged in premarital sex by the mid-1990s (Yan 2003: 70).

Moreover, in comparison to their parents and older siblings, village youths of the 1990s tended to be more open and vocal in expressing their emotions to their lovers and/or future spouses and to pay more attention to their future partner's individual characteristics. Pop culture and mass media seem to have had a direct influence on the development of the language of love and intimacy, which both enriches and alters the discourse on an ideal spouse and the practice of courtship. Young women are particularly interested in the intimate and autonomous aspects of courtship; so much so that a young man's ability to converse romantically or to support his wife against his own parents has become the most important traits of an ideal husband (Yan 2003: 64–85).

These changes mean that marriage is no longer a family strategy employed by parents to establish affinal ties or to improve the economic and social status of the household. Parents' failure to arrange their children's marriages is the beginning of loss of control over almost all aspects of family life. Indeed, the transformation of courtship has led to new conflicts between generations because, in the final analysis, intimacy is about the individual, or the gratification of the young couple (see Giddens 1992).

The second important contributing factor to the transformation of bridewealth is the new form in family division. Young couples have been advancing the time of family division since the 1970s, resulting in the rapid nuclearization of the family structure. By 1994, more than 40 per cent of newlywed couples established an independent household within one year after marriage, and nearly 80 per cent of family divisions had occurred within two years of marriage (Yan 2003: 143).

To meet the challenge of early family division, a new form of property distribution evolved, which can be called the 'serial form of family division'. Traditionally, family division occurred after all the sons in a family had married. At that time, the parents would divide the family estate equally among all sons, and then they would live with one married son or they would rotate their residence among all married sons (see Cohen 1976). Under the serial form of family division, the first married son moves out soon after marriage to set up a separate household. The family estate remains undivided because there are still unmarried siblings who need financial support from the family. The younger sons repeat the process, and a family typically undergoes property division several times.

A young couple who leave under this new form of family division are entitled only to their share of the family grain, stock, and cooking fuel as well as personal belongings obtained through bridewealth and dowry. It is thus natural for the couple to negotiate hard for lavish bridewealth because they can claim little other property under the serial form of family division.

At the last serial property division in a family, the parents create their own conjugal fund by retaining all cash savings, conserving their share of the farmland and production tools, and holding on to the family house, unless they had made a deal to live with a married son. This marks a significant departure from the traditional practice whereby the parents were trustees/managers of the family property and with family division they would give up their power of management, leaving them no individual property. The current parental claim of family property indicates that a more individualized perception of family property is emerging among family members of all generations.

The fact that parents want to hold on to their share of family property also reflects their sense of insecurity for old age, which constitutes the third important contributing factor to the transformation of bridewealth. The traditional notion of filial piety lost its ideological and institutional grounds under the attack of radical socialism from the 1950s to the 1970s and then suffered a fatal blow from the values of the market economy that emphasize balanced reciprocity. As a result, contemporary rural youth perceive elderly support from a new perspective of individual achievement and balanced exchange, insisting that they have the right to treat their parents in the same way that they were treated by their parents.

To avoid the possibility of unfavourable judgement from their sons and the unbearable consequences of losing old-age security, many parents have made extra efforts to satisfy their children's various demands. The most common strategy of parental investment in old-age security is to provide the largest possible size of bridewealth because the younger generation regards the value of bridewealth as the most important marker of parental support. Another strategy is to take more active steps to help their married son(s) build up an independent conjugal household so that intergenerational conflicts in everyday life can be avoided. The third parental strategy is, as indicated above, to allow married sons to take away only the moveables generated by their own marriage, keeping the major part of the family property as their own retirement fund in case they cannot rely on their married sons during old age. Unfortunately, all these strategies in seeking old-age security only motivate the young women and men to be more aggressive and demand an even larger size of bridewealth as they perceive it as the only chance to claim their share of the family property legitimately; hence a vicious circle in the escalation of bridewealth.

The above analysis reveals that a social norm rarely changes on its own; more often than not, a change in one norm is accompanied by changes in other norms and, at the same time, re-shapes the other norms as well. For example, the serial form of family division and the escalation of bridewealth seem to reinforce one another; but neither could have taken place without the concomitant youth autonomy in mate choice and the increased intimacy in courtship. Ultimately, all these changing social norms regarding the transaction and distribution of family properties reflect a more fundamental change in the private life sphere, that is, the decline of parental power and authority, on the one hand, and the development of a certain form of individuality, on the other, which are in turn the results of social changes in a larger context.

The State and Social Change at the Macro Level

After the 1949 Revolution, the leaders of the Chinese Communist Party (CCP) were determined to reconstruct the family – the very foundation of Chinese society – thereby creating a new socialist society and a new notion of personhood (Davis & Harrell 1993: 1–10; Yang 1965). Collectivization effectively ended family ownership of land and other means of production. Through the collectives and local government, the state could reach the public and private lives of every peasant household. State-sponsored campaigns were part of social engineering at the national level which aimed to promote collectivism and to shift the loyalty of individual villagers from the family to the collectives and ultimately to the socialist state. Accordingly, it was necessary to destroy the old social and family hierarchy and to reform all associated customs so as to transform villagers from loyal family members into individual citizens.

This led to a twofold result. On the one hand, never before had the family and individuals been exposed to state power and the formal administration system so closely; on the other hand, to a great extent individual villagers were also liberated from the control of the corporate family, kinship organization, and other informal communal powers. The family lost most of its economic, political, and social functions, which in turn led to the decline of parental power and authority (Parish & Whyte 1978; Yan 2003).

The custom of bridewealth and dowry was targeted by the CCP precisely because the traditional system of marriage transactions served to strengthen parental power and kinship organization. The 1950 Marriage Law banned the exaction of money or gifts in connection with marriage, together with concubinage and child marriage; this legal prohibition was re-stated in the 1980 Marriage Law. Although the marriage laws empowered young women and men to pursue freedom in mate choice (see Diamant 2000; Whyte 1995), they were much less effective in eliminating marriage transactions. During the periods of political radicalism, such as the late 1950s and mid-1960s, a small number of violators of the legal ban on bridewealth in Xiajia village were publicly humiliated at mass rallies or deprived political privileges. Yet villagers found ways around the law, by changing the name of betrothal money or adding new categories of gifts for the bride.

To compensate for the rather weak effect of the legal ban on bridewealth, ideological attacks and political campaigns against marriage transactions were a frequent feature of party propaganda after the 1950s, condemning bridewealth as 'buying and selling in marriage' and lavish dowries as 'feudal extravagance'. Mass education and new wedding styles attempted to change marriage patterns. A few young couples who declined the offer of bridewealth were hand-picked by the local government and promoted as progressive and modern couples through mass media and at political meetings. Throughout the 1970s and 1980s, official regulations on the amount of marital gifts and the size of wedding banquets were issued. Even in the early 1990s, Xiajia villagers were told by the local county government that they were not allowed to pay bridewealth or hold wedding banquets for more than forty guests, responding to a last attempt by the state to promote Maoist-style socialist culture.

At the same time, the state also views Western individualism as the ideological enemy of socialist collectivism. Capitalizing on the negative image of self-interest in traditional Chinese culture and the utilitarian interpretation of Western individualism by Chinese intellectuals at the turn of the twentieth century (Liu 1995), the party-state rather successfully re-defined individualism, characterized by selfishness, lack of concern for others, aversion to group discipline, and runaway hedonism, as a corrupt value of the dying capitalist culture. Through its propaganda apparatuses, political campaigns, and administrative power at all levels of government, the state was able to denounce all kinds of intention and behaviour that did not conform with the officially defined collective good – ranging from one's love of comfort in life, lack of political enthusiasm, distance from one's leaders, to any attempt at defending one's rights – as *zisi zili* and *gerenzhuyi* (selfish and individualistic). To fight against Western individualism, the state also promoted model individuals who devoted themselves completely to the state and relied wholeheartedly on the state for the arrangement of their lives, such as the famous soldier martyr Lei Feng.[4]

Such a characterization of individualism is obviously incomplete because it focuses only on utilitarianism while completely ignoring the liberalism of modern individualism. More importantly, state-sponsored critiques of individualism completely ignored the notions of independence and self-reliance, which are, as indicated above, the two common basic elements shared by utilitarian and liberal schools of individualism. As a result, in the eyes of several generations of Chinese youth, individualism was synonymous with being selfish, hedonistic, irresponsible, and antisocial.

These efforts at socialist transformation, including the attack on Western individualism, ironically and unexpectedly resulted in the rise of the individual in a characteristically Chinese way. By promoting loyalty to socialist collectives as opposed to one's family and by replacing famil-ism with collectivism, the state opened up a new social space and created social conditions necessary for the development of youth autonomy, as in the case of romantic love and spouse selection. The availability and accessibility of social space outside the family and kinship constitute the vital condition for the enrichment of the subjective world and the devel-opment of individual identity (Parish & Whyte 1978: 180; Yan 2003: 42–63, 217–35).

The autonomy and power of rural youth, however, were derived pri-marily from the top-down impact of collectivization, the marriage law, state policies, and political campaigns, rather than from a bottom-up, spontaneous movement in which individuals took the initiative to fight and sometimes to make sacrifices to win their rights. For instance, when young women were mobilized by the state to participate in production and politics, they rarely took the initiative to pursue their goals and thus did not demonstrate a clear gender perspective in their worldview.

Similarly, young villagers' pursuit of individual rights in the domestic sphere was not accompanied by an equal effort to gain autonomy and independence in the public sphere. Instead, under collectivization and the household registration system, villagers fell into the situation that Andrew Walder (1986) refers to as 'organized dependence', in which they had to depend on the collectives and the cadres to meet their everyday needs. All public activities were sponsored and organized by the collectives, and the new sociality invariably bore the imprint of the official ideology of the socialist state, emphasizing the submission of individuals to an officially endorsed collectivity, which, culturally, was an extension of the paternalistic tradition in Chinese society (see Madsen 1984). Chinese people were organized to play various social roles in public life, such as workers, farmers, and soldiers, and to fulfil their social obligations to the state, instead of being rights-bearing citizens. It was only in the private life sphere that youth and women were encouraged to exercise their rights against the traditional patriarchal culture and parental authority. As I argue elsewhere (Yan 2003: 232–4), the disjunction between public and private life spheres, and, more importantly, the exclusion of individual agency in public life, have led to an unbalanced and incomplete development of individuality.

Since the early 1980s the socialist state has gradually loosened its control over ordinary people's private lives. Consequently, the values of the market economy and globalizing consumerism have become dominant forces in family life in particular and in social change in general, making the Chinese case more like its counterparts in the West. The rising consumerism in everyday life directly triggered village youth to compete for lavish bridewealth. Many young villagers have worked in cities and have been exposed to the proliferation of modern life images in the mass media. The spread of consumerism has led them to believe that money is meant to be spent, goods are meant to be consumed, and the quality of life is to be judged in terms of consumption satisfaction.

This is not surprising, as China is rapidly becoming a consumer society and the state has been encouraging widespread consumerism. As I note elsewhere (Yan 2000), the graduated encouragement of mass consumption by the state played an important role in reducing social discontent and restoring political stability in post-1989 Chinese society. To expand the domestic market and speed up the sluggish Chinese economy in the late 1990s, the state went one step further to promote consumerism as an engine of economic growth, and the official media were filled with commentaries and reports that encouraged people to take personal loans – then a new social invention in China – for their consumer needs (see Yan 2000).

The drive for consumerism also creates more inter-generational conflicts as the older villagers still believe in the virtues of thrift. The rapid expansion of their imaginary world raises the life aspirations of village youth, sometimes creating a sense of helplessness because the modern lifestyles from Hong Kong or Shanghai are so desirable yet unattainable. Hence the ruthless extraction of money from one's parents is not only justified by the particular understanding of individualism in China but also necessitated by the drive for consumer desires.

Precisely due to the state's intrusive influence in everyday life during the collective period, its retreat in the post-collective era has produced an equally strong yet perhaps more negative impact on the private lives of individual villagers, that is, the development of an ultra-utilitarian individualism in the unique context where the survival of traditional culture, the legacy of radical socialism, and global capitalism compete with one another.

The previous evil image of individualism was suddenly turned on its head during the post-Mao reform era of the 1980s, because it was rediscovered as a catalyst of modernization in the West, stimulating individual incentives and economic growth. Yet there has been no serious effort to explore what individualism actually is and how it works in Western culture and thus earlier misunderstandings continue to exist. Individualism is still understood as a selfish and hedonistic ethic that places self-interest above the needs of the group, and one must pursue it at the expense of other people's interests. The only change is that this ethic is now in fact being praised (see Wang 2002).

It is in this special historical context that the young villagers in Xiajia, as they became involved in commodity production and the market, quickly embraced the values of late capitalism and emphasized the 'I deserve . . .' perspective, extracting money from their parents for lavish bridewealth while ignoring their obligations to respect the equal rights of other people. This is not the place to discuss the culturally rooted reasons why individualism was understood only as utilitarianism in China, or the political reasons why utilitarian individualism was denounced from the 1950s to the 1970s and praised thereafter.[5] The point is that such an interpretation of individualism at the macro level provides us with a key better to understand why young villagers choose to exercise their agencies by demanding larger bridewealth from their parents while still proudly expressing themselves as individualistic and modern youth.

CONCLUSION

The practice of bridewealth in this north China village has been transformed from the exchange of marital gifts between two families to the division of property within the groom's family, and the bride has replaced her parents as the recipient of bridewealth, effectively turning bridewealth into the wealth of the bride. A close examination of the transformation of bridewealth shows that, at the individual level, it has evolved over a long process in which the individual brides and grooms negotiated with their parents over control of bridewealth. In addition, a misunderstanding about Western individualism provides village youths with a new ideological tool to justify their relentless extraction of money from their parents. At the level of family life, the changing norm of bridewealth has been shaped and in turn has helped to re-shape mate choice, family division, and support of the elderly. Equally important is to note that these important changes have occurred within the context of other social changes at the macro level and are closely linked to the role of a powerful state.

A central argument in the present study is the active role of the individual in transforming the system of bridewealth, an important phenomenon that by and large has been overlooked in most studies of marriage transactions. Recognition of the individual, however, is only part of the argument; what is more important is how individuals exercise their agency in a culturally specific context, such as choosing to take advantage of the custom of bridewealth instead of abandoning it when they gain more autonomy in mate choice and marriage negotiations.

Two implications emerged from the unfolding of the Xiajia case. First, village youths' exercise of individual agency has not destroyed the earlier pattern of mutual dependency between parents and adult children; rather, it has led to an increase in the traditional dependence on parental support for marriage and has perpetuated the practice of bridewealth. The co-existence of youth autonomy in marriage and the continuity of bridewealth poses a challenge to the modernist grand theory of family change, causing us to rethink social norm change in particular and family change in general (see, e.g., Ensminger & Knight 1997).

Second, the Xiajia case also shows that the individual or individual agency does not exist in isolation; it was only in the culturally specific contexts of other social changes that individual couples were able to accomplish what they did. Consequently, any single-cause analysis runs the risk of misunderstanding reality through over-simplification. For instance, one is easily tempted to identify the shifting balance in the inter-generational power relationship as the ultimate cause of the transformation of bridewealth; but the decline of parental power is too general to explain how the transformation of bridewealth actually occurred in real life and how individual villagers of both generations contributed to and coped with the change. Moreover, given that parental control over their children's marriage was the primary reason for marriage transactions (see Gates 1996; Goody 1973; Harrell & Dickey 1985; Meillassoux 1981; Schlegel & Eloul 1988), the decline of parental power should have led to the disappearance of bridewealth (Goode 1963), instead of its escalation. It is only when we fully consider the social changes in a larger setting that we can understand why the transformation of bridewealth has taken its current form.

NOTES

An early draft of this article was presented as the 2003 Malinowski Memorial Lecture at the London School of Economics and Political Science (LSE) in May 2003. I am grateful to the audience and the participants in the subsequent Friday Seminar in the Department of Anthropology at LSE for their valuable comments and to Professor Charles Stafford for his hospitality. I owe special thanks to Dr Susan Bayly and four anonymous reviewers for their critical reading of the early drafts and insightful suggestions for revision, and I also thank Nancy Hearst for editorial assistance. I was able to concentrate on the writing of this article thanks to a 2003–4 Fellowship from the American Council of Learned Societies.

1. I began fieldwork in Xiajia village in the spring of 1989 and returned to the village in 1991, 1993, 1994, 1997, 1998, 1999, and 2004.

2. Hetherington (2001) describes how Western Christian ideology and practice affects the younger generation of Kenyan women when the payment of bridewealth is at stake; Ensminger and Knight (1997) point out that the Islamic notion of indirect dowry (*mahr*) provides an ideological alternative which is critical for the change from bridewealth to indirect dowry among the Orma pastoralists in Kenya.

3. The population control policy, important in other aspects of village life, has not yet had an impact on the practice of bridewealth. When I completed my last detailed survey on the subject in 1999, the young villagers who were born in or after 1980, the year when the birth control policy was implemented, were still in their late teens. For a detailed and systematic account of all major changes in private life in the village including that of population control and fertility culture, see Yan (2003).

4. Lei Feng, a soldier who was unconditionally grateful for the state-sponsored social mobility, responded actively to various state-sponsored political campaigns. He became known for doing volunteer work and for helping others. While on duty in the early 1960s he died in an accident; thereafter he was promoted by the state as a national model of the socialist new person who is selfless and wholeheartedly devoted to the great cause of communism. Mao Zedong personally called upon the Chinese people to 'learn from Lei Feng', thus making Lei Feng into a cultural icon during the 1960s and 1970s.

5. For an insightful analysis of the epistemic and linguistic conditions under which the notion of individualism is introduced and understood in China, see Liu (1995: 77–99); for psychological analysis of the negative image of individualism in China, see Bond (1986).

REFERENCES

Bell, D. & S. Song 1994. Explaining the level of bridewealth. *Current Anthropology* **35**, 311–16.

Bond, M. 1986. *The psychology of the Chinese people*. Hong Kong: Oxford University Press.

Buggenhagen, B.A. 2001. Prophets and profits: gendered and generational visions of wealth and value in Senegalese Murid households. *Journal of Religion of Africa* **31**, 373–401.

Cohen, M.L. 1976. *House united, house divided: the Chinese family in Taiwan*. New York: Columbia University Press.

Croll, E. 1981. *The politics of marriage in contemporary China*. Cambridge: University Press.

Davis, D. & S. Harrell 1993. Introduction: the impact of post-Mao reforms on family life. In *Chinese families in the post-Mao era* (eds) D. Davis & S. Harrell, 1–25. Berkeley: University of California Press.

Diamant, N. 2000. *Revolutionizing the family: politics, love, and divorce in urban and rural China, 1949–1968*. Berkeley: University of California Press.

Dumont, L. 1986. *Essays on individualism: modern ideology in anthropological perspective*. Chicago: University Press.

Ensminger, J. & J. Knight 1997. Changing social norms: common property, bridewealth, and clan exogamy. *Current Anthropology* **38**: 1–24.

Gates, H. 1996. *China's motor: a thousand years of petty capitalism*. Ithaca, N.Y.: Cornell University Press.

Giddens, A. 1992. *The transformation of intimacy: sexuality, love and eroticism in Modern societies*. Stanford: University Press.

Goode, W. 1963. *World revolution and family patterns*. New York: Free Press.

Goody, J. 1973. Bridewealth and dowry in Africa and Eurasia. In *Bridewealth and dowry* (eds) J. Goody & S. Tambiah, 1–59. Cambridge: University Press.

Grosz-Ngate, M. 1988. Monetization of bridewealth and the abandonment of 'kin roads' to marriage in Sana, Mali. *American Ethnologist* **15**, 501–14.

Harrell, S. & S. Dickey 1985. Dowry systems in complex societies. *Ethnology* **24:** 105–20.

Hetherington, P. 2001. Generational changes in marriage patterns in the Central Province of Kenya, 1930–1990. *Journal of Asian and African Studies* **36: 2**, 157–80.

Hollan, D. 1992. Cross-cultural differences in the self. *Journal of Anthropological Research* **48: 4**, 283–300.

Kim, K. n.d. Politics of 'backwardness': an ethnographic study of the Socialist Spiritual Civilization movement in contemporary rural North China. Unpublished manuscript.

King, A.Y. 1985. The individual and group in Confucianism: a relational perspective. In *Individualism and holism: studies in Confucian and Taoist values* (ed.) D.J. Munro, 57–70. Ann Arbor: University of Michigan Press.

Kipnis, A. 1997. *Producing guanxi: sentiment, self, and subculture in a north China village*. Durham. N.C.: Duke University Press.

Liu, L.H. 1995. *Translingual practice: literature, national culture, and translated modernity – China, 1900–1937*. Stanford: University Press.

Lukes, S. 1973. *Individualism*. Oxford: Basil Blackwell.

Macfarlane, A. 1978. *The origin of English individualism: the family, property and social transition*. Cambridge: University Press.

——— 1986. *Marriage and love in England: modes of reproduction 1300–1840*. Oxford: Basil Blackwell.

Macpherson, C. 1962. *The political theory of possessive individualism: Hobbes to Locke*. Oxford: Clarendon Press.

McCreery, J.L. 1976. Women's property rights and dowry in China and South Asia. *Ethnology* **15: 2**, 163–74.

Madsen, R. 1984. *Morality and power in a Chinese village*. Berkeley: University of California Press.

Meillassoux, C. 1981. *Maidens, meal and money: capitalism and the domestic community*. Cambridge: University Press.

Musschenga, A.W. 2001. The many faces of individualism. In *The many faces of individualism* (eds) A. van Harskamp & A.W. Musschenga, 1–23. Leuven: Peeters.

Parish, W. & M. Whyte 1978. *Village and family in contemporary China.* Chicago: University Press.

Schlegel, A. & R. Eloul 1988. Marriage transactions: labor, property, status. *American Anthropologist* **90**, 291–309.

Triandis, H.C. 1995. *Individualism and collectivism.* Boulder, Colo.: Westview Press.

Walder, A. 1986. *Communist neo-traditionalism: work and authority in Chinese industry.* Berkeley: University of California Press.

Wang, X. 2002. The post-Communist personality: the spectre of China's capitalist market reforms. *The China Journal* **47**, 1–17.

Watson, R.S. 1984. Women's property in Republican China: rights and practice. *Republican China* **10**, 1–12.

Whyte, M. 1995. From arranged marriage to love matches in urban China. In *Family formation and dissolution: perspectives from East and West* (ed.) C.-C. Yi, 33–83. Taipei: Academia Sinica.

Yan, Y. 1996. *The flow of gifts: reciprocity and social networks in a Chinese village.* Stanford: University Press.

——— 2000. The politics of consumerism in Chinese society. *China Briefing, 1998–2000* (ed.) T. White, 159–93. Armonk, N.Y.: M.E. Sharpe.

——— 2003. *Private life under socialism: love, intimacy, and family change in a Chinese village, 1949–1999.* Stanford: University Press.

Yang, C.K. 1965. *Chinese Communist society: the family and the village.* Cambridge, Mass.: MIT Press.

CHAPTER 8

HOW TO BE A CALCULATING YET NICE PERSON?

INTRODUCTION

It was in March 1991 that, after a long and unproductive month of fieldwork in Xiajia Village in northeast China, I suddenly discovered that villagers kept detailed records of received gifts in written form, an important family document locally known as a *lidan* (gift list). The gift lists are homemade books on red paper (funeral gift lists are recorded on yellow paper), containing the names of gift donors and the values of their gifts; the information is inscribed with a traditional Chinese calligraphy brush at a designated and often decorated table called the accounting station (*zhangfang*) in the venue of a given ceremony. The guests always first visit the accounting station before joining the ceremony, where they present their gifts and watch as they are recorded on the gift list.

As I note elsewhere (Yan 1996), the writing of a gift list documents the exchange activities of daily life as a part of family and local history. Therefore, gift lists serve as a repository of data on the changing nature of interpersonal relations. For an anthropologist, the gift list can be seen as a social map that records and displays the networks of personal connections. However, emically, a gift list is much more than a simple tool of memory and rational calculation for future giving and receiving. In the eyes of the villagers, their documentation endows gift-giving activities with a ritual significance and sacredness. The scene at the accounting station where a gift list is compiled is full of cultural symbolism: an educated and respectable bookkeeper writes the formal document using a calligraphy brush and red paper. All these symbols convey the power of writing – a long-standing tradition in Chinese society – into the numeration of gift giving.

As any ethnographer would have done intuitively under the circumstances, I made every effort to collect gift lists and the stories associated with them, which led to the collection of other kinds of family documents as well, such as personal diaries, engagement agreements, and family-division contracts. Amazed by my obsession with these family documents, a villager friend one day asked if I would be interested in Mr. Wang's account book (*zhangben* in Chinese). "Of course I am interested," I replied without thinking, "but what kind of *zhangben* does Wang have?" I was told that Mr. Wang had since 1984 recorded in an account book all receipts and expenses in his family. Fellow villagers feel that this account book contains the secrets of how Wang was able to lift his family out of poverty to become one of the most prosperous households in the community. The association of Wang's account book with his economic success gave him the reputation of being capable in his calculating and planning, thus earning him the nickname "bookkeeping man" (*jizhangde*). As several informants commented, the villagers most admire Mr. Wang for his persistence in carrying on the practice for such a long time, a rare and valuable quality (*suzhi*) in itself. Influenced by Wang's example, more than a dozen other villagers tried to keep written accounts of their household transactions, but none of them was able to continue for more than a year.

My first meeting with Wang went fairly well but did not go in the direction I wished. We spent several hours talking about almost everything except his account book because he showed no interest at all in discussing this topic. It was only as the mutual trust between us grew stronger after several subsequent visits to his home that Wang shared his account book with me, and even allowed me to hand transcribe a small part of it. Finally in 1998, after becoming familiar with my research over a period of six years, Wang generously let me take the entire account book to the county seat to make Xerox copies. Interestingly, he explained this by referring to a famous folk legend called "*Sangu maolu*" (Three visits to a rural retreat).

In this story, Liu Bei, a distant member of the royal family of the Han dynasty and an ambitious warlord during the third century, went to seek the advice of a famous hermit named Zhuge Liang. Testing Liu's sincerity, Zhuge Liang refused to come out during Liu Bei's first two visits to his retreat in the countryside (*maolu* in Chinese). Despite the huge gap in social status between the two (note Liu's kinship tie to the emperor and his power as a warlord), Liu visited Zhuge Liang for a third time and finally won the hermit's heart. To show his appreciation, Zhuge Liang offered Liu Bei a pre-prepared political proposal and agreed to be Liu's top advisor. By using various political and military strategies, Zhuge Liang helped Liu defeated the other warlords and established his own kingdom. Zhuge Liang's successful career was popularized in a series of folk legends and a famous novel, and he was made into a cultural icon of wisdom, strategy, and moral virtues.

By citing this well-known story, Wang wanted to let the anthropologist know that his offer of the account book was an emotional response and a gesture of appreciation for the anthropologist's repeated visits to him over a period of several years. However, it also delivered a clear message that Wang was fully aware of the cultural meanings of the account book and the prestige that the book had brought to him. To demonstrate that his reputation is well deserved, he positioned himself as a hermit full of wisdom and knowledge, making an analogy between his account book and Zhuge Liang's political proposal. Here again, as in the case of gift lists, written documents (read: literacy) provide additional power to the numeration of economic activities.

In the following pages, I will first review Wang's bookkeeping practices in an attempt to understand the format, content, and functions of his account book. Then I will examine how Wang learned and developed the art of calculating and budgeting, which is referred to locally as *suanji*. The skill of *suanji* is interwined with a set of cultural symbolisms in folk accounting, and it has to be learned as part of the local culture of reciprocity and moral economy, instead of merely a technique of budgeting and planning. In the concluding section, I argue that in the context of the rural household economy, economic agency is embedded in a more complicated process of social practice and, as a consequence, calculating and budgeting are as social-cultural as they are economic. The Wang case demonstrates the close link between learning and economic agency, and, more importantly, the close link between learnedness and social-economic achievement.

The present study is based on a series of fieldwork visits from 1989 to 1998 to Xiajia Village, Heilongjiang Province, in northeast China. With a population of 1,492 in 1998, the village had been fairly successful in collective farming prior to the implementation of the decollectivization reforms in the early 1980s; today it still remains a farming community.

The heavy reliance on farming has been one of the major obstacles to economic development in the village, keeping the average per capita income slightly below the national average during the 1980s and 1990s. But the villagers' livelihood has been closely tied to the market through cash crop farming, household sideline businesses, labor migration, and the impact of the mass media and urban consumerism (for more details about the history and current state of the community, see Yan 1996 and 2003).

THE BOOKKEEPING MAN AND HIS ACCOUNT BOOK

Wang was born in 1955 and, as the eldest son in a poor family, he began to learn the ethics of enduring hardship at an early age. He recalled that, as a primary school student, he had little time to complete his homework because after school he had to work for the family, mainly collecting wild herbs as feed for the family pigs. Because he was an excellent student in the village school, in 1970 he was selected to attend high school in the township where the commune headquarters was located. He loved to study but was forced to leave school the following year due to economic difficulties in his family.

Wang started to work in the collective at the age of 16. He was an energetic youth with a secondary school education and good class background (his family's class label is poor peasant), a qualification few of his peers could match at that time. More importantly, Wang was good at mathematics and was widely regarded by fellow villagers as *nengxie huisuan* (being capable at writing and calculating) and thus a man of culture. In addition, his class label was important capital that helped him become a member of the elite section of the village militia. This rather rare combination of a better education, known ability in math, and good political standing brought him a series of desirable job assignments. He started as a technician in the village-organized scientific research team specializing in cultivating grain seeds. Then he was appointed property controller (*baoguanyuan*) in the fourth production team of the then-Xiajia brigade. His duties included supervising the storage and distribution of various goods, keeping track of all production tools and other collective properties, and serving as a cashier for the production team. Wang told me that it was in this position that he learned his bookkeeping skills, taking care of two account books, one for the properties and the other for purchasing and sales in the collective. Under the collective system,

Wang was also given the desirable position of tractor driver for several years, a professional career that he has put to good use, driving his own tractor to earn cash income since the late 1980s.

In 1975 Wang married a girl from the same village; in 1976 the couple had a son and in 1980 a daughter, thus establishing a typical family in contemporary rural China. When they started their conjugal household in the summer of 1976, Wang and his wife owned only a share of grain and cooking fuel, plus their personal belongings. At the end of the year, their gross income from working for the collective was 299 yuan. After repaying the collective 127 yuan for grain and other expenses, they received a net cash income of 172 yuan, which was supposed to cover the entire year of 1977, including paying back their part of the 500-yuan family debt when they moved out, a debt originally incurred by Wang's parents to pay for his marriage. To maximize this modest amount of cash, a rigid plan was in order. "That was how the whole thing got started," Wang explained, referring to his decision to keep accounts for his household.

The economic conditions of the Wang household have been improving since the early 1980s. In my first household survey on economic stratification in the village in 1989, Wang's family ranked slightly above the average.[1] He owned one-third of a small tractor and a black/white TV; although he faced a number of expected expenditures because of his two school-age children, he had already built a four-room brick house. By the time of my last survey in 1998, however, the Wang family had moved up to the level of a rich household, owning a tractor and several farm machines, three milk cows, an undisclosed amount of cash savings, and several large consumer items such as a color television, a motorcycle, and a washing machine. More importantly, Wang had helped his son marry in style (spending more than 10,000 yuan on the bridewealth alone) and sent him off to establish his own conjugal household. This means that Wang and his wife had completed the most important and difficult mission in their life as parents, and there would be no more serious spending in the household.[2] Another indicator of his prosperity is that he sent his daughter to a private middle school in another county and paid nearly 5,000 yuan in tuition and fees between 1995 and 1997. However, when he realized that the investment could hardly bring any return because students graduating from that school were not offered government jobs, he asked his daughter to drop out.

From 1976 to 1983 Wang's bookkeeping was rather simple. He recorded the monetary total of his annual income and major expenditures in a small notebook, without any transaction details. Wang explained to me that because most economic transactions at that time were conducted within the collective system, there was little room for him to actually plan and manage his household economy; taking detailed notes on such transactions was thus unnecessary. This was particularly true for the monetary income, as the year-end distribution of cash by the collective was the only way by which villagers would receive substantial cash income, apart from the petty cash that women generated from raising chickens or pigs.

A significant change occurred at the end of 1983 when Xiajia collectives were dismantled virtually overnight. Most of the collective property was privatized, including the tractors and other heavy agricultural machines. The farmland, the fundamental means of production, was divided into two categories: subsistence-grain land (*kouliang tian*) and contract land (*chengbao tian*). Everyone in the village was entitled to two *mu* of subsistence-grain land and every adult male laborer received 10 *mu* of contract land. The villagers' obligations to provide the state with cheap requisitioned grain only applied to their contract land. Because they had two children, Wang and his wife received nearly 20 *mu* of land, plus 1,186 yuan cash income from the collectives in 1983.

Realizing that he would have to plan day-to-day production all by himself, Wang started to record his household's everyday transactions into a new, comprehensive account book. This account book looks like an entry-level general journal in the contemporary accounting system, or a day book of cash flows in traditional Chinese accounting practices (see Gardella 1992:326). On each page, there are five entries representing respectively dates, summary of transactions, receipts, payments, and balances. From the perspective of modern accounting, Wang uses the basic single-entry method of bookkeeping, separating receipts and expenses into two columns and recalculating the new balance after each receipt or payment. Table 1 below is a literal translation of the first two pages in Wang's account book, including all the transactions in March 1984.

Although it summarizes economic transactions for only one month, Table 1 contains rich information that tells us a great deal about production and consumption patterns in the Wang household. First, we see that farming (or, the sale of grain) was the major source of income for the

Table 1   Recorded transactions in Wang's account book, March 1984

Date	Transaction summary	Receipts	Payments	Balance
2/29	From last year's account	198.77		198.77
3/01	Textbook for student		1.00	197.77
3/01	Notebooks for student		1.10	196.67
3/03	Purchasing gift to visit brother-in-law		2.29	194.38
3/04	Sorghum stems, 500 bundles (for house construction)		70.00	124.38
3/05	Gift for so-and-so's engagement		1.50	122.88
3/06	Gift to so-and-so		2.00	120.88
3/08	A wooden chess		28.50	92.38
3/08	Roofing material (for house construction)		105.00	(12.62)
3/08	Bamboo sticks (for house construction)		28.00	(40.62)
3/08	Receiving payment for sale of grain (corn)	290.00		249.38
3/09	One bag of chemical fertilizer		7.30	242.08
3/12	Repairing wrist-watch		2.50	239.58
3/13	Soy souse, salt, sugar, and liquor		2.25	237.33
3/14	So-and-so returning loan	272.00		509.33
3/15	So-and-so returning borrowed money	2.90		512.23
3/15	Borrowing money from so-and-so	50.00		562.23
3/18	Returning borrowed money to so-and-so		50.00	512.23
3/21	Cooking oil		1.70	510.53
3/22	Sale of grain (corn), 0.20 per catty	40.80		551.33
3/23	Lent loan to someone (name not shown), middle-man so-and-so		180.00	371.33
3/23	Deposit into bank saving account		100.00	271.33
3/23	Gift to so-and-so		2.00	269.33
3/23	Sale of chicken eggs	4.20		273.53
3/25	Green beans (for house construction)		5.80	267.73
3/27	Wages for manual labor	10.00		277.73
3/28	Medicine		0.65	277.08
3/29	Purchasing bitumen from so-and-so (for house construction)		105.00	172.08
3/29	Matches, dried noodle		0.90	171.18
3/29	A returned loan from someone (name not shown)	50.00		221.18
Total		918.67	697.49	221.18

Wang family in 1984, whereas wage labor and family sidelines played only a supplementary role (see the receipt entries on March 23 and 27). Yet the transaction records show that the Wang family was also engaged in money lending. On March 14 and 29, the family received a total of 322 yuan in returned loans, and the family also gave out a loan of 180 yuan on March 23. These transactions were labeled as *taiqian*, which means a loan with interest, whereas two other financial transactions (see records for March 15 and 18), were marked as *jieqian*, meaning to borrow money without interest (more on this local distinction below). The records in Table 1 show that the Wang family was engaged in both kinds of personal finance, but the profitability of money lending remained elusive (more on this below).

Moreover, the transaction summaries also reveal the Wang family's consumption strategies, plus the prices of certain commodities at that time. Since Wang built his house in summer 1984, nearly half of the expenses (314 yuan out of 697 yuan) during the month of March were for construction materials. In addition, he spent 7.3 yuan on chemical fertilizer, which should be classified as a production cost. He also gave a personal loan of 180 yuan, and he deposited 100 yuan in the bank, both of which are actually investments instead of expenses. The Wang family also spent 9.8 yuan on gift giving which should be considered as an investment in social capital (note Wang recorded them as expenses in his account book). These expenses for productive or investment purposes amounted to a total of 610 yuan. Only 35.85 yuan could be regarded as consumption or living expenses, including for the purchase of a wooden chest that cost 28.50 yuan. Another important detail was the sale of a small quantity of chicken eggs (see the receipt entry for March 27), which would have been consumed in better-off families. Actually, Wang's account book shows that the family continued to sell chicken eggs until May 1989.[3] These transaction records prove that the Wang family reduced its consumption needs to the lowest level possible, spending most of its resources on production and investment. This is precisely the original goal that Wang wanted to achieve when he first began keeping daily accounts. Apparently, the account book served his purpose well.

Finally, it should be noted that the consumption of non-purchased items of subsistence, such as grain, vegetables, and cooking fuel, is not included in Wang's account book because he, like the other villagers, regards only commodities bought with cash as expenses. Since decollectivization in 1983, villagers have been directly producing grain, vegetables, eggs, and cooking fuel (corn stems and other crop stems) and thus they do not regard them as consumption costs. For the same reason, these items are not regarded as income. This is why the sample monthly records in Table 1 include only cash transactions. Moreover, Wang did not enter the taxes, levies, and various fees in his account book because the village office withholds these when the villagers sell their grain to the state through the village office. Wang argues that, since he cannot determine the amount of taxes and levies, it does not really make much difference whether he enters them in the book or not (but he does make a summary of all taxes and levies at the end of each year).

During my multiple interviews with him, Wang gave the following explanations for his bookkeeping practice. The initial motivation for keeping a systematic account of all transactions was to know where and why the money was spent over the year. Wang recalled that in the first few years the family had so little cash that they had to make sure that each cent was spent properly. After the first two or three years, Wang also realized that bookkeeping was an effective way of budgeting since he could thus review past transactions and, based on the review, predict future expenditures. This was particularly important when there were important investments or family ceremonies on the agenda, such as purchasing a milk cow, house construction, or his son's marriage. Over the years bookkeeping has also strengthened Wang's ability to plan his household economy and he has modified his production and investment strategies in response to changes in local society. In his words, making changes in response to outside opportunities (*suiji yingbian*) is an essential part of calculating and planning (*suanji*). Wang also noted that because he and his wife would review the account book together to discuss the future of their household economy, they began to feel much closer. In this sense, the account book has played a role in creating a channel of conjugal communication.

For years Wang tried in vain to get his son involved in the bookkeeping, hoping to pass on his experience and lessons in managing a household economy to the young man. But, like most village youth, his son was fascinated with the urban lifestyle he had seen on television, and thus he dismissed his father's way of calculating and planning as outdated and backwards. To make his son understand the importance of family budgeting, Wang took a radical step: in 1996 he gave his son and daughter-in-law half of the family estate and two-thirds of the dairy business and asked them to move out and start their own conjugal household. Wang hoped that early family division would force his son to learn the importance of calculating and budgeting, just as what he had during the late 1970s and early 1980s.

CULTURAL ASPECTS OF CALCULABILITY AND BUDGETING

From this brief review of Wang's life course and career trajectory we can see that he has benefited greatly from the new social institutions that were made available to ordinary villagers after the 1949 revolution, especially the mandatory and free secondary-school education and the political preference for children from formerly poor-peasant families. However, Wang's personal advancement also relied on the long-shared belief in the power of literacy and mathematical skills among Chinese villagers, which marked Wang as a promising young candidate for several upwardly mobile and rewarding jobs. Capitalizing on his qualifications, Wang gradually earned the respect of his fellow villagers through his 20-year experience in bookkeeping and his achievements in money-making and self-cultivation.

In this section I will examine in detail how Wang accomplished this by analyzing his account book. I will argue that it was the combination of literacy, numerical skills, calculability, personal character, and morality that made Wang a *hui suanji* (i.e., calculating and planning) person of the highest level by local standards. This case study will also shed new light on scholarly discourse about the relationship between accounting methods and economic agency (see Acheson 1972; Goody 1996:72–82; Weber 1978).

To better understand Wang's account book and economic agency, however, we must bear in mind that the Wang family, like other families in the village, operates its household economy in the social context of *guanxi* (personal networks) that are governed by *renqing* ethics. As I note elsewhere (1996), *guanxi* networks in Xiajia Village are characterized by both a high rate of multiplexity in relational configurations and high density interpersonal transactions. Most people in a given *guanxi* network are members of the same community and interact with one another in everyday life. In addition to exchanging gifts in various situations, they also cooperate in economic activities, support one another in village politics, and spend recreational time together. It is in this sense that *guanxi* distinguishes itself from the common form of personal networks in network analysis studies and assumes a stronger organizational form as a quasi-group, to borrow Boissevan's term (1968), in village society. Personal networks are so important in the social life of villagers that the term *guanxi* has become synonymous with the notion of society (*shehui*). A villager who has built an elaborate *guanxi* network locally is referred to as a "person in the society" (*shehuishang de ren*); one who is not successful in this aspect of social life is called a "dead door" (*si menzi*).

Whereas *guanxi* serves as the social matrix upon which one interacts with others, *renqing* ethics provides the guiding principles and regulations by which one learns to be a proper person interacting with others in a socially accepted way. Here, the Chinese notion of *renqing* should be understood as, first and foremost, a set of moral norms that guide and regulate one's behavior. *Renqing* is also the socially accepted pattern of emotional responses in the sense that one takes others' emotional responses into consideration. Furthermore, *renqing* serves as an important standard by which villagers judge whether one is a proper social person. In other words, it is *renqing* that gives meaning to everyday engagements, interactions, and transactions among villagers. Without *renqing*, life is less meaningful and people are dehumanized.

Therefore, Xiajia villagers, Wang included, must learn to exercise their agency in a local moral world characterized by moral obligations and emotional attachments in interpersonal relations and by stable mutuality between members of personal networks over a long period. Within the boundaries of this local moral world, the pursuit of personal interest mingles with the fulfillment of social obligations, and the highest level of calculability and planning (*suanji*) lies in the delicate balance between seeking economic rewards and being a proper person. This goal seems to be precisely what Wang has attempted to achieve, as shown in the economic strategies reflected in Table 2.

Table 2 summarizes the cash income and expenditures in the Wang household from February 29, 1984, the first day that Wang began to take detailed notes in his account book, to December 30, 1997. Several points are particularly noteworthy. First, a quick comparison between the second and the last columns in the table shows that, although the gross cash income (or the level of productivity) grew steadily over the 14 years, the actual year-end balance did not change much, except for 1997. Notwithstanding the small surges in 1988 to 1990, negative balances of several hundred yuan occurred in 1991 and 1992. In other words, it appears that no matter how much the income increased, there was always a shortage of funds by the end of the year. This phenomenon has puzzled many villagers and often causes family disputes when husbands and wives begin to accuse one another over missing or misused household funds. The account book, however, clearly shows that both production costs and

Table 2   Cash income and expenses in the Wang household, 1984–1997

Year	Gross income (yuan)	Expenses (yuan)					Year-end balance (yuan)
		Production	Living	Medical	Education	Gift-giving	
1984	1,250	194	291	8	5	48	704
1985	1,535	102	411	7	5	69	941
1986	1,605	147	378	125	5	216	734
1987	1,931	248	598	35	12	223	815
1988	2,383	335	725	27	30	250	1,016
1989	2,820	296	895	29	41	270	1,289
1990	3,067	389	626	16	56	344	1,636
1991	4,142	2,294	1,708	31	59	603	(553)
1992	6,054	2,773	1,868	108	1,195	725	(615)
1993	7,215	2,932	1,683	20	1,545	705	330
1994*	18,731	8,044	3,791	40	1,481	4,636	739
1995*	12,674	2,680	6,358	135	470	2,080	951
1996*	15,317	5,846	4,406	271	0	4,490	304
1997	11,855	4,779	2,470	157	0	2,273	2,176
Total	90,579	31,059	26,208	1,009	4,904	16,932	10,467

* These are the years in which a large amount of cash was spent for a special purpose: (1) 3,098 yuan in the category of "gift giving" were spent for Wang's son's engagement; (2) 3,028 yuan in the category of "living expenses" were spent on renovating the house; and (3) 1,360 yuan in the category of "gift giving" were spent on imposed fines and gifts for Wang's son's early marriage which was 1.5 years earlier than the minimum legal age of getting married in China. It should also be noted that Wang's son married in 1995 and costed a total of 11,000 yuan, which, however, was not reflected in Wang's account book and thus not included here in the table.

living expenses grew at almost the same pace as productivity. As a result, any additional expenditures, such as a sudden increase in educational expenses, were bound to send a shock to the household economy.

Second, since 1986 gift-giving expenses have amounted to at least 10 percent of annual gross income and more than 20 percent of net cash income. The increase in productivity always paralleled an increase in gift giving, and the ratio between production costs, which included capital investment in a tractor and milk cows and the costs of purchasing crop seeds, chemical fertilizer, and pesticide, and gift giving remained around two to one. A close look at the last row in Table 2 gives another view of the importance of gift giving in a rural household economy. After deducting the total production costs of 31,059 yuan between 1984 and 1997, the total household income during this 14-year period was reduced from 90,579 yuan to 59,520 yuan, which was the net cash income. A total of 16,932 yuan in gift-giving expenditures during the same period, in other words, amounted to 28 percent of the net income of the Wang household!

The other side of the gift economy is gift receiving. According to the account book and two gift lists that I obtained from Wang, his family received 2,595 yuan for their son's engagement ritual in 1994, the first harvest of returning gifts since the Wang family became seriously engaged in gift-giving activities in 1986. Then, the family received 1,820 yuan for house renovation in spring 1995, 5,060 yuan for their son's wedding in winter 1995, and 1,415 yuan for the celebration of the birth of their grandson in 1996. These gifts brought the family a total income of 10,890 yuan in gift exchange. Since Wang had spent 16,932 yuan during this period of 14 years, only two-thirds of the outgoing gifts were eventually returned. In other words, from a purely economic perspective, gift giving is a poor investment, a point that villagers repeatedly made during my early study of the gift economy in the community (Yan 1996:147–152).

In my 1996 study I explain in detail that villagers were motivated to engage in excessive gift-giving activities for social instead of economic concerns, because over the long term no one would receive an equal return on what he or she had given out. So the question is, why do villagers still continue their gift-giving practices? Wang's account book provides another perspective from which to appraise the issue, that is, to determine the link between gift giving and other more productive activities.

The real significance of gift giving lies in its role in maintaining and expanding one's *guanxi* networks and embodying the *renqing* ethics by which one's personhood is defined. For this reason, all villagers have actively participated in gift giving, and it is common to see that 20 percent of household net income is spent on outgoing gifts (Yan 1996:77). This is also why every family has at least one type of account book – the gift list. However, only a small number of villagers have been able to effectively turn the social investment of gift giving to their economic advantage, making the gifts make money for them. Wang is certainly one of this small group of profit-making gift-givers; this becomes clear when we take a close look at his strategies to organize the productive activities in his family.

As indicated above (see Table 2), the Wang household has been engaged in four types of productive work or business since the early 1980s: household farming, paid services, family sidelines, and money lending. Whereas farming is self-evident, the other three require some explanation. Paid services mainly refer to Wang plowing and/or harvesting other people's farmland with his tractor or transporting goods for other business owners. But it also includes his son's and, occasionally his daughter's, work as paid manual laborers. Family sidelines include Wang's wife raising chickens and pigs and, more importantly, running a small-scale dairy operation that at its peak had four milk cows and required the labor input of the entire family.

Money lending, the fourth business in the household, is not clearly reflected in the account book. Although Wang has kept occasional records of loans and payments received in the account book, the records are far from complete. The annual interest rate varies from 20 percent to 40 percent, yet most loan entries in the account book do not specify the interest rate. The lack of consistency and details regarding the loans contrasts sharply with Wang's records for all other transactions. He explains this in terms of the division of labor in his family – it is his wife's duty to take care of the loans. But this is not entirely true because Wang managed to keep detailed records of other family sidelines also mainly his wife's responsibility until the late 1990s. Wang once mentioned that sometimes he recorded the loans in a separate book, but he also made it clear to me that it would be a bad idea for me to ask about that secret account book, so I never tried. In any case, the incomplete records on personal loans make it virtually impossible to analyze the money-lending business. Consequently, the summary in Table 3 below covers the changing patterns of gross income, production costs, and net income only from household farming, paid services, and family sidelines.

Like most of their fellow villagers, during the early 1980s Wang and his wife relied on household farming as the major source of their income; this was supplemented by traditional family sidelines such as raising pigs and chickens. What distinguished Wang from the majority of Xiajia villagers, however, was his vision and strategy to diversify the household economy. After two years of household farming, Wang concluded that farming could never make his family rich and he had to find other opportunities to generate more cash income. In 1987 he made his first investment outside farming by spending 100 yuan on one-third ownership of a used small tractor; in subsequent years, this jointly owned tractor brought in enough additional cash to the family that Wang was able to purchase his first milk cow in 1991 and a new tractor in 1993. These rather large investments put his household budget in the red in 1991 and 1992 but produced enough returns to cover the largest expenditure of his life time – his son's marriage – during the period from 1994 to 1996.

Table 3   Costs and profits of productive activities in the Wang household

Year		Household farming (yuan)	Paid service (yuan)	Sideline business (yuan)	Yearly total (yuan)
1984*	Gross Income	520	104	246	870
	Production cost	82	25	87	194
	Net income	438	80	159	677
1985	Gross income	732	520	283	1,535
	Production cost	58	18	26	102
	Net income	674	502	257	1,433
1986	Gross income	767	607	231	1,605
	Production cost	65	60	22	147
	Net income	702	547	209	1,458
1987	Gross income	1,132	534	265	1,931
	Production cost	112	106	30	248
	Net income	1,020	428	235	1,683
1988	Gross income	1,360	721	302	2,383
	Production cost	247	26	62	335
	Net income	1,113	695	240	2,048
1989	Gross income	1,650	848	312	2,810
	Production cost	229	32	35	296
	Net income	1,421	816	277	2,514
1990	Gross income	1,571	1,392	104	3,067
	Production cost	288	87	14	389
	Net income	1,283	1,305	90	2,678
1991	Gross income	1,727	838	1,577	4,142
	Production cost	690	120	1,484	2,294
	Net income	1,037	718	93	1,848
1992	Gross income	1,354	1,198	3,502	6,054
	Production cost	396	32	2,345	2,773
	Net income	958	1,166	1,157	3,281
1993	Gross income	1,658	1,327	4,230	7,215
	Production cost	760	1,355	817	2,932
	Net income	898	(28)	3,413	4,283
1994*	Gross income	1,713	1,886	12,537	16,136
	Production cost	1,478	2,004	4,562	8,044
	Net income	235	(118)	7,975	8,092
1995	Gross income	1,064	1,650	9,960	12,674
	Production cost	670	1,030	980	2,680
	Net income	394	620	8,980	9,994

(Continued)

Table 3 (*Continued*)

Year		Household farming (yuan)	Paid service (yuan)	Sideline business (yuan)	Yearly total (yuan)
1996*	Gross income	1,160	1,512	11,230	13,902
	Production cost	1,164	1,325	3,357	5,846
	Net income	(4)	187	7,873	8,056
1997	Gross income	2,395	2,152	7,308	11,855
	Production cost	1,469	1,305	2,005	4,779
	Net income	926	847	5,303	7,076

* These are the years when an additional income was generated from monetary gifts received due to family ceremonies: (1) 380 yuan received in 1984 for house construction; (2) 2,595 yuan received in 1994 for the engagement ritual of Wang's son; and (3) 1,415 yuan received in 1996 for the birth of Wang's grandson. The largest amount of monetary gifts was received in 1995 for Wang's son's wedding, which was not recorded in Wang's account book and thus not included in this table either.

Reinvestment to expand production was Wang's number one priority, as he continually told me during our interviews, and he frequently referred to his account book as the best source for his constant adjustments and investments. As he himself said, the secret to developing a household economy is to find different ways of making money beget money.

Each of Wang's three businesses has had their own peak time in generating income: household farming culminated in 1989, and the business of paid services reached its peak in 1990. But both of them significantly suffered from diminishing returns during the 1990s, with a net loss of 4 yuan in farming in 1996, and net loss of 28 yuan in 1993 and 118 yuan in 1994 in paid services. The only profit-making business during the second half of the 1990s was the dairy enterprise because in 1994 Wang increased the number of milk cows to three, bringing an average net income of 6,000 yuan each year. But this business entailed certain substantial risks because each cow was worth 5,000 to 6,000 yuan, and with the animals vulnerable to various diseases, if they are not properly raised, they can be unproductive. Using annual net income as the indicator, a comparison of profitability among the three businesses is presented in Figure 1 below.

When comparing the pros and cons of the family's three major businesses, Wang asserted that he never considered dropping any of them even when they did not make profits. Why? He explained that with the rapid increase in production costs, such as expenses for crop seeds and chemical fertilizer, and higher taxes and local levies, household farming brought in diminishing returns. Yet, Wang still regarded farming as the basis for stability and security as well as his personal identity because it

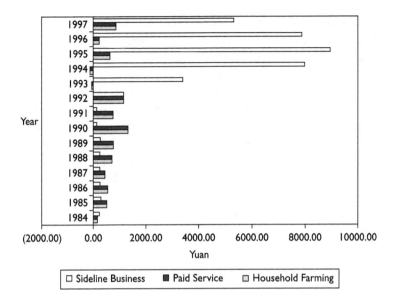

Figure 1   Net income from three major businesses in the Wang household

provided his family with their basic livelihood, the grain and vegetables that allowed the family to be less dependent on the market.

As for the paid services business, Wang attributed diminishing returns there to the constraints of *renqing* ethics in village society. According to unwritten rules, one should always make certain allowances when providing paid services to people within one's *guanxi* network. The standard wage for using one's own tractor to plow farmland for someone else, for instance, was 2 yuan per *mu* in 1997. But Wang only charged non-related fellow villagers this standard amount, and he reduced the fee to 1.5 yuan per *mu* for his relatives and neighbors. He also feels obliged to offer greater discounts to his close relatives and best friends, often charging only a minimum fee to recover his fuel and tractor repair costs.[4] With the growth of his social network, more and more fellow villagers became eligible to receive the discounted services, and Wang thus began to lose money. Despite these problems, Wang still wanted to continue this business because his relatives and friends who did not own a tractor needed his services, which is also a consideration in *renqing* ethics.

Wang's altruistic explanation, however, did not convince me because by the summer of 1998 area farmers owned 42 small tractors, and competition for work among tractor owners was stiff. Two other factors have to be taken into consideration. At first glance, the extremely low – almost close to zero – opportunity costs may be relevant. As several tractor owners pointed out, after plowing their own farm land, both the laborers and the machines are idle for a long time, so making even a small profit is better than being idle. However, unlike many fellow villagers, Wang also raises dairy cows and always complains about the lack of sleep time during the busy seasons. He would have been able to invest more time and capital in the lucrative dairy farm business had he quit providing tractor services. Why did he not do this? A likely reason was Wang's well-planned strategy to maintain and expand his *guanxi* network, which was vitally important to his money-lending business as well as his reputation and social standing in the community. Here again, the account book provides us with some interesting clues.

A careful reading of the transaction record shows an overlap of participants/clients in the three circles or networks that the Wang family has cultivated over the years: paid services, gift giving, and money lending. Because most people to whom Wang provides paid services are also in his network of gift exchange, he has to reduce the service charges and thus take a loss. However, the same group of people also constitutes the client base for Wang's money-lending business, and this provides the key to understand Wang's strategy.

Money lending in rural China remains a legally grey area since there is no law to either legitimize or ban the practice; as a result, it relies on the shared understanding of *guanxi* and *renqing* among villagers. Until recently no private banks existed, and all banking resources were under the tight control of the government. Yet financial support is very important to villagers, especially when they must host an important ceremony or expand investment in production. Since few villagers can acquire loans from the local state bank or credit union, they must depend on the traditional system of credits and loans, namely, seeking financial aid through networks of personal connections. Xiajia residents distinguish between two types of private loans. Borrowing money is called *jieqian*, for which no interest is charged. If interest is charged, it is called *taiqian*, and the annual interest rate varies from 20 to 40 percent. The close relationship between the lender and the borrower provides a moral basis for financial support without interest charged. For loans with interest, personal connections are also needed. All transactions depend on mutual trust between lenders and borrowers; otherwise, the lender has to rely on a middleman who is responsible for shortening the social distance and also guaranteeing the repayment of the loan. Either way, the lender's *guanxi* network provides the only safety net for this otherwise risky business.

On its surface, money lending seems to be the most lucrative business because it can generate much higher profits than all other types of productive activity in the local economy. Yet only a few individual villagers are able to become money lenders and even fewer are able to stay in the business for a long time. This is because the high interest (or profits) can seriously damage a lender's reputation as a good person in the moral world of *guanxi*. Once a money lender is viewed as a money-grubbing shark, he or she will be socially isolated because people in his or her *guanxi* network will avoid further interactions. This in turn will negatively affect his or her money-lending business. Therefore, a wise person in this business must minimize the profit-making nature of money lending and maintain a reputable and respected social standing in village society.

In Wang's case, the low returns from his tractor service enabled him to create a stable and sizable *guanxi* network and to maintain a good reputation as a reasonable person who loves to help people in his network. In other words, the diminishing returns in one business actually serve as a crucial condition for profit making in another. This is how Wang makes his cost-return analysis, and all his calculations and planning are done within the framework of *renqing* ethics. By diversifying the sources of his income, expanding his *guanxi* network, and fulfilling the obligations of *renqing*, Wang has been able not only to evenly distribute the risks but also to moralize his otherwise questionable business of money lending. As a result, he is widely recognized as one of the few individuals who have enriched themselves through hard work and a thrifty lifestyle, remaining all the while a good person. From the perspective of moral economy (Scott 1976), Wang is no doubt a socially rational actor who has been able to make the most rational choice on most occasions, providing that the notion of rationality is culturally specific and sensitive.

A good example of the embeddedness of rational choice in local culture is Wang's decision to let his son marry at the age of 19, three years earlier than the minimum age stated in the 1980 Marriage Law. Wang was able to bypass local authorities by not registering the marriage, but when his grandson was born the following year, Wang had to spend 1,360 yuan for bribes and in fines (all recorded in his account book) to obtain an official marriage license so that the newborn baby could be registered. When asked why his son could not wait until he turned into 22, Wang replied that it was he who could not wait because, as a well-respected and prosperous father, he was under strong pressure to help his son marry early so he, Wang, could have a grandson by the age of 40. "Otherwise, our family reputation would have been damaged, and my son might not have been able to find the best wife once he passed his prime. This is just the custom here, and I did what I was supposed to do as someone who really knows *renqing* well. The money [the bribery and the fines] was actually well-spent," concluded Wang.

Here, economic rationality constitutes only one aspect of Wang's exercise of agency, and having his son marry early, with seemingly irrational financial cost, was an equally important aspect of the same process of calculating and planning (*suanji*). Working on both fronts, Wang is able to cultivate himself as a proper person in the local moral world. It is not by accident that his account book is filled with old sayings and maxim on self-cultivation, such as "do not be overjoyed over what you receive, and do not worry over what you lose" (*de er buxi, shi er buyou*), "everything will go well when the family is in harmony" (*jiahe wangshixing*), and "the gentleman loves wealth but only pursues it in the proper way" (*junzi aicai, quzhi youdao*). Sometimes he is reflective, writing brief comments in his account book; one of which reads: "[Life] is as hard as walking on thin ice" (*ru lü po_bing, shifeng jiannan*).

CONCLUDING REMARKS

The cultural aspect of calculability is precisely what Max Weber tries to highlight when he examines the implications of accounting systems in different economies. According to Weber, there is a basic distinction between budgetary accounting and capital accounting. The former is oriented toward the rational use of income in order to meet the needs of consumption, the latter is oriented "not to marginal utility, but to profitability" (Weber 1978:92). The absence of such a fully rational system of capital accounting characterized by the double-entry bookkeeping method, argues Weber, is one of the factors that impeded the development of capitalism in China (1951:243). Although some scholars have made efforts to challenge Weber's thesis by demonstrating the existence of rationality in the Chinese accounting system and bookkeeping methods (see, e.g., Gardella 1992; Goody 1996), little scholarly attention has been devoted to the cultural principles on which the Chinese accounting system is based. What are the precise features of the Chinese accounting system? And, more importantly, how does it interact with the economic and social environments in which it is situated? The analysis of Wang's account book in the present study certainly cannot fully answer these questions, but it may shed new light on these issues from the perspective of a rural household economy embedded in *renqing* ethics.

A close look at Wang's account book and his strategies and choices in developing his household economy reveals that the local notion of *suanji* should be understood at three levels in ascending order: (1) a careful calculation of income and expenditure in order to economize; (2) a strategic planning of the household economy in order to maximize the returns to capital which, however, often do not include labor inputs due to extremely low opportunity costs; and (3) the consideration and practice of self-cultivation in order to be a proper person in the culture of *guanxi* and *renqing*. Being capable of *suanji* at the first level, according to my informants, is prerequisite for a decent life in the harsh and impoverished society of rural China, and being capable of *suanji* at the second level may make a person rich. But because no one can really escape from the moral constraints of *guanxi* and *renqing*, a person who is good only at economic calculation is regarded as *too* calculating and thus anti-social and immoral. It is only at the third level that one can simultaneously secure economic prosperity and a good reputation, and become a wise person who really knows how to calculate and plan (*hui suanji*) over the long run.

The Weberian distinction between budgetary and capital accounting cannot capture the rich meanings of calculability and planning (*suanji*) nor can it distinguish between its three levels because it is based on a single-dimensional, individual-centered definition of economic rationality. According to such a model, the economy is separate from society, and being a proper person is totally irrelevant to any type of accounting system. Obviously, this is not what we have found in the case of Wang's account book.

Interestingly, when I discussed the issue of calculating and planning with villager informants, many of them specifically used the difference between two local terms, *hu* and *sha*, to make their point. *Sha* simply means stupid, and the most evident indicator of stupidity is an incapability for numeral accounting, or *bu shishu* in local terms. *Hu* is not the mirror image of *sha* or stupidity; instead, it often results from overplaying one's smartness. The best example of being *hu*, according to these informants, is someone who is so calculating that she or he forgets *renqing* (read: becomes anti-social). A stupid person can still be well accepted in the community, but anyone who has been labeled as *hu* is bound to have a hard time in life because other villagers will try to avoid close interactions with such a person. After all, in a moral economy calculability must operate under the constraints of *renqing* ethics, thus providing a cultural element that coexists with economic rationality.

I began this paper by describing my encounter with the local custom of making and keeping gift lists, a special kind of accounting. What makes the gift lists so special, I argue, is the combination of literacy and numeracy skills because the power of writing has for so long been deeply embedded in the everyday life of ordinary people. In Xiajia Village, as elsewhere in rural China, literacy has always been considered not only a crucial element of the power and influence of local elites but also the key to successful farm management and commerce (see Smith 1970 [1899]), so much so that "the written work was in itself often an object of religious veneration" (Cohen 1970:xv). This is why, even though every family owns several gift lists and most people could themselves make notes on incoming gifts, they still prefer to have these lists compiled by invited assistants, often a well-respected or better-educated individual like a school teacher, and the lists must be compiled at a special accounting station, even if it is only an ordinary table placed at the corner of the ritual venue. Wang's account book demonstrates his literacy, numerical skills, and his persistence in keeping accounts for nearly 20 years, all of which has increase its symbolic power as a morally justified form of calculability on the part of a proper person.

On one hand, Wang's willingness to learn the techniques of accounting and budgeting and his ability to exercise these skills in the cultural practice of *suanji* shows that economic learning is centrally important in the local society. The cultural valuation of enumeration, calculation, education, and writing, on the other hand, provides us with a lens to understand how villagers understand and strategize their pursuit of economic agency.

NOTES

1. Household net income alone is not an accurate measure of a rural family's economic position because villagers need capital to invest in agricultural production. In my survey I used both household income and family assets to measure the economic position of a family. The second measurement includes primary tools of production, farm machinery and/or draft animals, and capital for family sidelines such as dairy cows, private enterprises, housing, savings, and consumer durables. For a more detailed account, see Van (1992:8–14). My first survey on household economic positions in 1989 has been updated three times, in 1991, 1994, and 1998.

2. Helping children, especially sons, marry in style is considered to be a crucial part of parenthood in rural China. Due to the escalating increase in marriage-related expenses, especially bridewealth, many parents have to work for 20 years or more to accomplish this culturally defined mission. For more detailed discussion on bridewealth and its relation to parenthood, see Yan (n.d.).

3. Interestingly, the Wang family has been purchasing eggs regularly since 1995, a sign that home-produced eggs were insufficient for consumption. Since the family always raises a small number of hens, the shift from selling to buying eggs is perhaps the best indicator of the changing life style and economic status of the family.

4. Interestingly, Wang's reckoning of the standards for services corresponds with the structure of *guanxi* networks in the village, which is comprised of three zones based on the degree of reliability in interpersonal relations: the personal core, the reliable zone, and the effective zone (see Van 1996:99–103).

REFERENCES

Acheson, James M. 1972 Accounting Concepts and Economic Opportunities in a Tarascan Village: Emic and Etic Views. *Human Organization* 31(1):83–91.

Cohen, Myron 1970 Introduction. In *Village Life in China*. Arthur H. Smith. Pp. ix–xxvi. Boston: Little, Brown and Company.

Boissevain, Jeremy 1968 The Place of Non-Groups in the Social Sciences. *Man* (n.s.) 3:542–556.

Gardella, Robert 1992 Squaring Accounts: Commercial Bookkeeping Methods and Capitalist Rationalism in Late Qing and Republican China. *Journal of Asian Studies* 51(2):317–339.

Goody, Jack 1996 *The East in the West.* Cambridge: Cambridge University Press.

Scott, James C. 1976 *The Moral Economy of the Peasant: Rebellion and Subsistence in Southeast Asia.* New Haven, CT: Yale University Press.

Smith, Arthur H. 1970 [1899] *Village Life in China.* Boston: Little, Brown and Company.

Weber, Max 1951 *The Religion of China: Confucianism and Taoism.* Hans Gerth, trans. Glencoe, IL: Free Press.

——— 1978 *Economy and Society.* Claus Wittich, ed. Berkeley; Los Angeles: University of California Press.

Yan, Yunxiang 1992 The Impact of Rural Reform on Economic and Social Stratification in a Chinese Village. *Australian Journal of Chinese Affairs* 27:1–23.

——— 1996 *The Flow of Gifts: Reciprocity and Social Networks in a Chinese Village.* Stanford: Stanford University Press.

——— 2003 *Private Life under Socialism: Love, Intimacy, and Family Change in a Chinese Village, 1949–1999.* Stanford: Stanford University Press.

——— n.d. *Individualism and the Transformation of Bridewealth in Rural North China.* Manuscript under review at the Journal of Royal Anthropological Institute.

CHAPTER 9

THE POLITICS OF CONSUMERISM

On March 15, 1999, *Beijing Youth Daily*, one of China's two most popular newspapers, published a feature article under a headline printed in unusually big characters: "The Springtime of Consumption." The author seriously advised readers that recent policy changes signaled the state's intention to stimulate mass consumption. To justify this policy shift, the author argued that "consumption used to be condemned as a kind of corrupt lifestyle and was always described with epithets such as 'hyper-consumption,' 'in-advance consumption,' and 'luxury consumption.' Some leaders even ordered banks to stop issuing personal loans for buying houses and automobiles. It is only now that consumption has been lifted to the unprecedentedly high level that it so much deserves. Consumption will be China's locomotive of economic growth."[1]

Consumption was indeed a hot topic in both official discourse and public opinion in the spring of 1999. The subject was first formally raised in a directive of the People's Bank of China, publicized in the *People's Daily* on March 4. The new directive loosened the central bank's control over loans, allowing all Chinese banks to make more personal loans, to lower the amount required for down payments, and to begin making loans for consumer durables, education, and even tourism. Throughout March and April, relevant government agencies and the mass media all launched into a propaganda campaign, encouraging people to take out loans for commodities and services, a practice that was nicknamed "*jieqian yuanmeng*" (borrowing money to realize one's dream).[2] At the same time, the central bank lowered interest rates for the seventh time since 1997, hoping to reduce the extremely high rate of personal savings, which amounted to more than 60 billion yuan by early 1999. The government's purpose was obvious: to expand the domestic market by "stimulating consumption and eventually to speed up the sluggish Chinese economy. However, the campaign had not been successful by the summer of 1999, and the focus of public discussion switched to the question of why the Chinese refused to take loans or spend their bank savings.[3]

This was the first time in the history of the People's Republic of China that the government openly recognized consumption as the key to economic growth and even went so far as to encourage people to consume more by taking out loans. This marked a sharp contrast to the communist ideology of the prereform period (1949–78), when "hard work and plain living" was promoted as the ideal. The officially endorsed role models during that period, such as the selfless soldier Lei Feng, barely consumed anything beyond basic subsistence needs; they all wanted to help the country by putting their modest savings in the state bank. To borrow money for consumption, many Beijing residents note, is a strange idea that they have never heard of before. Such a radical shift in economic policy obviously represents the triumph of consumerism.

The impact of mass consumption on the Chinese economy and domestic politics, however, is by no means a new phenomenon at the end of the 1990s. From the beginning of the economic reforms in the late 1970s, state policies on consumption have shifted back and forth. Advocates of reform have had to fight the legacy of the anticonsumption, ascetic ideology that dominated the first three decades of socialism. During the reform era, China has been swept by three successive waves of mass consumption, each of which has led to public debates and in some cases political changes. During the late 1980s and early 1990s, consumption and possession gradually replaced political symbols as the path toward defining one's social status and drawing group boundaries. The endless pursuit of material goods also helped to reduce the role of ideology in social life and to create more social space for individual citizens. Beginning in the early 1990s, a consumer revolution exploded across urban China; along with it, consumerism became a new ideology influencing the everyday life of ordinary citizens as well as the policy-making process, so much so that the consumer market slowdown in 1998 was regarded as a dangerous signal by both Chinese economists and government leaders, which led to the official push in 1999 for the expansion of consumption.

It seems to me that consumerism carries more sociopolitical meanings in China than in free-market societies. The present study, therefore, aims to unpack these meanings by examining how consumerism arose and what it has done to Chinese society.[4] In the first part of this chapter, I review the three waves of mass consumption during the past two decades. I argue that the third wave, in the early 1990s, differed in nature from the first two, in the 1980s, in that it carried the basic features of consumerism and marked the outbreak of a consumer revolution in urban China. The second part of the chapter concerns the main consequences and implications of the consumer revolution and analyzes the initial triumph of consumerism in relation to the formation of social classes, the change of dominant ideology, the creation of social space, the awareness of individual rights, and post–1989 politics in China.

Throughout the chapter, I use the term "consumerism" in a broad sense. It refers on the one hand to the ideology and practice that encourage people to consume more than what they need and on the other hand to the social movement for consumer protection that seeks to augment the rights and powers of consumers in relation to those of businesses that are interested only in making profits.[5] Defined as such, consumerism arises along with the emergence of a buyer's market, with the shift of emphasis in spending from foods to nonfood commodities, the increasing importance of fashion and taste, the awareness of consumer rights, and the organized action of consumers. It is, therefore, inadequate to depict consumerism only as the expression of consumers' seemingly unlimited and excessive desires/needs for commodities, which is mass consumption instead of consumerism. The key point is to avoid reducing consumers to mindless automatons in an undifferentiated mass society; rather, people (ordinary people as well as the elite) use consumption as a critical way of defining their social positions and changing power relations.[6] This is also why the present study focuses on the politics of consumerism in Chinese society.

FROM MASS CONSUMPTION TO CONSUMERISM: 1978 TO 1999

Anyone who visits Beijing, Shanghai, Guangzhou, or another Chinese city today cannot fail to be impressed by the dynamism and commercialism of the urban scene. The gigantic billboards along the newly constructed highways, the neon lights and skyscrapers in commercial districts, the well-dressed consumers in fancy shopping malls – all of these seem to boast to the world that at least urban China has become an affluent consumer society. The urban scene was, however, quite different two decades ago. A U.S. scholar recalled what he had observed in 1976: The streets were nearly deserted by seven in the evening; during the day a few buses moved along the streets, and tens of thousands of bicyclists dressed in blue cotton silently pedaled to and from their destinations. Vegetable and fruit stalls lined the main streets, offering little if any variety.[7] To better understand the remarkable changes over the past two decades, we need to look first at the prehistory of consumerism in China.

The Underdevelopment of Consumption during the Prereform Era

During the Maoist period (1949–76), consumption was reduced to the minimum. Influenced by the Soviet model of development, Chinese economic planning long gave top priority to the construction of heavy industry. The state built up a highly concentrated system of planning and redistribution, monopolizing the circulation of the means of production and major items of the means of subsistence as well. In urban areas, low wages and full employment constituted the core of labor policy, and Chinese workers received a more or less fixed salary for more than twenty years. To accommodate the low income of its citizens, the state provided subsidies for basic goods, housing, and transportation. For instance, state subsidies for food supplies in urban areas alone amounted to billions of yuan each year. The result was that the more people consumed, the more the state had to provide in subsidies, which made consumption counterproductive. This, plus the lack of incentive to produce under a planned economy, led to a shortage of basic subsistence goods for many years and forced the state to limit consumption and to issue ration coupons to make sure everyone got a share, no matter how minimal, of the small pie.

Under such a distribution system, consumption bore three distinctive features. First, there were few differences in consumption patterns and lifestyles – people basically wore the same kind of clothes, ate more or less the same kind of food, and lived in similar kinds of housing. True, there were small differences in material life across different occupations and regions, but they were so minor as to hardly reflect a clear sign of social differentiation. Rather, it was the political symbols (such as class labels or party membership) that served as marks of one's social status.

Second, consumption remained at the level of basic subsistence for almost three decades. More than 55 percent of household income was spent on food, mostly grain and vegetables. It normally took years to get a new outfit or a new pair of shoes. The popular saying for basic consumption was "three years new, three years old, and another three years by mending and patching" (*xin sannian, jiu sannian, fengfeng bubu you sannian*). Expenditure on entertainment was so small that it could be ignored: people did not have much money left over for leisure activities, and besides, most leisure activities, such as movies or concerts, were organized and paid for by work units as part of employee benefits.

Third, to sustain its policy of low consumption and high accumulation (of capital for national development), the state launched consistent ideological as well as administrative attacks on the individual pursuit of luxury goods or comfortable lifestyles, condemning them as manifestations of "corrupt bourgeois culture." Shops selling jewelry, furs or other expensive clothing, and cosmetics were closed down after the mid-1950s; bars and dance halls, together with brothels, were considered corrupt and were banned. In their place grew a large number of small shops for the masses. Ideologically, the state imposed a kind of socialist asceticism in everyday life, as reflected in the leading slogan of the time, "hard work and plain living." In a well-known movie called *Must Never Forget*, a man became the captive of corrupt bourgeois thoughts when he bought himself a wool suit. This kind of thinking reached such heights that, during the radical period of the late 1960s to the early 1970s, a young girl wearing a colorful hairpin could be subject to severe criticism for having unhealthy, petty bourgeois thoughts; old, patched clothes were considered a symbol of being revolutionary, or at least politically correct.

Two Waves of Mass Consumption in the 1980s

This ascetic ideology, or communist-style puritanism, was turned upside down after Mao's death in 1976. In order to revitalize the national economy, which was, according to the reformers, on the edge of collapse, Chinese Communist Party (CCP) leaders under Deng Xiaoping decided to launch economic reforms and to break China's isolation from the world. Consumption became an important part of the political agenda underlying the government's promotion of economic reforms. A famous slogan promoted by the reformers at that time was *nengzheng huihua*, which means "able to make money and knowing how to spend it." This slogan was in direct conflict with the official ideology of Maoist socialism that emphasized "hard work and plain living."

As mentioned earlier, there have been three distinct waves of mass consumption in the reform era. The first wave (1979–82) was initiated by peasants. The quick success of rural reform doubled peasant income during the short period from 1979 to 1984, which had a profound impact on both the circulation and consumption of goods nationwide. Having been poverty-stricken for years and suddenly having cash in their pockets, peasants hurried into markets and shops for all kinds of industrial products, ranging from washbasins to small tractors. Later, urbanites, who had just received their first wage raise in twenty years, joined the consumption wave. This tidal wave of mass consumption, which peaked in 1979–80, featured massive demand in the countryside for the products of light industry and an obvious increase of expenditure on foodstuffs in urban areas. Consumer demand increased by 22 percent in 1979 and 1980, far exceeding the 15.3 percent increase in consumer supplies during the same period. The result was an inflation rate of 6 percent in 1980, China's first taste of inflation since the late 1950s.[8] This led to a three-year (1982–85) period of government-enforced economic retrenchment. As a result, although peasant income continued to grow quickly until 1985, it was the state itself that put an end to the first wave of mass consumption.

The suddenly increased purchasing power of peasants broke the psychological balance of urban residents, who had for more than two decades enjoyed a superior status, and their discontent, plus the window effect of rural reforms, pushed the CCP leaders into launching urban economic reforms in the mid-1980s. In other words, the first wave of mass consumption made an important political contribution by facilitating the urban reforms of the mid-1980s.

The second wave of mass consumption started in early 1985, shortly after the urban reform programs launched by the state in 1984, and ended suddenly in 1989. Unlike the first wave, in which peasants played a key role, urban consumers formed the major force in this second wave. An important goal of the urban reforms was to adjust the previous state redistribution structure to allocate a larger proportion of revenue to wages. As a result, the average income of urban residents almost doubled during the period from 1985 to 1988. The private sector grew quickly and vigorously, more regions opened to foreign investment, and rural industry also made impressive progress during this period. All these factors added up to create a strong demand for consumer goods of all kinds. During this period, the state also loosened its control of the mass media. Newspapers and popular magazines were filled with reports of the "modern lifestyle" in developed countries, which produced another window effect on ordinary consumers.

In imitation of the state's goal of "four modernizations," ordinary citizens during the 1980s worked hard to realize their own "family modernization," which meant the possession of major appliances such as refrigerators, television sets, washing machines, and tape recorders. The demand and desire for appliances and other consumer goods seemed to be unlimited in the late 1980s. As a result, the inflation rate jumped to 18.5 percent in 1988, and when the state decided to launch a new reform of consumer prices in March 1988, panic purchasing broke out nationwide. Ordinary citizens terrified by the inflation rushed to buy whatever they could get their hands on. During my fieldwork in 1989, several interviewees showed me the stored goods that they had bought in 1988, such as dozens of blankets, a hundred bars of soap, and multiple boxes of toilet paper (this actually created tremendous difficulties for these people because most Chinese families do not have extra space for storage). It was also in this period that a large number of consumer goods for daily life flowed in from abroad, and consuming imported goods quickly became a new fashion among those who had gotten ahead economically and among a whole generation of youth.

The panic purchasing in 1988 in a way contributed to the popular protest movement in 1989, and the June 4 incident ended the second wave of mass consumption. In the following two years, the real income of both urban and rural families decreased by nearly 3 percent, and the state also imposed much stricter controls on the private sector of the economy. (Strangely, standards of living did not deteriorate, owing to special consumption policies. This is discussed further below.) The 1988 panic purchasing was frequently cited to show the importance of stability and order, and "overheated consumption" was blamed for economic difficulties during this period.[9] For a short time, China's reform era seemed to have come to a dead end.

CONSUMER REVOLUTION IN THE 1990s: THE THIRD WAVE AND ITS AFTERMATH

The economic stagnation after the end of the second wave of mass consumption (and the political repression associated with it) was ended by

Deng Xiaoping's 1992 tour to the southern city of Shenzhen, where he called upon both the CCP and the nation to be bolder in carrying out the policies of openness and speeding up the market-oriented economic reforms. As if it had broken a spell, Deng's speech quickly led to a new round of rapid economic growth. This began with the unprecedented phenomenon of *xiahai* ("jumping into the sea"); in other words, a large number of government officials, professionals, and intellectuals gave up their secure positions in government to go to work in the private sector. For a year or two, it seemed that the entire Chinese population was being lured into private business, and for most people moneymaking had become the highest ideal. The fever of investment, plus the quick growth of the real estate and stock markets, not only worked an "instant miracle" (which was in reality a bubble economy) but also stirred up people's desire and demand for more and better consumer goods; this caused the third wave of mass consumption, which started in 1992 and continued until 1996. The consumer market has slowed down since 1996, in part because of the state's "soft landing" policy in 1996–97, which aimed to control the overheated economy, and in part because of the impact of the Asian financial crisis in 1997–98.

It is the third wave of mass consumption, in my opinion, that bears the essential features of consumerism, such as the emergence of a buyer's market, the shift of emphasis in expenditure from food to other goods, the awareness of individual rights, and the development of a consumer movement. More important is that through this wave of mass consumption, consumerism has become the dominant ideology in Chinese society and one of the means available to the Communist Party to maintain its legitimacy. This is why consumerism continues to play an important role in social life and politics, as shown in the beginning of this chapter, even though the high tide of the third wave of mass consumption had already passed by 1996. Therefore, for several reasons the third wave of mass consumption deserves a closer look.

First, a buyer's market has emerged. As mentioned above, the two waves of mass consumption during the 1980s arose in the context of a shortage of consumer goods, which included both regular light industrial products for rural residents and electronic appliances for urban residents. Thanks to the previous ten-year economic reform, the tension between demand and supply began to change in the early 1990s. According to a 1992 report by the Ministry of Commerce, among six hundred major categories of consumer goods, 32 percent of the categories were produced in excess of market demand, 10 percent fell short of demand, and supply and demand for the rest were in balance. The supply-demand pattern has continued to improve. A recent report shows that by 1998, the supply and demand of 84 percent of six hundred major consumer goods were in balance, supply exceeded demand in only 14 percent, and in no category of consumer goods was there a shortage of supply.[10]

Because of the abundance of supplies and the pressure on retailers to turn a profit, consumers now have more choices as well as more bargaining power. "Customers are our god" has become a new commercial slogan, and sellers have had to resort to various techniques to promote sales, such as offering gifts or discounts, issuing discount cards, and using sandwich men. By 1993–94, the improvement in the shopping environment had become a big issue. In just a few years (by 1998), the glut of industrial goods and the satiation of consumer demand became a serious problem for the Chinese economy, as they led to a severe price war that forced a large number of retailers out of business. Clearly, for the first time since 1949, a fully developed buyer's market has emerged in China.[11]

Second, shopping has become an increasingly important part of everyday life for ordinary citizens, and people have begun to purchase goods they want but do not necessarily need.[12] Strolling through fancy shopping malls has become a popular leisure activity, especially among young women. During my fieldwork in 1994, 1998, and 1999, I asked my interviewees how often they went to shopping malls and why they did so. Nearly two-thirds of the women (aged 20–35) whom I interviewed said that they went weekly, and did so mainly "just to check it out" or "to have fun." Although the frequency of regular touring of shopping malls seems to have decreased a bit among young professional women in the last two years, their overall concern with and awareness of fashion, style, and taste has definitely increased. Several interviewees told me that they did not "worship" the goods in shopping malls; instead, they went there to "relax and make ourselves feel good." Another interesting and impressive piece of evidence of this change is that children are very knowledgeable about Beijing's new shopping malls and the products available there. A primary school teacher told me in 1994 that children in her class knew much more about brand names than did many of the teachers. Every Monday, a common topic of conversation among children was their experience in shopping malls over the past weekend. To test children's knowledge of commodities, I asked my two nephews, both aged nine in 1994, to identify the cars in a newly published auto magazine. To my surprise, they quickly named the models and manufacturers of more than half of the cars depicted.

Third, the expenditure structure of urban households has changed significantly in the 1990s: total spending on food, after years of steady yet slow decrease, fell to 49.9 percent of household income in 1995. This was the first time in the People's Republic that a significant number of urban residents had more than half of their income available for expenditure on nonfood items. The Engle's coefficient (the percentage of household income used for food expenditure) continued to drop, decreasing all the way to 45 percent among urban households by 1998.[13]

Indeed, in the 1990s urban consumers began to change their consumption patterns and spending habits in many ways. According to 1994 statistics released by the China Consumers Association, the average expenditure per capita has increased 4.1 times since 1984. The ratio of "hard consumption" (of food, clothes, and other daily necessities) to "soft consumption" (spending money on entertainment, tourism, fashion, and socializing) has changed from 3:1 in 1984 to 1:1.2 in 1994.[14] As a result, the hot areas of mass consumption have shifted to interior decoration, personal computers, communications devices, air conditioners, body-building machines, and tourism.[15]

A good indicator of the escalating demand for consumption is the changing definition of the "three big items" (san dajian), referring to the three products that are the most desirable. During the 1960s and 1970s, the "three big items" were wristwatches, bicycles, and sewing machines. Families saved for years to buy these expensive items (which cost an average of two hundred yuan each). In the 1980s, color television sets, refrigerators, and washing machines, each costing at least one thousand yuan, had become the new "three big items." By the early 1990s, the "three bigs" were telephones, air conditioners, and VCRs. For the new entrepreneurial class, the stakes have become so high that the three bigs are apartments, private cars, and cellular phones.[16] By the late 1990s, communications devices and leisure activities represented the latest development of consumerism. Pagers, personal computers, cellular phones, and Internet connections took turns as symbols of social status among trendy consumers in Chinese cities. What surprised me in this regard was that, during my visit to a remote farming village in northeastern China in 1998, I was frequently questioned by villagers as to why I did not have a cell phone. Later I found out that the two village leaders and several better-off individuals all had followed the trend and purchased cell phones, which made them a necessary status symbol in the village.

Fourth, gone with the traditional patterns of consumption is "tidal-wave consumption" (*pailangshi xiaofei*), a term used by Chinese scholars to describe seemingly mindless conformity in consumer choices. During the first two waves of mass consumption, there was a ticket item each year, such as television sets or refrigerators. Consumers from all walks of life wanted the same consumer items regardless of whether those items fit the individuals' needs, economic capability, and residential circumstances. This concentrated consumer demand easily created temporary shortages of one consumer product or another, which in turn stimulated further demand (sometimes even panic demand) until the wave broke. However, because of three new factors, tidal-wave consumption did not arise in the latest trend of mass consumption.

The first factor is that most Chinese families had basically completed their "family modernization": they had already acquired all the "essential" items, such as television sets, refrigerators, and washing machines. When they felt the need to choose from items that were more upscale and less necessary, such as air conditioners or recreational activities, they had no fixed formula to follow. Second, consumers had grown mature. Because of the rapid development of the domestic economy in the 1990s, they no longer worried about the exhaustion of supplies, and they had accepted inflation as a normal part of economic life. People remained calm even in 1994 when the inflation rate shot up above 20 percent, in contrast with the panic in 1984 when the inflation rate was 18.5 percent. The third and perhaps most important factor is that Chinese society has become rapidly differentiated economically (in a sense even polarized). People have found themselves falling into separate strata in terms of income and lifestyle. In the 1980s, the less fortunate may have resorted to the power of their kinship networks to compete with the better-off in purchasing household appliances; in the 1990s, there was no way for the majority of the Chinese people even to approach the luxurious lifestyle of the newly rich, who could easily spend 100,000 yuan for a wristwatch or 3,000 yuan for a bottle of imported wine.

The Rise of the Consumer Protection Movement

The most important aspect of consumerism in the 1990s was the rise of a consumer protection movement. In the buyer's market that existed, consumer discontent with shoddy products, bad service, and fake goods grew rapidly. Many consumers complained that even the quality of imported products, mainly household appliances, had declined. It was reported that some foreign manufacturers exploited the popularity of imported goods in the Chinese market by shipping factory seconds and rejects to China or denying customers' claims for after-sale services under warranty. Worse than shoddy products were faked goods, particularly foodstuffs. For instance, early in 1998, several peasants in Shanxi province produced fake liquor by mixing water with nine hundred times the officially permitted amount of methyl alcohol. As a result, 27 people died, and more than 200 were hospitalized.[17]

To fight faulty products and fake goods, a consumer protection movement gradually emerged, both in the form of a semiofficial consumer association and through individual action. The China Consumers Association was established as early as 1984, but it only gained wide support and popularity during the 1990s. Interestingly, as with the rural reforms and some other reform programs, the first push for consumer protection came from the grassroots level. In May 1983, the first local consumer association was established in Xinle County, Henan province, an area notorious for violating consumers' rights and for producing fake goods. Three months later, a similar organization appeared in Guangzhou, the most developed and open city at that time. As a response to calls from below, the China Consumers Association was established on December 26, 1984. By 1998 it had built up a nationwide network of more than 3,000 branch associations at the provincial, municipal, and county levels, plus a reported 45,000 grassroots association branches below the county level.

Although the association's constitution states that it is a mass organization, its organizational structure, budget, and personnel show that it is actually a de facto government agency. The leading positions in the association are all occupied by high-ranking officials, an indicator of both the government's support of consumer protection and the official nature of this organization. For instance, its first president was the deputy director of the State Administration for Industry and Commerce, its first honorary president was the vice-chairman of the Standing Committee of the People's Congress and the director of the Finance and Trade Committee of the State Council, and its first secretary-general was a deputy head of the Bureau of Market Administration of the State Administration for Industry and Commerce. Many staff members were transferred into the association from various government agencies concerned with commerce and market administration. This power structure has remained intact at both the national and local levels since 1984. At lower levels, the association may share the same office space and personnel with the Bureau of Administration of Industry and Commerce, a common practice called "one personnel crew with two organizational titles" (*yi ban renma, liangkuai paizi*).[18] Employees at consumer associations above the county level are paid by the government, and the operating funds are provided by relevant government agencies. For instance, the consumer association in Heilongjiang province had 750 employees by 1996, all of whom were paid by government at various levels. Of its total budget of 1.5 million yuan in 1996, 600,000 yuan was provided by the Provincial Bureau of Administration of Industry and Commerce (*Gongshang guanli ju*), 100,000 yuan by the Provincial Bureau of Commodity Prices (*Wujia ju*), and the rest by the Department of Public Health, Bureau of Commodity Inspection, Bureau of Technology Supervision, and so forth.[19]

The China Consumers Association has achieved considerable success in many areas. It has sent investigation teams to visit stores and markets to inspect the quality of products and search out fake goods; it has also launched consumer-education programs through its mouthpieces – the *China Consumer Daily* (founded in 1984) and the journal *Chinese Consumer* (founded in 1995) – as well as through national and local mass media, schools, and other organizations. But its greatest achievement thus far is in representing consumers in lodging complaints against manufacturers and service providers. Because of its close links to the various government agencies mentioned above, the China Consumers Association was able to obtain compensation for consumers in nearly 90 percent of the cases. Encouraged by this high success rate and backed up by their increased awareness of consumer rights, consumers have filed a steadily increasing number of formal complaints, up from 8,000 in 1985 to over 700,000 in 1997.[20] Because of the state's support, the association's achievement has also helped to improve the government's image as the protector of consumers.

In addition to seeking help from government agencies and the semi-official China Consumers Association, some people have begun to set up voluntary organizations to promote consumer protection. In 1996, a consulting company started accepting consumer complaints over a twenty-four-hour hot line and providing assistance such as finding good lawyers for consumers who sought compensation. Another private foundation was established in Zhejiang province in 1995, with the goal of detecting and fighting fake goods. By the end of 1998, several dozen voluntary organizations for consumer protection had appeared, but they were mostly small and had very limited power and influence.[21]

The "Wang Hai Phenomenon" and the Rule of Law in Consumption

To raise public awareness about faulty and fake products and to protect their own interests, some individuals have taken bold and sometimes dramatic action. Among them, Mr. Wang Hai deserves special attention for his strategic strikes on shoddy and fake goods. According to Article 49 of the Protection of Consumer Rights and Interests Law passed by the People's Congress in early 1995, a consumer who purchases a faulty or fake product is entitled to be compensated by the seller in an amount double the original price of the product. Inspired and encouraged by the new law, Wang Hai decided to attack the peril of fake goods in his own way.

On March 25, 1995, Wang purchased two Sony earphone sets at the state-owned Longfu Department Store in Beijing and verified that they were fake. Unlike most other customers, who would try to return fake products, he went back to the store and purchased the remaining ten sets of fake earphones. He then asked the store to compensate him with double the amount of the original price, citing the new law to support his claim. The store manager agreed to pay for the first two earphone sets that Wang had purchased but not for the other ten sets that he had bought later with the knowledge that they were fake. The manager argued that Wang was trying to buy fake goods solely for the purpose of claiming the double compensation, and he accused Wang of being a tricky hooligan who was cheating the store, manipulating the law, and damaging the interests of the state (because the store is a state-owned enterprise).

Wang went to law enforcement agencies for help but was similarly turned down. He admitted to the media that before he purchased the earphones he was already pretty familiar with the new law and planned to claim the double compensation in accordance with the law. He was therefore quite disappointed when his claim was denied both by the seller and by law enforcement agencies in Beijing. Later, in early September 1995, shortly after regulations entitled Methods of Implementing the Consumer Protection Law were issued by the Beijing municipal government, Wang returned to Beijing and resumed his adventure. He chose to buy fake goods from large department stores and shopping malls, because he felt that consumers would be angrier with these big retailers. From late September to late November 1995, he purchased fake products parading as famous brands (such as Gucci shoes and Goldlion belts) twelve times and successfully claimed double compensation in eleven cases, turning a tidy profit of more than 8,000 yuan ($1,000).[22]

The mass media responded quickly to Wang's adventures, covering his move from one city to another and rapidly turning him into a public hero. Wang's fame reached a peak when the Chinese government chose him to be among those to meet President Clinton during the latter's state visit to China in the summer of 1998. Later in the same year, he was also selected as one of twenty representative figures of the reform era to appear in the political documentary *Twenty Years, Twenty People*, aired by Chinese Central Television. However, Wang also ran into difficulties in his struggle against retailers of counterfeit goods and lost several legal battles, evidently because judges believed that Wang himself was cheating when he knowingly purchased fake goods.

The media sensation in turn transformed Mr. Wang's individual actions into a widespread "Wang Hai phenomenon." A number of individuals followed his example and purchased fake goods for the purpose of claiming double compensation. Some even set up companies to provide professional services in this respect. A man established a business for "beating fake goods" (by purchasing them and then claiming double compensation) in June 1996; by January 1997, he had spent 180,000 yuan on fake goods and had earned 140,000 yuan over that amount in compensation. He had a team of more than a dozen employees, each of whom could earn a net income of more than 1,000 yuan per month. Another consumer had gone further and set up a telephone line for free consultation, as well as a company to represent consumers in claiming the double compensation.

It is interesting that Wang Hai himself set up a firm in 1997 and worked for some large companies to investigate the forgery of the companies' products. By so doing, he shifted from representing ordinary consumers to representing big business.[23] As someone commented, "beating fake goods" itself had become a new business.[24] However, the most valuable outcome of the Wang Hai phenomenon was perhaps the awareness of consumer rights among ordinary consumers. As Wang Hai himself correctly concluded, "What I represent is a peculiar phenomenon that exists only in the era of openness and reform, that is, popularizing and raising the awareness of consumer rights."[25]

Wang's acts and the Wang Hai phenomenon led to public debates during 1995–98 that generated different opinions from retailers, consumer organizations, government agencies, lawmakers, law enforcement agencies, social scientists, and ordinary consumers. A series of interesting questions was raised: Is Wang Hai a hero fighting for consumer protection or a tricky person who just wants to turn a profit? Is it really cheating when a retailer sells fake goods? Is it also cheating when one purchases fake goods on purpose? Who should lead the fight to "beat fake goods" – individual consumers or the relevant government agencies? Should China import the notion of "punitive damages" and increase the amount of compensation? Some commentators argued that the emergence of the Wang Hai phenomenon actually revealed the impotence of government agencies and people's lack of confidence in the rule of law. It was equally urgent and important, many maintained, to perfect consumer protection laws and actually to implement those laws.[26] The consumer protection movement has therefore been part of the current reform toward a society ruled by law.

It should be noted that the media have played a double role by promoting both sides of consumerism. On one hand, both the China Consumers Association and individual consumers rely on the support of the mass media in the fight against abusive, cheating retailers and service providers. Almost all newspapers have long consumer columns; consumer hot lines on the radio publicize individual complaints and provide advice; television programs regularly air lengthy investigative reports regarding consumer protection issues; and there are a number of specialized journals on consumer protection. An interesting footnote in this respect is that, according to a high-ranking official in the China Consumers Association, the Wang Hai case was itself a dramatized event produced through cooperation between the association and the news media.[27]

Ironically, it is the same mass media that played an active role in promoting the fetishization of commodities and the endless desire for possessions in the first place, through its sensationalized coverage of fashion, modern lifestyles, and conspicuous consumption among the newly rich. A successful example is the *Purchasing Guide to Upscale Goods*, admittedly the most popular newspaper of its kind, which features special columns instructing consumers in fashion, taste, leisure activities, and interior decoration and provides up-to-date information on trendy goods. More important, the Chinese mass media have also been commercialized in the 1990s and have become an increasingly competitive business. According to a report of the Bureau of Information and Publications, there were 9,175 magazines (including 3 magazines directly imported from abroad) and more than 5,000 newspapers circulating on the market in 1998. Periodicals must fight hard to attract advertisements and readership. It is in this context that the media play the double role of promoting both sides of consumerism.

THE CONSEQUENCES AND IMPLICATIONS OF CONSUMERISM: A PRELIMINARY ASSESSMENT

It is a commonplace that consumerism is directly related to the performance of the economy in general and to the level of personal income in particular. The Chinese case is by no means an exception. The Chinese economy has been developing rapidly since 1978, with a double-digit growth rate on average over the past two decades. Under the impact of the Asian financial crisis in 1997, the growth rate fell to less than 8 percent for the first time in the reform era, but the economy as a whole was still considered strong. Like the economy, personal income has been increasing steadily, although it varies across different social groups in different periods. From 1978 to 1985, rural per capita income more than doubled, and as a result, rural per capita consumption also doubled. This, as mentioned above, made rural residents the major players in the first wave of mass consumption. However, the rate of income growth in rural areas slowed down after 1985 and has not recovered since. By contrast, urban per capita income increased much more rapidly between 1984 and 1988, and the trend continued in the next five-year period, albeit at a lower rate because of the economic retrenchment after 1989. It was during this period that – with a focus on household appliances and other nonfood commodities – the second wave of mass consumption swept over urban China. Beginning in 1992, urban per capita income began to rise rapidly, jumping from 1,826 yuan in 1992 to 3,830 yuan in 1995 and to 5,454 yuan in 1998. At the same time, personal savings grew to unprecedented levels: 23 billion yuan in 1992, 50 billion yuan in 1997, and more than 60 billion yuan by the spring of 1999.[28]

Although the rapid growth of the economy and the increase of personal income are obviously the main factors that made the rise of consumerism possible, a closer look from a sociopolitical perspective reveals that the rise of consumerism also involves a number of other factors. For instance, outside observers have been puzzled that so many people in China could afford to buy similar costly items at the same time, such as big-screen television sets and cellular phones in 1997–98. This contradicts the received wisdom that consumer choices are differentiated by differences in income. Here one must take into consideration that in Chinese society buying big consumer items is not just an individual matter; instead, it often involves the economic power of a larger kinship and *guanxi* network.[29] Moreover, the sign value of some status-related commodities is exploited to its maximum by people who are trying hard to reposition themselves in the transitional period. For instance, it is common to see cellular phones being loaned among good friends or relatives. In short, the booming consumerism is not merely a reflection of the booming economy; rather, it also reflects the changing social system and facilitates further changes in the system, such as redrawing the boundaries between social groups, creating social space outside state control, and forming a new ideology.

YOU ARE WHAT YOU PURCHASE: THE SYMBOLISM OF CONSUMPTION

The most obvious change that consumerism has wrought on Chinese society is its subversion of the existing socialist hierarchy established during the prereform period. Consumerism enables some people to redefine their social status in terms of consumption and lifestyle. In this connection, a well-known case of the early 1990s is particularly noteworthy.

On November 22, 1992, a motorcade led by six black Cadillacs and followed by more than twenty Mercedes-Benzes, Audis, and other luxury cars rolled toward Tiananmen Square from the eastern end of Chang'an Avenue, the most important thoroughfare in Beijing. A policeman who was directing traffic panicked when he first saw the motorcade because he had not received any notice from above that a presidential motorcade would pass his post. He was so panic-stricken, in fact, that he could not find the right end of his walkie-talkie when he tried to contact his superiors. By that time, the motorcade had passed under his nose. It was only after talking with colleagues from other posts that he discovered it was just a wedding motorcade for Mr. Shen, a young Beijing millionaire. This event attracted a lot of public attention precisely because the policeman misidentified Mr. Shen's private wedding motorcade as a government motorcade, a strong signal that the existing hierarchy was being undermined by the emerging power of private businesspeople.[30]

It turned out that Mr. Shen used to be a poorly educated and un-employed youth who was looked down upon by his peers and neighbors. He started a small retail business in the 1980s and soon made a fortune from it – a story typical of successful so-called *getihu*, a term that literally means "individual households." Like Mr. Shen, a large number of *getihu* came from humble family backgrounds, had been unemployed, lacked good education, and may even have had troubled pasts. Faced with such disadvantages, these urban youth started private retail and service businesses in the early 1980s, and they became the first group of rich people in the cities. To improve their social status and secure their positions, these *getihu* were eager to show off their wealth through conspicuous consumption of fancy clothes, luxurious banquets, leisure activities, household appliances, gambling, and various forms of senseless competition. It was reported, for example, that one man spent 188,000 yuan for a dinner in order to outdo a rival, and in another case, a rich man covered the walls of his house with 10-yuan bills.[31] Because of their conspicuous spending habits, along with their somewhat negative personal backgrounds, such people became targets of criticism by the elite strata and the focus of public envy of almost all of society. Nevertheless, they did make a strong point through their consumption, namely, that in this new era of market-oriented reforms, money speaks louder than anything else. In most cases, one can buy both comfort and respect with money – a point made conspicuously, for instance, by Mr. Shen with his wedding motorcade, and a point most people (if not all) quickly accepted as the truth.

Starting in the late 1980s, popular magazines and weekend-edition newspapers repeatedly featured and sensationalized stories of conspicuous consumption among the newly rich. The composition of the newly rich,

however, changed substantially after 1992, and so did the specific manifestations of conspicuous consumption. Shortly after Deng Xiaoping's
south China tour in early 1992, all across the country members of the elite
rushed to get into private business. Thousands of intellectuals, scientists,
artists, government officials, and even high-ranking cadres quit their
jobs, which not long before had been considered symbols of their social
achievement. This was called *xiahai* ("jumping into the sea" – the sea of
private business and commercial activities). An important psychological
push for these people was the thought, "so many *getihu* have become rich,
now it's our turn." Based on their personal connections in government or
their areas of expertise, plus their education and brainpower, many of these
newcomers succeeded in a short time and gained a new label – "private
entrepreneurs" – that distinguished them from the *getihu* of the 1980s.

Private entrepreneurs and leaders of state-owned enterprises or firms
came to constitute the backbone of the newly rich in the 1990s. Like
their *getihu* predecessors, these newly rich are notorious for conspicuous
consumption. This is particularly true of those in charge of government-
sponsored businesses or state-owned enterprises, because it is much
safer for them to spend public money under their control than to convert
it into their private property (though many have done both, as is evident
from the numerous corruption cases exposed by the Chinese media).
However, the newly rich of the 1990s have shown more interest in learning
to be the upper class through more refined and glamorous consumption.
For instance, the best a *getihu* could do in the 1980s was to spend 188,000
yuan on a banquet; by the late 1990s, one of the basic qualifications for
being rich in Shenzhen is to have a golf-course membership, which can
run more than $100,000.[32]

In addition to the newly rich, young professionals (or the emerging
"white-collar" class) who are better educated and well paid also actively use
consumption as a means of status maintenance. These young professionals
emerged along with the development of the market economy, especially
with the expansion of joint-venture and foreign-owned businesses during
the past decade. To prove and further secure their newly obtained social
status and prestige, they have taken the construction of a different lifestyle most seriously. Unlike the newly rich, the young professionals do
not (and probably cannot afford to) engage in mindless conspicuous
consumption; rather, they tend to follow the changing trends of fashion
and taste in the outside world closely.

As mentioned above, the phenomenon of tidal-wave consumption in the 1980s disappeared in the 1990s; in its place grew a much more differentiated consumer market. A direct result of this change is that people have become even more conscious of what consumption habits and lifestyle can do to one's social status. This social construct of consumption struck me deeply on two quite different occasions during my fieldwork in the summer of 1999.

The first was in a village in Heilongjiang province, where I found that the cost of financing a son's marriage had gone up again in comparison with what I had recorded the previous year – the highest cost of 30,000 yuan recorded in 1998 had become a must in 1999. This heavy economic burden inevitably falls on the shoulders of parents who feel morally obligated to get their sons married in style. When asked why, all my village friends answered that they would lose face and social status, not to mention the very prospect of getting their sons married at all, if they failed to follow the trend. Two months later, I went to a dinner at a country club in the southern city of Shenzhen, where an old friend went on for hours telling me of his new life since joining the world of golf. Country-club membership has been one of the most popular gifts private entrepreneurs bestow on government officials, according to him. When I tried to remind him that bowling used to be considered a high-class activity in Shenzhen several years ago,[33] he and his friends all laughed and insisted that golf was the only true sport for high-status people with good taste. I became convinced that whether they are in a remote village or the prosperous city of Shenzhen, people are uniformly conscious of the importance of consumption in defining their social status.

Consuming properly and stylishly has become so important that consumption know-how itself has become a commodity. As indicated above, a number of magazines and newspapers are devoted solely to consumption-related issues, and one can find consumption-related news reports, columns, and discussions in almost all the popular magazines and newspapers, not to mention various advertisements. An interesting article in a specialized newspaper, for instance, offers a long list of dress codes, matching brand-name clothes, shoes, wristwatches, belts, and bags with different people at different income levels.[34] One of the most recent examples in this connection is the popularity of a translated book – Paul Fussell's *Class: A Guide through the American Status System.* Tens of thousands of copies (including pirated copies) of this book were sold in early 1999, and it was regarded as the bible of lifestyle by many readers, particularly young people. As a result, several copycat books written by Chinese authors quickly appeared on the market, all with words such as "taste," "manners," and "status" in their titles, and they also sold well.[35]

Although many in the elite insist that the differentiation of the consumer market symbolizes the maturity of Chinese economic reform, the expanding income disparity between the rich and poor and the increasing social inequality are quite alarming. The rural-urban gap in consumption continued to grow in the 1990s, as the rate of rural income increase fell far behind that of urban residents. And in cities, the reform of state-owned enterprises over the past three years has led to widespread unemployment, leaving workers disadvantaged in every aspect of social life including consumption. The unpleasant side of this differentiated consumer market was demonstrated graphically in Beijing shopping malls during the hottest days of summer 1997. When the temperature climbed above one hundred degrees, a strange group of visitors arrived at shopping centers every evening; they walked into the fancy malls in family groups, wearing slippers and pajamas, waving hand fans, and sometimes even bringing little stools with them. They did not come to buy anything, not even to window-shop; instead, they just wanted to cool off in the climate-controlled malls because they could not afford home air conditioners.[36] This unexpected and unusual "invasion" of fancy shopping malls by the urban poor shows that differences in consumption capabilities and styles have become a major way of measuring people and of distinguishing them from one another both socially and spatially.

During the summer of 1999, I also witnessed a middle-aged man standing in the middle of a narrow street with his bicycle, refusing to give up the road to a red BMW that was headed in his direction. He argued angrily with the driver of the car, shouting repeatedly, "Don't think you can do whatever you want just because you have a car!" Within a few minutes, the incident drew a crowd of more than a hundred onlookers; it also caused a long line of cars to form, jammed behind the BMW. What struck me was that most of the onlookers showed their sympathy and moral support for the bicyclist, despite the fact that his angry reaction was causing a serious traffic jam. Later I was told that the explosive growth in the number of private cars in Beijing had created serious tension between those who own cars and those who don't, as they all had to fight for space on the overcrowded streets. A sociologist friend joked that if there were another land-reform-like campaign in the future, it would be a struggle by bicyclists and bus riders against car owners.

THE POWER OF COMFORT: SOCIAL SPACE AND INDIVIDUAL FREEDOM

While it sorts consumers into different social groups (and sometimes different spaces as well), consumerism also opens up new public spaces for individuals and helps free them from the previous dominance of communist ideology and collectivism. A significant change in public life during the postreform era has been the disappearance of frequent mass rallies, voluntary work, collective parties, and other forms of what I prefer to call "organized sociality," in which the state (through its agents) plays the central role. In its place are various newly emerged forms of private gatherings in public yet commercialized venues, such as shopping malls, restaurants, cafés, bars, and clubs. Unlike the previous "organized sociality," which emphasized the centrality of the state, official ideology, and the submission of the individual to an officially endorsed collectivity, the new sociality in these commercialized venues features the celebration of individuality and private desires in unofficial social/spatial contexts. The center of public life and socializing, accordingly, has shifted from state-controlled, larger public spaces (such as city squares, auditoriums, and workers' clubs) to smaller, commercialized arenas.

As James Farrer has noted, dance halls in Shanghai during the 1990s offered places of escape where customers could explore and display their desires, aspirations, and even identities through dancing. Also conducting research in Shanghai during the same period, Kathleen Erwin discovered that radio call-in shows and counseling hot lines provided ordinary residents a new public space to talk about their problems, express their emotionality, and by implication, expand their individual freedom in public life. My own research of McDonald's outlets in Beijing shows that imported fast-food restaurants provide another such arena that meets the increasing demand for a new kind of sociality outside state control, that is, the public celebration of individual desires and life aspirations as well as personal communications in a social context. However, consuming at McDonald's also addresses a new dimension of sociality, namely, the public embrace of modernity and foreign culture (this is further discussed below).[37]

In most cases, mundane and commercialized activities of consumption provide the concrete content, the specific form, and the particular space that make this new kind of sociality possible. The power of the comfort and joy that consumption activities normally generate obviously marks a sharp contrast to the collective activities of organized sociality during the prereform era. The ideology of consumerism, which simply encourages people to indulge themselves in the pursuit of personal happiness, also effectively dilutes the influence of communist ideology, which emphasizes personal sacrifice and ascetic values. Moreover, as described in the first part of this chapter, consumerism also awakens an awareness of individual rights, which in turn has sparked the consumer protection movement. It may not be a long distance from protecting one's consumption rights to protecting other areas of individual freedom. As a U.S. reporter recently noted, lawsuits against state-owned enterprises are "multiplying across China as ordinary people learn to stand up for their legal rights in a society long accustomed to not having any."[38] Clearly, the increased purchasing power of individual consumers can, to a certain extent, erode the power and authority of the state.

Basing her analysis on case studies of consumption in the volume that she has edited, Deborah Davis concludes that Chinese consumers' enthusiastic embrace of commercial opportunities and products has accentuated the role of individual choice and diversified the venues in which individuals from a broad spectrum of urban society socialize. Through a million repetitions in cities throughout China, these seemingly innocuous, apolitical transactions create the social preconditions for realigning institutional power and authority.[39] From the party leaders' perspective, this is actually an unexpected consequence of mass consumption and consumerism. Nevertheless, the expansion of commercialized social space and of consumerism-generated individual freedom also distracts the public's attention from politically sensitive issues to material comfort, which has to a great extent helped the CCP maintain political stability and regain legitimacy in post-1989 China.

CONSUMERISM AND POLITICAL STABILITY

After the tragic ending of the pro-democracy movement in 1989, for several years many outside observers kept predicting that the CCP would not survive the simultaneous crises of economic difficulties, social discontent, and lack of legitimacy. Actual events demonstrated the contrary: the CCP leadership quickly regained political control, maintained social stability, and after 1992, restarted the engine of economic development. By the Fifteenth Party Congress in 1997, the CCP had completely reconsolidated its power and launched more aggressive market-oriented reforms. Among the many factors that contributed to the stability after 1989, consumerism, in my opinion, is an important one that has received little scholarly attention.

It is true that the post–1989 Chinese economy slowed down for a few years, and the second wave of mass consumption ended in 1989. Nevertheless, consumption became an even more important issue for leaders at all levels after 1989, because the top priority then was to alleviate social discontent and maintain stability. To achieve these goals, people's needs had to be met. It was in such a context that so-called benefits consumption (which meant the expansion of consumption in the name of employee benefits) played an active role in easing the political emergency. I observed during my fieldwork in 1991 that the living conditions of most people had improved. The improvement derived not only from wage raises but also from various bonuses and allowances distributed within the work unit. On top of these bonuses and allowances, material goods and money were distributed in the name of work benefits in three major ways.

First, consumer goods were distributed by work units to employees during holidays, especially the Chinese New Year. Although this had been practiced before 1989, it had never been so substantial in terms of the quantity and variety of goods. During the holiday seasons of 1989 to 1992, work-unit leaders did their best to purchase and distribute holiday goods such as meat, fish, fruit, and beer; workers were equally busy transporting the goods home and then worrying about how to consume so much perishable food. To secure supplies, many work units went so far as to open their own farms in the countryside. These farms were dubbed *zhigong shenghuo jidi* (employee livelihood bases). The second channel of benefits consumption involved distributing high-quality goods in the name of "labor protection." The scope of labor protection goods was expanded to include wool uniforms, overcoats, blankets, electric ovens and rice cookers, Coca-Cola, and Nestlé coffee. The third way goods were distributed was by increasing the amount of existing allowances and setting up new categories of allowances. One of the most popular categories was a vacation allowance, which was given to those who did not take a paid vacation trip.[40] To ease the existing social tension, the central government had called on leaders at various levels to do some practical things for the masses (*wei laobaixing ban shishi*); benefits consumption was obviously one of these "buying-off" efforts, which, to a certain extent, indeed helped to cure the wound of 1989. This is also why "social stability" became a consensus between the party-state and the people, as shown repeatedly in social surveys made in the years after 1989.

As mentioned above, a large number of former cadres, intellectuals, and professionals quit their jobs and moved into the private sector in 1992–93, and the third wave of mass consumption arose in the same period. The consumption patterns and lifestyles of the newly rich and the newly emerged class of white-collar professionals attracted the attention of people from all walks of life. In an earlier review of structural changes in China, I noted four important changes in people's mentality: (1) more people seemed to accept the income gap as a natural consequence of the market economy; (2) being poor had become a disgrace, and many people would rather pretend they were successful and rich; (3) people were motivated by market competition and were driven to make more money by the sense of crisis; and (4) the role of ideology and politics in everyday life had further diminished (by the end of 1993, few people whom I interviewed wanted to recall anything about 1989). I concluded that a "Chinese dream" had emerged and implanted itself in the psyches of many people, thus contributing to the sociopolitical stability of the early 1990s.[41]

Looking at these issues in retrospect, I now realize that it was the possibility of and pursuit of consumption that offered the strongest material form of the Chinese dream. For those capable individuals who had gotten ahead, consumerism provided instant rewards. It was not by accident that during the same period reports of conspicuous consumption filled the Chinese mass media. For less fortunate people, consumerism offered a whole new set of life aspirations and motivated them to work harder. More important, when consumerism began to take its full shape in the early 1990s, it encountered little criticism or resistance from either official or intellectual circles. Although a discussion of the loss of humanistic spirit emerged during the high tide of commercialization,[42] it never reached beyond the small circle of elite intellectuals. The triumph of consumerism has drawn the public's attention away from political and ideological issues, overshadowed the increased social inequality and widespread corruption, and eased the legitimacy crisis facing the CCP after 1989. Furthermore, the state's direct involvement in the consumer protection movement, exemplified by its control over and support of the China Consumers Association, has improved its image as the ultimate judge of consumer disputes and the most powerful protector of ordinary consumers. This in turn also contributes to political stability. It is no wonder that the party-state has shown tremendous tolerance toward consumerism since 1989 and by 1999 has begun to recognize its importance in the economy and society openly.

CONSUMPTION AND THE GLOBAL LINK

Finally, consumption of imported material goods and cultural products has, on the one hand, provided the majority of ordinary people with a direct link to the outside world and, on the other hand, raised some nationalist concerns. During the prereform era, ordinary people rarely saw imported goods from the West (I do remember, however, consuming brown sugar from Cuba during the late 1960s), and until the early 1980s, the state tightly controlled retail sales of foreign goods. In 1982, for instance, the municipal government of Guangzhou officially prohibited *getihu* from selling imported goods.[43] Ordinary customers knew little about imported goods, just as they lacked knowledge of the outside world in general. Thus, it appeared strange to people when, on March 10, 1980, Chinese Central Television aired the first advertisement for a foreign product (a Citizen wristwatch). Many viewers called in to protest, and some thought that broadcasting a television commercial for a Japanese company was a great shame.[44] However, within a few years, Chinese customers found themselves making every effort to purchase Japanese color television sets and refrigerators; foreign goods have continued to grow in favor ever since, from household appliances, cosmetics, and soft drinks to toothpaste and laundry detergent.

Although Chinese manufacturers had taken back the domestic market for color television sets, microwave ovens, and washing machines by the early 1990s, the influence of foreign goods only increased and expanded to encompass almost all aspects of everyday consumption.[45] It was reported that imported fax machines and videotape recorders took 98 percent of the market share in China, and foreign cellular phones took 80 percent. At the same time, popular Chinese brand names were either defeated or bought out by foreign companies: Coca-Cola and Pepsi bought out seven of the eight leading Chinese soft drink brands, and more than 70 percent of the beer brewers were bought out by foreign companies. Although it caused a new round of national debate about the fate of the domestic film industry, the Chinese government finally decided to allow Kodak to purchase six Chinese film manufacturers in 1998, leaving Lekai the only domestic brand on the market. The competition between domestic and imported products was so severe that it was proclaimed "a war without gun smoke."[46]

For ordinary consumers, the influx of imported goods opened a completely new horizon of consumption and also brought in new cultural values that in turn could influence their lives. Pop music from Hong Kong and Taiwan, Hollywood movies, the NBA, and World Cup soccer games were among the "hot items" of cultural consumption sought by the majority of ordinary consumers. A *Titanic* ticket sold for 80 yuan (approximately $10) at state-owned theaters in 1998 – about one-fourth of a worker's monthly wage. As in other parts of the world, Michael Jordan was the ultimate hero for Chinese sports fans, and his retirement became the cover story of many magazines and newspapers in early 1999.[47] Another interesting example came in May 1999 when Chinese Central Television canceled its scheduled broadcast of the NBA games as a protest against the NATO bombing of the Chinese embassy in Belgrade. A large number of viewers called in to complain, insisting that sports should have nothing to do with politics. This is in sharp contrast to the above-mentioned incident in 1980 when people called to protest the broadcast of advertisements for foreign products.

The long-term and subtle influence of these imported cultural products has yet to be explored. For example, during my 1991 fieldwork, I found that when the U.S. television detective series *Hunter* was aired in China, it introduced the notion of individual rights and legal knowledge to Chinese audiences. A man in the village where I was conducting fieldwork, for instance, refused to allow local policemen to search his house without a search warrant, and when his attempt failed, he filed a complaint with the county government; he told me that he had learned how to do all this from watching *Hunter.*

Consumption of imported material goods also carries social meanings. As I note elsewhere, when the fast-food giant McDonald's entered the Beijing market, local customers flooded into the restaurants to taste

American cuisine. As a result of constant interaction between McDonald's management and local customers, the fast-food outlets have been transformed into middle-class establishments where consumers from different social backgrounds can, in addition to dining, linger for hours, relaxing, chatting, reading, enjoying the music, or having parties. Through these activities, Chinese customers redefine the concept of fast food and use McDonald's restaurants as a bridge to bring them the experience of consuming a Chinese version of American food culture and, in a larger sense, to link them with the outside world.[48]

The influx of foreign goods and transnational capital, however, has also generated local resistance and nationalistic reactions. Thus far, there have been a number of nationwide discussions on the "crisis of domestic products" in the mass media, all of which were triggered by the unpopularity of domestic electronic appliances, automobiles, computers, cosmetics, fast food, and soft drinks. Domestic manufacturers also appeal to consumers' nationalistic sentiment in marketing. For instance, in March 1996, Red Sorghum – a chain of noodle shops that specialized in country-style lamb noodles – opened its first outlet on Wangfujing Street, immediately across the street from what was then McDonald's flagship restaurant. The manager of the Red Sorghum company announced at the same time that twelve more shops would be opened in Beijing by the end of the year, all of which were to be situated beside McDonald's outlets. "We want to fight McDonald's," the manager claimed, "we want to take back the fast-food market."[49] In Shenzhen, another fast-food restaurant, Happy Chopsticks, adopted "Chinese people eat Chinese foods" as the leading slogan in its market promotion.[50]

These discussions and nationalistic commercials by local industries, however, seem to have had little effect on the actual practice of consumption. According to a 1994 Gallup survey, of the eight brand names recognized by over 50 percent of Chinese consumers, only one – Tsingtao beer – is a domestic product. The Japanese brands Hitachi, Panasonic, Toshiba, and Toyota take the lead, and the remaining three are American: Coca-Cola, Mickey Mouse, and Marlboro cigarettes.[51] A similar survey in 1997 showed the continuing popularity of foreign goods but also revealed that the influence of U.S. brands seemed to have surpassed that of Japanese brands. Among the top five brands, Coca-Cola, Jeep, and Shoulder to Shoulder all were of U.S. origin; the other two were Panasonic and Santana cars (produced by Shanghai Volkswagen).[52] To further test the degree of nationalism in patterns of consumption, a survey agency conducted a three-year-long investigation (1996–98), which found that "Beijing residents in general tend to regard the purchase of foreign goods as a personal choice and do not link it to moral judgments such as 'not being patriotic' or 'being the slaves of foreigners.'"[53]

This marks a sharp contrast to the radical movements to boycott foreign goods that swept Chinese cities in the early twentieth century, in which the masses were mobilized to save the country through consumer nationalism. It is clear that, in the 1990s, Chinese consumers tend to emphasize their own satisfaction with the goods and services they purchase more than anything else, which is yet another sign of the initial triumph of consumerism in Chinese society.

To summarize, there have been three waves of mass consumption during the past two decades, and each of them has brought further political and social consequences. By the end of the 1990s, a consumer revolution had occurred in urban China, and consumerism had replaced communist doctrine to become the paramount cultural ideology of contemporary Chinese society. Along with the flow of material goods and cultural products, consumerism had changed consumers' spending patterns, increased their awareness of individual rights, served as a new mechanism of social differentiation, linked consumers to the outside world, and played a role in promoting political stability in post–1989 China. Thus far, consumerism has overall played a more positive than negative role in China's transition toward a free-market economy and a more open society. But it has also opened a Pandora's box of new social perils, such as the fetishization of money, the commodification of personal relations, and the widespread phenomenon of corruption.

As mentioned at the beginning of this chapter, the CCP has for the first time officially recognized the crucial importance of consumption in stimulating economic growth. This may well indicate an important shift from a production-oriented to a consumption-oriented economy and lead to the further development of consumerism in Chinese society. If this is the case, the consumption-related social phenomena discussed in this chapter will continue to develop, and more questions will arise. For instance, as more and more consumers stand up to fight for their individual rights, will the consumer protection movement come to play a stronger role in domestic politics? If consumption continues to separate individuals socially and spatially, can it still help the state in maintaining social stability, or might it have the opposite effect? Is it possible that the new policy of encouraging consumption will exacerbate the widespread corruption among power holders at all levels of society, as consumption of public funds has been one of the strongest forces driving mass consumption since the early 1980s? Thus far, the consumer consumer protection movement is confined to the cities, but what will happen when it reaches the vast majority of Chinese peasants? Whatever the answers to these questions prove to be, the politics of consumerism will surely play an important and unprecedented role in Chinese society in the twenty-first century.

ACKNOWLEDGEMENT

This study is based on documentary data collected and interviews conducted during fieldwork in China in 1989, 1991, 1994, 1997, 1998, and 1999. The Smith Richardson Foundation, the National Science Foundation, the Wenner-Gren Foundation, and the Academic Senate of UCLA provided generous support for fieldwork in 1998 and 1999. I owe special thanks to Xiaoyan Liang and Tyrene White for their insightful and valuable comments on early drafts of this paper, and I am also grateful to Richard Gunde for his skillful editorial assistance.

NOTES

1. Wu Tao, "Xiaofei de chuntian" (The springtime of consumption), *Beijing qingnian bao* (Beijing Youth Daily), March 15, 1999, p. 21.
2. See Men Rui, "Chong ti gaoxiaofei" (Reevaluating hyperconsumption), *Zhongguo shichang* (China Market), no. 2 (1999), pp. 37–38; and Hu Yanping, "Baixing de qianbao shui neng dakai" (Who can open the wallets of ordinary people?), *Beijing Youth Daily*, April 4, 1999, p. 13.
3. See, for example, Wen Yuan, "Xiaofei xindai: Yuanhe bulü jiannan?" (Consumption loans: Why is it so difficult to start?), *Huanqiu shichang* (Global Market), no. 6 (1999), pp. 22–24; Wang Wei, "Xiaofei xindai heyi shouzu?" (Why are consumption loans encountering difficulties?), *Zhongguo jingji xinxi* (China Economic Information), no. 9, 1999, pp. 4–8; and Zhang Xiaofei, "Jiangxi ciji bule wo xiaofei" (Reducing interest rates cannot stimulate me to consume), *Nanfang zhoumo* (Southern Weekend), July 2, 1999, p. 8.
4. The literature on the subject is rather limited. For a good review of the economic origins of the consumer revolution in China, see Linda Chao and

Ramon Myers, "China's Consumer Revolution: The 1990s and Beyond," *Journal of Contemporary China*, vol. 7, no. 18 (1998), pp. 351–68; for case studies regarding the impact of consumption on social life in Chinese cities, see Deborah Davis, ed., *Consumer Revolution in Urban China* (Berkeley: University of California Press, 2000); for a more critical analysis of the trend of mass consumption and its impact on children, see Bin Zhao, "Consumerism, Confucianism, Communism: Making Sense of China Today," *New Left*, no. 222 (March 1997), pp. 43–59; and Bin Zhao and Graham Murdock, "Young Pioneers: Children and the Making of Chinese Consumerism," *Cultural Studies*, vol. 10, no. 2 (1996), pp. 201–17.

5. See, for example, James McIlhenny, "The New Consumerism: How Will Business Respond," *At Home with Consumers*, vol. 11, no. 2 (1990), p. 5; and Julius Onah, "Consumerism in Nigeria," in *Marketing in Nigeria: Experience in a Developing Economy*, ed. Julius Onah (London: Cassell, 1979), p. 126.

6. See Michael Featherstone, "Life Style and Consumer Culture," *Theory, Culture, and Society*, vol. 4, no. 1 (1987), pp. 55–70; and Arjun Appadurai, "Introduction: Commodities and the Politics of Value," in *The Social Life of Things: Commodities in Cultural Perspective*, ed. Arjun Appadurai (Cambridge: Cambridge University Press, 1986), pp. 3–63.

7. Linda Chao and Ramon Myers, "China's Consumer Revolution," p. 351.

8. Qiu Xiaohua and Wan Donghua "Dui jinshinianlai woguo xiaofei xinshi de jiben huigu yu zhanwang" (Retrospect and prospect of China's consumption situation in the past decade), *Xiaofei jingji* (Consumer Economy), no. 2 (1990), p. 2.

9. See Huang Weiting and Li Fan, *Dangdai Zhongguo de xiaofei zhi mi* (The riddle of consumption in contemporary China) (Beijing: Zhongguo shangye chubanshe, 1990). The authors offer a comprehensive analysis of conflicting consumption phenomena, such as low income with high consumption, and call for radical control of mass consumption by the government in both social psychology (ideology) and spending patterns.

10. Zhu Qingfang, "1998–1999: Zhongguo renmin de shenghuo zhuangkuang" (The living conditions of the Chinese people in 1998–1999), in *1999 nian: Zhongguo shehui xingshi fenxi yu yuce* (Analyses and predictions of social circumstances in China, 1999), ed. Ru Xin, Lu Xueyi, and Shan Tianlun (Beijing: Shehui kexue chubanshe, 1999), p. 354.

11. See Zhu Qingfang, "The Living Conditions of the Chinese People," pp. 354–55.

12. See news reports in *Zhongguo xiaofei shibao* (China Consumption Times), February 3 and March 3, 1993.

13. Zhu Qingfang, "The Living Conditions of the Chinese People," p. 355.

14. *Zhongguo xiaofeizhe bao* (China Consumer News), September 12, 1994.

15. See, for example, Gao Changli, "Woguo jiushi niandai chengxian duoyuanhua xiaofei qushi" (Consumption trends have become diversified in China during the 1990s), *Shangpin pingjie* (Commodity Review), no. 10 (1992), p. 6; and Dong Fang, "Zhongguo chengshi xiaofei wuda redian" (The five hot points in Chinese urban consumption), *Jingji shijie* (Economic World), no. 1 (1994), p. 22.

16. Lin Ye, "Xiaofei lingyu xin sanjian" (The new three big items in consumption), *Zhongguo shichang* (China Market), no. 7 (1994), p. 28.

17. See Beverly Hooper, "From Mao to Market: Empowering the Chinese Consumer," *Howard Asian Pacific Review*, vol. 2, no. 2 (summer 1998), pp. 29–34. The rise of a consumer movement in China has received little attention from China scholars in the West. Hooper's article is the only one that I have found thus far.

18. See Beverly Hooper, "From Mao to Market"; for more details, see China Consumer Association, ed., *Zhongguo xiaofeizhe yundong shinian* (Ten years of consumer movement in China) (Beijing: Zhongguo tongji chubanshe, 1994); and Zhou Rong, "Zhuanxin shiqi Zhongguo xiaofeizhe zuzhi de jiegou yu gongneng" (The structure and function of Chinese consumer organizations in the transitional period) (Master's thesis, Sociology Department, Beijing University, 1998).

19. Zhou Rong, "The Structure and Function of Chinese Consumer Organizations," p. 46.

20. See Beverly Hooper, "From Mao to Market," p. 33.

21. See Zhou Rong, "The Structure and Function of Chinese Consumer Organizations," pp. 35–36.

22. Liu Dong, "Mian dui Wang Hai" (Facing Wang Hai), *Zhongguo shangbao* (China Commerce Daily), December 9, 1995, p. 2.

23. Tao Junfeng, "Wang Hai – wo wei 'diao min' zuo zongjie" (My conclusions on the tricky person Wang Hai), *Beijing Youth Daily*, January 20, 1999, p. 5.

24. Li Wanbing, "Jingcheng yongxian zhiye dajia" (The emerging profession of beating fake goods in Beijing), *Beijing Youth Daily*, January 10, 1997, p. 4. Extensive news coverage of the "Wang Hai case" in 1995 and then the "Wang Hai phenomenon" in 1996–98 can be found in issues of major newspapers and popular magazines during that period, such as *China Commerce Daily, China Industrial and Commercial Times, China Consumer, Beijing Youth Daily,* and *Southern Weekend.*

25. Tao Junfeng, "My Conclusions on the Tricky Person Wang Hai."

26. Some of these diversified views are nicely summarized in *Falü wenhua yanjiu zhongxin tongxun* (Newsletter of the Research Center for Legal Culture/Beijing), no. 10 (1996).

27. See the *Newsletter of the Research Center for Legal Culture*, no. 10 (1996).

28. For a more comprehensive analysis of the link between economic growth and consumer revolution in China, see Linda Chao and Ramon Myers, "China's Consumer Revolution."

29. Bin Zhao dubs this feature "Confucian consumerism." See Zhao, "Consumerism, Confucianism, Communism."

30. Gong Wen, "Guonei gaoxiaofei daguan" (Hyperconsumption in China), *Xiaofei zhinan* (Consumption Guide), no. 2 (1993), pp. 1–12.

31. Cao Liang, "Jixing xiaofei yousilu" (Worrying notes on unhealthy consumption), *Xiaofei jingji* (Consumer Economy), no. 4 (1993), pp. 33–34.

32. Personal interview in August, 1999.

33. For an interesting study of bowling in Shenzhen, see Gan Wang, "Cultivating Friendship through Bowling in Shenzhen," in *Consumer Revolution in Urban China*.

34. See *Jingpin gaowu zhinan* (Purchasing guide to upscale goods), June 7, 1995, p. 7.

35. For critical comments on the book's popularity in China, see Shen Hongfei, "Yiqie cong gediao kaishi" (It all starts with "class"), *Southern Weekend*, July 2, 1999, p. 17.

36. See reports in *Beijing Youth Daily*, July 15, 1999, p. 1; and *Purchasing Guide to Upscale Goods*, August 22, 1997, p. B7.

37. See James Farrer, "Uncivil Society: Dancing in Shanghai in the 1990s"; Kathleen Erwin, "Heart-to-Heart, Phone-to-Phone: Family Values, Sexuality, and the Politics of Shanghai Advice Hotlines"; and Yunxiang Yan, "Of Hamburger and Social Space: Consuming McDonald's in Beijing," all in *Consumer Revolution in Urban China*.

38. Henry Chu, "China: Ordinary Citizens Learn to Stand Up for Their Rights," *Los Angeles Times*, October 1, 1999, p. A24.

39. See Deborah Davis's introduction in *Consumer Revolution in Urban China*, pp. 1–22.

40. For a detailed account, see Huang Weiting and Li Fan, *The Riddle of Consumption in Contemporary China*, pp. 143–69.

41. Yunxiang Yan, "Dislocation, Reposition and Restratification: Structural Changes in Chinese Society," in *China Review 1994*, ed. Maurice Brosseau and Lo Chi Kin (Hong Kong: Chinese University Press, 1994), pp. 15.1–15.24.

42. See articles in *Dushu* (Reading), no. 3 (1994).

43. See *Xin zhoukan* (New Weekly), no. 22 (1998), p. 27.

44. See *New Weekly*, no. 6 (1999), p. 40.

45. Zhao Bo, "Xingxing sese yang xiaofei" (Varieties of consumption of foreign goods), *Shichang jiage* (Market Price), no. 3 (1994), p. 9.

46. Wang Yuxian and Lin Yang, "Guohuo yu yanghuo: Meiyou xiaoyan de zhanzheng" (National products versus foreign products: A war without the smoke of gunpowder), *Shidian* (Perspectives), no. 6 (1996), pp. 16–18.

47. For instance, *Beijing Youth Daily*, one of the most popular newspapers, published reports and news on Jordan's retirement almost daily between January 13 and January 27, 1999. Other printed media also covered the event extensively.

48. Yunxiang Yan, "McDonald's in Beijing: The Localization of Americana," in *Golden Arches East: McDonald's in East Asia*, ed. James L. Watson (Stanford: Stanford University Press, 1997), pp. 39–76.

49. Anonymous, "Honggaoliang yuyan zhongshi kuaican de qushi" (The Red Sorghum predicts the trend of Chinese fast food), *Zhongguo jingying bao* (Chinese Business) June 11, 1996.

50. Liu Guoyue, "Shenzhen kuancan shichang jiqi fazhan" (The fast-food market in Shenzhen and its development), *Zhongguo pengren* (Chinese Cuisine), no. 8 (1996), pp. 20–22.

51. Gallup Organization, *China: Nationwide Consumer Survey* (Princeton: Gallup Organization, 1995).

52. Zhang Qin, "Gailuopu diaocha: Zhongguo jiating xiang mai shenme?" (Gallup survey: What do Chinese families want to buy?" *Zhongguo shangjie* (Chinese Business World), no. 2 (1998), pp. 16–19.

53. Hai Ping, "Zhongguohuo da minzu pai: Shuiren hecai?" (Chinese products playing the card of nationalism: Who is cheering?), *Zhongguo qingnian bao* (China Youth Daily), April 2, 1999, p. 6.

CHAPTER 10

OF HAMBURGER AND SOCIAL SPACE:
THE MAKING OF NEW SOCIALITY

In a 1996 news report on dietary changes in the cities of Beijing, Tianjin, and Shanghai, fast-food consumption was called the most salient development in the national capital: "The development of a fast-food industry with Chinese characteristics has become a hot topic in Beijing's dietary sector. This is underscored by the slogan 'challenge the Western fast food!'"[1] Indeed, with the instant success of Kentucky Fried Chicken after its grand opening in 1987, followed by the sweeping dominance of McDonald's and the introduction of other fast-food chains in the early 1990s, Western-style fast food has played a leading role in the restaurant boom and in the rapid change in the culinary culture of Beijing. A "war of fried chicken" broke out when local businesses tried to recapture the Beijing market from the Western fast-food chains by introducing Chinese-style fast foods. The "fast-food fever" in Beijing, as it is called by local observers, has given restaurant frequenters a stronger consumer consciousness and has created a Chinese notion of fast food and an associated culture.

From an anthropological perspective, this chapter aims to unpack the rich meanings of fast-food consumption in Beijing by focusing on the fast-food restaurants as a social space. Food and eating have long been a central concern in anthropological studies.[2] While nutritional anthropologists emphasize the practical functions of foods and food ways in cultural settings,[3] social and cultural anthropologists try to explore the links between food (and eating) and other dimensions of a given culture. From Lévi-Strauss's attempt to establish a universal system of meanings in the language of foods to Mary Douglas's effort to decipher the social codes of meals and Marshal Sahlins's analysis of the inner/outer, human/inhuman metaphors of food, there is a tradition of symbolic analysis of dietary cultures, whereby foods are treated as messages and eating as a way of social communication.[4] The great variety of food habits can be understood as human responses to material conditions, or as a way to draw boundaries between "us" and "them" in order to construct group identity and thus to engage in "gastro-politics."[5] According to Pierre Bourdieu, the different attitudes toward foods, different ways of eating, and food taste itself all express and define the structure of class relations in French society.[6] Although in Chinese society ceremonial banqueting is frequently used to display and reinforce the existing social structure, James Watson's analysis of the *sihk puhn* among Hong Kong villagers – a special type of ritualized banquet that requires participants to share foods from the same pot – demonstrates that foods can also be used as a leveling device to blur class boundaries.[7]

As Joseph Gusfield notes, the context of food consumption (the participants and the social settings of eating) is as important as the text (the foods that are to be consumed).[8] Restaurants thus should be regarded as part of a system of social codes; as institutionalized and commercialized venues, restaurants also provide a valuable window through which to explore the social meanings of food consumption. In her recent study of dining out and social manners. Joanne Finkelstein classifies restaurants into three grand categories: (1) "formal spectacular" restaurants, where "dining has been elevated to an event of extraordinary stature"; (2) "amusement" restaurants, which add entertainment to dining; and (3) convenience restaurants such as cafes and fast-food outlets.[9] Although Finkelstein recognizes the importance of restaurants as a public space for socialization, she also emphasizes the antisocial aspect of dining out. She argues that, because interactions in restaurants are conditioned by existing manners and customs, "dining out allows us to act in imitation of others, in accord with images, in responses to fashions, out of habit, without need for thought or self-scrutiny." The result is that the styles of interaction that are encouraged in restaurants produce sociality without much individuality, which is an "uncivilized sociality."[10] Concurring with Finkelstein's classification of restaurants, Allen Shelton proceeds further to analyze how restaurants as a theater can shape customers' thoughts and actions. Shelton argues that the cultural codes of restaurants are just as important as the food codes analyzed by Mary Douglas, Lévi-Strauss, and many others. He concludes that the "restaurant is an organized experience using and transforming the raw objects of space, words, and tastes into a coded experience of social structures."[11] Rick Fantasia's analysis of the fast-food industry in France is also illuminating in this respect. He points out that because McDonald's represents an exotic "Other" its outlets attract many young French customers who want to explore a different kind of social space – an "American place."[12]

In light of the studies of both the text and context of food consumption, I first review the development of Western fast food and the local responses in Beijing during the period 1987 to 1996. Next I examine the cultural symbolism of American fast food, the meanings of objects and physical place in fast-food restaurants, the consumer groups, and the use of public space in fast-food outlets. I then discuss the creation of a new social space in fast-food restaurants. In my opinion, the transformation of fast-food establishments from eating place to social space is the key to understanding the popularity of fast-food consumption in Beijing, and it is the major reason why local competitors have yet to successfully challenge the American fast-food chains. This study is based on both ethnographic evidence collected during my fieldwork in 1994 (August to October) and documentary data published in Chinese newspapers, popular magazines, and academic journals during the 1987–96 period. Since McDonald's is the ultimate icon of American fast food abroad and the most successful competitor in Beijing's fast-food market, McDonald's restaurants were the primary place and object for my research, although I also consider other fast-food outlets and compare them with McDonald's in certain respects.[13]

FAST-FOOD FEVER IN BEIJING, 1987 TO 1996

Fast food is not indigenous to Chinese society. It first appeared as an exotic phenomenon in novels and movies imported from abroad and then entered the everyday life of ordinary consumers when Western fast-food chains opened restaurants in the Beijing market. *Kuaican*, the Chinese translation for fast food, which literally means "fast meal" or "fast eating," contradicts the ancient principle in Chinese culinary culture that regards slow eating as healthy and elegant. There are a great variety of traditional snack foods called *xiaochi* (small eats), but the term "small eats" implies that they cannot be taken as meals. During the late 1970s, *hefan* (boxed rice) was introduced to solve the serious "dining problems" created by the lack of public dining facilities and the record number of visitors to Beijing. The inexpensive and convenient *hefan* – rice with a small quantity of vegetables or meat in a styrofoam box – quickly became popular in train stations, in commercial areas, and at tourist attractions. However, thus far boxed rice remains a special category of convenience food – it does not fall into the category of *kuaican* (fast food), even though it is consumed much faster than any of the fast foods discussed in the following pages. The intriguing point here is that in Beijing the notion of fast food refers only to Western-style fast food and the new Chinese imitations. More important, as a new cultural construct, the notion of fast food includes nonfood elements such as eating manners, environment, and patterns of social interaction. The popularity of fast food among Beijing consumers has little to do with either the food itself or the speed with which it is consumed.

American fast-food chains began to display interest in the huge market in China in the early 1980s. As early as 1983, McDonald's used apples from China to supply its restaurants in Japan; thereafter it began to build up distribution and processing facilities in northern China.[14] However, Kentucky Fried Chicken took the lead in the Beijing market. On October 6, 1987, KFC opened its first outlet at a commercial center just one block from Tiananmen Square. The three-story building, which seats more than 500 customers, at the time was the largest KFC restaurant. On the day of the grand opening, hundreds of customers stood in line outside the restaurant, waiting to taste the world-famous American food. Although few were really impressed with the food itself, they were all thrilled by the eating experience: the encounter with friendly employees, quick service, spotless floors, climate-controlled and brightly-lit dining areas, and of course, smiling Colonel Sanders standing in front of the main gate. From 1987 to 1991, KFC restaurants in Beijing enjoyed celebrity status, and the flagship outlet scored first for both single-day and annual sales in 1988 among the more than 9,000 KFC outlets throughout the world.

In the restaurant business in Beijing during the early 1980s, architecture and internal decoration had to match the rank of a restaurant in an officially prescribed hierarchy, ranging from star-rated hotel restaurants for foreigners to formal restaurants, mass eateries, and simple street stalls. There were strict codes regarding what a restaurant should provide, at what price, and what kind of customers it should serve in accordance with its position in this hierarchy. Therefore, some authorities in the local dietary sector deemed that the KFC decision to sell only fried chicken in such an elegant environment was absurd.[15] Beijing consumers, however, soon learned that a clean, bright, and comfortable environment was a common feature of all Western-style fast-food restaurants that opened in the Beijing market after KFC. Among them, McDonald's has been the most popular and the most successful.

The first McDonald's restaurant in Beijing was built at the southern end of Wangfujing Street, Beijing's Fifth Avenue. With 700 seats and 29 cash registers, the restaurant served more than 40,000 customers on its grand opening day of April 23, 1992.[16] The Wangfujing McDonald's quickly became an important landmark in Beijing, and its image appeared frequently on national television programs. It also became an attraction for domestic tourists, a place where ordinary people could literally taste a piece of American culture. Although not the first to introduce American fast food to Beijing consumers, the McDonald's chain has been the most aggressive in expanding its business and the most influential in developing the fast-food market. Additional McDonald's restaurants appeared in Beijing one after another: two were opened in 1993, four in 1994, and ten more in 1995. There were 35 by August 1997, and according to the general manager the Beijing market is big enough to support more than a hundred McDonald's restaurants.[17] At the same time, Pizza Hut, Bony Fried Chicken (of Canada), and Dunkin' Donuts all made their way into the Beijing market. The most interesting newcomer is a noodle shop chain called Californian Beef Noodle King. Although the restaurant sells Chinese noodle soup, it has managed to portray itself as an American fast-food eatery and competes with McDonald's and KFC with lower prices and its appeal to Chinese tastes.

The instant success of Western fast-food chains surprised those in the local restaurant industry. Soon thereafter, many articles in newspapers and journals called for the invention of Chinese-style fast food and the development of a local fast-food industry. April 1992 was a particularly difficult month for those involved in this sector: two weeks after the largest McDonald's restaurant opened at the southern end of Wangfujing Street, Wu Fang Zhai, an old, prestigious restaurant at the northern end of Wangfujing Street, went out of business; in its stead opened International Fast Food City, which sold Japanese fast food, American hamburgers, fried chicken, and ice cream. This was seen as an alarming threat to both the local food industry and the national pride of Chinese culinary culture.[18]

Actually, the local response to the "invasion" of Western fast food began in the late 1980s, right after the initial success of KFC. It quickly developed into what some reporters called a "war of fried chickens" in Beijing. Following the model of KFC, nearly a hundred local fast-food shops featuring more than a dozen kinds of fried chicken appeared between 1989 and 1990. One of the earliest such establishments was Lingzhi Roast Chicken, which began business in 1989; this was followed by Chinese Garden Chicken, Huaxiang Chicken, and Xiangfei Chicken in 1990. The chicken war reached its peak when the Ronghua Fried Chicken company of Shanghai opened its first chain store directly opposite one of the KFC restaurants in Beijing. The manager of Ronghua Chicken proudly announced a challenge to KFC: "Wherever KFC opens a store, we will open another Ronghua Fried Chicken next door."

All of the local fried chicken variations were no more than simple imitations of the KFC food. Their only localizing strategy was to emphasize special Chinese species and sacred recipes that supposedly added an extra medicinal value to their dishes. Thus, consumers were told that the Chinese Garden Chicken might prevent cancer and that Huaxiang Chicken could strengthen the yin-yang balance inside one's body.[19] This strategy did not work well; KFC and McDonald's won out in that first wave of competition. Only a small proportion of the local fried chicken shops managed to survive, while KFC and McDonald's became more and more popular.

Realizing that simply imitating Western fast food was a dead end, the emerging local fast-food industry turned to exploring resources within Chinese cuisine. Among the pioneers, Jinghua Shaomai Restaurant in 1991 tried to transform some traditional Beijing foods into fast foods. This was followed by the entry of a large number of local fast-food restaurants, such as the Beijing Beef Noodle King (not to be confused with the California Beef Noodle King). The Jinghe Kuaican company made the first domestic attempt to develop a fast-food business on a large scale. With the support of the Beijing municipal government, this company built its own farms and processing facilities, but it chose to sell boxed fast foods in mobile vans parked on streets and in residential areas.[20] Thus it fell into the preexisting category of *hefan* (boxed rice) purveyors. Although the price of boxed fast foods was much lower than that of imported fast food, the boxed fast foods did not meet consumers' expectations of fast food. The Jinghe Kuaican Company disappeared as quickly as it had emerged. In October 1992, nearly a thousand state-owned restaurants united under the flag of the Jingshi Fast Food Company, offering five sets of value meals and more than 50 fast-foods items, all of which were derived from traditional

Chinese cuisines. This company was also the first fast-food enterprise to be run by the Beijing municipal government, thus indicating the importance of this growing sector to the government.[21] The Henan Province Red Sorghum Restaurant opened on Wangfujing Street in March 1996, immediately across the street from the McDonald's flagship restaurant. Specializing in country-style lamb noodles, the manager of Red Sorghum announced that twelve more restaurants were to be opened in Beijing by the end of 1996, all of which would be next to a McDonald's outlet. "We want to fight McDonald's," the manager claimed, "we want to take back the fast-food market."[22]

By 1996 the fast-food sector in Beijing consisted of three groups: The main group was made up of McDonald's, KFC, and other Western fast-food chains. Although they no longer attracted the keen attention of the news media, their numbers were still growing. The second group consisted of the local KFC imitations, which managed to survive the 1991 "chicken war." The most successful in this group is the Ronghua Chicken restaurant chain, which in 1995 had eleven stores in several cities and more than 500 employees.[23] The third group included restaurants selling newly created Chinese fast foods, from simple noodle soups to Beijing roast duck meals. Many believe that the long tradition of a national cuisine will win out over the consumers' temporary curiosity about Western-style fast food.

Thus far, however, Chinese fast food has not been able to compete with Western fast food, even though it is cheaper and more appealing to the tastes of ordinary citizens in Beijing. Red Sorghum was the third business to announce in public the ambitious goal of beating McDonald's and KFC (after the Shanghai Ronghua Chicken and Beijing Xiangfei Chicken), but so far none have come close. By August 1996 it was clear that Red Sorghum's lamb noodle soup could not compete in the hot summer with the Big Mac, which was popular year-round.[24]

The lack of competitiveness of Chinese fast food has drawn official attention at high levels, and in 1996 efforts were made to support the development of a local fast-food sector.[25] Concerned experts in the restaurant industry and commentators in the media attribute the bad showing of the Chinese fast-food restaurants to several things. In the mid-1990s, at least: (1) the quality, nutritional values, and preparation of Western fast foods were highly standardized, while Chinese fast foods were still prepared in traditional ways; (2) Chinese fast-food establishments did not offer the friendly, quick service of Western fast-food restaurants;

(3) the local establishments were not as clean and comfortable as the Western fast-food restaurants; and (4) most important, unlike McDonald's or KFC, Chinese restaurants did not employ advanced technologies or modern management methods.[26] From a Marxist perspective, Ling Dawei has concluded that the race between imported and local fast foods in Beijing is a race between advanced and backward forces of production; hence the development of the local fast-food industry will rest ultimately on modernization.[27]

There is no doubt that these views have a basis in everyday practice; yet they all regard food consumption as purely economic behavior and fast-food restaurants as mere eating places. A more complete understanding of the fast-food fever in Beijing also requires close scrutiny of the social context of consumption – the participants and social settings, because "The specific nature of the consumed substances surely matters; but it cannot, by itself, explain why such substances may seem irresistible."[28]

THE SPATIAL CONTEXT OF FAST-FOOD CONSUMPTION

As Giddens points out, most social life occurs in the context of the "fading away" of time and the "shading off" of space.[29] This is certainly true for fast-food consumption. Fast-food restaurants, therefore, need to be examined both as eating places and as social spaces where social interactions occur. A physical place accommodates objects and human agents and provides an arena for social interactions, and it follows that the use of space cannot be separated from the objects and the physical environment.[30] However, space functions only as a context, not a determinant, of social interactions, and the space itself in some way is also socially constructed.[31] In the following pages I consider, on the one hand, how spatial context shapes consumers' behavior and social relations, and how, on the other hand, consumers appropriate fast-food restaurants into their own space. Such an inquiry must begin with a brief review of Beijing's restaurant sector in the late 1970s in order to assess the extent to which Western fast-food outlets differ from existing local restaurants.

Socialist Canteens and Restaurants in the 1970s

Eating out used to be a difficult venture for ordinary people in Beijing because few restaurants were designed for mass consumption. As mentioned earlier, the restaurants in Beijing were hierarchically ranked by architecture, function, and the type and quality of foods provided. More important, before the economic reforms almost all restaurants and eateries were state-owned businesses, which meant that a restaurant was first and foremost a work unit, just like any factory, shop, or government agency.[32] Thus a restaurant's position and function were also determined by its administrative status as a work unit.

Generally speaking, the restaurant hierarchy consisted of three layers. At the top were luxury and exclusive restaurants in star-rated hotels, such as the Beijing Hotel, which served only foreigners and privileged domestic guests. At the next level were well-established formal restaurants, many of which specialized in a particular style of cuisine and had been in business for many years, even before the 1949 revolution. Unlike the exclusive hotel restaurants, the formal restaurants were open to the public and served two major functions: (1) as public spaces in which small groups of elites could socialize and hold meetings; and (2) as places for ordinary citizens to hold family banquets on special, ritualized occasions such as weddings. At the bottom of the hierarchy were small eateries that provided common family-style foods; these were hardly restaurants (they were actually called *shitang*, meaning canteens). The small eateries were frequented primarily by visitors from outlying provinces and some Beijing residents who had to eat outside their homes because of special job requirements. The majority of Beijing residents rarely ate out – they normally had their meals at home or in their work-unit canteens.

In the 1950s the development of internal canteens (*neibu shitang*) not only constituted an alternative to conventional restaurants but also had a great impact on the latter. Most work units had (and still have) their own canteens, in order to provide employees with relatively inexpensive food and, more important, to control the time allotted for meals. Because canteens were subsidized by the work units and were considered part of employees' benefits, they were run in a manner similar to a family kitchen, only on an enlarged scale. The central message delivered through the canteen facilities was that the work unit, as the representative of the party-state, provided food to its employees, just as a mother feeds her children (without the affectionate component of real parental care). The relationship between the canteen workers and those who ate at the canteens was thus a patronized relationship between the feeder and the fed, rather than a relationship of service provider and customers. The tasteless foods, unfriendly service, and uncomfortable environment were therefore natural components at such public canteens, which prevailed for more than three decades and still exist in many work units today.

The work-unit mentality of "feeding" instead of "serving" people also made its way into restaurants in Beijing because, after all, the restaurants were also work units and thus had the same core features as all other work units – that is, the dominating influence of the state bureaucracy and the planned economy. Commercial restaurants also shared with the work-unit canteens the poor maintenance of internal space, a limited choice of foods, the requirement that the diner pay in advance, fixed times for meals (most restaurants were open only during the short prescribed lunch and dinner times), and of course, ill-tempered workers who acted as if they were distributing food to hungry beggars instead of paying customers.[33] It is true that the higher one moved up the ladder of the restaurant hierarchy the better dining environment and service one could find. But in the famous traditional restaurants and the star-rated hotel restaurants, formality and ritual were most likely the dominating themes. Still, until the late 1980s it was not easy for ordinary people to enjoy dining out in restaurants.

In contrast, Western fast-food restaurants offered local consumers a new cultural experience symbolized by foreign fast food, enjoyable spatial arrangements of objects and people, and American-style service and social interactions.

The Cultural Symbolism of Fast Food

It is perhaps a truism to note that food is not only good to eat but also good for the mind. The (Western) fast-food fever in Beijing provides another example of how in certain circumstances customers may care less about the food and more about the cultural messages it delivers. During my fieldwork in 1994 I discovered that although children were great fans of the Big Mac and french fries, most adult customers did not particularly like those fast foods. Many people commented that the taste was not good and that the flavor of cheese was strange. The most common complaint from adult customers was *chi bu bao*, meaning that McDonald's hamburgers and fries did not make one feel full: they were more like snacks than like meals.[34] It is also interesting to note that both McDonald's and KFC emphasized the freshness, purity, and nutritional value of their foods (instead of their appealing tastes). According to a high-level manager of Beijing McDonald's, the recipes for McDonald's foods were designed to meet modern scientific specifications and thus differed from the recipes for Chinese foods, which were based on cultural expectations.[35] Through advertisements and news media reports, this idea that fast foods use nutritious ingredients and are prepared using scientific cooking methods has been accepted by the public. This may help to explain that why few customers compared the taste of fast foods to that of traditional Chinese cuisine; instead customers focused on something other than the food.

If people do not like the imported fast food, why are they still keen on going to Western fast-food restaurants? Most informants said that they liked the atmosphere, the style of eating, and the experience of being there. According to an early report on KFC, customers did not go to KFC to eat the chicken but to enjoy "eating" (consuming) the culture associated with KFC. Most customers spent hours talking to each other and gazing out the huge glass windows onto busy commercial streets – and feeling more sophisticated than the people who passed by.[36] Some local observers argued that the appeal of Chinese cuisine was the taste of the food itself and that, in contrast, Western food relied on the manner of presentation. Thus consumers would seem to be interested in the spectacle created by this new form of eating.[37] In other words, what Beijing customers find satisfying about Western fast-food restaurants is not the food but the experience.

The cultural symbolism that McDonald's, KFC, and other fast-food chains carry with them certainly plays an important role in constructing this nonedible yet fulfilling experience. Fast food, particularly McDonald's fast food, is considered quintessentially American in many parts of the contemporary world. In France, the most commonly agreed "American thing" among teenagers is McDonald's, followed by Coca-Cola and "military and space technologies."[38] In Moscow, a local journalist described the opening of the first McDonald's restaurant as the arrival of the "ultimate icon of Americana."[39] The same is true in Beijing, although the official news media have emphasized the element of modernity instead of Americana. The high efficiency of the service and management, fresh ingredients, friendly service, and spotless dining environment in Western fast-food restaurants have been repeatedly reported by the Beijing media as concrete examples of modernity.[40]

Ordinary consumers are interested in the stories told in news reports, popular magazines, and movies that the Big Mac and fried chicken are what make Americans American. According to a well-known commentator on popular culture in Beijing, because of the modernity inherent in the McDonald's fast-food chain, many American youths prefer to work first at McDonald's before finding other jobs on the market. The experience of working at McDonald's, he argues, prepares American youth for any kind of job in a modern society.[41] To many Beijing residents, "American" also means "modern," and thus to eat at McDonald's is to experience modernity. During my field-work I talked with many parents who appreciated their children's fondness for imported fast food because they believed it was in good taste to be modern. A mother told me that she had made great efforts to adapt to the strange flavor of McDonald's food so that she could take her daughter to McDonald's twice a week. She explained: "I want my daughter to learn more about American culture. She is taking an English typing class now, and I will buy her a computer next year." Apparently, eating a Big Mac and fries, like learning typing and computer skills, is part of the mother's plan to prepare her daughter for a modern society.

Inspired by the success of the cultural symbolism of McDonald's and KFC, many Chinese fast-food restaurants have tried to use traditional Chinese culture to lure customers. As I mentioned in the preceding section, almost all local fried-chicken outlets during 1990–91 emphasized the use of traditional medicinal ingredients and the idea of health-enhancing food.[42] Others used ethnic and local flavors to stress the Chineseness of their fast foods, such as the Red Sorghum's promotion of its lamb noodle soup.[43] And some directly invoked the nationalist feelings of the customers. For instance, Happy Chopsticks, a new fast-food chain in Shenzhen, adopted "Chinese people eat Chinese food" as the leading slogan in its market promotion.[44] The power of cultural symbolism in the fast-food sector also has made an impact on the restaurant industry in general: the cultural position of the restaurant business is regarded as an important issue, and the debate about the differences between Western and Chinese cuisine continues in professional journals.[45]

A Place of Entertainment for Equals

According to older residents, in addition to different cuisine styles, traditional restaurants in pre-1949 Beijing also differed in their interior decorations, seating arrangements, and interactions between restaurant employees and customers. During the Maoist era, such features were considered inappropriate to the needs of working-class people and thus gradually disappeared. Under the brutal attack on traditional culture during the Cultural Revolution period, some famous restaurants even replaced their old names with new, revolutionary names, such as Workers and Peasants Canteen (*Gongnong shitang*). As a result, by the late 1970s most restaurants looked similar both inside and out, which, combined with the canteen mentality in restaurant management and poor service, turned Beijing restaurants into unpleasant eating places.

When KFC and McDonald's opened their outlets in Beijing, what most impressed Beijing consumers was their beautiful appearance. As mentioned earlier, both the first KFC and first McDonald's are located near Tiananmen Square in the heart of Beijing, and both boast that they are the largest outlets of their kind in the world, one with a three-floor, 500-seat building and the other with a two-floor, 700-seat building. The statues of Colonel Sanders and Ronald McDonald in front of the two establishments immediately became national tourist attractions.

Once inside the restaurants, Beijing customers found other surprises. First, both McDonald's and the KFC restaurants were brightly lit and climate-controlled. The seats, tables, and walls were painted in light colors, which, together with the shiny counters, stainless-steel kitchenware, and soft music in the background, created an open and cheerful physical environment – a sharp contrast to traditional Chinese restaurants. Moreover, social interaction at McDonald's or KFC was highly ritualized and dramatized,[46] representing a radical departure from the canteen-like restaurants in Beijing. Employees wore neat, brightly colored uniforms, and they smiled at customers while working conscientiously and efficiently. As one observant informant remarked, even the employee responsible for cleaning the toilets worked in a disciplined manner. In his study of restaurants in Athens, Georgia, Allen Shelton commented: "The spectacle of McDonald's is work: the chutes filling up with hamburgers; the restaurant and the other diners are secondary views."[47] In contrast, both the work and the restaurant itself constituted the spectacle at McDonald's and KFC in Beijing.

One of the things that most impressed new customers of the fast-food outlets was the menu, which is displayed above and behind the counter, with soft backlighting and photographic images of the food. The menu delivers a clear message about the public, affordable eating experience that the establishment offers. This was particularly important for first-timers, who did not know anything about the exotic food. Another feature is the open, clean, kitchen area, which clearly shows the customers how the hamburgers and fried chickens are prepared. To emphasize this feature, Beijing's McDonald's also provides a five-minute tour of the kitchen area on customer request.

The Western fast-food restaurants also gave customers a sense of equality. Both employees and customers remain standing during the ordering process, creating an equal relationship between the two parties. More important, the friendly service and the smiling employees give customers the impression that no matter who you are you will be treated with equal warmth and friendliness. Accordingly, many people patronize McDonald's to experience a moment of equality.[48] The restaurants also seem to convey gender equality and have attracted a large number of female customers (I will return to this point later).

All these details in internal space are important in understanding the success of McDonald's and KFC in Beijing: objects have a voice that originates in those who use them, just as the scenery on a stage shape the movements of an actor.[49] The impact of spatial context on people's behavior in McDonald's restaurants is well addressed by Peter Stephenson. He observed that some Dutch customers lost their cultural "self" in such a culturally decontextualized place because "there is a kind of instant emigration that occurs the moment one walks through the doors, where Dutch rules rather obviously don't apply."[50] Rick Fantasia observed that French customers undergo similar changes or adjustments in behavior in McDonald's outlets in Paris.[51] Given the sharper and deeper cultural differences between American and Chinese societies, it is natural to expect the cultural decontextualization to be even stronger in Beijing's McDonald's and KFC restaurants.

The interesting point is that, owing to the powerful appeal of modernity and Americana projected by McDonald's and KFC, when experiencing the same "instant emigration," Beijing customers seem to be more willing to observe the rules of American fast-food restaurants than their counterparts in Leiden or Paris. For instance, in 1992 and 1993 customers in Beijing (as in Hong Kong and Taiwan) usually left their rubbish on the table for the restaurant employees to clean up: people regarded McDonald's as a formal establishment at which they had paid for full service. However, during the summer of 1994 I observed that about one-fifth of the customers, many of them fashionably dressed youth, carried their own trays to the waste bins. From subsequent interviews I discovered that most of these people were regular customers, and they had learned to clean up their tables by observing the foreigners' behavior. Several informants told me that when they disposed of their own rubbish they felt more "civilized" (*wenming*) than the other customers because they knew the proper behavior. My random check of customer behavior in McDonald's and in comparably priced and more expensive Chinese restaurants shows that people in McDonald's were, on the whole, more self-restrained and polite toward one another, spoke in lower tones, and were more careful not to throw their trash on the ground. Unfortunately, when they returned to a Chinese context, many also returned to their previous patterns of behavior. As a result, the overall atmosphere in a Western fast-food outlet is always nicer than that in Chinese restaurants of the same or even higher quality.[52]

A Multidimensional Social Space

In part because of the cultural symbolism of Americana and modernity and in part because of the exotic, cheerful, and comfortable physical environment, McDonald's, KFC, and other foreign fast-food restaurants attract customers from all walks of life in Beijing. Unlike in the United States, where the frequenters of fast-food restaurants are generally associated with low income and simple tastes, most frequenters of fast-food restaurants in Beijing are middle-class professionals, trendy yuppies, and well-educated youths. Unfortunately, there has yet to be a systematic social survey of Chinese fast-food consumers. Nevertheless, according to my field observations in 1994, a clear distinction can be drawn between those who occasionally partake of the imported fast foods and those who regularly frequent fast-food restaurants.

Occasional adventurers include both Beijing residents and visitors from outlying provinces and cities. It should be noted that a standard one-person meal at McDonald's (including a hamburger, a soft drink, and an order of French fries, which is the equivalent of a value-meal at McDonald's in the United States) cost 17 renminbi (rmb) ($2.10) in 1994 and 21 rmb ($2.60) in 1996.[53] This may not be expensive by American standards, but it is not an insignificant amount of money for ordinary workers in Beijing, who typically made less than 500 rmb ($60) per month in 1994. Thus, many people, especially those with moderate incomes, visited McDonald's restaurants only once or twice, primarily to satisfy their curiosity about American food and culinary culture. A considerable proportion of the customers were tourists from other provinces who had only heard of McDonald's or seen its Golden Arches in the movies. The tasting of American food has recently become an important part of the tourist beat in Beijing; and those who partake of the experience are able to boast about it to their relatives and friends back home.

There are also local customers who frequent foreign fast-food outlets on a regular basis. A survey conducted by Beijing McDonald's management in one of its stores showed that 10.2 percent of the customers frequented the restaurant four times per month in 1992, in 1993 the figure was 38.3 percent.[54] The majority of customers fell into three categories: professionals and white-collar workers; young couples and teenagers; and children accompanied by their parents. Moreover, women of all age groups tended to frequent McDonald's restaurants more than men.

For younger Beijing residents who worked in joint-venture enterprises or foreign firms and had higher incomes, eating at McDonald's, Kentucky Fried Chicken, and Pizza Hut had become an integral part of their new lifestyle, a way for them to be connected to the outside world. As one informant commented: "The Big Mac doesn't taste great; but the experience of eating in this place makes me feel good. Sometimes I even imagine that I am sitting in a restaurant in New York or Paris." Although some emphasized that they only went to save time, none finished their meals within twenty minutes. Like other customers, these young professionals arrived in small groups or accompanied by girl/boy friends to enjoy the restaurant for an hour or more. Eating foreign food, and consuming other foreign goods, had become an important way for Chinese yuppies to define themselves as middle-class professionals. By 1996, however, this group had found other types of activities (such as nightclubs or bars), and gradually they were beginning to visit foreign fast-food restaurants for convenience rather than for status.

Young couples and teenagers from all social strata were also regular frequenters of McDonald's and KFC outlets because the dining environment is considered to be romantic and comfortable. The restaurants are brightly-lit, clean, and feature light Western music; and except during busy periods they are relatively quiet, making them ideal for courtship. In 1994, McDonald's seven Beijing restaurants had all created relatively isolated and private service areas with tables for two. In some, these areas were nicknamed "lovers' corners." Many teenagers also considered that, with only the minimum consumption of a soft drink or an ice cream, fast-food establishments were good places simply to hang out.

As in many other parts of the world, children in Beijing had become loyal fans of Western fast food. They were so fond of it that some parents even suspected that Big Mac or fried chicken contained a special, hidden ingredient. The fast-food restaurants also made special efforts to attract children by offering birthday parties, dispensing souvenirs, and holding essay contests, because young customers usually did not come alone: they were brought to McDonald's and KFC by their parents or grandparents. Once a middle-aged woman told me that she did not like the taste of hamburgers and that her husband simply hated them. But their daughter loved hamburgers and milkshakes so much that their entire family had to visit McDonald's three to five times a month. It is common among Beijing families for children to choose the restaurant in which the whole family dines out. Fast-food outlets were frequently the first choice of children.

A gender aspect of fast-food consumption is highlighted in He Yupeng's 1996 study of McDonald's popularity among female customers. In conducting a small-scale survey at four restaurants in Beijing – a formal Chinese restaurant, a local fast-food outlet, and two McDonald's outlets – He found that women were more likely than men to enjoy dining at fast-food restaurants. According to his survey, while 66 percent of the customers (N=68) at the formal Chinese restaurant were men, 64 percent of the customers (N=423) at the local fast-food outlet were women. Similar patterns were observed in the two McDonald's restaurants, where women constituted 57 percent of a total of 784 adult customers.[55] The most intriguing finding of this survey was that women chose McDonald's because they enjoyed ordering their own food and participating in the conversation while dining. Many female customers pointed out that in formal Chinese restaurants men usually order the food for their female companions and control the conversation. In contrast, they said, at a McDonald's everyone can make his or her own choices and, because smoking and alcohol are prohibited, men dominate less of the conversation.[56]

Furthermore, the imported fast-food restaurants provide a venue where women feel comfortable alone or with female friends. Formal Chinese restaurants are customarily used by elite groups as places to socialize and by middle-class people as places to hold ritual family events such as wedding banquets. In both circumstances, women must subordinate themselves to rules and manners that are androcentric, either explicitly or implicitly (the men order the dishes; the women do not partake of the liquor). These customs reflect the traditional view that women's place is in the household and that men should take charge of all public events. There is a clear division between the private (inside) and the public (outside) along gender lines.

A woman who eats alone in a formal Chinese restaurant is considered abnormal; such behavior often leads to public suspicion about her morality and her occupation. For instance, a young woman I interviewed in a McDonald's outlet in 1994 recalled having lunch alone in a well-known Chinese restaurant frequented mostly by successful businessmen. "Several men gazed at me with lascivious eyes," she said, "and some others exchanged a few words secretly and laughed among themselves. They must have thought I was a prostitute or at least a loose woman. Knowing their evil thoughts, I felt extremely uncomfortable and left the place as quickly as I could." She also commented that even going to a formal Chinese restaurant with female friends would make her feel somewhat improper about herself, because the "normal" customers were men or men with women. But she said that she felt comfortable visiting a McDonald's alone or with her female friends, because "many people do the same." This young woman's experience is by no means unique, and a number of female customers in McDonald's offered similar explanations for liking the foreign fast-food restaurants. Several elderly women also noted the impropriety of women dining in formal Chinese restaurants, although they were less worried about accusations about their morals.[57]

In his survey, He Yupeng asked his respondents where they would choose to eat if there were only a formal Chinese restaurant and a McDonald's outlet. Almost all the male respondents chose the former, and all the female respondents chose the latter. One of the main reasons for such a sharp gender difference. He argues, is the concern of contemporary women for gender equality.[58] The new table manners allowed in fast-food restaurants, and more important, the newly appropriate gender roles in those public places, seem to have enhanced the image of foreign fast-food restaurants as an open place for equals, thus attracting female customers.

The Appropriation of Social Space

Finally, I would point out that Beijing customers do not passively accept everything offered by the American fast-food chains. The American fast-food restaurants have been localized in many aspects, and what Beijing customers enjoy is actually a Chinese version of American culture and fast foods.[59] One aspect of this localization process is the consumers' appropriation of the social space.

My research confirms the impression that most customers in Beijing claim their tables for longer periods of time than Americans do. The average dining time in Beijing (in autumn 1994) was 25 minutes during busy hours and 51 minutes during slack hours. In Beijing, "fastness" does not seem to be particularly important. The cheerful, comfortable, and climate-controlled environment inside McDonald's and KFC restaurants encourages many customers to linger, a practice that seems to contradict the original purpose of the American fast-food business. During off-peak hours it is common for people to walk into McDonald's for a leisurely drink or snack. Sitting with a milkshake or an order of fries, such customers often spend 30 minutes to an hour, and sometimes longer, chatting, reading newspapers, or holding business meetings. As indicated earlier, young couples and teenagers are particularly fond of frequenting foreign fast-food outlets because they consider the environment to be romantic. Women in all age groups tend to spend the longest time in these establishments, whether they are alone or with friends. In contrast, unaccompanied men rarely linger after finishing their meals. The main reason for this gender difference, according to my informants, is the absence of alcoholic beverages. An interesting footnote in this connection is that 32 percent of my informants in a survey among college students (N=97) regarded McDonald's as a symbol of leisure and emphasized that they went there to relax.

Beijing consumers have appropriated the restaurants not only as places of leisure but also as public arenas for personal and family ritual events. The most popular such event is of course the child's birthday party, which has been institutionalized in Beijing McDonald's restaurants. Arriving with five or more guests, a child can expect an elaborate ritual performed in a special enclosure called "Children's paradise," free of extra charge. The ritual begins with an announcement over the restaurant's loudspeakers – in both Chinese and English – giving the child's name and age, together with congratulations from Ronald McDonald (who is called Uncle McDonald in Beijing). This is followed by the recorded song "Happy Birthday," again in two languages. A female employee in the role of Aunt McDonald then entertains the children with games and presents each child with a small gift from Uncle McDonald. Although less formalized (and without the restaurant's active promotion), private cere- monies are also held in the restaurants for adult customers, particularly for young women in peer groups (the absence of alcohol makes the site attractive to them). Of the 97 college students in my survey, 33 (includ- ing nine men) had attended personal celebrations at McDonald's: birth- day parties, farewell parties, celebrations for receiving scholarships to American universities, and end-of-term parties.

The multifunctional use of McDonald's space is due in part to the lack of cafes, tea houses, and ice-cream shops in Beijing; it is also a conse- quence of the management's efforts to attract as many customers as pos- sible by engendering an inviting environment. Although most McDonald's outlets in the United States are designed specifically to prevent socializ- ing (with less-comfortable seats than formal restaurants, for instance) it is clear that the managers of Beijing's McDonald's have accepted their customers' perceptions of McDonald's as a special place that does not fit into pre-existing categories of public eateries. They have not tried to educate Beijing consumers to accept the American view that "fast food" means that one must eat fast and leave quickly.[60] When I wondered how the management accommodated everyone during busy periods, I was told that the problem often resolved itself. A crowd of customers natur- ally created pressures on those who had finished their meals, and more important, during busy hours the environment was no longer appropri- ate for relaxation.

In contrast, managers in Chinese fast-food outlets tend to be less toler- ant of customers who linger. During my fieldwork in 1994 I conducted several experimental tests by going to Chinese fast-food outlets and order- ing only a soft drink but staying for more than an hour. Three out of four times I was indirectly urged to leave by the restaurant employees; they either took away my empty cup or asked if I needed anything else. Given the fact that I was in a fast-food outlet and did all the service for my- self, the disturbing "service" in the middle of my stay was clearly a mes- sage to urge lingering customers to leave. I once discussed this issue with the manager of a Chinese fast-food restaurant. He openly admitted that he did not like customers claiming a table for long periods of time and certainly did not encourage attempts to turn the fast-food outlet into a coffee shop. As he explained: "If you want to enjoy nice coffee and music then you should go to a fancy hotel cafe, not here."

CONCLUDING REMARKS: DINING PLACE, SOCIAL SPACE, AND MASS CONSUMPTION

In the United States, fast-food outlets are regarded as "fuel stations" for hungry yet busy people and as family restaurants for low-income groups. Therefore, efficiency (speed) and economic value (low prices) are the two most important reasons why fast foods emerged as a kind of "industrial food" and remain successful in American society today. These features, however, do not apply in Beijing. A Beijing worker who loads the whole family into a taxi to go to McDonald's may spend one-sixth of his monthly income; efficiency and economy are perhaps the least of his concerns. When consumers stay in McDonald's or KFC restaurants for hours, relaxing, chatting, reading, enjoying the music, or celebrating birthdays, they take the "fastness" out of fast food. In Beijing, the fastness of American fast food is reflected mainly in the service provided; for consumers, the dining experience is too meaningful to be shortened. As a result, the American fast-food outlets in China are fashionable, middle-class establishments – a new kind of social space where people can enjoy their leisure time and experience a Chinese version of American culture.

As I emphasize repeatedly throughout this chapter, eating at a foreign fast-food restaurant is an important social event, although it means different things to different people. McDonald's, KFC, and other fast-food restaurants in Beijing carry the symbolism of Americana and modernity, which makes them unsurpassable by existing standards of the social hierarchy in Chinese culture. They represent an emerging tradition where new values, behavior patterns, and social relationships are still being created. People from different social backgrounds may enter the same eating place/social space without worrying about losing face; on the contrary, they may find new ways to better define their positions. For instance, white-collar professionals may display their new class status, youngsters may show their special taste for leisure, and parents may want to "modernize" their children. Women of all ages are able to enjoy their independence when they choose to eat alone; and when they eat with male companions, they enjoy a sexual equality that is absent in formal Chinese restaurants. The fast-food restaurants, therefore, constitute a multivocal, multidimensional, and open social space. This kind of all-inclusive social space met a particular need in the 1990s, when Beijing residents had to work harder than ever to define their positions in a rapidly changing society.[61]

By contrast, almost all local competitors in the fast-food sector tend to regard fast-food restaurants merely as eating places, and accordingly, they try to compete with the foreign fast-food restaurants by offering lower prices and local flavors or by appealing to nationalist sentiments. Although they also realize the importance of hygiene, food quality, friendly service, and a pleasant physical environment, they regard these features as isolated technical factors. A local observer pointed out that it is easy to build the "hardware" of a fast-food industry (the restaurants) but that the "software" (service and management) cannot be adopted overnight.[62] To borrow from this metaphor, I would argue that an understanding of fast-food outlets not only as eating places but also as social space is one of the "software problems" waiting to be resolved by the local competitors in the fast-food business.

Why is the issue of social space so important for fast-food development in Beijing? It would take another essay to answer this question completely; here I want to highlight three major factors that contribute to fast-food fever and are closely related to consumers' demands for a new kind of social space.

First, the trend of mass consumption that arose in the second half of the 1980s created new demands for dining out as well as new expectations of the restaurant industry. According to 1994 statistics released by the China Consumer Society, the average expenditure per capita has increased 4.1 times since 1984. The ratio of "hard consumption" (on food, clothes, and other necessities of daily life) to "soft consumption" (entertainment, tourism, fashion, and socializing) went from 3:1 in 1984 to 1:1.2 in 1994.[63] In 1990, consumers began spending money as never before on such goods and services as interior decoration, private telephones and pagers, air conditioners, body-building machines, and tourism.[64] As part of this trend toward consumerism, dining out has become a popular form of entertainment among virtually all social groups, and people are particularly interested in experimenting with different cuisines.[65] In response to a survey conducted by the Beijing Statistics Bureau in early 1993, nearly half of the respondents said they had eaten at Western-style restaurants (including fast-food outlets) at least once.[66] A central feature of this development in culinary culture is that people want to dine out as active consumers, and they want the dining experience to be relaxed, fun, and healthful.

In response to increasing consumer demands, thousands of restaurants and eateries have appeared in recent years. By early 1993 there were more than 19,000 eating establishments in Beijing, ranging from elegant five-star hotel restaurants to simple street eateries. Of these, about 5,000 were state-owned, 55 were joint ventures or foreign-owned, and the remaining 14,000 or so were owned by private entrepreneurs or independent vendors (*getihu*).[67]

These figures show that the private sector has played an increasingly important role in the restaurant business. Unlike the state-owned restaurants, some private restaurants have used creativity to meet consumers' demands for a new kind of dining experience. The best example is the emergence of country-style, nostalgic restaurants set up by and for the former sent-down urban youths. In these places customers retaste their experience of youth in the countryside: customers choose from country-style foods in rooms and among objects that remind them of the past. Like customers in McDonald's or KFC, they are also consuming part of the subculture and redefining themselves in a purchased social space. The difference is that the nostalgic restaurants appeal only to a particular social group, while the American fast-food outlets are multivocal and multidimensional and thus attract people from many different social strata.

The rise of new consumer groups is the second major factor that has made the issue of social space so important to understanding fast-food fever in Beijing. Urban youth, children, and women of all ages constitute the majority of the regular frequenters of American fast-food restaurants. It is not by accident that these people are all newcomers as restaurant customers – there was no proper place for them in the pre-existing restaurant system, and the only social role that women, youth, and children could play in a formal Chinese restaurant was as the dependents of men. Women's effort to gain an equal place in restaurant subculture was discussed earlier, so here I briefly examine the place of youth and children.

Young professionals emerged along with the development of the market economy, especially with the expansion of joint-venture and foreign-owned business in Beijing in the 1990s. To prove and further secure their newly obtained social status and prestige, the young elite have taken the construction of a different lifestyle seriously, and they often lead the trend of contemporary consumerism in Chinese cities. Urban youth may be less well off than young professionals, but they are equally eager to embrace a new way of personal life. According to a 1994 survey, the purchasing power of Beijing youth increased dramatically over the previous decade, and nearly half of the 1,000 respondents in the survey had more than 500 rmb per month to spend on discretionary items.[68] With more freedom to determine their lifestyles and more economic independence, these youngsters were eager to establish their own social space in many aspects of life, including dining out.[69] A good example in this connection is the astonishing popularity among young people in mainland China of pop music, films, and romance novels from Hong Kong and Taiwan.[70]

The importance of teenagers and children in effecting social change also emerged in the late twentieth century, along with the growth of the national economy, the increase in family wealth, and the decline of the birth rate. The single-child policy – which is most strictly implemented in the big cities – has created a generation of little emperors and empresses, each demanding the attention and economic support of his or her parents and grandparents. Parental indulgence of children has become a national obsession, making children and teenagers one of the most active groups of consumers. Beijing is by no means exceptional in this respect. According to Deborah Davis and Julia Sensenbrenner (see Chapter 3 in this volume), ordinary working-class parents in Shanghai normally spend one-third of their monthly wages to provide their children with a lifestyle that is distinctly upper middle class in its patterns of consumption. For many parents, toys, trips, fashionable clothes, music lessons, and restaurant meals have become necessities in raising their children. This suggests a significant change in patterns of household expenditure, and accordingly there is an urgent need to meet the market demands and special tastes of this important group of consumers.

The emerging importance of women, youth, and children as consumers results from a significant transformation of the family institution in contemporary Chinese society, which is characterized by the nuclearization of the household, the centrality of conjugality in family relations, the rising awareness of independence and sexual equality among women, the waning of the patriarchy, and the rediscovery of the value of children.[71] As far as fast-food consumption is concerned, the link between new groups of independent consumers and shifts in family values is found in other East Asian societies as well. After analyzing the relationship between the McDonald's "takeoff" in five cities (Tokyo, Hong Kong, Taipei, Seoul, and Beijing) and the changes in family values (especially the rising status of teenagers and children), Watson concluded: "More than any other factor . . . McDonald's success is attributable to the revolution in family values that has transformed East Asia."[72]

A third important factor in the success of Western fast-food enterprises is the new form of sociality that has been developing in market-controlled public places such as restaurants. A significant change in public life during the post-Mao era has been the disappearance of frequent mass rallies, voluntary work, collective parties, and other forms of "organized sociality" in which the state (through its agents) played the central role. In its place are new forms of private gatherings in public venues. Whereas "organized sociality" emphasized the centrality of the state, the official ideology, and the submission of individuals to an officially endorsed collectivity, the new sociality celebrates individuality and private desires in unofficial social and spatial contexts. The center of public life and socializing, accordingly, has shifted from large state-controlled public spaces (such as city squares, auditoriums, and workers' clubs) to smaller, commercialized arenas such as dancing halls, bowling alleys, and even imaginary spaces provided by radio call-in shows (e.g., see chapters in this volume by Kathleen Erwin, James Farrer, and GanWang). The new sociality has even emerged in conventionally state-controlled public spaces, such as parks, and has thus transformed them into multidimensional spaces in which the state, the public, and the private may coexist (see Richard Kraus's chapter in this volume).

Restaurants similarly meet the demand for a new kind of sociality outside state control – that is, the public celebration of individual desires, life aspirations, and personal communications in a social context. As indicated above, in earlier decades the socialist state did not encourage the use of restaurants as a social space in which to celebrate private desires or perform family rituals. Rather, by institutionalizing public canteens in the workplace, the state tried to control meal time and also change the meaning of social dining itself. This is particularly true in Beijing, which has been the center of national politics and socialist transformation since 1949. Any new form of social dining was unlikely to develop from the previous restaurant sector in Beijing, which consisted primarily of socialist canteens. It is thus not accidental that by 1993 nearly three quarters of the more than 19,000 eating establishments in Beijing were owned by private entrepreneurs (local and foreign) or were operating as joint ventures.[73] McDonald's and other foreign fast-food restaurants have been appropriated by Beijing consumers as especially attractive social spaces for a new kind of socializing and for the celebration of individuality in public. Moreover, consuming at McDonald's and other foreign fast-food outlets is also a way of embracing modernity and foreign culture in public.

To sum up, there is a close link between the development of fast-food consumption and changes in social structure, especially the emergence of new social groups).[74] The new groups of agents demand the creation of new space for socialization in every aspect of public life, including dining out. Fast-food restaurants provide just such a space for a number of social groups. The new kind of sociality facilitated by fast-food restaurants in turn further stimulates consumers' demands for both the food and the space. Hence the fast-food fever in Beijing during the 1990s.

NOTES

This chapter is based on fieldwork in Beijing, August to October 1994, supported by a grant from the Henry Luce Foundation to the Fairbank Center for East Asian Research, Harvard University, and on further documentary research supported by the 1996 Senate Grant, University of California, Los Angeles. I am grateful to Deborah Davis, Thomas Gold, Jun Jing, Joseph Soares, and other participants at the American Council of Learned Societies conference at Yale University for their valuable comments on earlier drafts of this chapter. I also owe special thanks to Nancy Hearst for editorial assistance.

1. Liu Fen and Long Zaizu 1996.
2. For a general review, see Messer 1984.
3. See, e.g., Jerome 1980.
4. See Douglas 1975; Lévi-Strauss 1983; and Sahlins 1976.
5. See Harris 1985; Murphy 1986; and Appadurai 1981.
6. Bourdieu 1984, pp. 175–200.
7. Watson 1987. For more systematic studies of food in China, see Chang 1977 and E. Anderson 1988.
8. See Gusfield 1992, p. 80.
9. Finkelstein 1989, pp. 68–71.
10. Ibid. p. 5.
11. Shelton 1990, p. 525.
12. See Fantasia 1995, pp. 213–15.
13. For an anthropological study of sociocultural encounters at McDonald's in Hong Kong, Taipei, Beijing, Seoul, and Tokyo, see chapters in Watson, ed., 1997.

14. See Love 1986, p. 448.
15. See Zhang Yubin 1992.
16. See *New York Times*, April 24, 1992. For a detailed account, see Yan 1997a.
17. See *China Daily*, September 12, 1994; and *Service Bridge*, August 12, 1994.
18. See Liu Ming 1992; Mian Zhi 1993.
19. Duan Gang 1991.
20. Zhang Zhaonan 1992a.
21. See Zhang Zhaonan 1992b; You Zi 1994; and Zhang Guoyun 1995.
22. Yu Bin 1996; "Honggaoliang yuyan zhongshi kuaican da qushi" 1996.
23. Yu Weize 1995.
24. See Liu Fen and Long Zaizu 1996.
25. The development of Chinese fast food is incorporated into the eighth national five-year plan for scientific research. See Bi Yuhua 1994; see also Ling Dawei 1996.
26. For representative views on this issue, see Guo Jianying 1995; Huang Shengbing 1995; Jian Feng 1992; Xiao Hua 1993; Ye Xianning 1993; Yan Zhenguo and Liu Yinsheng 1992a; and Zhong Zhe 1993.
27. Ling Dawei 1995.
28. Mintz 1993, p. 271.
29. Giddens 1984, p. 132.
30. See Sayer 1985, pp. 30–31.
31. See Lechner 1991; Urry 1985.
32. For a comprehensive study of the work-unit system, see Walder 1986.
33. In prereform Beijing even the hotel restaurants and guesthouse canteens were open only during "proper" meal times. So if a visitor missed the meal time, the only alternative was to buy bread and soft drinks from a grocery store.
34. For more details on the results of the survey, see Yan 1997a.
35. See discussions in Xu Chengbei 1994.
36. *Zhongguo shipinbao* (Chinese food newspaper), November 6, 1991.
37. *Jingji riban*, September 15, 1991.
38. Fantasia 1995, p. 219.
39. Ritzer 1993, pp. 4–5.
40. Every time McDonald's opened a new restaurant in the early 1990s, it was featured in the Chinese media. See e.g., *Tianjin qingnianbao* (Tianjin youth news), June 8, 1994; *Shanghai jingji ribao* (Shanghai economic news), July 22, 1994; *Wenhui bao* (Wenhui daily), July 22, 1994. See also Han Shu 1994; Xu Chengbei 1993, p. 3.
41. Xu Chengbei 1992. In fact, I applied to work in a McDonald's outlet in Beijing but was turned down. The manager told me that the recruitment of employees in McDonald's involves a long and strict review process, in order to make sure that the applicants' qualifications are competitive.

42. The relationship between medicine and food has long been an important concern in Chinese culinary culture. See E. Anderson 1988, pp. 53–56.
43. See Yu Bin 1996; and "Honggaoliang yuyan" 1996.
44. Liu Guoyue 1996.
45. See Zhao Huanyan 1995; Xu Wangsheng 1995; Xie Dingyuan 1996; and Tao Wentai 1996.
46. For an excellent account, see Kottak 1978.
47. Shelton 1990, p. 520.
48. *Gaige Daobao* (Reform herald), no. 1 (1994), p. 34.
49. See Douglas and Isherwood 1979.
50. Stephenson 1989, p. 237.
51. Fantasia 1995, pp. 221–22.
52. For an interesting study of eating etiquette in southern China, see Cooper 1986, pp. 179–84. As mentioned near the beginning of this chapter, Finkelstein offers an interesting and radically different view of existing manners and custom in restaurants. Since manners and behavior patterns are socially constructed and imposed on customers, they make the "restaurant a diorama that emphasizes the aspects of sociality assumed to be the most valued and attractive" (Finkelstein 1989, p. 52). Accordingly, customers give up their individuality and spontaneity and thus cannot explore their real inner world in this kind of socially constructed spatial context (ibid., pp. 4–17).
53. The 1994 figure comes from my fieldwork; the 1996 figure is taken from Beijing Dashiye Jingji Diaocha Gongsi (Beijing big perspective economic survey company), quoted in "Kuaican zoujin gongxin jieceng" (Fast food is coming closer to salaried groups), *Zhongguo jingyingbao*, June 21, 1996.
54. Interview with General Manager Tim Lai, September 28, 1994.
55. He Yupeng 1996.
56. Ibid. p. 8.
57. See Yan 1997a.
58. He Yupeng 1996, pp. 8–9.
59. See Yan 1997a.
60. According to John Love, when Den Fujita, the founder and owner of McDonald's chain stores in Japan, began introducing McDonald's foods to Japanese customers, particularly the youngsters, he bent the rules by allowing his McDonald's outlets to be a hangout place for teenagers. He decorated one of the early stores with poster-sized pictures of leather-jacketed members of a motorcycle gang "one shade removed" from Hell's Angels. Fujita's experiment horrified the McDonald's chairman when he visited the company's new branches in Japan. See Love 1986, p. 429.
61. Elsewhere I have argued that Chinese society in the 1990s underwent a process of re-structuring. The entire Chinese population – not only the peasants – was

on the move: some physically, some socially, and some in both ways. An interesting indicator of the increased social mobility and changing patterns of social stratification was the booming business of namecard printing, because so many people changed jobs and titles frequently and quickly. Thus consumption and lifestyle decisions became more important than ever as ways for individuals to define their positions. For more details, see Yan 1994.

62. Yan Zhenguo and Liu Yinshing 1992b.

63. See Xiao Yan 1994.

64. See, e.g., Gao Changli 1992, p. 6; Dong Fang 1994, p. 22.

65. Gu Bingshu 1994.

66. *Beijing wanbao*, January 27, 1993.

67. *Beijing qingnianbao* (Beijing youth daily), December 18, 1993.

68. Pian Ming 1994.

69. For a review of changes in consumption and lifestyles among Chinese youth, see Huang Zhijian 1994.

70. See Gold 1993.

71. On changing family values and household structure, see chapters in Davis and Harrell 1993. For a detailed study of the rising importance of conjugality in rural family life, see Yan 1997b.

72. Watson 1997, p. 19.

73. See *Beijing qingnianbao*, December 18, 1993.

74. See especially Mintz 1994; see also sources cited in notes 2 to 13.

CONCLUSION: THE INDIVIDUALIZATION OF CHINESE SOCIETY

In this chapter, I will first briefly review the individualization thesis found in contemporary social theory. This thesis has provided me with both the initial inspiration and the conceptual tool to rethink social transformation in China. Next, I will explore the key role of increased social mobility in changing the relationships among the three major components of society, that is, the individual, social groups, and state institutions. The third section focuses on the impact of identity politics on social institutions, revealing the interacting and interactive relationship between the rise of the individual and the individualization of society. The fourth section examines the emergence of new kinds of sociality that also pose new challenges to the more individualized society. While describing the contours of Chinese society in the process of individualizing, I will also note some differences between the Chinese case and that which the individualization thesis prescribes for Western Europe.[1] I conclude by comparing the Chinese and Western European cases and highlighting the Chinese model of individualization that excludes cultural democracy, a welfare state and individualism.

THE INDIVIDUALIZATION THESIS

There is nothing new in noting the rising importance of the individual in modern times, and the emancipation of the individual as an autonomous rights-bearer is generally seen as inherent to the process of modernization in the West. Some scholars argue that the rise of the individual started even before industrialization (see, for example, Macfarlane 1978). The individual–society relationship occupies a central place in the classic theories of Durkheim and Weber, and continues to do so in contemporary social thought; there are also numerous theories specifically about the individual and the self. The individualization of society, however, appears to be a relatively new concept intrinsically related to processes of globalization.

In an excellent overview, Cosmo Howard (2007) makes the distinction between individualization as a discursive field, in which there are a number of theoretical frameworks competing with one another, and the particular individualization thesis of Bauman (2001), Beck (1992), Giddens (1991), and Beck and Beck-Gernsheim (2002). The latter is one of the frameworks that aims to challenge the dominant neoliberal model of individualization.

Although benefiting from Howard's insights, I see the individualization thesis as both antithetical to and a development from the earlier neoliberal model of individualization. The neoliberal theory assumes that the individual is naturally autonomous and a self-determining agent, and in an ideal situation, the individual is able to perform best without the constraints of social institutions (see Harvey 2005). Focusing on the tensions between the individual, on the one hand, and the society and the state, on the other hand, in various ways neoliberal theory promotes the protection and development of individual rights and freedom. As an antithesis, the recent individualization theory of Beck and others emphasizes the tensions between the increasing demands for individuality, choice, and freedom both from and being imposed on individuals, on the one hand, and the complex and unavoidable dependence of these same individuals on social institutions, on the other hand. The importance of promoting and protecting individual rights and freedom is equally important in the new individualization thesis, but it is no longer a pressing issue because, as Giddens argues (1991), in Western Europe the emancipation politics has ended and the new dominant form of politics is that of lifestyles, as opposed to that of life chances. In a similar vein, Beck argues that the individualization process relies on "cultural democratization," meaning that democracy is widely accepted and practiced as a principle in everyday life and social relations (Beck and Beck-Gernsheim 2002: 205). Here the connection between the two theoretical models is quite clear.

Three key arguments in the individualization thesis are particularly noteworthy (see also Howard 2007). The first is what Giddens calls "detraditionalization," or what Beck refers to as "disembedment." Increasingly, individuals are disembedded from external social constraints, which include both cultural traditions in general and some encompassing categories in particular, such as the family, kinship, community and social class. As a result, society has become further differentiated and diversified. Yet, this does not mean that tradition and social groups no longer play a role; instead, they still may be important if they serve as resources for the individual. The key difference, in my view, is that individuals no longer believe that they ought to work for the sake of preserving tradition (such as the continuity of the family line); instead, individuals use selected traditions to work for their own lives.

The second feature is a paradoxical phenomenon referred to by Bauman as "compulsive and obligatory self-determination" (Bauman 2000: 32). This means that modern social structures compel people to become proactive and self-determining individuals who must take full responsibility for their own problems and who develop a reflexive self (Giddens 1991). This is done through a set of new social institutions, such as the education system, labor market and state regulations. By removing the option to seek the protection of tradition, family or community, the influence of modern social institutions on the individual has actually increased. This is the key point at which the individualization thesis departs from the neoliberal proposition.

The third feature is characterized as a "life of one's own through conformity" (Beck and Beck-Gernsheim 2002: 151), meaning that the promotion of choice, freedom and individuality does not necessarily make every individual unique. On the contrary, because the dependence on social institutions determines that the contemporary individual cannot float free in the search for and construction of a unique self, men and women must construct their own biographies through guidelines and regulations; thus they end up with a life of individual conformity. This argument is also consistent with some earlier observations about the lack of genuine individuality in modern society, such as the shift from the "inner-directed" to "other-directed" individual in US society (Riesman 1989).

The individualization thesis as a theoretical construction captures the particular changes in the nature of social relations in Western European societies which, in a number of ways, differ from those of a developing country such as China. Most noticeably, in Western European societies individual rights and freedom are regarded as a given and they have long been protected by political democracy; the inequality gap is under the control of the welfare state; and individual identity is increasingly defined by lifestyle and an individual biography instead of by social groups, such as the family or social class. Consequently, the increasingly institution- ally defined individual must rely on the security and wealth provided by the welfare state to maintain "ontological security" (Giddens 1991), a paradoxical development referred to as institutional individualism by Beck and Beck-Gernsheim (2002). This emphasis on the protective and supportive role of the welfare state also sets the individualization thesis apart from scholarly accounts of the individual–society relationship in the United States (see, for example, Bellah et al. 1996; Putnam 2000; Riesman 1989), which regard the community instead of the state as the provider of security and moral support for the individual.

Yet, the globalization of the world economy has radicalized the competition for profit and has raised the bar much higher for efficient individuals. As a result, the social democratic countries in Western Europe have had to reduce the dependence of individuals on the support of the welfare state by promoting individual choice, agency, responsibility and a "do-it-yourself biography." Consequently, the individualization of so- ciety and social relations under postmodern conditions has been accel- erated and intensified, leading to a risk society full of precarious freedom (Beck 1992) and many sorts of uncertainty/fluidity (Bauman 2001).

To what extent can the individualization thesis be applied to other types of society, such as that in China which is still undergoing the mod- ernization process? Alternatively, is Chinese society moving toward individualization? If so, in what specific ways?

MOBILITY AND DISEMBEDMENT

The first and foremost feature of the individualizing social structure in China is that, due to the increased opportunities for mobility in both phys- ical and social terms, the individual can now break away from the con- straints of social groups and find her or his own ways of self-development in a new social setting. The invisible hand obviously plays a decisive role in promoting mobility because the market needs free and mobile laborers. The visible hand of the party-state, however, is equally im- portant because it has a high stake in stimulating economic growth and maintaining the social structure on its own terms.

There are numerous accounts about how, in the 1980s and 1990s, Chinese individuals were pulled by market forces to leave their family, kin group, community or work unit to venture into the unknown waters of market competition and, by so doing, they had to take full responsibility for their own well-being and self-development. A common example is the historical phenomenon of the tidal waves of migrant workers (*mingong chao*) when millions of villagers flooded into the cities in search of better work and new lifestyles. The nationwide fever to leave state-secured jobs for private business in 1993, known as "jumping into the sea" (*xiahai feng*), might be another example of the pulling force of the market. In contrast, the party-state contributed to the trend of mobility and disembedment by implementing policy and institutional changes, such as loosening up the household registration system and laying off workers from state-owned enterprises. A more telling example in this connection is the issuance of personal identity cards in the 1980s.

It is widely known that the core reasoning behind the household registration system was to fix Chinese citizens to their birthplace and to make them dependent on either the rural collective or the urban work unit for employment and subsistence needs. It also controlled citizens' travel and practically banned all rural–urban migration without official permits, increasing and perpetuating the social equalities between the rural and urban areas. What is less well known, however, is that, under the household registration system during the Maoist era, Chinese individuals did not have personal identity cards. They were all registered as members of a family/household – either a conventional type of household or an institutionally created entity called a "collective household" (*jiti hu*). In the cities each household was given a family registration booklet (*hukou ben*) that contained the key identity information of all its members. When traveling, a person would take the family registration booklet as an official paper testifying to her/his identity, which meant that, at any given time, only one person per household could travel and the others would have to remain "identity-less" during this period. Unmarried people who did not reside with their parents were even less fortunate because they were all registered as members of a collective household, and the registrations were kept by their work units. As a substitute, urban people could use the employment certificate (*gongzuo zheng*) issued by their work unit to travel or for some other purposes. In either case, one was identified only as a member of a group – the family/household or the work unit – and did not stand alone as an individual in her/his own right. The situation was even worse for the majority of the Chinese populace who lived in the countryside and who were collectively labeled as "peasant." In rural China, key information about a person's identity was recorded in a collective book kept at the village office (at the time, the headquarters of the collective) and there were no household-based registration booklets for rural families. Thus, rural residents did not have an individual identity and they were denied the basic freedom of mobility. The best a villager could do was to obtain an introduction letter issued by the village office signifying official recognition of the person's membership in the collective.

The situation began to change in 1985 when the National People's Congress passed a law mandating that all Chinese citizens be issued with an identity card. Since then, Chinese individuals, both in cities and the countryside, have all been entitled to obtain an individual identity card – called a "*jumin shenfenzheng*" (resident identity card) – and, by law, they must carry the card when traveling or engaging in important transactions as legal proof of their identity. The intriguing point is that, even though in Western societies the issuance of a national ID card often causes heated debates about its potential to usurp individual freedoms, in China it actually represented important progress in liberating the individual from the constraints of the family, community, work place and ultimately the state. Once freed from these constraints, many people were able to leave their villages or work units, to change their jobs or occupations, and to reinvent themselves through their achievements, or the DIY-type biographic work in Beck and Beck-Gernsheim's terms (2002).

More than six decades ago, Francis L.K. Hsu (1948) stated that five core elements of Chinese culture constitute the Chinese individual: the central importance of the father–son relationship; the estrangement between the two sexes; the ideal of the large family; an education system that teaches children as if they were adults; and parental authority and power. Hsu's synthesis reflected a received wisdom that remains influential today, both inside and outside China, i.e. that Chinese culture places group interest over individual interest and the individual belongs and remains secondary to the group or collective. At least at the level of ideology, the group (be it the family or the state) does not exist to support the individual; it is the other way round – the individual exists to continue the group. Therefore, the individual was born into, grew up with and remained living under the ancestors' shadow, as suggested by the title of Hsu's volume. It should be added that, after the 1949 revolution, the ancestors' shadow was mostly replaced by that of the party-state.

The shadow of the ancestors or the modern state cannot be sustained without the various constraining powers of the collectives, and the latter will not endure if the individual can leave or break away from the collectives. In other words, mobility serves as an important agent of transformation as it enables disembedment, making it possible for the individual to break out of the shadow of the various sorts of collectives.

Admittedly, in practice the Chinese individual in both traditional and modern times has always been active in exercising agency and taking actions against the hegemony of the collective (Hwang 1987). Structurally, the individual also acts at the center of the concentric circles of interpersonal relations (Fei 1948), and Confucian ethics recognize the agency of the individual under some circumstances (King 1985). It would be incorrect, therefore, to overlook or deny what the individual can do, or indeed did, to social groups or the state before the social transformation of individualization.

It would be equally incorrect, however, to replace the structural arrangement of the individual–group–state relationship with the particular agency and acts of some individuals under the same structure, because the group or state, although they may change the life chance or status of a particular individual, will not alter the overall structure. For example, a submissive and oppressed daughter-in-law may one day become a powerful mother-in-law, or some hard-working individuals may move up the social ladder and become part of the elite by obtaining a degree through the imperial education system, but neither will change the existing structure of social relations that prescribes the individual to be secondary and subordinate to social groups and the state. Quite often, the ones who moved up would make every effort to reinforce the existing structure so that they could enjoy the fruits as the representatives of a social group or the state.

The significance of the changes described in this book lies in the simple fact that not only some elite or capable individuals but also ordinary people have gained the legitimacy and opportunities of mobility to seek alternatives outside the existing constraints of social groups or state-sponsored institutions, albeit not all individuals can fully take advantage of the new opportunities of mobility and disembedment due to various social and personal reasons. The "breakaway" individuals in turn reshape their relationship with social groups and institutions, promoting changes in both of them. For example, post-marital coresidence, a key element in the Chinese family institution, has been altered in a variety of ways to accommodate the demands of the individual, and a new family ideal has taken shape under the influence of independent residency for both young and old generations (see also Thøgersen and Ni 2008). In response to the increasing individual efforts to combat governmental wrongdoings and injustices, the party-state enacted the Administrative Litigation Law in 1990 which, for the first time in Chinese history, gives citizens a legal right to sue local governments and government agencies. In short, although social inequalities and injustices still exist (and may have increased in some circumstances), the increased mobility has changed the previous balance in the structured relations among the individual, social groups and institutions. The individual has gained more weight in society and has emerged as an important and independent social category for policy making and cultural reasoning alike, which in turn has led to the emergence of identity politics.

INDIVIDUAL IDENTITY AND THE POLITICS OF RECOGNITION

A simple indicator of the rising importance of individual identity is the shifting usage of the first-person term from "we" to "I" in public discourse. In traditional China a person was embedded and defined by the net of family and kinship relations, representing merely a temporary point between ancestors and future decedents on the long rope of descent line (see Baker 1979; Pye 1996). After the revolution, individuals were liberated from kinship and community power by the party-state but they found themselves re-embedded in the redistributive system of the "socialist big family," whereby every individual was part of an organization politically controlled and economically run by the party-state. Although urbanites enjoyed more privileges and welfare benefits than did rural people, no one had an independent status or identity – one could only be either a work-unit person in the cities (*danwei ren*) or a commune member (*gongshe sheyuan*) in the rural areas. In a strict sense, self-identity did not exist in public life, and therefore the individual could never be an independent unit in public discourse. Consequently, people tended to use the plural term to substitute for the singular "I," such as "we," "our work unit," "our family," etc., instead of saying "I," "my work unit," or "my family."[2] This customary usage of the plural "we" gradually disappeared in the 1990s and, by the late 1990s, a new Chinese phrase, "*wo yi dai*" (the I-generation or the me-generation), was coined to describe those who were born in the 1970s and who had grown up during the reform era because of their proud usage of the first person.

The denial of the individual as an independent social category in public discourse is a common practice; a recent example is the changing social label for private entrepreneurs. Regardless of the nature of their businesses, the pioneers in the private economy during the 1980s were all officially labeled "*geti hu*," which consists of the two Chinese words "individual" and "household." It did not make any sense either linguistically or socially to label a person's social and economic status as a "household" with the prefix of "individual," but no one questioned it at the time. In reality, because most private entrepreneurs in the early 1980s were individuals who, for various reasons, could not find a position in a state-owned enterprise or collective unit, the label "*geti hu*" carried certain negative connotations as well, as if these individuals were not completely accepted by society. Beginning in the early 1990s, the term "*siying qiyejia*" (private entrepreneur) emerged as a new label for successful individuals who had accumulated a considerable amount of capital, and the former term "*geti hu*" was gradually replaced by other more specific and individualistic terms, such as "*xiaoshangfan*" (petty vendor). In the twenty-first century, private entrepreneurs gained more recognition from the party-state as an important social and political force, and some were even recruited into the Chinese Communist Party. Yet, there are clear limits to their political participation set by the party-state; when individual entrepreneurs try to exceed the boundaries by organizing their own sub-political communities or engaging in self-politics on a larger scale, they will be punished (see Delman and Yin 2008).

Social labeling is important because it defines the individual's rights, status, and identity in society. The social category of peasant, for example, had a negative connotation in modern China (see Cohen 1993) and was used to push rural people down the socialist hierarchy, and to discriminate against rural migrants in the cities or migrant workers. This is why increasingly more individual migrant workers have stood up to demand social or official recognition of their rights and respect for their individual identity.

A very recent case of Internet activism may help illustrate both changes and continuities in the individual–state relationship. Although the infamous household registration system was loosened after the mid-1980s, allowing rural residents to work and live in the cities, a temporary residence permit was still required for those who went to the cities from the countryside. In Beijing, where rural–urban migration was controlled more tightly, the government in 2001 issued new regulations, requiring all migrants (*wailai renkou*, which literally means people from the outside) to obtain a temporary residence permit. This new permit was issued according to three types: an A-type was given to those who had lived in the city for three years, were legally employed and had no criminal records; a B permit was given to those who had lived in the city between one and three years but met the latter two conditions; and a C permit was for those who had lived in the city for less than one year. Because the A permit was green, the B permit yellow and the C permit red, some migrants referred to the A permit as a "Beijing green card," after the popular usage of the US legal alien card. The 2001 regulation, which was renewed in 2007, makes it clear that holders of the various types of temporary residence permits will be treated differently. "The government will mainly protect and serve the A permit holders; for the B permit holders, the government focuses on increasing their capacity for self-management, self-education, and self-control; the government regards the C permit holders as the key objects of governance and must increase our work of inspecting, guarding against, and controlling this population."[3]

These regulations separate the migrants from the Beijing residents in a hierarchically arranged social space; the distinctions between the three permit types differentiate the migrants and create a hierarchical identity among them. For the migrants, it is a dual-attack on their identity and individual rights. As a result, protest and conflict became inevitable.

On April 2, 2008, Liu Shuhong, a 38-year-old freelancer who is better known by his pen name Laodan ("old egg"), posted on his blog a personal protest letter entitled "A Statement about my Beijing Temporary Residence Permit."[4] Liu had moved to Beijing in 2006 and, since then, had been holding a C-type temporary residence permit, the lowest in the ranking of temporary residency. Liu argued that the temporary residence permit system perpetuates the low status of migrants in Beijing, subjecting them to a variety of open and institutionalized discriminations. Moreover, because the temporary residence permit is issued according to three types (A, B and C types in different colors) in accordance with the migrant's economic status and history of living in the city, and because the migrants are forced to carry the permit at all times, the Beijing government openly discriminates against and humiliates migrants, similar to the South African government's discrimination of Indian immigrants at the turn of the twentieth century.

Within three days, Liu's statement had been read by 22,400 people and 668 people had submitted follow-up commentaries on the Internet, effectively making Liu's personal politics both public and collective. The majority agreed with Liu and supported his protest, and some even called Liu a Martin Luther King–type hero and wanted to join him in further collective action. However, about 20 percent of the readers disagreed with Liu, calling him an ungrateful migrant who merely wanted to take advantage of the social welfare in Beijing, an opportunist who wanted to create his 15 seconds of fame and to find business opportunities. Most of his opponents identified themselves as Beijing residents and complained about the high crime rate, over-crowding, poor hygiene and other social vices that had been created in their lovely hometown by the large influx of migrants. These views were countered by other arguments from migrants who emphasized their contributions to the city through their hard work and who complained about the local discrimination. A war of words quickly accelerated into a hostile confrontation between Beijing residents and migrants in the virtual world.

These points are particular noteworthy, and they also apply to many other cases of identity politics. First, the individual has begun to link the self with a set of rights and thus to expand the traditional definition of the individual as part of a social group. Echoing Liu's complaint that he was arbitrarily given a C-type temporary residence permit even though he qualified for an A permit because of his ownership of real estate in Beijing, a number of migrants offered similar personal accounts and then raised a question with a strong flavor of possessive individualism (see Macpherson 1962): "Who am I if by law I can only temporarily reside in my own house?" Second, most individuals seemed to regard their individual rights as being earned through their hard work, instead of being given at birth. Those who opposed Liu argued that the rights and privileges of Beijing residents are derived from their hard work and/or their parents' hard work in the city, indicating that individual rights are earned, not given at birth. Interestingly, many migrants counter-argued that they had contributed to the city by paying taxes, creating employment opportunities, and purchasing commodities and property. Following the same logic of individual rights as earned instead of given, some successful migrants used their biographies to show how they eventually earned a Beijing household registration due to their extraordinary achievements. Third, the identity politics mainly took the form of a public appeal to the party-state for policy or institutional changes, which is similar to the rights-assertion activism among workers (Lee 2007) or the rural rightful resistance (O'Brien and Li 2006) that have become widespread since the late 1990s. This is still consistent with the traditional Chinese pattern of an individual–state relationship whereby the state is bestowed with both virtues and absolute authority, and the individual is dependent on the state for protection and well-being (Pye 1996). Such a relationship in turn enables the state to exert a profound influence on society and on the changing structure of social relations.

NEW SOCIALITY AND MORAL CHALLENGES

The emergence of new types of sociality constitutes the third aspect of the individualization of social structure. By "new sociality" I mean social interactions among individuals as individuals (instead of as representatives of the family or other social groups). Chapter 10 depicts the rise of one type of new sociality, that is, consumption-based sociality in a commercialized public space; the holiday picnic party among young couples in Xiajia village that I briefly mention in the Introduction to this volume indicates another new type of sociality – friendship among individuals who still conceive of themselves and act as individuals even after marriage. At the time of their respective initial occurrences, both brought down the collective boundaries that confined the individual within a given group and both recognized the individual as an independent unit in social life.

Along with the increase of mobility in social scale and geographic scope, more individuals found themselves interacting in public life with other individuals who were either unrelated or total strangers, whereby collective identity and group membership became secondary to individual identity and capacity. As a result, how to interact with individual strangers has become both a feature of the individualizing society and its new challenge.

On the positive side, new types of sociality with unrelated individuals have emerged and developed, ranging from online chatting and socializing with people with similar hobbies to public participation in the form of NGOs and volunteerism (Chan 2005). Although in many cases the new sociality will eventually turn a stranger into an acquaintance or will form a new group membership, such as online dating or NGO work, in other cases it remains a temporary connection among unrelated individuals. A recent example in this connection was the rise of individual volunteerism in the aftermath of the Sichuan earthquake in May 2008. Shortly after the disaster, more than 250,000 people rushed to the quake areas at their own expense to help the victims. When asked why, many responded that they had been moved by the suffering of the victims and thus they wanted to offer help, with a number of them specifically pointing out that helping others makes their personal lives more meaningful (Cha 2008). Such compassion toward strangers represents a new kind of sociality that is universal and individualistic at the same time, in other words humanity's bonds in brotherhood transcending geographical, racial, economic and social boundaries. Their actions also made a breakthrough in the individual–society–state relationship because volunteer work has long been organized and led only by the government and its associated agencies, and it has always been regarded as a type of collective activity (see Rolandsen 2008).

In addition to the creation of new types of sociality, the increasing interactions among unrelated individuals also individualized the prevailing moral values and trust in Chinese society. When individuals belong to various social groups, they rely on a type of personal trust that only respects people who are in one's own social web, ranging from family, kinship and community, to a wider yet still well-defined network of friends. Personal trust derives from long-term interactions with the same group of people so is based on low mobility and a narrower scope of social interactions. In such a society of acquaintances, moral standards are determined by the social distance between two parties (meaning particularistic), and strangers are regarded as potential enemies and thus are not trustworthy. In contrast, in a highly mobile and open society, most social interactions occur among individuals who are not related to one another by any particularistic ties; in many cases, people do not expect to interact with the other party again in the future. In such a society of strangers, social trust is more important than personal trust and morality is based on universal values. Social trust is understood as a more generalized trust in social institutions that will behave in accordance with the stated rules; in experts who will guard the rules to make the institutions work well; and also in strangers who will work for peaceful and non-harmful social interactions. The expansion of personal trust to social trust provides one of the key mechanisms in making a modern economy and society work and thus is a necessary condition for modernity (Giddens 1990).

The promotion of social trust and universal values has become an urgent moral and social issue in China as it is becoming a more open, modern and highly mobile society. The above-mentioned examples of the new sociality and individual volunteerism are budding changes on the positive side; there are, however, disturbing and negative changes as well. For example, in 2004, a group of reporters from the China Central Television station asked workers in a rural factory producing colloidal food additive out of various types of leather waste, such as old shoes, whether they knew that the contaminated products would end up in foods to be consumed by the people. The producers replied lightly: "So what? They are strangers, and we do not know them at all. In this region, no one would eat foods with colloidal additives because we all know the secret" (CCTV 2004). Elsewhere, I examine the morally disturbing encounters with strangers, known as "*zuo haoshi bei e*" in Chinese, meaning a Good Samaritan who helps a person in an accident or in other kinds of distress but is accused of causing the initial damage and is the victim of extortion by the very person whom the Good Samaritan originally sought to help. It is intriguing that most extortionists are senior citizens who otherwise should be the most common recipients of social compassion and respect. I single out the particularistic morality, the lack of social trust and the institutional failure to protect the Good Samaritan as major factors contributing to this social phenomenon that has been occurring since the mid-1990s (Yan 2009). To juxtapose this with the above-mentioned individual volunteerism, one can clearly see the tensions between the two moral systems and the challenges of dealing with strangers in an increasingly individualized society.

Although the market economy has been developing rapidly in China, social trust has in general declined. A Chinese sociologist summarizes a crisis of social trust by describing six kinds of distrust prevailing in contemporary China: distrust of the market due to faulty goods and bad services, of service providers and strangers, of friends and even relatives, of law enforcement officers, of the law and legal institutions, and of basic moral values (Peng 2003: 292–5; see also Wang and Liu 2003; Zheng 2001). The lack of social trust in turn leads one to trust only those individuals in one's personal networks and to behave in accordance with a particularistic morality. Institutions may provide the key to safeguarding social trust, yet there is also a widespread low level of trust in institutions because of the corruption of the power holders and the individual manipulation of the law and regulations through *guanxi* practice. When all of these take place in an increasingly individualized society, social relations are in danger of being further instrumentalized and fragmented, and the society becomes a risk to the individuals, albeit not in exactly the same way as a risk society develops in Western Europe (see Beck 1992).

A CHINESE MODEL OF INDIVIDUALIZATION

Comparing the Chinese case with that of Western Europe, one can find both similarities and differences. Clearly, Chinese society is undergoing an individualization transformation. Detraditionalization, disembedment, the creation of a life of one's own by DIY biographic work, and the irresistible pressure to be more independent and individualistic are all indicators of individualization in Western Europe that have also occurred to Chinese individuals. Identity politics and institutional changes play a key role in promoting the process of individualization in both cases. Finally, the impact of globalization on individualization is equally important in Western Europe and China, albeit in different ways.

There are, however, important differences. First, in Western Europe, disembedment mainly refers to the change whereby social groups no longer define the identity of the individual, who, by breaking away from the previously encompassing social categories, remakes herself or himself through institutional mechanisms, such as an education, career or lifestyle. Breaking away from the social in identity construction, however, does not mean cutting off interactions with other individuals in everyday life or abandoning sociality; on the contrary, it only redefines relationships by recognizing the full autonomy of the individual in the face of the social and with one another, such as the new type of pure relationship of intimacy (Giddens 1992). This is an equally important part of the individualization process, which is referred to as "re-embedment" by Beck and Beck-Gernsheim (2002). Both disembedment and re-embedment, however, take place at the level of life politics, the everyday politics of lifestyle and personal identity (Giddens 1991).

In contrast, disembedment in the Chinese case manifests itself mainly in the domain of emancipatory politics, i.e. the everyday politics of life chances and social status, as revealed in the ethnographic account presented in this volume. The individual effort of DIY biography is first and foremost about the improvement of living standards and social status. Personal identity does matter, but it matters mainly because it affects one's life chances. As a result, mobility, which seems to be merely one of many factors in the Western European case, plays a pivotal role in the Chinese case of individualization. Identity, the core of the politics of recognition, relates more to the claim of individual rights and the redefinition of the individual–group–institution relationship than to the search of the self.

The existence or absence of cultural democracy and a welfare state regime constitutes the second major difference in the impact of globalization on individualization. In Western Europe, the individualization process relies on what Beck calls "cultural democratization," meaning that democracy has been widely accepted and practiced as a principle in everyday life and social relations for so long that it has become part of the culture, instead of merely a political regime. Individualization also relies on the systems of education, social security, medical care, employment and unemployment benefits that are backed up by the welfare state (see Beck and Beck-Gernsheim 2002, especially pp. 22–9 and 204–5). These social conditions are not found in China. Despite the astonishing economic growth and dramatic changes in social life, political reforms have lagged over the past three decades; as far as political democracy is concerned, the party-state simply stopped its reform efforts after 1989. As I indicate in the Introduction, one of the major institutional changes that the party-state promoted was the untying of the individual, the state-owned enterprises and the local governments in order to stimulate incentives, creativity and efficiency from below. At the same time, the party-state also withdrew from the previous socialist welfare system and in many ways shed its responsibilities in the provision of public goods for the purpose of reducing its financial burden. The best-known examples are housing reform, medical reform and education reform since the mid-1990s. In other words, the individualization process in China does give the individual more mobility, choice and freedom, but it does so with little institutional protection and support from the state. To seek a new safety net, or to re-embed, the Chinese individual is forced to fall back on the family and personal network or *guanxi*, the same point where disembedment begins. Moreover, without the institutional support of a welfare state, the Chinese process of individualization has also accelerated socio-economic differentiation and has tended to polarize society in terms of economic standing and social status, instead of merely diversifying society in terms of identity construction and life politics.

Third, the current wave of individualization in Western Europe is characteristic of the second or reflexive modernity, meaning that it has developed from and reacted to the early trend of individualization associated with industrialization, urbanization and liberalization – i.e. the first modernity. Several kinds of individualism, such as religious, political, economic, expressive and utilitarian, arose during the early stages of modernization and became an undercurrent yet a solid basis for the second wave of individualization. In contrast, individualism was introduced into Chinese society at the end of the twentieth century and has been understood only as utilitarian individualism or simply selfishness. This incomplete or unbalanced understanding of individualism not only makes the individual egotistic and uncivil, but also amplifies the negative aspects of individualization, such as the relentless individual competition and the decline of social trust. The underdevelopment of individualism in the Chinese process of individualization also means that the individual must face the tensions between the indivisible and isolated self, on the one hand, and the all-encompassing social categories, on the other hand, at the level of identity construction and psychological development. The individual has gained an opportunity for mobility to physically leave the family, for example, yet, at the same time, the family remains the most important reference point for the individual's self-identity. It is therefore plausible that individualization in China may not necessarily lead to the isolation of the individual.

Finally, the individualization process in China is managed to a great extent by the party-state, differentiating the Chinese case from its counterparts in Europe. By state-managed individualization, I do not mean merely the state's role in promoting institutional changes, which can also be found in Western Europe. More importantly, the party-state in China also directs the flow of individualization by soft management (as opposed to control) of the interplay among the players: the individual, the market, social groups, institutions and global capitalism. One of the key strategies is what I refer to as "railroading with self-interest"

(Yan 2002: 40–1), meaning that the party-state uses attractive economic or political rewards to allow the individuals to freely choose the way favored by the party-state and to exert self-control or self-management while staying within the boundaries that have been drawn by the party-state.

In general, the party-state manages the individualization process at three levels: (1) while promoting and supporting the rise of the individual in economic life, private life and some selected domains of public life, the party-state has made various efforts to prevent an individualistic claim of political rights; (2) while individuals from all walks of life appeal to the party-state in rights-assertion movements or in seeking new opportunities for self-development, they receive different treatments from the state in accordance with the ranking of their respective social groups. In general, civil servants, private entrepreneurs, college students and intellectuals are granted more privileges and opportunities for self-expression and development, whereas villagers and workers receive less support and are more tightly controlled by the government; (3) The party-state tends to be more receptive to isolated individual actions of rights assertion and pursuit of self-interest, but has much less tolerance for the collective actions of organized individuals, especially those that cross the boundaries of social class or geographic region. By so doing, the party-state has managed to control the development of an independent civil society whereby individuals may simultaneously re-embed themselves and maintain an autonomous identity.

In short, the individualization of Chinese society appears to be an ongoing process characterized by the management of the party-state and the absence of cultural democracy, a welfare state regime and classic individualism. Moreover, whereas the notion of a "second modernity" refers to a new era of post-democracy and a post-welfare state (Beck and Beck-Gernsheim 2002), the Chinese individuals examined in this volume are still working to achieve goals that belong to the first modernity of Western Europe, such as comfortable material lives, secure employment, welfare benefits, and freedom to travel, speak and engage in public activities. Yet, as I argue elsewhere (Yan 2008), Chinese individuals are also living in an environment where a fluid labor market, flexible employment, increasing personal risks, a culture of intimacy and self-expression, and a greater emphasis on individuality and self-reliance have been created by the market economy and global capitalism in the context of the political authoritarianism of the party-state. In other words, the Chinese case simultaneously demonstrates pre-modern, modern and post-modern conditions, and Chinese individuals must deal with all of these conditions at the same time. This multilayered and multi-temporal mix characterizes the complex process of individualization in China; the corresponding ways by which Chinese individuals, social groups and the party-state cope with this great social transformation may well establish a different model of individualization.

NOTES

1. Individualization is obviously a widespread phenomenon and may likely become a global trend. In this chapter, however, I compare the China case only with that of Western Europe instead of the West in general for two reasons. First, the individualization thesis in contemporary social theory is developed mainly with specific references to social changes in Western Europe where social democracy and the welfare state prevail. The US obviously stands for a different type of individualization as far as the ideological and institutional contexts are concerned. Second, the practice of Maoist socialism in China created an organized dependence of the individual on social institutions and the state, which determines that the rise of the individual in China is intrinsically related to, if not initiated by, state-sponsored institutional changes. In this aspect, the Western European model is more relevant to China than the US model of individualization; it may take another paper to compare the Chinese and US cases. However, the Chinese model differs from that of the West in general in a number of ways, as will be shown below.

2. This observation is derived from several sources: informal discussions with Chinese colleagues, encounters with villagers in north China and my own life experiences. It is particularly interesting that, in rural north China, villagers often use the plural term "ours" to describe their spouse, such as "*zanmen jialide*," which actually means "my wife" but appears on the surface to be "our wife" (the local term "*jialide*" literally means the one who stays at home or inside the house). The purpose of this usage is of course to create a closely shared base between the two parties in a conversation and, therefore, it only occurs in friendly conversations. In a dispute, for instance, one would use "*wo jialide*" or "*wo xifu*" to describe one's wife, emphasizing the ownership of the relationship.

3. See the official news release by the Xinhua New Agency at http://www.cpirc. org.cn/news/rkxw_gn_detail.asp?id=413 (accessed May 10, 2008).

4. See http://liushuhong.blog.sohu.com/83552839.html (accessed May 10, 2008).

REFERENCES

Baker, Hugh D.R. 1979. *Chinese Family and Kinship*. New York: Columbia University Press.

Bauman, Zygmunt. 2000. *Liquid Modernity*. Cambridge: Polity Press.

Bauman, Zygmunt. 2001. *The Individualized Society*. Cambridge: Polity Press.

Beck, Ulrich. 1992. *Risk Society: Towards a New Modernity*. Trans. Mark Ritter. London: Sage Publications.

Beck, Ulrich and Elisabeth Beck-Gernsheim. 2002. *Individualization: Institutionalized Individualism and its Social and Political Consequences*. London and Thousand Oaks, CA: Sage Publications.

Bellah, Robert N., Madsen, Richard, Sullivan, William M., Swidler, Ann and Tipton, Steven M. 1996. *Habits of the Heart: Individualism and Commitment in American Life* (updated edition). Berkeley, CA: University of California Press.

CCTV [China Central Television station]. 2004. "Life" Program, June 17. For a text of the program, see http://www.wanghai.net/article.aspx? articleid=3517. Accessed August 21, 2009.

Cha, Ariana Eunjung. 2008. "Young Volunteers in Quake Zone Ultimately Find a Modest Mission." *Washington Post*, May 22, p. A14.

Chan, Kin-man. 2005. "The Development of NGOs under a Post-Totalitarian Regime: The Case of China." In Robert P. Weller (ed.), *Civil Life, Globalization, and Political Change in Asia: Organizing Between Family and State*. London: Routledge, pp. 20–41.

Cohen, Myron. 1993. "Cultural and Political Inventions in Modern China: The Case of the Chinese 'Peasant'." *Daedalus* 122(2): 151–70.

Delman, Jørgen and Xiaoqing, Yin. 2008. "Individualisation and Politics in China: The Political Identity and Agency of Private Business People." *European Journal of East Asian Studies* 7(1): 39–73.

Fei Xiaotong. 1948. *Xiangtu Zhongguo* (Folk China). Shanghai: Guancha Press (English translation *From the Soil: The Foundations of Chinese Society*. Trans. Gary G. Hamilton and Wang Zheng. Berkeley, CA: University of California Press, 1992).

Giddens, Anthony. 1990. *The Consequences of Modernity*. Stanford, CA: Stanford University Press.

Giddens, Anthony. 1991. *Modernity and Self-Identity: Self and Society in the Late Modern Age*. Stanford, CA: Stanford University Press.

Giddens, Anthony. 1992. *The Transformation of Intimacy: Sexuality, Love and Eroticism in Modern Societies*. Stanford, CA: Stanford University Press.

Harvey, David. 2005. *A Brief History of Neoliberalism*. Oxford: Oxford University Press.

Howard, Cosmo. 2007. "Introducing Individualization." In Cosmo Howard (ed.), *Contested Individualization: Debates about Contemporary Personhood*. New York: Palgrave Macmillan, pp. 1–24.

Hsu, Francis L.K. 1948. *Under the Ancestors' Shadow: Chinese Culture and Personality*. New York: Columbia University Press.

Hwang, Kwang-kuo. 1987. "Face and Favor: The Chinese Power Game." *American Journal of Sociology* 92(4): 944–74.

King, Ambrose Yeo-chi [Yao-ji Jin]. 1985. "The Individual and Group in Confucianism: A Relational Perspective." In Donald J. Munro (ed.), *Individualism and Holism: Studies in Confucian and Taoist Values*. Ann Arbor, MI: Center for Chinese Studies Publications, University of Michigan, pp. 57–70.

Lee, Ching Kwan. 2007. *Against the Law: Labor Protests in China's Rustbelt and Sunbelt*. Berkeley, CA: University of California Press.

Macfarlane, Alan. 1978. *The Origins of English Individualism: The Family, Property and Social Transition*. Cambridge: Cambridge University Press.

Macpherson, C.B. 1962. *The Political Theory of Possessive Individualism: Hobbes to Locke*. Oxford: Clarendon Press.

O'Brien, Kevin J. and Li, Lianjiang. 2006. *Rightful Resistance in Rural China*. Cambridge: Cambridge University Press.

Peng Siqing. 2003. "Wo ping shenmo xinren ni?" (By What Should I Trust You?). In Zheng Yifu and Peng Siqing (eds.), *Zhongguo shehui zhong de xinren* (Trust in Chinese Society). Beijing: Zhongguo chengshi chubanshe, pp. 292–301.

Putnam, Robert D. 2000. *Bowling Alone: The Collapse and Revival of American Community*. New York: Simon & Schuster.

Pye, Lucian W. 1996. "The State and the Individual: An Overview Interpretation." In Brian Hook (ed.), *The Individual and the State in China*. Oxford: Clarendon Press, pp. 16–42.

Riesman, David, with Nathan Glazer and Reuel Denney. 1989 [1961]. *The Lonely Crowd: A Study of the Changing American Character*. New Haven, CT: Yale University Press.

Rolandsen, Unn Malfrid H. 2008. "A Collective of Their Own: Young Volunteers at the Fringes of the Party Realm." *European Journal of East Asian Studies* 7(1): 101–29.

Thøgersen, Stig and Ni Anru. 2008. "'He is He, and I am I': Individual and Collective among China's Rural Elderly." *European Journal of East Asian Studies* 7(1): 11–37.

Wang Shaoguang and Liu Xin. 2003. "Xinren de jichu: Yizhong lixing de jieshi" (The Foundation of Trust: An Interpretation of Rationality). In Zheng Yifu and Peng Siqing (eds.), *Zhongguo shehui zhong de xinren* (Trust in Chinese Society). Beijing: Zhongguo chengshi chubanshe, pp. 209–49.

Yan, Yunxiang. 2002. "Managed Globalization: State Power and Cultural Transition in Contemporary China." In Peter L. Berger and Samuel P. Huntington (eds.), *Many Globalizations: Cultural Diversity in the Contemporary World.* New York: Oxford University Press, pp. 19–47.

Yan, Yunxiang. 2008. "Introduction: Understanding the Rise of the Individual in China." *European Journal of East Asian Studies* 7(1): 1–9.

Yan, Yunxiang. 2009. "The Good Samaritan's New Trouble in China: A Case Study of the Changing Moral Landscape in the Reform Era." *Social Anthropology* 17(1): 9–24.

Zheng Yefu. 2001. *Xinren lun* (On Trust). Beijing: Zhongguo guangbo dianshi chubanshe.

PERMISSIONS

The following chapters are included in this collection by permission of the original publishers:

Chapter 1 was published as "The Impact of Rural Reform on Economic and Social Stratification in a Chinese Village." *Australian Journal of Chinese Affairs* 27 (1992): 1–23.

Chapter 2 was published as "Everyday Power Relations: Changes in a North China Village." In Andrew Walder (ed.), *The Waning of the Communist State: Economic Origins of Political Decline in China and Hungry.* Berkeley: University of California Press (1995), pp. 215–41.

Chapter 3 was published as "The Triumph of Conjugality: Structural Transformation of Family Relations in a Chinese Village." *Ethnology* 36(3) (1997): 191–212.

Chapter 4 was published as "Practicing Kinship in Rural North China." In Susan McKinnon and Sarah Franklin (eds.), *Relative Values: Reconfiguring Kinship Studies.* Durham, NC: Duke University Press (2001), pp. 224–43.

Chapter 5 was published as "Rural Youth and Youth Culture in North China." *Culture, Medicine, and Psychiatry* 23(1) (1999): 75–97. Reprinted by permission of Springer Science and Business Media.

Chapter 6 was published as "Girl Power: Young Women and the Waning of Patriarchy in Rural North China." *Ethnology* 45(2) (2006): 105–23.

Chapter 7 was published as "The Individual and Transformation of Bridewealth in Rural North China." *Journal of the Royal Anthropology Institute* 11(4) (2005): 637–57.

Chapter 8 was published as "Calculability and Budgeting in a House-hold Economy: A Case Study from Rural North China." *Taiwan Journal of Anthropology* 2(1) (2004): 69–72.

Chapter 9 was published as "The Politics of Consumerism in Chinese Society." In Tyrene White (ed.), *China Briefing, 1998–2000.* Armonk, NY: M.E. Sharpe (2000), pp. 159–93.

Chapter 10 was published as "Of Hamburger and Social Space: Consuming McDonald's in Beijing." In Deborah S. Davis (ed.), *The Consumer Revolution in Urban China.* Berkeley: University of California Press (2000), pp. 201–25.

INDEX

food safety 285–7
foreign influences xxx–xxxiv,
233–7
see also fast food
France 253, 256
Freedman, Maurice 100
Fricke, T. 75, 146
funerals 85–7
Fussell, Paul 227

Giddens, Anthony xiii, xvii, 250,
274
gift giving 32, 43, 44, 92, 97, 98,
99, 194–5
marriage, *see* bridewealth
record keeping 183, 204
globalization 276
Gong Xiaoxia 42
Goode, William 60, 76
Great Leap Forward 35, 109, 120
Guanxi, *see* networks
Gusfield, Joseph 244

Happy Chopsticks 235, 254
Harrell, S. 76
He Yupeng 259, 260
holidays 231
Homans, George 50
Hooper, Beverley xxxii
household registration system
277–8
houses
family division and 65–9,
141–3, 171
organization of 65
Howard, Cosmo 274
Hsu, Francis 100, 278
Hu Jintao xiii
Hungary 15, 17, 25, 31

identity cards
household registration system
277–8
individual 278
individualism xxviii–xxx
Chinese model of
individualization 287–91
individual identity and politics
of recognition 280–4
individualization thesis 273–6
mobility and disembedment
276–80
new sociality and moral
challenges 284–7
inflation 217

Jiang Zemin xii
Jinghe Kuaican 248
Jinghua Shaomai Restaurant 248
Jingshi Fast Food Co 248–9
Jordan, Michael 234

Kentucky Fried Chicken (KFC)
243, 246, 252, 253, 255, 256,
263
kinship xix–xxiii, 85–8
emotional dimension of
kinship practice 98–100
flow of practical kinship 91–8
elasticity of kinship
distance 92–3
flattenization of kinship
95–6
uncertainty of kinship
alliances 93–4
women and changing
kinship practice 96–8
scholarly models 100–4
Xiajia village 89–91, 101, 104

London School of Economics Monographs on Social Anthropology series
Series Editor: Charles Stafford

With over 70 volumes published since 1949, including classic work by Gell, Barth, Leach and Firth, the LSE Monographs now form one of the most prestigious series in the discipline of Anthropology. Presenting scholarly work from all branches of Social Anthropology the series continues to build on its history with both theoretical and ethnographic studies of the contemporary world.